FOREVER FIT

Cher

FOREVER FIT

THE LIFETIME PLAN FOR HEALTH, FITNESS, AND BEAUTY

Robert Haas M.S.

BANTAM BOOKS

NEW YORK · TORONTO · LONDON · SYDNEY · AUCKLAND

Fitness, diet, and health are matters which necessarily vary from individual to individual. Readers should speak with their own doctor about their individual needs before starting this or any other diet or exercise program. Consulting one's physician is especially important if one is on any medication or is already under medical care for any illness.

FOREVER FIT

A Bantam Book / February 1991

Grateful acknowledgment is made for permissions to reprint the following: recipes for "Chocolate Cherry Cake" and "Need-No-Syrup Banana Pancakes" from EAT TO WIN, copyright © 1983 by Robert Haas, published by Rawson Associates, New York. Food Composition Tables and recipe for "Haas Mayonnaise Spread" from EAT TO SUCCEED, copyright © 1986 by Think Tank International, Inc., published by Rawson Associates, New York.

Library of Congress Cataloging-in-Publication Data

Cher, 1946–
    Forever fit / Cher, Robert Haas.
      p.   cm.
    Includes bibliographical references and index.
    ISBN 0-553-07073-8
    1. Health. I. Haas, Robert, 1948–   . II. Title.
RA776.C6432   1991
613.7—dc20
                         90-20864
                         CIP

Published simultaneously in the United States and Canada

Bantam Books are published by Bantam Books, a division of Bantam Doubleday Dell Publishing Group, Inc. Its trademark, consisting of the words "Bantam Books" and the portrayal of a rooster, is Registered in U.S. Patent and Trademark Office and in other countries. Marca Registrada. Bantam Books, 666 Fifth Avenue, New York, New York 10103.

PRINTED IN THE UNITED STATES OF AMERICA

0 9 8 7 6 5 4 3 2 1

ACKNOWLEDGMENTS

My sister Georganne, my manager Bumper Sammeth, all the women in my house: Paulette, Angela, Debbie, Etsuko, and Andy, who is all man, Bea and Sal, my children Chastity and Elijah (who are just now getting into exercise and understanding its value), Robert Haas, the Blechmans and their enduring endurance, Dr. Arnold Klein and Dr. Norman Orentreich, and probably every person I've met and talked to, because I learn something from every encounter I have in my life.

—CHER

I wish to thank the following people who helped make this book a reality:

Ann and Albert Haas, Mark Budwig, Charles Rembar, Connie Clausen, Cher, Bill Sammeth, Steve Diamond, Howard Abrams, David, Jean, Steve, Dean, Neal, Brian, and Ross Blechman, Roy Ulin, Kristin Massey, Debbie Paul, Georganne LaPiere, Arnold Klein, M.D., Ruth Rafidi, Steve Ford, Liza Joseph, Angela Best-Arnaud, Jean Brown, Mary Ellen Siegal, Susan Blum, Margaret Danbrot, and Amanda Urban.

Very special thanks: Hilarie Porter, Steve Blechman, and Coleen O'Shea.

—ROBERT HAAS M.S.

The authors would also like to acknowledge
Jim Jerome's contributions to this book.

CONTENTS

1

WHY WE WROTE THIS BOOK

CHER

As my grandmother was approaching her 72nd birthday a couple of years ago, I asked her, "Grandma Lynda, what do you want for your birthday?" And she said, "Well, honey, I could really use some new sweat clothes—you know, some nice leotards."

She had joined a gym near her house, had started to make a bunch of new friends, and she just loved going there every day to work out. By the time she was 72 she was thinner than she had ever been in her life, and she couldn't believe what was happening with her body and spirit.

Eating had become much less important to her, which is what usually happens when you start yourself on an exercise program. There are chemical changes taking place in your body that make you feel more rested and relaxed, less anxious, more energetic. Grandma Lynda was just having the time of her life. She did aerobics, exercise classes, and some light weight machines for muscle tone.

She brought her new friends to a screening of *Moonstruck* before it opened, and I'll never forget that. They were just beside themselves. It was so great to see these women at that stage of life being so active and feeling so vital.

My grandmother is one of my heroes because she's exactly what Robert Haas and I think of as being forever fit. She is living proof that it is never too late in life to change the way your body and mind can work together so you look and feel your best.

That's why we decided to write this book—to give people the kind of information they need to get off their butts and commit to a lifestyle of health and fitness and the best mind–body connection they can have at any age. I know I can't work on my body without also working on my mind. There are all kinds of self-help disciplines, therapies, and books and tapes aimed at improving your mind. But for me, and for most people I know, a commitment to exercise has always been my first attempt at developing a happier, healthier spirit. We know that the automatic result of eating right and working out is looking good and, even better, feeling good. And that's just an incredible combination.

I don't ever want to stop moving in that direction. I want to be one of those old women who climb Mt. Everest at 75 if that's what I decide to do. I can't imagine how awful it would be to lose that freedom of choice when I'm older just because I couldn't make my body do something.

Looking good today just makes me happy. I look in the mirror and go, "You know, you really look good for any age. You're past 40, but your body's in the best shape it's ever been in your entire life, and you have more control over how you look than ever before."

If I can look and feel my best, at this age *anyone* can do it. But it doesn't just get done—you have to DO IT! And once you do it, it doesn't last. You have to KEEP doing it.

That's why Robert, one of the nation's leading sports nutrition experts, and I have shared our experiences, fitness philosophies, and information to write the one book that can serve as a guide to overall, lasting well-being based on the close connection between your body and mind.

I can only see a better, richer life coming from that. We know dieting is a curse. You can't just stop eating. So we have a diet and weight-maintenance program that does not force you to live in denial your whole life.

We've all started new workout programs only to give up and fail because we've set impossible goals. For instance, we know that running is difficult for a lot of people. *Our* exercise program is based on low-impact aerobic walking and a series of exercises geared to your own needs and abilities so you won't get frustrated and give up. We know the excuses, we know it's really tough to go it alone, we've struggled with motivation. We have had to deal with all of it.

But we also learned the tricks that will help you stick to a realistic exercise program that you'll look forward to every day. I know this works. People I know who have had a war going on with their bodies begin to work out, and suddenly they start to love the new power they have over their bodies. It's the power to look in the mirror and like the changes you see, wear great clothes that show off parts of your body you couldn't show before because it never looked good. The changes may be minor at first, but they will only lead to a self-confidence you never had before. What's important is to start.

I don't know anybody who doesn't feel better when they look better. I hear women say, "I feel so bad now; I just let myself go," or "I lost two dress sizes, and I feel really good about myself." And when you feel better, you do better work, you have more energy, more to give your family, and your concentration on everything is sharper.

We've seen how exercise can help you reduce and manage stress and pull you out of negative attitudes and depressions. I know. I've been dealing with them for most of my life, and I can tell you that nothing lifts me out of a bad mood better than a hard workout on my treadmill. It never fails: to us, exercise is nothing short of a miracle.

ROBERT

We've been our own best guinea pigs for years. We put ourselves through all the diets, workouts, and fads, as well as our share of skin and hair experiments. That's why we have written *Forever Fit*. The *Forever Fit* Permanent Weight-Loss Plan, Weight-Maintenance Plan, and exercise plan are the result of long and often frustrating experiences we have both had with dieting, training, and weight maintenance.

Now we've developed a comprehensive program for total well-being that has truly succeeded for both of us. It is a remarkable, cutting-edge weight-loss diet derived from a scientifically balanced combination of carbohydrates, protein, and fat, inspired by Cher's proven success with the aerobic power-walking and muscle-toning workout program we designed together and based on our de-aging strategy for skin care.

We won't pull any punches. We'll tell you about each and every product we currently use, *by brand name.** Because we've already asked all the questions and made the mistakes for you, you won't have to suffer from the wrong choices. We even walked up and down supermarket aisles, taking an inventory of those products that meet our exacting standards; we've compiled food lists and read between the lines of fine print where ingredients are listed so you'll know the difference between buying "health" and buying hype when you stock your *Forever Fit* pantry.

There are very good reasons to be vigilant about what we choose to eat. The issue of food safety—from carcinogenic ingredients to hazardous

---

*We've referred to several products by Twin Laboratories, Ronkonkoma, N.Y., a company Robert consults with. Although we have used many of their products with success, we've tried to offer alternative products.

pesticides to the inadequacy of government regulations—has become so critical and controversial that by the middle of 1990 no fewer than 30 food safety bills were before Congress, the most ever at any one time. The message is clear: making the right decisions about food can turn into a matter of life and death.

We take the same no-nonsense approach to exercise. This is not a book about fitness fantasies. It is not a manual on how to make it as a supermodel or professional athlete. We have not scaled our standards and expectations beyond your reach. For us, "perfection" means feeling, looking, *being* the very best YOU can be. That's a realistic goal we can all achieve.

FOREVER FIT IS A
TOTAL HEALTH PACKAGE

**IT'S GETTING
STARTED THAT
COUNTS**

We believe this book will become your "bible" for getting fit—and staying fit. Sure, some men and women are luckier than others with what they've been "given" through heredity. So, yes, it's an unfair fact of life: some of us have to work harder than others; some of us are skeptical veterans of the trendiest health and diet kicks. But with our *Forever Fit* program we're less interested in where you've been than in where you're headed. It's getting started now that counts most for us. That's why we've created an equal-opportunity fitness and diet strategy for women and men regardless of age and lifestyle.

But such a strategy doesn't just happen. The answers to the most critical health questions don't just come to us. There's so much confusion and controversy nowadays about food products, body chemistry, physical training, aging, and weight loss. It's become *too hard and time-consuming* for the average working person to figure it all out. But we have already done it and written the one book that will tell you everything you need to know.

The revolutionary diet and fitness regime I developed through research and experience with professional athletes helped pull Cher out of a long physical and mental slump. Her turnaround in creative energy, mental focus, and self-confidence was amazing—and I don't amaze easily. It gave her just the kind of strength, peak stamina, and self-assurance she needed to haul herself out of the doldrums and move her career and life in dynamic, award-winning directions.

She came to understand why many of the world's foremost athletes and celebrities have had stunning success working with my nutritional and workout programs. I made just a few basic—but tasty—changes in her diet and overall approach toward eating. Just doing *that* immediately gave her the boost she needed to hone and accelerate our own easy-to-follow exercise program. The result: in no time flat, the condition—and look—of her body was markedly improved.

Forever Fit is actually several books in one. It provides a regimen that lets you take control of your diet, reach your optimum weight and desired level of fitness, and improve your looks and the quality of your life.

Forever Fit is:

- *A diet, fitness, and beauty book* complete with our remarkable Permanent Weight-Loss Plan and Weight-Maintenance Plan and our suggestions for enjoying younger skin at any age. The *Forever Fit* Diet has propelled us to new levels of energy and self-confidence. Our recommendations are based on the latest breakthroughs in nutrition research, and they will provide you with greater variety, freedom, and pleasure than you've ever enjoyed on a weight program before.

- *A cookbook-within-a-book* offering more than 75 delicious and healthy recipes developed by Hilarie Porter, M.S., a world-renowned expert in gourmet creations for slimming cuisine. Finally, you can forget about the grim deprivations of dieting. We did. We love to eat and we love to cheat. And we'll tell you how to do both! After all, Cher, a world-class ice cream and chocolate lover, has discovered tricks *and* treats on *Forever Fit's* regimen that allow her to give in to that nagging sweet tooth. I've watched her develop a most impressive discipline when it comes to dieting, especially when a video or film shoot or rock tour is coming up and she needs to look her sexy, revealing best. But there are still certain foods even *she* won't give up just to look fabulous.

  So if she can have it both ways, so can you. You probably can't imagine the ordeal of keeping to a regimen that forever forbids treats like lasagne, pancakes, French fries and sauces, puddings, cakes, and brownies, right? Well, that's okay because you won't have to give them up on our *Forever Fit* Diet. Plus, we *encourage* drinking our own thick and tasty shakes as meal supplements—because they're *good* for you!

  Each recipe includes a complete breakdown of calories, protein, carbohydrate, fat, cholesterol, and sodium, so you will never have to guess how a particular dish fits into your overall program.

- *An easy-to-follow exercise video guide,* the result of years of our own best and worst experiences with training regimens. We designed it for the person who no longer wants to risk injury and chronic pain from running but who wants the energizing, exhilarating "high" of a basic yet effective, calorie-burning, cardiovascular workout.

- *A food composition index* for hundreds of everyday supermarket, fast-food, health-food, and restaurant offerings. It will also break down foods listed for all of the special recipes in this and Robert's other two bestselling nutrition books *Eat to Win* (New York: Rawson Associates, 1983) and *Eat to Succeed* (New York: Rawson Associates, 1986). By knowing exactly what you're putting into your body when you cook and eat, you'll be able to make the wisest and tastiest decisions about food. This simple-to-use resource will furnish the precise per-serving tally of calories, carbohydrates, fats, proteins, cholesterol, and sodium. From now on, when you shop for groceries or dine out, you'll be selecting the right foods with knowing confidence instead of confusion and ignorance.

We want to share with you the benefits of our years of experimentation with fitness, antiaging, and skin products—especially those that are least known and hardest to find.

CHER

When I first started working with Robert, I had put on weight because I had injured my arm and couldn't work out. My film work had left me drained, I wasn't in great shape, and I felt lethargic. He did a blood work-up on me, put me on his great-tasting diet, and had me bouncing on a trampoline for an aerobic workout that wouldn't hurt my arm.

I learned why aerobic walking can actually be better for you than running. I found out why some foods can be healthy *or* unhealthy, depending on how they are prepared. Like tortillas. If you steam a tortilla, it's pretty healthy. If you fry the same tortilla, it turns into Hell Night.

I was skeptical. I had tried all the major diets but found, for example, the Beverly Hills diet was torture. They tell you to eat only fruit all day, one fruit type at a time. Plus, in New York in winter, where do you find fresh watermelon, mango, and pineapple? But Robert showed me how you don't have to live in denial and constantly deprive yourself. Right away he gave me these banana pancakes (page 175) that are unbelievably delicious. It's like someone brought you the Taj Mahal on a plate. How can you eat banana pancakes and go, "God, this is a tough diet"? The key is getting yourself into a different thought process and being open to making some changes. And I learned again how exercise can be the one thing that keeps me feeling balanced, calm, and in control no matter how crazy my life gets.

Robert's program brought amazing results. By 1987 I had the most demanding year or so I had ever had in my life. I made three films back to back, recorded an album, made two videos, launched a fragrance for women, and traveled four times back and forth all over Europe for promotion. I sat for hundreds and hundreds of interviews, and I did commercials and TV appearances and posed for god-knows-how-many magazine cover sessions.

It was a schedule that would have choked a horse. There's no way I could have done it all without working out, always getting some exercise in, no matter how tired I was. And by being strict about what I was eating. Because of the way Robert and I redesigned my diet and exercise routine on the *Forever Fit* Plan, I had so much more energy than I had ever had.

During that period of time I turned 40. Was I worried about a milestone like 40? Listen, the absolute best shape I was ever in was when I shot the video for "I Found Someone," and that was a year later.

Even now, at 44, I don't see myself slowing down a whole lot. Between the fall of 1989 and the fall of 1990 I shot *Mermaids* for four difficult months, put together a world-wide concert tour, recorded another album, promoted the new movie, and finished work on the book you're now reading. Plus, I bought a new house, decorated it myself, moved in, began building another new house nearby, kept my business running, tried to maintain my personal life, and filmed a fitness video. My days *always* started with a printout from my assistant with a schedule that kept me running from 8:00 to 8:00.

There is no way I could have done all that without a fitness program that keeps me at my peak, helps me cut stress and cope with depressions and exhaustion, and keeps my mind and body strong. My life may be more hectic than other people's, but it's not really all that different from any working mother's life. The same little tricks that help me get through it will help any woman who's got a job, a husband, and children. Because she too is racing the clock, facing deadlines all the time. My life is a constant game of "Beat the Clock." I can be up for days working on something—exhausted, filled with tension and anxiety. It can make you crazy, like mice in a laboratory maze. For me, physical training really helps reduce the stress.

The reason a book like *Forever Fit* is helpful is that you can't turn 40 or 42 years old and just think that God or the U.S. government or *anyone else* is going to take care of your body. I have this feeling that people think someone is watching out for their best interests when it comes to food, medicine, vitamins, and exercising.

You're the only person in charge of your body and your health. We weren't meant to be so sedentary. We were meant to be hunters and

YOU'RE THE ONLY PERSON IN CHARGE OF YOUR BODY AND YOUR HEALTH

gatherers, to bend over, to walk, move, use our bodies. We've created an environment where we don't do that anymore. Too many people are constantly on the run, eating fast-food junk, and looking for a magic cure in the form of cocaine to keep them up and partying, marijuana or alcohol to settle them down and loosen up their inhibitions, tranquilizers to let them sleep, cigarettes for nerves, and fatty, unhealthy foods when they eat to forget their sorrows.

Our bodies are like engines. What happens if you pour cheap gasoline into your car engine? Doesn't your car just fall apart? We can't keep dumping poison into our bodies from every angle—and expect them to keep running properly. Put the right fuel into your body and you'll feel a whole lot better right away. The more vigilant I am about what I eat the better I feel.

It's not surprising many of us are careless or reckless about what we're doing to ourselves. It's easy to look around, see the news, and feel helpless, stressed out, or angry. So we pig out from nerves; we get lazy. We grab a Big Mac that has a whole day's fat allowance or go through a pint of Häagen-Dazs. It's a vicious cycle.

A lifetime commitment to fitness has become all the more important because our world today is so complex and overwhelming. So many serious issues and crises seep into your mind every day. You can't just be an island and not see the problems. You see things on the news and feel helpless and say, "Well, what can I do about that?" or "Can I do anything at all?" You may feel helpless in your job—even in your life. Something may happen with your kids; your husband's doing drugs or drinking; it could be *millions of things.*

Our leaders have let industry poison our air and water. Our food is processed so much so that it's almost not food anymore. We've got people killing each other in every part of the world. The United States ranks 49th in literacy among member countries of the United Nations. Our prison system is down the tubes. The savings and loan officials were just using their positions to financially rape people in their communities, and now we're going to have to spend a fortune to fix it up.

I saw the mayor of Washington, D.C., Marion Barry, smoking crack on TV, and he didn't see why he couldn't still be mayor, and I thought, "George Washington must be doing a 360 in his grave." I think about nuclear power plants, toxic waste that burns through iron barrels, oil spills in our harbors and rivers, the hole in the ozone layer. I think about the crack epidemic, and about the 13 million children in the U.S. who are malnourished, and about the homeless families living in cars and cardboard boxes. Or the fact that one in five Americans can't read, that kids growing up today are more out of shape than ever before because they're playing Nintendo games instead of baseball and football and they're stuffing their faces with Cocoa Puffs and Big Macs and all kinds of junk food. Sometimes it just doesn't seem like anything is sacred anymore.

But there is one area of life that is sacred—and that we still maintain complete control over: our bodies and minds. And I can say this about the gym: no matter what else is going on, there's never been a time when I didn't feel better when I left the gym than when I went in. I'm not stupid. I wouldn't waste my time if it didn't work. I'd read a book. I'd go shopping. I'd go to the movies. I sure wouldn't bust my ass the way I do.

And yet I know some women are really luckier than others and some have to work harder than others. But the way you treat your mind and body has to become a high priority. I also know there are hundreds of thousands, *millions* of people who think, as I once did, that you're pretty much stuck with the body you're born with and it starts to deteriorate as you get older.

You can believe that if you want to; or you can read the rest of this book and find out for yourself how you can get—and stay—in the best shape of your life at any age and for all ages.

We're not here to tell you that life isn't a bitch. Life *is* a bitch. Once you know that, half your battle is won, because then you're ready to transcend the fact that life can be difficult. You're prepared for it. And I don't care how much money you have, how famous you are, or if you've won an Academy Award. I have my own set of problems. They're different from other people's problems. But they are no less stressful.

So for me, exercise gives me at least some time alone where I'm working on myself, getting a better perspective, thinking about my responsibilities and my problems, and coming up with solutions. I don't go into the gym for my body alone; a better body is just an unbelievable fringe benefit.

Hopefully I'll still be able to have a happy, active life when I'm 75 because I took care of my body when I was 30 and 40. Maybe, like my grandmother, I'll still be looking for the latest in leotards on my birthday. Or maybe climbing Mt. Everest.

2

CHER: THE PERFECT PARTNER

ROBERT

As a prominent sports nutritionist, my normal workday has often consisted of advising such world-renowned athletes as Martina Navratilova and Ivan Lendl. My "track record" of helping good athletes become better—and better athletes become the very best in the world—speaks for itself. Many of my clients have used my advice to win world championships and set world records. I was quite surprised, however, when Cher called. I knew this was a woman of stunning versatility and limitless energy. But was she about to launch into training for the women's U.S. Open? I couldn't imagine what this was about.

It turned out Cher had called to ask for my help in recovering from a grueling year of hard work, little sleep, and poor diet. She had just finished making the motion picture *Mask,* for which she won the Best Actress award at the 1985 Cannes Film Festival in the role of a pill-popping biker mom with a son suffering from a serious, deforming birth defect.

As great as Cher's work in the film was, it had clearly taken a heavy toll. "I'm at the lowest point of my career, physically and mentally," she admitted to me. "My role in *Mask* was so demanding. The pressure on me was so great to be extra-thin to play my part that I starved myself. Now I've gained back all the weight I lost, plus an extra eight pounds, and I'm totally burned out from dieting and stress."

I quickly realized that beyond the superficial circumstances she described, Cher's plight was actually no different from what I regularly find among topflight touring athletes: professional burnout. Many athletes I've worked with undereat and/or overtrain to achieve and maintain what they consider to be their ideal "fighting" weight—often at the expense of health and fitness. Improper diet and weight-loss methods, compounded with jet lag, irregular sleeping patterns, and stress can all result in the burnout syndrome similar to the one that led Cher to seek my help.

Like many weight- and health-conscious people today, Cher was concerned with holding on to her youthful vitality, looks, and high energy levels. She had learned the importance of creating a high-quality life of fitness and good health. But like many people so concerned, she had embraced a variety of ill-advised weight-loss schemes (including starvation) and diet programs in an effort to stay slender and fit.

TAKING THE CHER CHALLENGE

I agreed to work with Cher, but I wasn't overly optimistic about her ability to comply with the same strict dietary guidelines that I impose on professional athletes. My field experience has taught me that most athletes are "no pain, no gain" gluttons for punishment who will adopt just about any dietary regimen, however strict, and make any sacrifice if it means winning. Quite simply, athletes earn their living with their bodies— bodies that must be trained and fueled to move faster, stronger, and longer than the competition's. When the body begins to deteriorate, so do performance and income. Nonathletes, however, are generally less motivated to curb their appetites for unhealthy foods and lifestyles than the pros.

That's why it was with some reluctance—and scaled-down expectations— that I considered Cher for the same strict and demanding regimen that I create for world-class athletes. A quick dietary history revealed that she had a chronic weakness for the kinds of food that aren't exactly at the top of an athlete's training diet and strict weight-loss program: rich chocolate desserts, deep-fat-fried foods, and all manner of salty or sweetened snacks. And her first cholesterol test revealed a less than healthy blood cholesterol count.

Plus, with Cher I was not taking on a jock-client burning with a dream to topple Martina or break the tape ahead of Greta Waitz at the Boston marathon. Sure, I knew that Cher, like most entertainers—most human beings—wanted to *look* her best; but I wasn't convinced she was ready to commit to an all-out, full-time assault on conditioning. In fact, like many onetime runners preferring to approach mid-life without nagging aches, pains, and orthopedic worries, she had grown to detest jogging. When she called, she was obviously suffering a crisis of motivation. She really didn't know *what* to do.

The challenge was formidable: to devise a can't-miss, no-willpower weight-loss and weight-maintenance diet coupled with a simple but efficient exercise and conditioning program she could follow anywhere in the world—*and* throw in an antiaging skin-care regimen. If it would allow Cher to enjoy a lifetime of sleek, healthful vitality while functioning at a high level of artistic achievement, it could very well do the same for anyone.

As I struggled to create this all-encompassing program, I realized I could learn something from Cher's own checkered history with dieting, exercise, fads, and products. Her practical experience of trial and error had turned her into a "streetwise" dieter. She had learned much about the diets and products that *don't* work, which is second only in importance to learning which ones *do*. And we both soon realized that by pooling our knowledge and resources we could devise a program that would benefit the general population as well.

Cher impressed me from the start. Despite the problematic lapses that led her to me in the first place, Cher brought to our work a remarkably sane and candid attitude about food that assured our success. Cher struck me as a woman who had a fundamental respect for her own body and treated it accordingly. She had always dealt decisively and intelligently with "substances" like cigarettes, alcohol, coffee, and drugs. Basically, she just said no. And was she ever tough on herself!

But obviously she had some concern and confusion about diet, fitness, and health, which is why she contacted me. I was struck—and relieved—to discover that Cher, in dealing with diets, had come to regard food as just another substance that people can abuse during weak, stressful, or self-destructive phases. Making that analogy was important. Given Cher's positive history with other vices, I was optimistic about her ability to kick whatever bad habits she had acquired about food. She convinced me she was not only eager but sufficiently strong-willed to make bold, sweeping changes in her diet.

KICK BAD HABITS ABOUT FOOD

CHER

I have a certain kind of personality. It's like if I were a drug addict I would probably be a dead one, because I would do all the drugs you could do. When I smoked, I smoked three packs of cigarettes a day. Some people might say I'm fanatical or obsessed with exercise. But at least that's a healthy obsession.

The most important thing for your health is to give yourself a fighting chance. I quit smoking and never smoke. I don't do drugs. I never drink coffee and almost never have alcohol or eat red meat, so I'm way ahead of the game right there.

But it's not like I don't have weaknesses. When it comes to food, I love to eat. For many people food is like a substance to abuse. If I've been eating really well and suddenly go off that, I have to constantly make sure I don't go for the wrong foods out of stress or nervousness. It can be really insidious. The craving just gets into you, and you have to be real careful.

I can eat Häagen-Dazs coffee, strawberry, or chocolate ice cream up the wazoo. Or I'll have 10 tons of M&Ms. It's really a shame these things aren't good for you. A shame. But we have to be grown up about them.

People who put drugs into their body always amaze me because they get the drugs from some pimpy guy on a dark street corner that you wouldn't take *directions from*. But you're going to go up to him, give him money, and ingest some substance into your body from this cretin?

To me cocaine is a nightmare. I thought, "People are really having a good time with this?" I never got it. I don't want my heart beating like that, feeling out of breath and nervous. That's just not something I find appealing. I want to be able to sleep. I have never tried cocaine. I did once have liquid cocaine administered to me by a doctor who wanted to shrink swollen nasal membranes and get a look at what was wrong inside my nasal passage. When he told me what he had given me, I was frightened and angry and I started to cry. My own doctor later told me it was B.S.; the other doctor could have given me something else.

I never really got into drugs. I did try Benzedrine once. That was some weekend. I was 14. I chewed the same piece of gum for the whole weekend. By the time I was ready to go to bed on Sunday night after not sleeping for three days I was so upset that I went to my mother and started crying when I told her what I had done. My jaw felt like it was broken, I had chewed gum so hard, and my mother asked, "Did you learn your lesson?" I said, "Absolutely."

I guess 14 was a big year for me. The first time I ever got drunk was that same year. I drank two big cans of this stuff called Country Club Stout Malt Liquor and puked my guts up all over this place in L.A. called the Players' Ring. What a fiasco. So it wasn't hard to push alcohol out of my life altogether. I never had another drink until I was 27. Now, if I ever drink, it's a glass of wine, nothing more than that. I just don't like alcohol. It's fattening and makes you real puffy and ugly. It doesn't hold any fascination for me. Plus, my stepfather was a terrific guy, but he was an alcoholic who died of cirrhosis of the liver and my mother's father was also an alcoholic.

I had a scary incident involving alcohol during the filming of *The Witches of Eastwick*. The car I was riding in was rear-ended by a man who had left a party with his wife and was way too drunk to drive. When they got in their car, she put him on the passenger side and he passed out. She stopped at a 7-Eleven to get cigarettes. While she was inside, he woke up, got in the driver's seat, not even remembering she was with him, and drove off. He smashed into our car, ramming us into oncoming traffic. His car was totaled, but somehow we all came out of it okay, though I had a bad whiplash. I was lucky, but thousands and thousands of innocent people are killed every year by drunk drivers. *Alcohol is just unbelievably bad.*

It's the legal substances that are hardest to kick for many people. For me cigarettes were difficult. I heard someone talking recently about smoking—that it's worse than kicking heroin and that you can't do it. That's just B.S. I smoked. I loved it. I gave it up. People can do difficult things. People can survive the Holocaust, they can certainly give up smoking.

There are obvious medical reasons to quit smoking. Not only does it *kill you*, but before that it destroys your looks. It does terrible, terrible things to a woman's face. It ruins your skin. It gives you all these little lines from squinting and pinching up your mouth to smoke. And if you smoke and go in for a face-lift, you usually heal badly. If you don't smoke, your chances of healing well are better.

Coffee is out of the question for me. My body has an unbelievably low tolerance for certain substances, including prescription drugs. An aspirin once made me shake because it had caffeine in it. There was a scene in *The Witches of Eastwick* where I had to wake up in a bed full of live snakes. It wasn't supposed to be my scene, but all of a sudden it was given to me. The part of the scene we shot first was a night shot consisting of me running out of my house in terror after having woken up with these snakes all over me. As an actress this posed a couple of problems for me: number one, as we would be shooting the *exterior* of my house only, there wouldn't even be any snakes there for me to react to, and number two, even if there had been snakes on the set that night, I'm not really afraid of them at all!

So I started looking around to find the motivation I needed to appear hysterical when I really wasn't. And I thought, "Well, what makes me nervous and crazy?" And I realized the answer was coffee. So I drank four or five cups, one after another after another, and about halfway through shooting this scene I got about as uncomfortable as I have ever been in my life. I was a mess. I was shaking so badly they finally had to shut down production, and I went home to bed, but of course I couldn't even sleep.

Other beverages can also be a problem. For instance I used to be hooked on Dr. Pepper, drinking like four a day, which is a lot of sugar. I got off Dr. Pepper by going to carbonated water, which I hated in the beginning. Then I started looking forward to having Perrier so much that I didn't even recognize myself without one in my hand. So I realized it wasn't the sugar but the carbonation I liked so much.

As for food groups, I had to get out of the habit of eating certain foods and into the habit of eating others. I try to avoid foods with a high fat content because they make me sluggish and keep my weight up. Dairy products are not good for us. After a certain age we don't need milk. I weaned myself from whole milk to nonfat milk—if I'm having milk at all. I think cheese is one of the worst things for the body. It doesn't digest well, and most cheeses are too high in fat and cholesterol.

One exception that Robert recommends is Parmesan to flavor meals. It has roughly the same amount of fat and cholesterol as most cheeses— about eight grams of fat and twenty-five milligrams of cholesterol per ounce (or packaged slice). But you never need an ounce of Parmesan because it's so flavorful. So when you sprinkle a tablespoon of it over pasta you're getting only about 1.5 grams of fat and 4 milligrams of cholesterol. You can do so many great things with it and not have to think about it, like slicing up an eggplant and putting a little oregano, sweet basil, and Parmesan over it and sticking it in the broiler. It tastes great, and there's nothing in there that'll hurt you.

I really don't eat meat, but only partly because of the animal fat and cholesterol. I once took Elijah when he was very small to a working farm in the San Fernando Valley. There were these tiny little calves there that had been taken away from their mothers, and they put straps under their front and hind legs and hung them in dark cages before slaughtering them.

When I saw what they did to the calves, I was furious. Elijah was horrified. It's bad enough people have to kill animals to eat them. I don't like it, but I can understand it. And it's not like I'm a major animal rights activist, either. Still, I can't justify the torture of animals just so I can put a meal on my table.

My worst addiction is sweets. Chocolate. I've always had a major sweet tooth. And I know when I feel really healthy I'm strong enough to leave sweets alone. So why give in? I guess I just love the taste. I also know if I eat lots of chocolate or candy I'll get a rush for about 20 minutes. Stress burns up the chemicals and nutrients that give you energy, so you tend to replace them with sugar for quick energy—but eventually you crash and burn. The sugar and caffeine of a Coke will give you a rush, but it doesn't last. That's why you have the craving all day.

Sweets have been the toughest "substance" for me to kick. Later on in this book we'll talk about acceptable ways to cheat on the *Forever Fit* Plan that give you a much better chance at successful dieting. Robert's feeling about it is great: "Treat yourself every once in a while. Don't deny yourself something you like so much." So when we went to Cannes for the film festival, we had chocolate soufflés, and they were just out-of-this-world unbelievable. That's my kind of diet.

ROBERT

The first thing I did when Cher invited me to her house was to inspect her kitchen and "sweep" it clear of all unhealthy foods and trendy but questionable nutritional supplements such as bee pollen and starch blockers. I went through her refrigerator and pantry and threw out dozens of dubious "health" foods (organic cakes and cookies loaded with tropical oils, "trail mixes" with as much fat as a Big Mac). They all sounded impressive—"all natural," "organically grown"—but I broke the news to her that they were all part of the problem rather than the solution.

Then I took Cher shopping and began to educate her about tricky labeling on food products and show her what I considered to be more beneficial, nutritious supplements and products (we'll tell you what we use by brand name throughout this book). Next we worked out the exercise program that Cher could follow anywhere (it is explained in full in Chapter 9).

As luck would have it, we soon had a chance to test our regimen and take it on the road—some 6,000 miles from Cher's home gym and kitchen. She was nominated for Best Actress at the Cannes film festival for her role in *Mask;* off we went in the spring to the French Riviera. So this had to be a *portable* program as well.

We made a simple diet-survival travel list: portable blenders to make our special weight-loss drink (portable weight-loss meals), vitamins (portable nutrition), fold-up trampolines and walking shoes (portable exercise equipment). We were thus able to enjoy delicious and healthy meals and, in some cases, rich desserts (after all, this is a health plan for human beings) throughout Europe (and later Japan) while still following our diet and exercise plan.

As it turned out, the inconvenience of world travel actually worked for us and made us more resourceful. It forced us to face the necessity of devising a weight-loss plan that we could take with us anywhere in the world, based on complex carbohydrates such as pasta, rice, bread, potatoes, vegetables, fruits, and high-quality protein foods such as seafood, poultry, and, occasionally even some red meat. At some point I wondered if we had actually started a new branch of nutrition called "creative international weight loss."

ALL DIETERS
MUST COPE
WITH
OCCASIONAL
LAPSES OF
WILLPOWER

With the diet and workout program in place, we next addressed Cher's need to maintain healthy-looking skin through proper nutrition and the use of topical antiaging creams. For years she had been using Retin-A, the well-known prescription skin cream doctors recommend for treating skin disorders such as acne. It is now also used to help eliminate skin wrinkling, another stubborn skin problem, so she had a head start in keeping smooth and healthy-looking skin. But Retin-A is a powerful prescription drug to be used only under a physician's care. And it's not without side effects.

So I began research on products that would help keep skin moist and supple and would protect against premature aging due to overexposure to ultraviolet (UV) radiation from the sun and tanning booths. I studied the most effective ingredients in the leading skin moisturizers and talked to some of the leading dermatologists. I learned about the ingredients most of the experts agreed should be in a product that qualified as a true antiaging skin moisturizer.

Now we both use products every day and night to maintain soft, supple skin. Once again Cher's special need led to the discovery of products that everyone could benefit from (these products, and skin care in general, are discussed in Chapter 8).

As it turned out, Cher was the perfect partner for developing this remarkable total health plan. In one way it was fortunate that she possessed the ordinary human weaknesses—chocolate and ice cream cravings and the occasional lapses of willpower—that all dieters must cope with. It confirmed for us that if Cher could succeed on this program there's an excellent chance that virtually anyone can come out a winner.

Cher has learned that by using the right food, exercise, and health products she can look and feel her best without radically altering her work schedule, without making drastic sacrifices at mealtime—whether at home or far from it. She has learned that the best way to stay slim and youthful is to follow a realistic, practical program based on ordinary foods, regular exercise, and products we have used and have come to rely on over the years.

And now it's time for you to become our partner as we help you achieve those goals to which we should all aspire: a life of ongoing good health, invigorating fitness, and peak vitality.

3

READ THIS BEFORE YOUR NUMBER IS UP

B efore we help you take command of your body in the battle for health and fitness, we urge you to visit your physician for a physical examination. In particular, one test will tell you and your physician one of the most important numbers in your life—your blood cholesterol count.

By now nearly everyone has heard that a high blood cholesterol count can be a significant risk factor for heart disease— still the number-one cause of death in the U.S. And many people have already taken the first step in the fight against heart disease by having their cholesterol measured. If you haven't yet done so, we strongly recommend you do that. *We urge you to consult with a physician before taking any test so that you will be properly informed and instructed on the nature and procedure of these tests.*

IT'S A NUMBERS GAME

There is still a great deal of disagreement among health experts as to what constitutes a "safe" or desirable cholesterol count, but the published data are compelling. These data indicate that the ideal total blood cholesterol level (the combined amount of LDL, HDL, and VLDL cholesterol carried in your blood) for *anyone* who wants to eliminate the possibility of a cholesterol-induced artery blockage, which could lead to a heart attack or stroke, is clearly in the range of 150 mg/dl for most people, regardless of sex or age. And populations the world over who have a cholesterol number of 150 or less rarely suffer heart attacks.

That's why we emphatically defend a cholesterol number of 150 or below. There's another equally important reason, however. Recent research has established that people with a serious degree of artery blockage can possibly *reopen* their clogged arteries when they reduce their blood cholesterol levels to 150 or below (the reversal process can actually start *before* cholesterol drops to 150) and embrace a regular aerobic exercise plan.

HOW TO PREPARE FOR THE BLOOD CHOLESTEROL TEST

Since it is essential that you obtain an accurate blood cholesterol count, we offer the following guidelines to help you obtain a valid and reliable reading:

1. Do not have the blood cholesterol test when you are sick (e.g., when you have a cold or influenza). Wait one week after you are better before having the test.
2. Do not eat or drink anything except water for 12 hours before the test.
3. Avoid taking the test during times of great emotional stress or job pressure.
4. Check with your physician to see if any medication you are taking or any medical treatment you are undergoing might interfere with the results of the test.

CHOLESTEROL EXPLAINED

Just what *is* cholesterol, and why is it so bad for you?

Cholesterol is a waxy substance that's produced mainly by your liver. It is *not* a fat, as many people mistakenly believe. It supplies no calories to the body. Cholesterol is made only by animals (a blue-green alga food source called *spirulina* is the exception we know of), so when you eat foods from animal sources, you're ingesting *dietary* cholesterol. *Serum* cholesterol is the amount of cholesterol carried in the blood, and this number, generally expressed as milligrams of cholesterol per 100 milliliters (one deciliter) of blood (mg/dl), reflects the amount of cholesterol your body manufactures, plus the amount you eat.

Always necessary (it's the structural component of cell membranes and an insulator of nerve cells), sometimes sexy (it's the building block of testosterone and estrogen, the hormones that make men men and women women), and still controversial (there are *still* physicians and nutritionists who believe that cholesterol does not cause heart attacks), cholesterol can also be extremely dangerous. The danger arises when cholesterol irritates and damages your arteries, narrowing them and making it easier for a blood clot to block the passage of blood to your heart (a heart attack) or your brain (a stroke).

Cholesterol is water-repellent and must travel throughout the body via the blood, which is mostly water. So cholesterol is combined with proteins into packets called *lipoproteins* that are able to circulate in the bloodstream. The most prevalent type of lipoprotein is low-density lipoprotein, or LDL; it's this lipoprotein that carries cholesterol into your arterial walls. Another type of lipoprotein, high-density lipoprotein (HDL), actually carries cholesterol away from arterial walls. Although the higher your HDL fraction the better, your LDL levels will always be higher than your HDL levels.

The point, then, is to keep your total blood cholesterol levels as low as possible, *up to a value of 100 plus your age, but in no case higher than 150.*

Maintaining a healthy blood cholesterol level would be no problem if you simply relied on your liver; each day it would make all the cholesterol your body requires. But since all animal foods contain some cholesterol (and many contain a hefty amount) and since your liver's daily cholesterol production quota is barely reduced in response to dietary intake, *if you eat too many foods from animal sources, you're getting more cholesterol than you need.*

How much more? Up to a point, your blood cholesterol levels will rise in direct proportion to how much dietary cholesterol you consume. So the more high-cholesterol foods you eat—such as beef, organ meats, egg yolks, and whole-milk products—the faster your blood cholesterol will climb up to and beyond your target limit of 100 plus your age.

CHOLESTEROL: HOW MUCH IS TOO MUCH?

The American Heart Association recommends that we all practice *moderation* and consume up to *300 milligrams per day* of cholesterol.

Such a level defines "moderation" only in a nation such as ours, where people consume, on the average, a staggering 600 to 800 milligrams or more of cholesterol a day. Keep cholesterol consumption under 300 milligrams a day, the AHA says, and your blood cholesterol will remain at a safe level.

MODERATION IN ALL THINGS EXCEPT CHOLESTEROL

In our opinion this recommendation is far too generous, because most healthy people cannot keep their blood cholesterol levels at 100 plus their age while eating anywhere close to 300 milligrams of cholesterol a day and a diet composed of up to 30 percent total calories from fat such as the AHA recommends. An overwhelming body of published scientific evidence clearly shows that people who practice this kind of "moderation" may still have difficulty in lowering their cholesterol number into the real safety range (under 150), while those people who consume zero to 150 milligrams of dietary cholesterol per day and about 10 to 20 percent of total calories from fat generally stand a better chance of achieving a cholesterol number of 150 or below. We recommend you adopt the healthy and scientifically sound anticholesterol plan we're going to tell you about.

IT'S THE FIRST 300 MILLIGRAMS IN YOUR DIET THAT KILL YOU

Beyond the levels your liver makes every day, there's just a small amount of dietary cholesterol your body can clear. Exceed that limit and your blood cholesterol levels will start to rise. Ironically enough, it's the first 300 or so milligrams of cholesterol that exert the most powerful effect on your blood cholesterol values.

Here's why: the first 300 milligrams of cholesterol consumed tend to saturate the blood's ability to use and transport cholesterol safely through the bloodstream. Don't forget, the body already manufactures about 750 to 1,000 milligrams of cholesterol each day—more than enough to fill your body's need for cholesterol (it uses cholesterol for membrane synthesis in the cells, to manufacture bile acids that aid in digestion, and to synthesize hormones, including male and female sex hormones). Once the blood is laden with cholesterol—and it appears that this occurs even on "moderate-cholesterol" diets allowing 300 milligrams per day—eating more cholesterol will have only a minor incremental effect on already saturated blood cholesterol levels. After those initial 300 milligrams, additional cholesterol will not raise your blood levels as quickly—cold comfort, indeed, since the *first* 300 can be more than sufficient to raise your levels dangerously high.

There is no escaping the fact that *many people must restrict consumption of these foods to the levels we recommend to maintain a healthy blood cholesterol level—below 150 milligrams.* Our recommendations do not mean you have to give up these foods forever. They do require that you limit intake of dietary cholesterol to 150 milligrams per day if you're already at your optimum level and to even less if you haven't yet achieved your target level of 100 plus your age. Some people may have to take in even less cholesterol (about 25 milligrams per day) to hit 150. Still others, because of their genetic makeup, must use medication along with diet to control cholesterol levels.

The good news is that limiting your consumption of cholesterol to 150 milligrams a day or less is not at all difficult. Consider: four ounces of either lean beef, chicken without skin, or most fish contain about 120 milligrams of cholesterol, leaving room for two glasses of skim milk (total cholesterol: eight milligrams) and a four-ounce serving of frozen yogurt for dessert (some brands, such as Columbo, come in a cholesterol-free version).

A day's food plan might include the following:

Breakfast: a meal replacer shake made with skim milk or a bowl of whole grain cereal with fresh fruit and skim milk.

YOU DO NOT HAVE TO GIVE UP THESE FOODS FOREVER

Lunch: a bowl of split pea soup, spaghetti with marinara sauce and two teaspoons of grated Parmesan cheese, and one serving of fresh fruit.

Dinner: a broiled chicken breast (now available at fast-food restaurants such as Burger King), salad with low-fat dressing (two grams or less per serving—also available at many fast-food restaurants), and if you're eating at home, corn on the cob with Butter Buds or Molly McButter butter substitute, steamed broccoli with lemon juice, and a four-ounce serving of cholesterol-free frozen yogurt or one serving of fresh fruit.

Total cholesterol for the day: under 150 milligrams.

The *Forever Fit* Diet will help you cut cholesterol in three ways:

1. The *Forever Fit* dietary guidelines, listed and outlined in Chapter 5, will show you how to make wise mealtime and snack choices that will automatically keep your cholesterol consumption within recommended guidelines.
2. By consulting our food composition tables (located in Appendix III), you will find the cholesterol count of most commonly eaten foods (including fast foods). You will never again be forced to eat "blindly," without knowing how much cholesterol is in the foods you love.
3. The *Forever Fit* recipe section (Appendix I) contains delicious low-cholesterol recipes that make it possible to cut down on cholesterol without cutting back on your eating enjoyment.

WHAT ABOUT HDL CHOLESTEROL?

By now most people know that HDL (high-density lipoprotein) cholesterol is called the "good" cholesterol. Since your HDL cholesterol is one measure of your risk of artery closure and heart attack—the higher the number, the better—you should ask your physician to include this as part of your blood cholesterol test.

The *Forever Fit* Permanent Weight-Loss Plan and Exercise Program is designed to help you lower your total cholesterol number to 100 plus your age. Your HDL cholesterol number will be more important at the start of your new diet than after you've reduced your total cholesterol number to 150 or less. That's because when total cholesterol is about 180 and above, HDL cholesterol has a predictive value—it can tell your physician about your risk, or probability, of suffering from heart disease. For example, if your total cholesterol number is 260 and your HDL cholesterol is 30, your risk of suffering a heart attack may be six times (or even more) that of a person with a total cholesterol number of 200 and an HDL cholesterol number of 45. Once your total cholesterol number drops to 150 or below, HDL cholesterol tends to have a less predictive effect.

The Tarahumara Indians of Mexico, for example, have total cholesterol numbers of about 125 on the average and HDL cholesterol numbers of 25. Not surprisingly, heart attacks are virtually unknown among the Tarahumara. Yet a North American male with an identical HDL number of 25 *and* an "average" U.S. total cholesterol number of 240 would be a high-risk candidate for cardiovascular disease.

We don't expect you to take off for rural, remote areas where diet and less stressful lifestyles will prolong your life. But our *Forever Fit* Diet does address the issue of cholesterol in a manner that makes it feasible to stay right where you are and drop your total cholesterol level toward our ultimate target of 150 or below.

DROP TOTAL CHOLESTEROL LEVEL TOWARD OUR ULTIMATE TARGET

THE FOREVER FIT
PERMANENT WEIGHT-LOSS
PLAN: HOW IT WORKS

CHER

After I read Robert's book, *Eat To Win*, we began working together, and I told him we were in for a fight against my worst food enemy, chocolate. His reassuring attitude helped me. "Sweets," he said, "are okay if eaten sensibly. You can learn to appease this powerful sweet tooth of yours on this diet. Properly."

He was right. My problem has never been gaining a lot of weight. Even when I don't exercise—I want to be really honest about this—I don't get fat. But it's not like I don't have to fight myself over my cravings.

Do I still love M&Ms? Yes.

Could I go for a Mounds bar or Junior Mints? Yes.

Do I love Häagen-Dazs and Dove Bars? Absolutely.

Are Jack-in-the-Box tacos and Cherry Cokes great? Yes.

I try not to deny myself these things, because every time I go on a strict diet to lose weight quickly, I want to eat them all the more because I think they're disappearing from the planet.

I've admitted that chocolate is my biggest downfall. Basically, I like anything that has chocolate in it, and the chocolatier the better. I know a lot of people who don't have a sweet tooth; I'm not one of them. But I'm getting better about it, and I believe it has to do with not being obsessed with denying myself chocolate.

Honestly, we're all grown-ups, and we can do exactly what we want. If I go and buy a Mounds bar and it tastes really good, I know they're not going to disappear from the planet, so I don't need to have one tomorrow. Just the fact that every once in a while I'm *allowed* to have one makes it easier.

I had a boyfriend who liked Entenmann's chocolate doughnuts. Well, they're pretty good—know what I mean? I used to think, "They're going to be around, I'm not going to live in a doughnut-free world, so if I have one it doesn't mean I have to have *all* of them right now or have one every day. It means I can see them and not have them."

A diet should not mean that sweets are forever off-limits—and on the *Forever Fit* Plan, they aren't. I honestly believe that if you put in your mind that you're going to deny yourself everything, then that's all you'll be able to think about.

The key to this diet is that you don't feel you have to make major sacrifices. A diet shouldn't torture you, and ours doesn't. One of the best things about *Forever Fit*'s diet plan is the delicious meal replacer protein shake in the morning that absolutely satisfies my craving for chocolate— and my hunger. It's a powder called Feelin' Fit from Twin Laboratories. The directions say to make it with nonfat milk and it comes to fewer than 200 calories with almost no fat or cholesterol.

It's actually a *complete meal*. I asked Robert why this meal replacement shake was so much better than the others, and he had lots to say on the subject: "It's really a source of soluble and insoluble fibers like oat bran, cellulose, and psyllium, and it's got high-quality protein derived from skim milk and egg white. And it gives you one-third the RDA for essential vitamins and minerals and even trace minerals like selenium, which helps protect against cancer and heart disease, and chromium, which is required for carbohydrate metabolism."

I doctor my shakes with my own recipe that Robert admits is better than his. I use *water* and more ice to make it frostier. I put in regular (not chocolate-flavored) malt, which has fewer calories, three packets of Equal, and a heaping teaspoon of unsweetened cocoa powder like your mother used to make hot cocoa. Then I blend it all for a minute, and I've got a nutritious chocolate malt with 200 calories. (Sometimes I leave out the malt and add fresh strawberries.)

Still, Robert has always stressed permanent weight loss on a diet of mostly *solid* meals. We both feel the fat- and cholesterol-free meal replacer shakes on the market are a right step in helping people lose weight, but the last thing you want is to become dependent on them. If you really want to maintain lower weight for the rest of your life, you have to learn to change your eating habits using solid foods.

Moderation usually doesn't work for me. I have to actively start a program, get into a system, make a big change. The trick is not to make the denial another form of compulsion or neurosis—not to spend too much time thinking about the denial. The less I dwell on "I shouldn't, I shouldn't, I shouldn't," the less I give in.

For anyone who subconsciously overeats, there are support groups that deal with overeating, because this isn't something you do just once. If it is, it's not a problem. But if it becomes the major way you cope with all your problems, it's a pattern. The problem isn't that ice cream bar you have today—it's the one you have every day for a year. Sometimes I know I deal with my problems with a pint of Häagen-Dazs in the middle of my bed. If I'm having Pepperidge Farm Goldfish today, then let that be the only bad thing for today and that's enough—instead of moving on to Ding Dongs and then ice cream and so on.

To make this or *any* diet work you have to change your eating habits and you have to change your tastes. I can't imagine that by eating better foods you're not going to feel much better and be less heavy than if you just go out and stuff yourself with pork rinds, potato chips, and Chee•tos. Bacon, corn chips, hot dogs—you just can't have that stuff in the house and be on this diet. For example, I never think to buy doughnuts anymore, and I used to love doughnuts. If the average American family wrote down what they're eating every day, they'd be shocked. And they shouldn't be surprised if their kids are overweight or having illnesses that we thought didn't come until old age or at least midlife.

I tried to keep junk food out of my house, but it isn't easy since advertisements target our kids so young. My son, Elijah, used to get angry when I wouldn't bring home Wonder Bread. I mean, what *is* Wonder Bread? To me it's like The Blob. I don't know what either one of them is made out of. One year he said to me, "You won't let me have Wonder Bread, and it's the *official bread* of the Olympics." I said, *"What the hell does that mean?"* Can someone tell me what that means? It's like Snickers is the "official candy bar" of the Olympics, but that doesn't make it healthy for you either. It's hard to tell your kid these things when he hears on TV that it builds bodies 12 ways and provides all these nutrients and vitamins. And so you have to say, "Just because they say that, sweetheart, doesn't mean it's good for you."

This is the worst time in our history for unhealthy foods and for seeing fat children from kindergarten on. There's also a horrendous backlash of 12-year-old anorexics and bulimics. People used to have exercise built into their lifestyles; kids were out playing on baseball diamonds instead of watching TV and playing video games. Kids are becoming less active. So you've got a small percentage of the population that's fanatical, like me, and the majority of the population being overweight, watching people like me on TV.

When Robert and Hilarie Porter visited my house for a month when we first started working together, she prepared most of the foods he put on the diet program. We tried everything. The thing is: you can't taste foods the old way. For instance, I got used to nonfat milk. I love it now. Someone recently gave me whole milk, and I looked at my girlfriend and went, "What the hell is that?" It looked like heavy cream to me. Now if my milk's not blue I don't want it. I love to pour it over plain Shredded Wheat. It's just a matter of getting used to it. It absolutely tastes like dairy but has no fat.

Cakes made without sugar or butter obviously won't taste the same. But Robert's chocolate cake, which Hilarie made for him, just knocked me on my butt. It was the best thing I ever had. Her chocolate pudding obviously is made differently from regular chocolate pudding, but it tastes so great that if you thought it was healthy you would make allowances for its not tasting the way you've always thought it should taste. And you become accustomed to the new taste.

EATING IS REALLY EMOTIONAL

For me, eating is really emotional. When you eat foods that are bad for your body—but you're doing it as an escape from what's bothering you—you look in the mirror, and you're devastated by what you're doing to yourself. But then you do it more. It's a ridiculous chain reaction, but you've got to stop it before it gets out of control.

A lapse grows into a pattern, and a pattern becomes your lifestyle very easily. If you have a tendency to drown your sorrows in food, you have to watch out, just as you would if you drowned them in alcohol. You have to discipline yourself to say no to stuff, too. You're trying to eat your problems away. And then you're not only going to still have your problems; you're going to be overweight at the same time.

People need psychological "crutches" or principles to help themselves when eating becomes emotional. If I get real emotional about something or when I feel myself getting anxiety-ridden, the first thing I try to do is get on my treadmill. Nine times out of 10 my nervousness disappears and the craving passes.

I'm now more likely to work that stuff out in the gym than I am with a bag of M&Ms. Not every time, but more times than not, because I know that if I go through a whole bag of M&Ms I'll have my problem *and* I'll feel real depressed—I'll have the sugar blues *and* I'll be fat.

So if I make it into the gym instead, the "crisis" or whatever it was passes and I'll look better.

So why not just do that? It's so much smarter. It seems dumb to add another problem to your list of problems because of the way you're dealing with the list you've already got. I don't want to add a problem like Fat, or Not Looking Good to Not Making My House Payment or Hard Time with One of My Children. I'd rather shorten the list of problems, and it seems to me that exercise helps you do just that. At least it doesn't *add* to the list.

When you're younger, you make strong associations with food. When you were sick, your mother may have made certain foods for you and you remember the comfort that they gave you. She'd go, "All right, once we go to the doctor, if you're really good when you get your shot we'll go get an ice cream." Or if you have a temperature, you've got to have Coca-Cola or ginger ale because the doctor always said it was good for an upset stomach or a fever. Or if you're good about homework, you get a cookie or we'll make fudge, or won't it be fun to stay home and make popcorn?

By the time you're a grown-up, you can't simply cut off those associations and memories. So at those times in your life when you're not getting the love or the understanding you need, or you're too stressed out, you reach for those foods as crutches because they're the only things you can get to. You can't call your mother. You can't go home. You can't travel backward. There is no way to replace those attachments.

But you try. You reach for the foods that represent what you can't have. What you're really looking for is the direct experience of the past. You use food as a substitute—you're replacing what you really *need* with what you can actually *get*. You can't go to the market and pick up Mother and Dad and the fabulous family stuff from your childhood. But you can go down Aisle 4 and pick up some Häagen-Dazs because it's the food, the sweets, that symbolize the emotional experiences.

When I was growing up, I was always skinny, back before being thin was in. My mother was the only healthy person I knew where we grew up. We shopped at the only health-food store in the San Fernando Valley, and on our table there was always a big bowl filled with raw nuts. My mother believed in salads back then, too, and once she gave up smoking she was against it. No one drank coffee either.

I was real healthy and was a pretty athletic tomboy who played all the sports. In fact, when I met Sonny I was 16 and I belonged to a softball team. I ate whatever I wanted and never worried about putting on weight. Then, all of a sudden, I was 18 and went on the pill and watched my weight go from 106 to 121 in a month. It was frightening. Of course the pill was 10 times stronger then than it is now. I was really heavy, and it was kind of a rough time for me. But I was working already, and people weren't so concerned with health back in the early sixties, and I was young and everyone thought I had been too skinny anyway. So I didn't pay much attention.

My weight came back down, and then a few years later I put on about 30 pounds when I was pregnant with Chastity. But *after* she was born in March 1969, I became real sick and so within three weeks I weighed 106 again. I had sort of a baby face before Chas was born. But I had a totally different look after her birth. My face became more angular; I lost baby fat.

When we started doing *The Sonny & Cher Show* on television, I began getting conscious of my body—like maybe I should do something with it. I had to do dance routines, and though I could pick up the steps, I felt I should start taking classes to build up my legs. I also started paying attention to what I was eating, because I was under constant stress and needed to maintain a good energy level.

But food and mood were always intertwined for me. Before I left Sonny, I weighed 92 pounds. And I'm almost 5′8″. I just couldn't eat. I mean, I was suicidal. I was in Vegas and *could not* eat. I was drinking water and eating maybe an egg a day or some toast, just trying to get stuff down. This happened only one other time in my life, when I was so emotionally upset I couldn't get food past my mouth. But I know this too: both episodes passed, and I ate fine again.

Even though those were difficult times, I found out years later that making movies is also very stressful and demands every waking hour. So I learned that it's while making movies and being away on locations that I usually have my worst eating patterns. I always have a bag of M&Ms around someplace. The better thing, of course, is to reach for an apple, a banana, an orange, nectarines, peaches, cherries, or a melon, and I'll do that when I'm paying attention to being healthy and I know it will give me that little boost I need. You get just as much fulfillment from fruit—but you've got to prepare it, peel it, etc. But an orange is so unglamorous at the market. It doesn't yell out at you with 75 colors and weird names and bright boxes. It's just sitting there, and you have to *do something* to it. We get *so lazy*. But every time I eat an orange I'm surprised how much I like it. Someone's peeling one, they give you a slice, and you go, "God, this is good."

Also, movie locations can get real lonely. I want to be with my family. It's a job that forces you to sit and sit and not be able to work. It's like being a bull they're going to let go at the rodeo—you have to stay in the chute all day long but always be charged up. That can drain all your energy. It's an unhealthy state to be in.

Making a movie is difficult only for that reason—the work isn't tough at all. It's not the acting you have to be good at—it's the waiting and being able to keep yourself constantly ready at a fever pitch, so concentrated that at any moment you can start a huge dramatic crying scene right before lunch. You do two takes, someone yells, "Cut," and when you come back after lunch you've got to pick up exactly where you left off.

That puts a lot of strain on your mind. It's almost impossible to relax. You can't even read a book, because you don't want to lose your concentration. You're forced to sit and wait and you get really anxious. And that can make you vulnerable to bad eating habits.

I have had some bad binges while making movies. Towards the end of *The Witches of Eastwick* Michelle Pfeiffer, Susan Sarandon, and I really went crazy. Our trailers all looked identical because we'd go from one to the other stuffing ourselves with Pepperidge Farm Cheddar Cheese Goldfish, M&Ms, Cokes, and Hershey's Kisses. Actually, you could say we went on a candy kiss binge. They were everywhere. We were under so much stress, and when that happens your body looks for a lift—and you get that false lift from sugar. So we were constantly eating sugar and chocolate.

But then Michelle and I found out we could microwave sweet potatoes in four minutes, and that changed our entire lives. We lived on sweet potatoes, baked potatoes, and Caesar salads. I did get lucky once and had great catering on a shoot—for *Moonstruck* in Toronto. We had great salads and vegetables that were really appealing, like summer squash and yellow squash and roasted potatoes. Stuff you could eat without ever feeling guilty.

But lately I've been concentrating on eating the foods that Robert has stressed as being terrific: brown rice (not white rice), legumes— lentils, pinto, navy, lima, and kidney beans—vegetables, pastas, fruit. Pastas give me a lot of energy, and so do fruits like bananas, papaya, and nectarines, because they have a lot of sugar but it isn't refined.

When it comes to red meat, I almost never eat it. I'll have a good hamburger maybe twice a year. I prefer fish: shellfish such as shrimp and lobster, halibut, swordfish, and tuna steaks. Fish is really low in fat and calories, high in protein, and good for you if you just broil or bake it with a little lemon. Shrimp is unbelievably low in calories—unless you load up on a creamy dip or fry it or make scampi and sop up the butter and lemon sauce with bread.

I remember what Robert said to me when we first started working together: "If you're going to cheat, have a Popsicle, have a soft drink instead of the ice cream, because you get the sugar but not the fat. You can find ways to cheat without doing yourself much damage."

Also, make sure it's a cheat (the exception and not the rule)—not your minimum daily requirement. And find ways to substitute things, like Parmesan for soft, fatty cheeses. And Robert's got those fabulous banana pancakes instead of buttery pancakes with maple syrup. They're cooked in Pam vegetable spray and if the pancakes don't know it's Pam, neither will your taste buds.

Another thing I learned a while back: the closer to the afternoon you have your biggest meal of the day, the better off you are. If you're eating with friends at night, then have a salad or pick at food. I like to have a humongous plate of spaghetti *no* later than six o'clock. You'll lose weight just by *not* eating anything after a certain time. In the afternoon you're working and burning. At night you're home, sitting, watching TV, doing homework, going to bed. You need time to burn food off. To my mind, the best way to eat pasta is with light tomato sauce, some vegetable and/or olive oil, but no heavy cream. Of all the bottled sauces I prefer the Prego version with no sugar or corn syrup added.

But now let me have Robert detail the way our *Forever Fit* Permanent Weight-Loss program will work for you.

ROBERT

THE FIRST RULE OF PERMANENT WEIGHT LOSS

Relax. I'm not going to give you a long-winded scientific explanation of the biochemistry of weight loss or burden you with testimonials from people who have embraced the *Forever Fit* Permanent Weight-Loss Plan. But I am going to explain the basics of how it works because I believe that it is important for you to understand what you're doing—*and why*. So let's cut right to the chase.

The first rule of the *Forever Fit* Permanent Weight-Loss Plan is: **The amount of fat you eat will ultimately determine how fat you are.**

Under normal conditions the body burns a mixture of fat, carbohydrate, and protein each day for fuel and stores the excess as body fat. But your body actually *prefers* to store the fat you eat long before it ever tries to store protein or carbohydrate. You see, your body's metabolic machinery actually works *against* turning protein and carbohydrate into fat, but it does a wonderful job of turning the fat you eat each day into body fat. That's why the total calories from fat—all types of fat (saturated, monounsaturated, and polyunsaturated) you eat each day—are much more important than total calories from protein and carbohydrate. And by now you may have guessed why some popular low-calorie diets don't always work so well: they simply contain too much *total* fat. The *Forever Fit* Permanent Weight-Loss Plan trains your body to *burn* fat as its *primary* fuel, so the last thing we want you to do is eat the very thing you need to lose!

Keeping consumption of total fat to our recommended level—about 20 grams a day—is the fastest and most direct way to remove excess body fat. By providing a special combination of high-quality protein and complex-carbohydrate foods and beverages, the *Forever Fit* Permanent Weight-Loss Plan allows you to enjoy a wide variety of tasty foods and recipes at home or in restaurants—from lobster to pasta (or lobster *with* pasta, if you prefer)—and still lose all the weight you want, permanently. Whether you are a vegetarian, part-time vegetarian, or card-carrying carnivore, once you construct your diet around our special protein-carbohydrate food combinations, you will never again have to suffer with an overweight, overly fat body.

WHY IS IT SO IMPORTANT TO BURN OFF YOUR EXCESS BODY FAT?

The benefits of fat loss are *progressive.* For each pound of fat that you burn off, you gain a new measure of health and fitness.

You don't have to wait until you reach your ideal weight to start enjoying the rewards. We now know that certain health benefits begin as soon as you've reduced your body weight by just 10 percent. Studies show that losing excess body fat can reduce the risk of cancer, Type II (adult-onset) diabetes, heart disease, digestive diseases, and orthopedic problems.

Losing excess body fat also has a dramatic fattening effect on your wallet. Health surveys reveal that losing weight can actually increase your long-term earning potential. One recent study revealed that being over-weight decreases annual income by an average of $4,000 a year per person. Research has also shown that, fair or not, thin people get promotions and pay raises faster than fat people.

People who successfully reach their ideal weight and maintain it report improved self-image and increased self-confidence, both of which can translate into better job performance and increased success. Think of how much better off you'd be if you spent a single year's "lost" income on home gym equipment (e.g., motorized treadmill, exercise bicycle, multiple weightlifting station, etc.) or even just a good pair of walking shoes to help lose excess weight and keep it off for good.

WHY CARBOHYDRATES WILL HELP YOU
ACHIEVE PERMANENT WEIGHT LOSS

Ordinarily it takes about 2,000 to 2,500 carbohydrate calories to fill up the body's specialized carbohydrate storage cells (located in the muscles and the liver). Each day, you burn off some of this stored carbohydrate—

called *glycogen*—during all types of physical activity. The longer the duration and the more frequently you exercise, the greater will be the loss of stored glycogen.

The wonderful thing about this process is that the body will do everything possible to avoid storing carbohydrates as fat in order to replenish burned-off glycogen. Thus you can enjoy carbohydrate-rich foods in relatively large amounts *once you have burned away some of your stored glycogen* because your body will turn carbo calories into glycogen instead of fat.

A simple example: Let's say you're very active and your daily work and exercise routine burns off 800 calories (equal to jogging for 60 minutes and then playing a set of doubles tennis). Roughly 50 to 60 percent of these calories—about 500—will come from glycogen (the other 300 from stored body fat). When you eat according to the *Forever Fit* weight-loss dietary principles, you can eat *at least* 500 calories from carbohydrate-rich foods like pasta and potatoes and *never worry* that the bulk of those foods will be converted to body fat.

As a bonus, I'm happy to tell you that your body uses up an additional 20 to 25 percent of the calories from carbohydrate foods you eat during the ordinary digestive and assimilation process. This means that *for every 500 carbohydrate calories you eat, only about 375 calories remain after digestion, absorption, and assimilation.* You get a bonus in the form of an additional 175-calorie deficit.

So, if you exercise regularly, you will be able to enjoy a wide variety and relatively large quantity of carbo-rich foods and lose weight permanently. That's why the *Forever Fit* Permanent Weight-Loss Plan allows you literally to feast on complex carbohydrates such as potatoes, pasta, breads, low-fat crackers, cereals, baked goods, and the like. We have listed dozens of brands to choose from in Chapter 6. Moreover, these foods will actually help control your appetite (in part because of their rich fiber content), thereby blocking sensations of hunger and deprivation during the weight-loss process.

Now you understand why we recommend that you cheat with carbohydrate foods rather than fatty foods. If you're going to pig out, then pig out on pasta, potatoes, and other "nonfattening" starches. And when Cher wants to cheat with something sweet, I recommend that she choose something like a Popsicle, Coke, Entenmann's no-fat/no-cholesterol bakery items, or chocolate pudding made with skim milk (Jell-O brand sweetened with NutraSweet is one of our favorites). The point is: *if you have to cheat, cheat with sugar, not fat.*

Now that I've told you about the role of fat in keeping you permanently fat and the role of carbohydrate in keeping you permanently thin, the last nutrient for you to know about is protein. And protein is very important.

IF YOU HAVE TO, CHEAT WITH SUGAR NOT FAT

THE IMPORTANCE OF CARBOHYDRATE FOR PERMANENT WEIGHT LOSS

The role of carbohydrate (and its storage form in the body, called *glycogen*) is central to swift and permanent weight loss. Here are three essential rules about carbohydrates we want you to remember:

1. *Fat burns in the flame of carbohydrate.* This means that to burn excess body fat efficiently you must eat a daily diet rich in complex carbohydrates. Your body requires a fuel mix composed of *both* carbohydrate and fat to burn fat efficiently.

2. *Glycogen (the storage form of carbohydrate) is a key regulator of appetite.* You must replenish your glycogen stores each day, especially after exercise, to prevent hunger and avoid overeating fat.

3. *Exercise each day to deplete enough glycogen so that most of the carbohydrate you eat will be converted back to glycogen and not fat.* For example, if you burn off 600 calories each day through exercise, about 300 calories of glycogen will be depleted from your liver and muscles. Even if you "cheat" on your diet and overeat 500 carbohydrate calories after exercise, the body will respond by temporarily increasing glycogen synthesis to accommodate this excess intake of carbohydrate. This means that most of the extra carbohydrate calories you cheated on will *not* be converted to body fat.

   But if you overate 500 calories of fat instead, a whopping 97 percent of those calories (485 calories) would be available for instant storage as fat! So from a weight-loss standpoint more than 80 percent of your calorie-burning exercise will have been worthless. Practically speaking, then, it is better to cheat on 500 calories from whole grain breakfast cereal, baked potatoes, and pasta with plain tomato sauce than it is to cheat on the same amount of calories from salad covered with conventional high-fat dressings (e.g., blue cheese, oil and vinegar, Russian), most commercially prepared breakfast muffins (which can contain as much fat as a cheeseburger), whole milk, and eggs. All of these foods generally contain 50 percent or more of the calories as fat.

4. *Eating carbohydrate helps spare protein.* During exercise, protein from muscle can be broken down and converted into carbohydrate for energy, especially when following a low-calorie weight-loss diet. While fat has its own unique storage cells and carbohydrate is stored in the muscles and liver as glycogen, the body has no specialized cell for storing protein. So a diet rich in carbohydrate can help prevent the body from using up muscle protein for energy.

THE ROLE OF PROTEIN IN THE *FOREVER FIT* DIET

The *Forever Fit* Permanent Weight-Loss Plan replaces many of the calories that usually come from fat in the ordinary diet with protein sources of high biological value. Biological value (BV) is a measure of how well the body absorbs and uses specific protein. Some foods, like whey protein (from milk) and egg white protein (called albumin), rate at the top of the BV scale; other proteins, from vegetables, rate lower. The most important thing to know about biological value is that the human body thrives on a *mixture* of proteins with high and low BV. Scientists don't yet fully understand why this is, but the research results clearly show that our diet should consist of a variety of protein sources.

BIOLOGICAL VALUE OF SOME COMMON PROTEIN SOURCES

	BIOLOGICAL VALUE (BV)
Whey protein (from human and cow's milk)	95
Egg (whole)	94
Lobster	88
Egg (white)	83
Casein (milk)	80
Beef	74
Pork	74
Soy beans	73
Kidney beans	73
Wheat germ	73
Brown rice	73

AS CALORIES DECREASE, PROTEIN NEEDS INCREASE

One of the most important recent nutritional discoveries with respect to weight loss is that if you consume fewer than approximately 800 to 1,000 calories per day—an amount not unusual on today's popular diets (some liquid diet "fasts" supply only 400 calories daily)—your body's requirement for the protein it uses each day can increase significantly and in some cases nearly *double* if you are exceptionally active.

Keep in mind that it's not just the amount of protein that's important—it's the *quality* of the protein as well.

Recent research suggests that during periods of reduced calorie intake and regular exercise the body may require a greater proportion of high-BV proteins because they may help prevent the body from breaking down muscle tissue in an effort to provide the body with energy (muscle protein can be converted to glucose via a process called *gluconeogenesis*). The high-quality protein content of the *Forever Fit* Permanent Weight-Loss Plan, however, signals the body to spare vital muscle and lean tissue as a fuel source during weight loss, thereby helping to protect against muscle loss during times of low calorie intake. The consumption of high-BV proteins thus provides a very desirable result: *muscle loss is minimized compared to reduced-calorie diets that provide less protein or lower-biological-value proteins.*

This is important because the higher your muscle-to-fat ratio, the easier it is to continue to lose excess body fat and keep it off for good. Muscle burns many more calories than adipose (fat) tissue, so as you begin to lose excess body fat while keeping the muscle tissue you already have, your muscle-to-fat ratio increases, forcing your body to burn fat more efficiently.

Bear in mind that it is excess body fat, not muscle, that robs your body of its shape and poses great risks to your health. The *Forever Fit* Permanent Weight-Loss Plan is designed to rid your body of this excess fat and give you a sleeker, healthier shape.

In summary, the *Forever Fit* Permanent Weight-Loss Plan is designed to help you:

1. train the body to burn fat as its primary fuel;
2. provide the body with the proper amount of carbohydrate to ensure efficient weight loss and optimal health; and
3. provide high-BV protein to meet increased protein needs by the body during weight loss.

FOREVER FIT CAN WORK FOR YOU

Even if you think you are a hopeless yo-yo dieter—someone with a sluggish, stubborn metabolism who has lost and gained weight on a succession of diets and exercise programs—*we believe the* Forever Fit *Permanent Weight-Loss Plan will work for you.*

5

THE FOREVER FIT
PERMANENT WEIGHT-LOSS PLAN

The *Forever Fit* Permanent Weight-Loss Plan is a delicious, super-fat-burning diet designed to help you burn off fat efficiently and sensibly. Our plan lets *you* make healthful food choices that fit your own tastes and lifestyle, whether you enjoy home-cooked meals or dine out.

Our plan may be different from anything you have tried before, but if you faithfully follow it we believe you will enjoy the same benefits—slenderness, optimal health, and high energy—that we have come to depend on to keep us forever fit.

VIVE LA DIFFÉRENCE

The *Forever Fit* Permanent Weight-Loss Plan uses a special combination of two solid-food meals, two "meals" of fresh fruit, plus a low-fat meal replacement drink (besides Twin Laboratories' Feelin' Fit, a variety of brands are available in most health-food stores, drugstores, and supermarkets).

Our weight-loss plan does not force you to follow the customary "three square meals a day." Instead, losing weight on the *Forever Fit* Plan is simple: one meal consists of an easy-to-make meal replacement shake that supplies fat- and cholesterol-free milk and egg white protein. The meal replacement shakes that we've used have been formulated by their manufacturers to meet increased protein and other nutritional needs imposed on the body during the weight-loss period.

The *Forever Fit* Plan will also work without the use of meal replacers, but weight loss may not come as quickly and the nutritional content of the diet may not be as low in fat and cholesterol or as high in vitamins and minerals. *Most commercially available meal replacers supply your body with substantial nutrition; however, they should never be used as the sole source of nutrition, nor should any one food or food product. A healthy diet can come only from a variety of foods.*

Many people who have used liquid meal replacer shakes report that *using a liquid meal replacer shake made weight loss far easier than any other approach they tried before.* We believe that liquid meal replacers can play a role in helping people achieve *permanent* weight loss. Here's why:

1. Today's liquid meal replacers have been scientifically formulated to provide a complete meal's nutritional complement of vitamins, minerals, protein, fiber, and carbohydrate *without the excessive fat* of a conventional meal. For example, government surveys reveal that many people eat about 90 to 150 grams of fat each day (up to about 1,500 calories). Simply by using a liquid meal replacer, you can eliminate about 500 fat calories from your diet each day, which would result in a one-pound weight loss each week—52 pounds in a year. When used in conjunction with the *Forever Fit* Permanent Weight-Loss Plan, a meal replacer shake can help maximize weight loss.

2. Using a liquid meal replacer can significantly reduce dietary cholesterol. A "typical" quick breakfast of an oat bran muffin and coffee with sugar substitute and milk (a breakfast that we do not recommend) contains about 85 milligrams of cholesterol. Replace the muffin with a breakfast of scrambled eggs, and you're chowing down on a staggering 285 milligrams of cholesterol. But substitute a fat-burning meal replacer shake, and your total cholesterol intake for breakfast shrinks to an incredible 5 milligrams.

3. Liquid meal replacer shakes provide high nutrient density for very few calories. This means that for every calorie you consume you get a cornucopia of vitamins and minerals not present in conventional breakfast foods. One of the most important "secrets" of permanent weight loss is to be able to provide the body with *all* of the vital nutrients it needs for the least amount of calories. A liquid meal replacer is the equivalent of any conventional nutritionally "perfect" meal packed with all the essential protein, carbohydrate, fiber, vitamins, and minerals your body needs *without*—and this is the key—all the excessive calories, fat, and cholesterol of that conventional meal.

4. Liquid meal replacer shakes take much of the tedium and guesswork out of weight loss. Most people don't have the time to weigh foods, shop for long lists of specialty food items, or spend all day cooking. Meal replacers simplify everything about the weight loss process. They're easy to make (30 seconds); they're portable (most brands supply a shake cup with cap you can take anywhere); they provide complete premeasured nutrition (avoiding confusing and time-consuming food balancing or combining schemes). No cooking, no messing, no guessing, no food weighing. They're perfect for the lifestyle of the nineties: convenient, effective, quick, and portable.

5. After you've lost all the weight you want, you can still use the liquid meal replacer shake as a meal option or even as a snack or dessert as we do. It will thus help keep down your intake of calories, fat, and cholesterol to recommended levels while continuing to provide the substantial nutrition necessary for fitness and health. We've been using liquid meal replacers for the last four years with *excellent* results. But, as recent studies reveal, many people who lose weight on very-low-calorie all-liquid diets regain most or all of their lost weight within a few years. That's why *we believe that people who choose to use liquid meal replacers should use them in conjunction with solid foods to help maintain permanent weight loss.*

We're asking you to break with the time-honored tradition of three "squares" a day and embrace our permanent weight-loss plan of two solid-food meals plus one meal replacer (optional) and two servings of fresh fruit. In all our years of experience with weight-loss diets, we have never found a more nutritious or effective diet than the *Forever Fit* Permanent Weight-Loss Plan for burning fat and keeping it off.

CHER

I'm no longer a big meal eater. We don't recommend eating big meals. It's better to eat smaller, more frequent meals so the body has a chance to deal with smaller amounts of calories, fat, and cholesterol at a time. Robert's research has convinced me that the body is simply not equipped to handle the huge amounts that many people consume at each and every meal. We'll tell you why a little later in this chapter.

I am not a big red meat eater either. I like a good hamburger maybe twice a year. *Forever Fit* allows for that as well as other types of animal protein foods such as seafood and fowl but in amounts that don't provide too much saturated fat and cholesterol. Of course we stress high-quality protein sources such as those found in the replacer shake (discussed in Chapter 7), seafood, and legumes.

From time to time I like to eat lacto-vegetarian style, meaning that I rely on our *Forever Fit* meal replacer (it contains skim milk—that's the "lacto" part) and rich vegetable protein sources such as beans, peas, and lentils. When I'm not "vegging out," I enjoy low-fat, high-quality protein sources such as lobster, halibut, fresh or canned (packed in water) albacore tuna, and other low-fat seafood.

ROBERT

THE DIET CHEMISTRY OF THE FOREVER FIT PERMANENT WEIGHT-LOSS PLAN

The *Forever Fit* Permanent Weight-Loss Plan works quickly—up to two pounds a week—because it provides your body with the most effective diet chemistry ever devised for burning fat and sparing muscle.

Scientists who specialize in the study of weight loss have discovered that the most effective diet chemistry necessary for the *selective* loss of excess body fat and the preservation of lean body mass (muscle) requires adherence to the following three principles:

1. *Consume moderate amounts of high-biological-quality protein foods* during periods of reduced calorie intake and regular exercise. Whey protein is one of the highest-quality protein sources available, and it is found in some of today's modern meal replacer shake formulations. Other high-quality protein sources include egg whites, turkey and chicken (remove the skin), seafood, lean cuts of beef, and, in the vegetable world, legumes such as beans, peas, and lentils.

During weight-loss periods on the *Forever Fit* Permanent Weight-Loss Plan, your total protein intake will be about 20 to 25 percent of your total daily calories to promote the selective burning of fat rather than fat-burning muscle tissue. Nonvegetarians will consume about three quarters of their protein from high-quality animal protein sources and about one quarter from grains, cereals, legumes, and vegetables.

Then, during weight maintenance, we'd like you to reduce your protein intake to about 12 to 14 percent of total daily calories. At this time you will derive more protein (about 50 to 75 percent) from cholesterol-free vegetable sources such as legumes, potatoes, pasta, and whole grain cereals.

2. *Consume minimal amounts of fats and oils* by reducing your intake of fat-rich sources such as conventional salad dressings, mayonnaise, poly-unsaturated oils such as corn and safflower, butter, whole milk and whole-milk products, lard, margarine, egg yolks, meats such as high-fat beef, pork, and lamb, fried foods, seeds, nuts, coconut, olives, hearts of palm, and avocado. Fat substitutes such as no-oil salad dressings, Butter Buds butter substitute, Pam vegetable spray for frying and sautéing, cholesterol-free/reduced-fat mayonnaise substitutes, skim milk, Scramblers (cholesterol-free egg substitute from Worthington Foods, Inc.), lean cuts of beef, chicken, and turkey without skin, and fat-free seafoods like lobster can all help reduce total fats and oils to *Forever Fit* recommended levels.

3. *Consume optimal amounts and types of complex carbohydrates and fiber* from a variety of whole grains and unrefined cereals, breads, pasta, potatoes, and vegetables and from low-fat complex-carbohydrate desserts and snacks such as the ones we've included in the recipe section of this book (Appendix I).

Complex carbohydrates, the only source of fiber, will become your *primary foods*—foods that supply the majority of the calories you eat each day. On the *Forever Fit* Permanent Weight-Loss Plan they will supply about 50 percent of total daily calories. Then, on the *Forever Fit* Weight-Maintenance Plan, complex carbs supply up to 75 percent of daily calories. Why? Because people the world over who base their diets on complex carbohydrates generally are not obese and suffer *far* less from the diseases of aging such as heart disease, cancer, osteoporosis, diabetes, and high blood pressure than those who eat the typical lower-carbohydrate (about 40 percent) American diet. *Complex carbohydrates are thus an important key to maintaining your new, lower body fat level and keeping it low permanently.*

4. *Consume at least 1,000 (women) or 1,300 (men) calories on the average, each day,* because any less could leave you hungry and undernourished and will not replenish your glycogen (stored carbohydrate) supply, which is critical in helping you control appetite, burn off body fat

(remember the saying "Fat burns in the flame of carbohydrate"), and maintain high energy levels. These suggested calorie levels are based on the caloric needs of most men and women who need to lose between five and twenty pounds.

Some people believe that the best weight-loss diets supply the lowest number of calories. Today it is not unusual to see liquid diet "fasts" that recommend 400 calories a day. People who follow these all-liquid, very-low-calorie plans, in our opinion, stand a poor chance of achieving *permanent* weight loss because they're practicing how *not* to eat.

Very-low-calorie liquid diets have been used with morbidly obese people under a physician's and hospital staff's strict supervision while hospitalized (these diets are commonly referred to as *protein-sparing modified fasts*), but for the general population we recommend a more generous and nutritious food intake of at least 1,000 to 1,300 calories each day from solid and liquid meals. Thus a woman weighing 140 pounds who wants to lose up to 20 pounds to reach her ideal weight should consume about 1,000 calories each day, while a man weighing 180 pounds who wants to reach an ideal weight of 160 should eat about 1,300 calories each day. *Anyone who is more than 20 pounds above his or her ideal weight is a good candidate for a physician-supervised weight-loss regimen.*

Even if you are within 20 pounds of your ideal weight and you are considering going on a medically unsupervised very-low-calorie liquid diet, which we do not recommend, it may surprise you to learn that the difference with respect to weight loss in following a 400-calorie-per-day liquid fast and enjoying the liquid and delicious solid foods and recipes—and dining out at your favorite restaurants—on the *Forever Fit* Permanent Weight-Loss Plan (400 vs. 1,000 calories each day) will usually be no more than losing a single pound per week!

Diets that provide only 400 calories each day from liquid meals never teach the dieter how to eat ordinary foods under a variety of real-life conditions. Just as Oprah Winfrey discovered, she could lose weight by *drinking* 400 calories a day while exercising an hour each day to boot (as anyone would), but once she tried to resume her normal lifestyle of eating solid, ordinary foods inside and outside her home, "lost" body fat quickly crept back on her newly slenderized body.

The *Forever Fit* Permanent Weight-Loss Plan shows you how to lose weight by enjoying the same liquid and solid foods that will help keep you *permanently* slim—for the rest of your life. And from day one of your new diet you can eat inside and outside the home while achieving your weight-loss goal.

CHER

The only person who can look out for what's best for you is *you*. This means reading beyond the hype and the big letters on food packaging and checking the ingredient lists in fine print. It means making sure you know exactly what kind of food you're putting into your body. If nobody's putting sugar in anything anymore, why is everything we eat sweet? Some food manufacturers claim their products are "all natural." Well, sugar and fat are "natural," but they aren't necessarily good for you.

The first time I got interested in labeling was when Chastity was having her seventh birthday party at school. The night before, a friend of mine had made the batter from scratch. She had bought frosting that came in a can, and when my girlfriend Paulette and I came home that night the cupcakes were all out in the kitchen. Paulette took the first bite and said, "God, this stuff tastes great."

"It does?" I said. I was curious to know what was in it. I picked up the can, and there were 30 ingredients in there that all sounded like a chemical waste problem. I had no idea what any of this stuff was. I said, "Paulette, we're not eating anything that's *real*. And it tastes good. This is *really frightening*."

This first experience made me so nervous I started reading everything, and the more I read the more frightened I got.

Another time my mother couldn't understand why she was all of a sudden putting on weight. She eats very carefully, and she is usually very thin. So I said, "Let's just look at what you've been eating that's different." She said she had been having a bowl of bran-based cereal every night before going to bed.

We read the cereal's ingredients and figured out she was pouring fat and sugar into her body before going to sleep—a lot of bran products are loaded with sugar. And she was having low-fat milk with it. People look at the carton and read, "2 percent milkfat," and you think it's 2 percent out of 100 percent—and that's not true.

Robert and I want you to know the truth about what you're eating—or at least to have as much information as you can get. And most of it is right there on the package. So we walked up and down the aisles of a typical supermarket and picked a bunch of foods at random to read the fine print on the labels. We decided that you absolutely need to take the time to do the same thing if you want to control what goes into your body and make all the right decisions about eating.

We started with breakfast cereals because everybody eats them and they're supposed to be so healthy for you as a way to start the day. To get

KNOW THE TRUTH ABOUT WHAT YOU'RE EATING

some perspective, first we picked up a box of Post's Fruity Pebbles—billed as a health food. It contains, in order, rice, sugar, partially hydrogenated sunflower oil, then corn syrup, which is cheap sugar extracted from corn, followed by salt and artificial coloring. So two ingredients are for sweetening only.

A cereal like Kellogg's Cracklin' Oat Bran *is* marketed to seem good for you. Sounds healthy, doesn't it? True, you get eight grams of fiber per cup of cereal from its two main ingredients, oat bran and wheat bran. But they've flavored it with brown sugar, sugar, corn syrup, malt flavoring, coconut, and salt, plus partially hydrogenated cottonseed and/or soybean oil. This stuff might leave you "cracklin'," but it might be from all those added sweeteners.

Post Raisin Bran has whole wheat, raisins, wheat bran, sugar, natural flavoring, salt, corn syrup, and honey—I mean, they don't even stop with one kind of sugar. They add all kinds. Another cereal we won't even bother to name—but which is marketed as "fiber rich"—has honey, malt flavoring, *plus* sugar, corn syrup, *and* sorbitol. Five sweetners. Take the most basic American cereal, Kellogg's Corn Flakes: corn, sugar, salt, malt flavoring, corn syrup. It offers maybe a gram of fiber at best.

I prefer Nabisco Shredded Wheat—one of the only popular cereals with no sugar or salt—and Quaker Oats, which is nothing but oatmeal. They're two of the healthiest cereals on the shelf.

But even Post Grape-Nuts, which I have always liked, has salt and malted barley, which is a sweetener. The label for Grape-Nuts says: "All sugars occur naturally in the wheat and malted barley," but malted barley is something they add, so it's like putting in sugar and trying to disguise it. It's amazingly clever.

Another product we looked at was Nabisco's 100% Bran with Oat Bran, which is touted on the package as the "highest fiber cereal with oat bran." True, the label tells you it gives you eight grams of dietary fiber per serving and "no artificial sweeteners," but after the wheat and oat bran, the ingredients are high fructose, corn syrup, sugar, brown sugar (all of which are sugars), and salt. You have to realize that these claims are misleading.

We looked at the so-called "diet bars"—which are really candy bars designed to make you think they're all right for dieters. Most are loaded with sugars, hydrogenated oil, which has been linked to heart disease, and fats. Figurines, made by Pillsbury, lists sugar, polydextrose, and lactose, all sugars found in a "diet bar."

Quaker's chewy Granola Bars pack in between three to eight grams of fat, which is way too much. Have two of them and you've got as much or more than the fat found in a bag of M&Ms (ten) and a Three Musketeers (nine). A Granola Bar's got brown sugar, hydrogenated vegetable oil, cottonseed oils, dried unsweetened coconut—again, saturated fats—almonds, which are high in fat, raisins, which have sugar, salt, and malt. I'll bet there are better things for you in real candy bars. And then at least you've got honesty, since a candy bar hardly pretends to be a "health food."

You can find sugar, corn syrup, honey, malted barley, and any number of other hidden sweeteners in almost anything—whether it's SpaghettiOs, Ragu and Buitoni tomato sauces, to pick only two, Rice-A-Roni, the "all natural" so-called "fruit drinks" like Hi-C and Hawaiian Punch, Mott's applesauce, some Campbell's soups, Spam, most breads (we recommend unsweetened breads like rye, sourdough, pumpernickel, and 100 percent whole wheat), yogurt-covered raisins, frankfurters, and on and on. People just don't realize how inundated with sugar we are.

YOU CAN FIND SUGAR IN ALMOST ANYTHING

The point is, as long as ingredients and food compositions are listed, you might as well know them and choose right. The differences can be huge. A 3½-ounce can of Starkist solid white albacore tuna packed in water has 70 calories and one gram of fat. You also get a third of the protein you need per day, and it's loaded with vitamins and minerals. The same can of tuna packed in oil gives you 170 calories and 13 grams of fat. Plus, the albacore tuna is known to be a rich source of the Omega-3 fatty acids that help prevent heart disease and strokes.

Walk down the "dietetic meal" aisle and you find out why you really have to watch your weight. Some Weight Watchers meals have as many as 13 grams of fat per meal, and we recommend only a daily total of 20 on the *Forever Fit* Plan. In general Lean Cuisine meals are just slightly lower in fat content than Weight Watchers.

People can focus too much on calories alone instead of fat. Like Triscuits, for example, are made from whole wheat, but people don't realize they're loaded with fat and that outweighs any value you might get from the whole wheat.

Take a "health food" like Tofutti, hyped as a cholesterol-free snack. Personally, I think Tofutti is B.S. So what if it's got no cholesterol? You're not doing yourself any big favor with Tofutti or low-fat frozen yogurt (as opposed to nonfat frozen yogurt, which is nonfattening). Tofutti's got 13 grams of fat per four ounces. Have it as a treat, but don't kid yourself that you're eating something healthy.

Tofu Light is low-sodium, cholesterol-free, lactose-free. Great. But it gives you 15 grams of fat per bar, more than an entire Weight Watchers dinner.

Another food that people often assume is healthy because of its "natural" appeal and its protein content is peanut butter. Unfortunately, peanut butter is very fattening. Two tablespoons of Skippy Super Chunk—that's a pretty thin sandwich—contains 17 grams of fat and 190 calories. And that's without the jelly. (For jelly, we recommend brands like Sorrell Ridge 100% Fruit, Smucker's Simply Fruit jelly, and Polaner, which add no sugar but get their sweetness entirely from the fruit preserves. See page 84 for a full list of recommended jellies.) So, if you are watching your fat intake, any brand of peanut butter—Scudder's doesn't add sugar the way Skippy does but still has 16 grams of fat for the same two tablespoons—is a disaster.

We looked at "seltzers," which people assume are practically calorie-free, and found brands like New York Seltzer that have between 120 and 180 calories in the flavored drinks. Seltzer should really have between zero and 10 calories. I used to be really into Sundance Sparklers, and I called them to find out how many calories were in their fruit-flavored drinks, because the bottles didn't say. They finally admitted it was 190. At least they weren't calling it a seltzer. But that's like having a soda, though the sugar is "natural" from the fruit concentrates.

As I said before, we recommend staying away from dairy products like eggs, soft cheeses, and whole milk. If you have to have any dairy products, skim milk and skim-milk products (they are the same as nonfat milk products) are what I call the "best of the worst" options. Even something as basic as American cheese varies, depending on the brand. One ounce of Kraft Deluxe American cheese contains 110 calories, nine grams of fat, and 460 milligrams of sodium. Borden's Lite-Line cheddar cheese contains 35 calories, two grams of fat, and about 300 milligrams of sodium. And the Weight Watchers version has only 50 calories, two grams of fat, and 400 milligrams of sodium.

As for milk, I'd like to point out that low-fat milk, which is usually hyped as "2%" fat, is actually more like 33 percent fat. When a label says "2% fat," it's referring to milkfat content *by weight,* not calories. In terms of calories, 33 percent of low-fat's calories come from milkfat. On the other hand, whole milk, which is only 3.5% milkfat by weight, gets 50% of its calories from milkfat. So, in fact, low-fat milk still contains almost two-thirds as much fat as whole milk.

Finally, people should know that yogurt—one of the first of the so-called "health foods," isn't good for you at all, from our point of view. Most yogurts are fattening as hell. People think yogurt is like having a glass of water—like "Should I have a Perrier or that yogurt over there?" Don't kid yourself. Have it, but plan on it as part of your day's diet. Don't think it's healthy.

Most brands, no matter how they're marketed, are loaded with fat and sugar, and their calorie counts are unbelievable. Most are 250 calories. Especially the ones crammed with sugary fruits. Sugar is the second ingredient in almost all yogurt brands. Even a low-fat six-ounce yogurt has 150 calories.

The only brand I think is any good is Weight Watchers yogurt, which has no fat for eight ounces. But others go out of their way to let you know they're cholesterol-free and low-fat when they're 200 calories or more with four grams of fat. Most of the sweeter ones go past 250 calories for eight-ounce containers. Knudsen's makes a yogurt that tastes absolutely great, but it's got 250 calories, and it's made with low-fat, not nonfat, milk. That's hardly our idea of a health food. The Armenians have something called *madzoon*—a plain, no-flavoring, nonfat yogurt. It is really healthy for you. You could live on it. But with the yogurt in *our* supermarkets, you might as well go out and have ice cream.

Now, enough about some of the foods you should avoid. Robert's going to detail the ones you need for the *Forever Fit* Permanent Weight-Loss Plan.

ROBERT

THE FOREVER FIT BASIC PLAN

The *Forever Fit* Permanent Weight-Loss Plan includes up to two choices from each of the following categories plus one or two servings of a fat-burning meal replacement shake:

Each day, select the designated amounts from each category:

1. **Meal replacer:** one serving

2. **Animal protein:** up to four ounces of poultry, seafood, lean meat

3. **Dairy:** up to two cups skim milk or twelve ounces nonfat yogurt or two ounces 1% cottage cheese (1 cup of skim milk is used in the meal replacer drink)

4. **Vegetables** (includes salads): two or more servings (one serving cooked vegetables = ½ cup; fresh vegetable salads may be eaten as desired)

5. **Starch:** two servings (serving size = ½ to ¾ cup most starches or one slice whole grain bread or ½ to ¾ cup most hot and cold breakfast cereals)

6. **Fruit:** two servings (one serving = ½ cup fresh fruit or two tablespoons raisins or three dried medium prunes or one small apple or ½ medium banana)

For those who like to count calories, here is what a typical day's food intake on the *Forever Fit* Permanent Weight-Loss Plan would include:

Approximate Daily Caloric Intake
Up to 950 calories from daily solid-food meals and snacks
up to 350 calories from two fat-burning meal replacement shakes
───
= Up to 1,300 total daily calories (Suggested range: 1,000–1,300)

Following the *Forever Fit* weight-loss dietary guidelines will help you consume adequate amounts of all vitamins, minerals, essential amino acids, and fatty acids required by the body to promote optimal weight loss, peak physical performance, and maximum health. A nutritional "label" for each day's food intake would look something like this:

NUTRITIONAL "LABEL" FOR THE *FOREVER FIT* PERMANENT WEIGHT-LOSS PLAN

Protein: 55–75 grams per day (up to 300 calories)

Fats and oils: 10–20 grams per day (up to 180 calories)

Complex carbohydrates: about 150–200 grams per day (up to 800 calories)

Fiber: up to 40 grams per day when diet is supplemented with Twin Laboratories' Fiber Booster (discussed in Chapter 7)

RDA's: 100%+ of the Recommended Daily Allowance (RDA) for vitamins, minerals, and protein

AS PERCENTAGE OF DAILY CALORIES

Protein: 20–25% (this is reduced to 12–14% during weight maintenance)

Fat: 10–20%

Complex carbohydrate: 60%

PICKING THE PROPER MEAL REPLACER

More than a dozen popular liquid meal replacement products are sold in the U.S. These can be found in health-food stores, supermarkets, groceries, and drugstores. During the last four years we have used the Feelin' Fit liquid meal replacer made by Twin Laboratories (available in health-food stores), and we have tried others, such as Ultra Slim•Fast, made by Thompson Medical Co., and Ensure, made by Ross Laboratories. We strongly urge you to consider the following criteria before selecting the liquid meal replacer you will use on the *Forever Fit* Permanent Weight-Loss Plan. Here are the essentials you should look for:

- **Protein:** High-biological-value protein sources, including nonfat dry milk, whey protein, egg white protein, and casein (a milk protein) are musts for any first-rate meal replacement formula.
- **Carbohydrate:** The primary complex carbohydrate you should look for is called *maltodextrin*. Complex carbohydrates from maltodextrin, as well as from the additional starches you will eat from foods such as pasta and potatoes, actually help spare protein requirements. Meal replacers may also contain simple carbohydrates for sweetness (fructose, or natural fruit sugar, which helps replenish liver glycogen stores).
- **Minerals and trace minerals:** Look for essential minerals such as calcium, magnesium, iron, and zinc for strong bones, proper muscular function, healthy blood, a strong immune system, and general good health. But you also need trace minerals, such as molybdenum, manganese, chromium, and selenium, which may help protect against heart disease, diabetes, and diet-related or environmentally induced cancers. While the body requires trace minerals in much smaller amounts than minerals such as calcium and magnesium, they are just as important as any other class of nutrients.
- **Fiber:** Fiber is essential for maintaining optimal intestinal functioning and in some cases may help control blood cholesterol levels. The meal replacement product you select should contain the most effective types of fiber that help to lower serum cholesterol and blood fats as well as improve bowel function. The water-soluble fibers such as oat bran, psyllium husk, and guar gum help you excrete cholesterol and its related metabolic products as well as carcinogenic waste products manufactured by bacteria that ordinarily live in your intestine. The type of fiber that stimulates proper bowel function, such as bran, cellulose, or psyllium seed husks, should also be present in any first-rate meal replacer.

BEVERAGES

You can survive without food for months, but without water, you'd last only weeks. Water is the beverage of choice on the *Forever Fit* Plan. We enjoy a variety of water: salt-free mineral waters, lightly flavored carbonated bottled waters (the ones flavored with fruit essences and *not* heavily sugared), bottled spring water, and of course, ordinary tap water.

We let our own thirst tell us how much water to drink except during exercise. We know all too well that during exercise, thirst does not keep apace of the body's water needs. During vigorous physical activity, we can consume one cup of water or sports/activity drink for every fifteen minutes of exercise.

For sports/activity drinks, we use Body Quench (Twin Laboratories) to help replace electrolyte (minerals) lost through sweat. This product is available in most health-food stores, but there are a variety of sports/activity drinks in most supermarkets and drugstores. Some contain appreciable amounts of sugar, others use artificial sweeteners, so check the label carefully.

Water comes in many "flavors": coffee, tea, soda, fruit juice, lemon- and lime-flavored activity drinks, just to name a few. In general, all of these beverages are acceptable on the *Forever Fit* Plan, but the ingredients which we try to avoid overconsuming are caffeine, sugar, and alcohol. We don't want to take away your morning coffee, afternoon tea, or favorite evening libation, but we do want to urge you to choose water whenever possible, as *your* beverage of choice.

CHOOSE WATER
AS YOUR
BEVERAGE
OF CHOICE

Today's supermarket and health-food store provide many alternatives to caffeinated, sugared, or fermented beverages: decaffeinated coffees, caffeine-free herbal teas and sodas, sugar-free drink mixes (Wyler's and Crystal Light brands, for example), sugar-free sodas (we recommend those sweetened with NutraSweet), and of course, the ever-popular bottled waters, plain, carbonated, or lightly flavored with fruit essences. We've even noticed that alcohol-free beer and wine substitutes are showing up on grocery shelves and in our favorite restaurants.

No one yet can say with scientific certainty how much caffeine, sugar, or NutraSweet we can safely consume, and that's why we recommend that you make water your primary beverage. If you enjoy other beverages, use common sense and moderation. An occasional diet soda, cup of coffee or tea, or sugared soft drink is fine.

Here are the guidelines we follow whenever we stray from pure water:

- **Fruit juice:** We try to eat the fruit instead, thereby getting the additional benefit of fiber, which contributes to intestinal health and helps keep our cholesterol levels down. Whole fruit tends to satisfy the appetite better than juice, and it's much easier to overconsume juice than whole fruit.
- **Caffeine:** No more than 100 milligrams per day (this means drinking no more than one cup of coffee or three small cups of tea or about two cans of caffeinated soda). Some people are sensitive to even this amount of caffeine and should therefore avoid it altogether. We like to avoid caffeine whenever possible, but sometimes it's hard to pass up a Coke

(fortunately, this and most other caffeinated soft drinks are available in caffeine-free formulations).

- **Skim milk:** We use skim milk in our meal replacer shake and on breakfast cereal. Of course, milk and cookies is a great combination too, but in general, we regard milk as a food (albeit in liquid form) and not a beverage.
- **Alcohol:** We rarely imbibe. Some recent studies suggest that for some people, there is no "safe" level of alcohol consumption. While it is likely that some people can enjoy a few drinks a week without apparent ill effect, we reserve alcohol use for occasional toasts such as holidays, birthdays, and anniversaries.
- **Sugar:** No more than 12 ounces of any soft drink made with sugar, and no more than several times a week. This applies to fruit juices as well, also a rich source of sugar.
- **NutraSweet (Equal):** Up to 16 ounces of any soft drink made with NutraSweet or Equal each day. Some people have reported a "sensitivity" to this sweetener; however, no definitive scientific study has been published that has measured or substantiated these claims. We've used beverages sweetened with NutraSweet for the last ten years without any apparent ill effects.

FOREVER FIT WEIGHT-LOSS MENUS

Nutritional surveys reveal us to be creatures of habit. People may choose among as few as four different meal choices each for breakfast, lunch, and dinner. During periods of weight loss we like to focus on two to three breakfast, lunch, and snack choices and then get our variety from dinner foods. With the ever-quickening pace of today's lifestyle, most people find it easier to lose weight when they stick to a regular or "standard" breakfast and lunch menu and then relax with more variety at dinner. So we've constructed the following "quick" menus to help simplify breakfast, lunch, and dinner choices.

Breakfast and lunch choices should be especially low in fat—about half your daily fat ration should come from breakfast and lunch combined, the other half coming from dinner. The *Forever Fit* breakfast and lunch choices are designed to give your body what it needs to start the day right and keep going— plenty of complex carbohydrates and protein but very little fat and cholesterol.

Now we want to show you the nutritional breakdown of a typical *Forever Fit* weight-loss breakfast:

BREAKFAST

1 serving (1 cup) for a typical liquid meal replacer (made with skim milk)

Calories	175	Carbohydrate	30.0 g
Protein	13.3 g	Fat	1.0 g
Sodium	201 mg	Cholesterol	5 mg

Caloric Breakdown: 66% carbohydrate, 29% protein, 5% fat.

or

Whole grain cereal with fresh fruit and skim milk

	Weight (g)	Calories	Carbo. (g)	Protein (g)	Fat (g)	Choles. (mg)	Sodium (mg)
½ average Banana	75	69	17.5	0.8	0.4	0	1.0
1 serving Bran Cereal, 100% Bran	28	76	20.7	3.5	1.4	0	196
¾ cup Skim Milk	183	64	9.0	6.2	0.4	4	94
Total Values:	286	209	47.2	10.5	2.2	4	291

Caloric Breakdown: 75% carbohydrate, 17% protein, 8% fat.

LUNCH

Water-packed albacore tuna (no salt added) sandwich with soup and fresh fruit

	Weight (g)	Calories	Carbo. (g)	Protein (g)	Fat (g)	Choles. (mg)	Sodium (mg)
3 ounces Tuna (all white meat fancy albacore in water, no salt)	85	108	0	23.8	0.7	54	35
2 tablespoons Lemon Juice	30	6	2.0	0.1	0.1	0	6
1 Bagel (whole wheat if available)	46	102	22.0	4.8	1.4	0	242
½ average Grapefruit	100	32	8.1	0.6	0.1	0	1
1 cup Split Pea Soup	245	184	27.2	10.0	4.2	7	975
Total Values:	506	432	59.2	39.4	6.4	61	1259

Caloric Breakdown: 52% carbohydrate, 35% protein, 13% fat.

DINNER

1 serving spaghetti with salad

	Weight (g)	Calories	Carbo. (g)	Protein (g)	Fat (g)	Choles. (mg)	Sodium (mg)
2 cups Spaghetti, cooked firm, 6–8 minutes	294	435	88.5	14.7	1.5	0	3
1 serving Tomato-Mushroom Spaghetti Sauce (Forever Fit Recipe)	113	34	7.5	1.5	0.3	0	133
2 teaspoons grated Parmesan Cheese	3	15	0.1	1.4	1.0	3	62

Dinner Salad

	Weight (g)	Calories	Carbo. (g)	Protein (g)	Fat (g)	Choles. (mg)	Sodium (mg)
¼ cup Carrots, raw	50	21	4.8	0.5	0.1	0	24
1 cup Lettuce, loose leaf or bunching varieties	56	10	1.9	0.7	0.2	0	5
⅓ cup Broccoli, raw	50	16	2.9	1.8	0.1	0	8
5 small Radishes, raw	50	9	1.8	0.5	0+	0	9
2 tablespoons no-oil salad dressing	34	8	2.0	0	0	0	244
Fruit: 1 average Apple	150	89	22.9	0.3	0.6	0	2
Total Values:	800	636	132.6	21.5	3.8	3	489

Caloric Breakdown: 82% carbohydrate, 13% protein, 5% fat.

Approximate daily totals: *Forever Fit target range:*

Calories: 1,250   1,000–1,300
Carbohydrate: 230   150–250 grams
Protein: 70   55–75 grams
Fat: 12 grams   10–20 grams
Cholesterol: 70 milligrams 0–150 milligrams
Sodium: 2,000 milligrams   500–3,000 milligrams

These are the numbers you should shoot for each and every day to safely and healthfully lose between one and two pounds of pure fat every week. As a bonus, your blood cholesterol level will probably drop (many people with average cholesterol levels of 200 milligrams and above usually experience a 10 to 30 percent or greater drop in three to four weeks) and you will probably feel more energetic. By adhering to the *Forever Fit* five rules of meal planning that follow, you can easily make correct mealtime choices and stay within the acceptable range for the above nutrients.

THE FOREVER FIT FIVE RULES OF MEAL PLANNING

The special diet chemistry of the *Forever Fit* Permanent Weight-Loss Plan requires that you do five things each day:

1. Have at least one serving of a meal replacer drink each day.
2. Eat at least 600 calories from carbohydrate foods each day.
3. Eat at least 240 calories from protein sources each day.
4. Limit total fat intake to 20 grams each day and cholesterol to 150 milligrams each day.
5. Limit total sodium intake each day to 3,000 milligrams (about 1 teaspoon of table salt).

SAMPLE SELECTIONS FOR MAIN-COURSE VARIETY

Most of the variety in your new diet will probably come from the main course. Each main course should consist of four ounces of a recommended high-quality protein food, providing approximately 20 to 30 grams of protein. Vegetarians should select low-fat protein sources such as skim milk products, beans, peas, and lentils. Select main-course choices from the following approved sample main-course chart (you may also select any protein source from the food composition tables in Appendix III, as long as it meets the criteria above).

SAMPLE MAIN-COURSE PROTEIN CHOICES

	Weight (g)	Calories	Carbo. (g)	Protein (g)	Fat (g)	Choles. (mg)	Sodium (mg)
Turkey, without skin, white meat, roasted *4 ounces*	113	193	0	33.2	5.7	86	79
Chicken, broiler, without skin, white meat only, broiled *4 ounces*	113	154	0	27.0	4.3	99	75
Tuna, canned in water, fancy albacore, solid white *4 ounces*	113	144	0	31.8	0.9	71	46
Cod, broiled *4 ounces*	113	193	0	32.3	6.0	92	125
Lobster, steamed *4 ounces*	113	103	0.6	19.2	2.2	95	240
Shrimp, boiled* *4 ounces* ** Note that shrimp is relatively high in cholesterol.*	113	132	0.8	27.4	1.2	170	159
Swordfish, broiled *4 ounces*	113	197	0	31.8	6.8	91	152
Scallops, steamed *4 ounces*	113	128	5.1	26.5	1.6	40	299
Halibut, broiled *4 ounces*	113	194	0	28.6	7.9	68	152
Crab, steamed *4 ounces*	113	105	0.6	19.6	2.2	113	238
Beef Porterhouse, lean, choice grade, broiled *4 ounces*	113	254	0	34.2	11.9	103	84
Black Beans, cooked *½ cup*	100	118	21.2	7.8	0.6	0	7
Beans, white, raw (note the difference between raw vs. cooked beans) *½ cup*	100	340	61.3	22.3	1.6	0	19
Kidney Beans, canned, rinsed *½ cup*	90	113	20.5	7.1	0.5	0	4
Peas, green, frozen, boiled w/o salt, drained *½ cup*	100	63	11.8	5.1	0.3	0	351

SAMPLE MAIN-COURSE VEGETABLE CHOICES

Select two servings each day from the following foods. (Note that nearly every vegetable is acceptable on the Forever Fit *Plan.) One serving = ¹/₂ cup.*

	Weight (g)	Calories	Carbo. (g)	Protein (g)	Fat (g)	Choles. (mg)	Sodium (mg)
Asparagus, raw spears, boiled w/o salt, drained *1 serving*	75	17	2.8	2.4	0.1	0	1
Broccoli, raw *¹/₂ cup*	75	24	4.4	2.7	0.2	0	11
Beet Greens, boiled w/o salt, drained *1 serving*	100	18	3.3	1.7	0.2	0	76
Cabbage, common varieties, raw *1 serving*	50	12	2.7	0.6	0.1	0	10
Cauliflower, raw *1 serving*	83	22	4.3	2.2	0.2	0	11
Corn, whole-kernel, low-sodium, canned, drained solids *1 serving*	125	95	22.5	3.1	0.9	0	3
Chard, Swiss, boiled w/o salt, drained *1 serving*	83	15	2.7	1.5	0.2	0	72
Eggplant, raw *2 slices*	100	25	5.8	1.2	0.2	0	2
Green Beans, raw *1 serving*	63	22	4.9	1.3	0.1	0	5
Kale, leaves, boiled w/o salt, drained *1 serving*	100	39	6.1	4.5	0.7	0	43
Okra, boiled w/o salt, drained *1 serving*	100	29	6.0	2.0	0.3	0	2
Spinach, boiled w/o salt, drained *1 serving*	100	23	3.6	3.0	0.3	0	50
Squash, summer, raw *¹/₂ cup*	65	12	2.7	0.7	0+	0	0+
Potato, baked, w/skin *1 average*	255	117	48.9	6.0	0.3	0	9
Black Beans, cooked *¹/₂ cup*	100	118	21.2	7.8	0.6	0	7

	Weight (g)	Calories	Carbo. (g)	Protein (g)	Fat (g)	Choles. (mg)	Sodium (mg)
Kidney Beans, canned, rinsed *1 serving*	90	113	20.5	7.1	0.5	0	4
Lentils *1 serving*	75	80	14.5	5.8	0	0	10
Peas, green, frozen, boiled w/o salt, drained *1 serving*	100	63	11.8	5.1	0.3	0	351
Beets, red, canned, drained solids *1 serving*	83	31	7.3	0.8	0.1	0	197
Brussels Sprouts, boiled w/o salt, drained *1 serving*	83	30	5.3	3.5	0.3	0	8
Butternut Squash, boiled, mashed w/o salt *1 serving*	125	51	13.0	1.4	0.1	0	1
Cabbage, Chinese, raw *1 serving*	22	3	0.7	0.3	0+	0	5
Celery stalks, raw *3 small*	50	11	2.4	0.6	0.1	0	79
Chicory, head, raw *1 serving*	77	12	2.5	0.8	0.1	0	5
Collards, leaves, boiled w/o salt, large amount water *1 serving*	100	31	4.8	3.4	0.7	0	25
Dandelion Greens, boiled w/o salt, drained *1 serving*	100	33	6.4	2.0	0.6	0	44
Endive leaves *10 small*	13	3	0.5	0.2	0+	0	2
Escarole leaves *8 small*	25	5	0.9	0.3	0+	0	3
Garbanzo Beans (Chick-Peas), canned *2 ounces*	57	102	17.3	5.8	1.4	0	149
Green Pepper, raw *1 large*	40	9	1.9	0.5	0.1	0	5
Kohlrabi, thick bulblike stems, boiled w/o salt *1 serving*	75	18	4.0	1.3	0.1	0	5
Mixed Vegetables, frozen, boiled w/o salt *1 serving*	82	52	10.9	2.6	0.2	0	43

	Weight (g)	Calories	Carbo. (g)	Protein (g)	Fat (g)	Choles. (mg)	Sodium (mg)
Onion, raw *1 average*	86	33	7.5	1.3	0.1	0	9
Parsnips, cooked w/o salt *1 serving*	78	52	11.6	1.2	0.4	0	6
Pumpkin *1 serving*	100	26	6.5	1.0	0.1	0	1
Rutabaga, boiled w/o salt, drained *1 serving*	100	35	8.2	0.9	0.1	0	4
Scallions, bulbs and tops, raw *3 average*	50	23	5.2	0.5	0.1	0	3
Shallot, bulbs, raw *1 serving*	100	72	16.8	2.5	0.1	0	12
Snow Peas, frozen *2 ounces*	57	51	11.6	3.3	0.2	0	68
Sweet Potato, baked, w/skin *1 average*	298	254	58.5	3.8	0.9	0	22
Water Chestnuts, Chinese, raw *16 average*	100	79	19.0	1.4	0.2	0	20
Watercress, raw *1 serving*	50	10	1.5	1.1	0.1	0	26
Wax Beans, boiled w/o salt, drained *1 serving*	100	22	4.6	1.4	0.2	0	3
Zucchini, steamed w/o salt, drained *1 serving*	100	12	2.5	1.0	0.1	0	1

SAMPLE SALAD CHOICES

Choose any combination of choices from the sample vegetable list above or from the examples listed below for a raw vegetable salad.* Use a no-oil or very-low-fat dressing (see suggestions from the "approved" salad dressing list in Chapter 6). On the Forever Fit *Plan you can enjoy salads with no-oil dressings as snacks as well.*

* Any vegetable is permitted for salads, with the exception of olives, hearts of palm, and avocado. Nuts and seeds are also not permitted.

	Weight (g)	Calories	Carbo. (g)	Protein (g)	Fat (g)	Choles. (mg)	Sodium (mg)
Lettuce, Romaine, raw *2 servings*	133	24	4.7	1.7	0.4	0	12
Lettuce, loose leaf or bunching varieties *2 servings*	111	20	3.9	1.4	0.3	0	10
Carrots, raw *1 serving*	100	42	9.7	1.1	0.2	0	47
Tomato, raw *1 average*	133	29	6.3	1.5	0.3	0	4
Radishes, common, raw *10 small*	100	17	3.6	1.0	0.1	0	18
Alfalfa Sprouts, raw *1 ounce*	28	10	1.0	1.0	0	0	1
Cucumber, raw *½ average*	56	8	1.8	0.3	0.1	0	3

THE FOREVER FIT WEIGHT-LOSS EATING IN AND OUT MENU PLANS

Here is a seven-day, 21-meal plan designed to give you a variety of options while eating inside and outside the home. People who want to follow a highly structured weight-loss plan can follow these suggestions day by day. You can also mix and match any of the following meal examples to add a variety of foods and tastes to your new eating plan.

We want you to get used to the idea that during the weight-loss phase of your new way of eating, a solid food meal can consist simply of a baked potato with approved topping, a large fresh vegetable salad with a no-oil or low-fat dressing, and one serving of fresh fruit (i.e., ½ cup). Once you adapt to this mode of "light" eating, we believe that you will become accustomed to eating smaller portions after you've reached your target weight, thus developing an eating habit that will make weight mainte-nance easier and weight loss permanent.

GUIDELINES

1. Use these menu plans to add variety as you desire. Any day or meal can be repeated when desired and you can mix or match meals from any day so long as you consume no more than four ounces of animal protein (e.g., poultry, seafood, lean beef) on any single day.

2. We recommend using a liquid meal replacer for breakfast. If you choose not to use a liquid meal replacer, hot or cold cereal with skim milk and fresh fruit may be eaten every day for breakfast if desired, or choose a *Forever Fit* breakfast recipe listed below for occasional variety.

3. Have one fresh fruit serving with breakfast and lunch each day.

4. An asterisk (*) indicates a *Forever Fit* recipe found in Appendix I of this book.

5. Enjoy fresh vegetable salads with lunch and dinner every day if desired. Approved salad dressings are listed on page 81. Fast-food restaurants, such as McDonald's and Burger King, offer low-fat salad dressings that are acceptable on the *Forever Fit* Plan.

6. Suggested baked potato toppings: low-fat yogurt (1% fat); low-fat cottage cheese (1% fat); Butter Buds or Molly McButter (our favorite) butter-flavored granules; two tablespoons of any low-fat salad dressing (up to three grams of fat per tablespoon).

7. Low-fat dessert suggestions: four ounces of frozen low-fat frozen yogurt; low-fat frozen desserts such as Weight Watchers brand; ¾ cup of unsweetened applesauce; two cups hot air-popped popped corn; your favorite brand of liquid meal replacer; one serving fresh fruit; one serving of any dessert recipe in this book.

MEAL SUGGESTIONS

BREAKFAST EVERY DAY: Choose your favorite liquid meal replacer

or

1 serving hot or cold whole-grain cereal with ¾ cup skim milk, ½ sliced banana, or ½ cup other fresh fruit

or

Choose one of the following *Forever Fit* breakfast recipes found in Appendix I:

- Oatmeal and Prunes Cereal
- Baked Breakfast Toast with one piece of fruit
- Baked Omelet
- Potato Scramble
- Brown Rice-Pineapple Cereal
- Old-Fashioned Scrambled Eggs
- Blueberry Pancakes
- Bran Pancakes
- Oatmeal Apple-Raisin Pancakes
- Pumpkin Pancakes

Additional "quick" breakfast suggestions for variety:

- Egg white omelet with your favorite vegetables topped with salsa
- 1 serving (3 pancakes) Aunt Jemima Lite Microwave Buttermilk Pancakes with 3 tablespoons Aunt Jemima Lite Syrup

LUNCH DAY 1

EATING IN 1 serving *Mashed Potato Pie and salad with approved dressing (see page 81)

EATING OUT Baked potato with low-fat topping (see page 80), salad bar with approved dressing (see page 81)

DINNER DAY 1

EATING IN 1 serving *Baked Garlic Snapper, 1 ear corn on the cob, and salad with approved dressing (see page 81)

EATING OUT ¼ pound poached salmon, 1 ear corn on the cob or 1 baked potato with low-fat topping (see page 80), and salad with approved dressing (see page 81)

LUNCH DAY 2

EATING IN 1 cup *Lima Bean Chowder with 1 slice whole wheat toast

EATING OUT 1 bean burrito with lettuce, tomato, onion, and enchilada sauce

DINNER DAY 2

EATING IN 1 serving *Chicken Cacciatore, 1 baked potato with low-fat topping (see page 80) and salad with approved dressing (see page 81)

EATING OUT 1 barbecued chicken breast half (without skin), ½ cup baked beans, 1 ear corn on the cob, 1 piece of fresh fruit

LUNCH DAY 3

EATING IN 1 serving *Teriyaki Chicken Kabobs served over 1 cup brown rice

EATING OUT 1 serving shrimp, lobster, or crab cocktail with red cocktail sauce and 1 baked potato with approved low-fat topping (see page 80)

DINNER DAY 3

EATING IN 1 serving *Spaghetti with Basil & Tomato Sauce (2 teaspoons grated Parmesan cheese optional) and salad with approved dressing (see page 81)

EATING OUT 1 serving spaghetti with marinara sauce (2 teaspoons grated Parmesan cheese optional) and salad with approved dressing (see page 81)

LUNCH DAY 4

EATING IN 1 serving *Quick Corn Soup, 1 slice whole wheat bread, and salad with approved dressing (see page 81)

EATING OUT 1 slice of pizza (whole wheat if possible) made with low-fat mozzarella cheese and mixed garden salad with approved dressing (see page 81)

DINNER DAY 4

EATING IN 1 serving *Spaghetti with Turkey Meatballs and salad with approved dressing (see page 81)

EATING OUT   1 serving lobster or stone crabs, shelled, with red cocktail sauce or lemon juice, 1 baked potato with low-fat topping (see page 80) or 1 ear corn on the cob, and salad with approved dressing (see page 81)

LUNCH DAY 5

EATING IN   1 cup *White Bean and Turkey Stew and salad with approved dressing (see page 81)

EATING OUT   ½ turkey sub (lettuce, tomato, peppers, etc.) with vinegar, mustard, and pepper

DINNER DAY 5

EATING IN   Steamed vegetable platter, 1 baked potato with low-fat topping (see page 80), and salad with approved dressing (see page 81)

EATING OUT   Vegetable stir-fry with no oil (ask that vegetables be stir-fried with chicken stock) served over brown rice and salad with approved dressing (see page 81)

LUNCH DAY 6

EATING IN   1 serving *Baked Sesame Chicken and large fresh vegetable salad with approved dressing (see page 81)

EATING OUT   1 broiled chicken sandwich with mustard (e.g., Burger King's B.K. Broiler sandwich), salad, and approved dressing (see page 81)

DINNER DAY 6

EATING IN   1 slice *Mashed Potato Pie and salad with approved dressing (see page 81)

EATING OUT   1 bean burrito with lettuce, tomato, and enchilada sauce

LUNCH DAY 7

EATING IN	1 3-ounce can fancy white albacore tuna packed in spring water (no salt added) mixed with 2 tablespoons lemon juice or no-oil dressing on 2 slices whole grain bread and large fresh vegetable salad with approved dressing (see page 81)
EATING OUT	1 serving boiled shrimp, crab, or lobster cocktail with red cocktail sauce, 1 slice whole grain bread, and large fresh vegetable salad with approved dressing (see page 81)

DINNER DAY 7

EATING IN	2 cups (cooked) *Linguine Alfredo and ½ cup steamed broccoli with lemon juice
EATING OUT	2 cups (cooked) spaghetti with marinara sauce (2 teaspoons grated Parmesan cheese optional) and salad with approved dressing (see page 81)

DOES DIETING CAUSE GALLSTONES?

Recent reports of some dieters developing gallstones have raised an important question: does dieting cause gallstones?

The gallbladder is a sac-like organ located under the liver whose primary function is to store bile, a mixture of cholesterol-related substances made by the liver that aid in fat digestion. When fat enters the digestive tract, the gallbladder contracts, sending bile into the intestines.

Gallstones occur in an estimated twenty percent of the women and eight percent of the men over age 40 in the United States. Gallstones are rock-like objects that form in the gallbladder when there is an imbalance in chemicals that make up bile. They can sit "silently" in the gallbladder and cause no pain. In some cases, however, a gallstone may block the path of bile out of the gallbladder, causing the organ to become inflamed, a condition that may have to be corrected with surgery or drugs. Healthcare professionals have recognized that people who are overweight are more likely to have gallstones than people at their normal weight.

Many people recently became aware of these facts when a number of dieters were reported to have developed gallstones while losing weight. There is still much speculation about why gallstones formed in these and other dieters. Fasting and very-low-calorie diets have been linked to increased risk of gallstone formation, but there seems to be general agreement among health-care professionals that the fewer calories you consume and the more rapidly you lose weight, the greater your risk of forming gallstones.

Most weight loss experts recommend that weekly weight losses not exceed one to two pounds. This is the same recommendation we make on the *Forever Fit Lifetime Weight Loss Diet*. Although no one can state unequivocally that this recommended rate of weight loss will protect against gallstone formation, such a recommendation is based upon the best available scientific evidence to date. Dieting to lose excess body fat may have its risks, but most health experts believe that the health risks associated with obesity, such as certain types of cancer, diabetes, and cardiovascular disease, far outweigh the risks of developing gallstones. If you are concerned about the gallstone question or have a history of gallstones or any other medical condition, we urge you to see a physician before beginning this or any other dietary plan.

6

THE FOREVER FIT
WEIGHT-MAINTENANCE PLAN

Now for what *used* to be the hard part—keeping it off. On the *Forever Fit* Weight-Maintenance Plan we'll show you how to stay slender for life—how to cook *Forever Fit* style, how to eat out, and how to quickly shed any unwanted pounds that may creep back.

THE SECRETS OF
PERMANENT WEIGHT LOSS

THE FIRST SECRET

This may seem like common sense to you, but many dieters meet with disaster because they don't know the first secret of permanent weight loss: a weight-maintenance diet must be nearly identical, with some liberal modifications, to the diet that got you slender in the first place. The same delicious foods and eating habits you acquired on the *Forever Fit* Permanent Weight-Loss Plan will keep you, well, forever fit. That's why our motto is: *Never change a winning game.*

If your prior weight-loss diet required you to starve yourself on 400 liquid calories a day, or if it required you to buy unusual or special foods that you couldn't ordinarily purchase at your favorite health-food store or supermarket, you probably ended up as just another diet-disaster statistic.

With our maintenance plan, once you reach your target weight you can eat about 500 more calories each day of your favorite high-complex-carbohydrate/low-fat foods and snacks while continuing to enjoy a nutritious liquid meal replacer as a dessert, breakfast drink, or snack.

THE SECOND SECRET

Your new eating plan should be able to be followed *everywhere*. The *Forever Fit* Weight-Maintenance Plan shows you how to select low-fat/low-cholesterol foods in a variety of situations, in the home and away from home.

Liquid diets never show you how to do this because they don't let you make food choices. Diet plans that rely mostly on special prefabricated foods or prepackaged meals unavailable in ordinary food outlets may also fail to give you practical knowledge about food composition. We think it is important that you learn how to select foods based on the amount of fat, cholesterol, protein, and carbohydrate they contain. Reading labels carefully is one key way.

While you don't have to acquire the knowledge of a dietitian to make healthy food choices, you should learn at least to count up the grams of total fat and milligrams of total cholesterol you eat each day to help keep you thin and healthy for the rest of your life. And that's why we've included a food composition index (Appendix III) and nutritional labels for each recipe in this book.

THE SECRET
OF
PERMANENT
WEIGHT LOSS
IS
REGULAR
EXERCISE

THE LAST SECRET

The final secret of permanent weight loss is *regular exercise*.

The health benefits of regular aerobic exercise such as walking, cycling, and low-impact aerobics cannot be overstated. The same can be said for the value of an exercise program to ensure permanent weight loss. We believe that any diet plan that doesn't contain regular aerobic exercise as an integral part of a weight-maintenance and cardiovascular health plan is unrealistic.

IT'S AS EASY AS ONE, TWO, THREE

To make your weight-maintenance plan easy to follow, we have divided the foods you will enjoy into three categories: *primary, secondary,* and *supplementary.* These categories will help you decide which foods you should choose at each meal, every day, regardless of whether you want to lose or maintain your weight.

Primary foods are those that supply most of your daily calories (50 percent or more). During both weight loss and weight maintenance, these will be the complex-carbohydrate foods that supply super nutrition and vital fiber for optimal health, energy, and vitality. Grains, cereals, breads, pasta, potatoes, and other vegetables will make up the bulk of your primary foods.

PRIMARY FOOD EXAMPLES

- Potatoes (white and sweet)
- Pasta (made without egg yolks): all types, including spaghetti, linguine, penne, lasagne noodles
- Rice (preferably brown) and all other whole grains
- Corn
- Beans: all types (soybeans should be limited because of their high fat content)
- Peas: all types (chick-peas [garbanzo beans] should be limited because of their high fat content)
- Lentils: all types
- Breakfast cereals (see approved cereals, page 81)
- All whole grain baking flours
- Cornstarch and arrowroot powder
- All vegetables, raw and cooked, except olives, avocado, hearts of palm, coconut; also exclude nuts and seeds

---

Secondary foods will provide much of your body's protein needs. The most common examples of the secondary foods you will enjoy on the

Forever Fit Permanent Weight-Loss Plan include the meal replacer protein shake; lean meats; poultry without skin; seafood, including lobster, oysters, and scallops; skim and low-fat dairy products; and legumes (beans, peas, lentils). When animal protein sources are chosen, you must limit your intake to four ounces per day because of their cholesterol content.

SECONDARY FOOD EXAMPLES
(up to four ounces of animal protein per day)

- Chicken (without skin)
- Turkey (without skin)
- Fish (all types)
- Lobster, shrimp, scallops, oysters, clams, and other shellfish
- Fancy all-white albacore canned tuna packed in water
- Lean beef (no more than 20 percent fat) with all visible fat trimmed
- Pork (all visible fat trimmed)
- Beans, peas, and lentils (note that these foods are included under the primary food list as well because they are unique in that they are a rich source of *both* complex carbohydrate and protein)
- Egg whites
- Skim and low-fat (1 percent) milk products such as skim milk, yogurt, cottage cheese

---

Supplementary foods can be enjoyed as snacks, nibbles, and desserts. Foods in this category, such as popcorn, frozen yogurt, and unsweetened applesauce, allow you to "cheat" during the weight-loss phase of your new diet and still achieve the rapid weight loss you desire.

SUPPLEMENTARY FOOD EXAMPLES

- Fresh fruit: all types
- Vegetables: all types except avocado, hearts of palm, coconut, and olives (use these sparingly as condiments rather than in serving portions); also exclude nuts and seeds
- Any commercial brand of fat-free or very-low-fat salad dressings (see approved list, page 81)
- Grated Parmesan cheese (up to 2 tablespoons a day)

- Popcorn (hot air popped)
- Unsalted pretzels
- Applesauce (unsweetened): 1 cup
- Low-fat frozen yogurt: 5 ounces
- Dried fruits (e.g., raisins, prunes, dates, apricots): 2 ounces
- Low-fat butter substitutes such as I Can't Believe It's Not Butter brand or Weight Watchers reduced-calorie margarine (up to 1 tablespoon a day)
- Butter Buds or Molly McButter brand powdered butter substitutes
- Pam vegetable spray
- Cholesterol-free/reduced-fat mayonnaise such as Hellmann's or Weight Watchers brand
- Olive oil (up to 1 teaspoon a day)
- Reduced-fat/no-cholesterol mayonnaise (up to 1 tablespoon a day)
- Jams, jellies, syrups
- Low-sodium soy sauce, tamari soy sauce, teriyaki sauce
- Alcohol (wine, beer, light beer, and hard liquor)

A SAMPLE DAY'S WEIGHT-MAINTENANCE DIET

BREAKFAST

- Liquid meal replacer

or

1 serving hot or cold whole grain cereal with ¾ cup skim milk, Equal sweetener (if extra sweetening is necessary), 1 serving fresh fruit (e.g., banana)

or

1 serving any *Forever Fit* breakfast recipe (see pages 171 to 179)

LUNCH

- 1 serving spaghetti marinara with 2 teaspoons grated Parmesan cheese

or

- cup split pea soup

or

- ½ cup steamed broccoli

or

- 1 piece fresh fruit

or

- 1 bean burrito (choose refried beans made without lard) tomato sauce, lettuce, mushrooms, peppers
- unlimited fresh vegetable salad with approved no-oil dressing (see page 81)
- 1 piece of fresh fruit

DINNER

- 4 ounces boneless turkey, no skin
- unlimited fresh vegetable salad with approved no-oil dressing (see page 81)
- baked potato with butter substitute and chives
- 1 slice Fresh Apple Pie (see page 226)

SNACKS

- 1 serving liquid meal replacer

or

1 piece of fresh fruit

or

3 cups hot air–popped corn

or

1 cup unsweetened applesauce

Snack Suggestions:
    frozen low-fat soft-serve yogurt (¾ cup)
    unsweetened applesauce (¾ cup)
    hot air–popped corn (2 cups)
    your favorite brand of liquid meal replacer
    1 piece of fresh fruit
    1 serving of any dessert recipe in this book

Suggested baked potato toppings: low-fat yogurt, low-fat cottage cheese, Molly McButter (butter flavor, sour cream flavor, or cheddar flavor), Butter Buds butter substitute.

FOREVER FIT APPROVED FOOD LISTS

CEREALS

The following breakfast cereals do not contain extraordinarily high amounts of sugar (some contain almost none) or fat (always check nutrition labels):

Oatmeal

Nabisco Shredded Wheat

Grape-Nuts

Kellogg's Nutri-Grain Wheat/Corn

Wheatena

Whole Wheat Total

Puffed Rice/Wheat

Cheerios

Rice/Wheat/Corn Chex

Corn Flakes (Whole oat or other whole grain flakes are more nutritious)

Any of the Arrowhead Mills, Erewhon, or Health Valley Brands made without fat and with little or no added sugar, nuts, seeds, or coconut

ACTIVITY DRINKS

Twin Laboratories—Body Quench (our favorite)

Ross Laboratories—Exceed

SALAD DRESSINGS

Only 1 tablespoon permitted when dressing contains one to three grams of fat per serving; otherwise no-oil dressings can be used up to 3 tablespoons per salad. These are just a few of the commercially available no-oil dressings found in supermarkets and health-food stores:

Wm. Reilly & Co.—Herb Magic (all varieties)

American Health Products—El Molino Herbal Secrets (all varieties)

Kraft—Oil-Free Italian (relatively high in sodium), Reduced Calorie, and Kraft Free fat free–cholesterol free dressing, Light Cholesterol Free Mayonnaise, Miracle Whip Cholesterol Free Dressing

H. J. Heinz—Weight Watchers Dressing (French, Tomato Vinaigrette)

Hain Pure Food Co.—No Oil Dressing Mix (Italian, French, Natural Herb)

Bunker Hill—all varieties

Walden Farms (varieties containing less than 1 gram of fat per serving)

Thomas J. Lipton, Inc.—Wishbone Lite (several varieties)

Campbell Soup Co.—Marie's Lite Dressings

Weight Watchers International, Inc.—Weight Watchers Dressings

General Foods Corp.—Good Seasons No Oil Italian salad dressing mix

The HVR Company—Hidden Valley Ranch Reduced Calorie Original Ranch Salad

Dressing Mix, Hidden Valley Ranch Take Heart cholesterol free dressing, Hidden Valley Ranch Reduced Calorie dressing

Pritikin Foods Division—Pritikin No Oil Dressing

Sandoz Nutrition Corp.—Featherweight Healthy Recipes Salad Dressings

The Estee Corp.—Estee low sodium, low calorie dressing

Astor Products, Inc.—Astor Light Dressing

Seven Seas Foods, Inc.—Seven Seas Light salad dressings

Deep South Products—Deep South Cholesterol Free Mayonnaise, Deep South Light Mayonnaise

United Food Industries, Inc.—Bright Day Cholesterol Free Mayonnaise

Best Foods, CPC International Inc.—Hellmann's Light Mayonnaise, Hellmann's Cholesterol Free Mayonnaise

Weight Watchers International, Inc.—Weight Watchers Reduced Calorie Mayonnaise, Weight Watchers Reduced Calorie Cholesterol Free Mayonnaise

Any salad dressing recipe from the recipe section (Appendix I) of this book

Wine vinegar or balsamic vinegar

Lemon or lime juice

BARBECUE SAUCES AND CATSUPS

Health Valley Foods—Catch-Up Tomato Table Sauce

Venture Packing Co.—Enrico's Ketchup

Westbrae Natural Foods—Fruit Sweetened Catsup, Unsweetened Un-Ketchup

Ridges Finer Foods—Bull's-Eye Original Barbecue Sauce

Hain Pure Food Co.—Catsup

BEVERAGES

HOT BEVERAGES AND COFFEE SUBSTITUTES (NO CAFFEINE)

Twin Laboratories—Body Quench (the most nutritious)

General Foods Corp.—Postum

Richter Bros.—Cafix

Nestlé Food Corp.—Pero

All types of tea (caffeine-free) and herbal tea

JUICES AND OTHER BEVERAGES

Monterey Canning Co.—Thrifty Maid Unsweetened Juices

Dole Packaged Foods Corp.—Dole Pure Unsweetened Juices, Dole Pure and Light

Mott's U.S.A., a Div. of Cadbury-Schweppes, Inc.—Mott's Unsweetened Juices

Nestlé Foods Corp.—Libby's Unsweetened Juices, Libby's Juicy Juice, Nestlé Quik Sugar Free

Seneca Foods Corp.—Seneca 100% Apple and Grape Juice, no sugar added

Campbell Soup Company—No Salt Added V 8 Juice

Ocean Spray Cranberries, Inc.—Ocean Spray Low Calorie juices

Cadbury-Schweppes, Inc.—Red Cheek Apple Juice No Sugar Added

Snapple Co.—Snapple Juices, No Sugar Added

Sun-Diamond Growers of California—Sunsweet Juice, No Sugar Added

Welch's—Welch's 100% Juices, No Sugar Added

Stokely-Van Camp, Inc.—Gatorade Light

Thomas J. Lipton, Inc.—Lipton Sugar Free Iced Tea, Lipton Low Calorie Iced Tea

General Foods Corp.—General Foods Sugar Free International Coffees, Sugar Free Crystal Light, Sugar Free Kool-Aid, Country Time Sugar Free

Beatrice/Hunt Wesson, Inc.—Swiss Miss Sugar-Free Hot Cocoa Mix

H. J. Heinz Co.—Alba Fit 'n Frosty

Carnation Company—Carnation Hot Cocoa Mix Sugar-Free

CONDIMENTS AND SEASONINGS

SALSAS

Tree of Life—Salsa

Hain Pure Food Co.—Salsa

Pet—Old El Paso Salsa

Nabisco Brands—Ortega Green Chile Salsa

Thompson Kitchens—Pritikin Mexican Sauce

Venture Packing Co.—Enrico's Salsa

Pace Foods—Picante Sauce

La Victoria Foods—Chili Dip (several varieties)

HOT AND SPICY SAUCES

McIlhenny Co.—Tabasco

Nabisco Brands—A.1. Steak Sauce

Durkee-French Foods—RedHot Cayenne Pepper Sauce

Reese Finer Foods—Prepared Horseradish

J. Sosnick & Sons—Kosher Horseradish

Trappey's Fine Foods—Red Devil Louisiana Hot Sauce

St. Giles Foods Ltd.—Matured Worcestershire Sauce

Sandoz Nutrition Corp.—Featherweight Chili Sauce

SEASONINGS

Maine Coast Sea Vegetables—Sea Seasonings (several varieties)

Parsley Patch—Parsley Patch (several varieties)

Hain Pure Food Co.—Chili Seasoning Mix

Modern Products—Vegit, Onion Magic, Natural Seasoning

The Estee Corp.—Seasoning Sense (Italian and Mexican)

Alberto-Culver Co.—Mrs. Dash (several varieties)

Kikkoman Foods, Inc.—Kikkoman Lite Soy Sauce (40% less salt)

Modern Products, Inc.—Vege-Sal Onion Magic, Spike, Vegit, Garlic Magic, Lemon Pepper, Herbal Bouquet

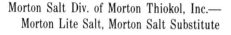
Morton Salt Div. of Morton Thiokol, Inc.—Morton Lite Salt, Morton Salt Substitute

Bekal Products—Bekal Spices, Complete Seasoning Low in Salt

AZKO International Salt Co.—Salt Sense (33% less sodium)

OILS AND BUTTER SUBSTITUTES

Boyle-Midway Household Products, Inc.—Pam No Stick Cooking Spray regular, butter flavor, and olive oil

Best Foods, CPC International—Mazola NoStick Corn Oil Cooking Spray

Weight Watchers International, Inc.—Weight Watchers Buttery Spray

Butter Buds Div. for Cumberland Packing Corp.—Butter Buds

Astor Products, Inc.—Fischer's Shake O'Butter

Alberto-Culver Co.—Molly McButter

Lever Bros. Co.—I Can't Believe It's Not Butter

Weight Watchers International, Inc.—Weight Watchers Reduced Calorie Margarine

Van Den Bergh Foods—Promise Extra Light Margarine

Land O'Lakes, Inc.—Land O'Lakes Spread and Country Morning Blend Light

Kraft, Inc.—Touch of Butter

Best Foods, CPC International—Mazola Light Corn Oil Spread

Nabisco Brands, Inc.—Fleischmann's Light Corn Oil Spread

JELLIES, JAMS, SPREADS, SYRUPS, AND SWEETENERS

Contain no added sugar or corn syrup:

Sorrell Ridge Farm—Sorrell Ridge 100% Fruit (several varieties)

Knudsen & Sons—All Fruit Fancy Fruit Spreads (several varieties)

M. Polaner, Inc.—All Fruit (several varieties)

Eden Foods—Barley Malt

J. M. Smucker Co.—Smucker's Simply Fruit (several varieties)

The J. M. Smucker Co.—Smucker's Low Sugar spreads, Smucker's Natural Peanut Butter lightly salted, no sugar added

Sandoz Nutrition Corp.—Featherweight Fruit Spreads and Imitation Jellies

The Estee Corp.—Estee Imitation Preserves

Goody's Mfg. Corp.—Necta Sweet

Thompson Kitchens—Superose Sugar Substitute

The NutraSweet Company—Equal Sweetener

Quaker Oats Co.—Aunt Jemima Lite Syrup

General Foods Corp.—Log Cabin Lite Syrup

The Estee Corporation—Estee Syrup (sucrose free)

Sandoz Nutrition Corp.—Featherweight Lite Syrup

Borden, Inc.—Cary's Sugar Free Reduced Calorie Syrup

NONDAIRY CREAMERS

Carnation Company—Coffee-Mate Lite Non-Dairy Creamer

Borden, Inc.—Cremora Lite Non-Dairy Creamer

SOUR CREAM

Dean Foods Co.—Extra Light sour cream product (⅔ less fat)

American Whipped Products, Inc.—King Sour sour dressing

Kraft, Inc.—Breakstone's Light Choice Sour Cream

MILK

Carnation Company—Carnation Evaporated Skimmed Milk

Familar Foods, Inc.—Low Fat Milkman (powdered milk)

Carnation Company—Carnation Nonfat Dry Milk

Pet Incorporated—Pet Light Evaporated Skimmed Milk

Dairymen, Inc.—Farmbest Lowfat Milk (cardboard carton)

Weight Watchers International, Inc.—Weight Watchers Skim Milk (cardboard carton)

SPAGHETTI SAUCE, TOMATO SAUCE, AND TOMATO PASTE

Del Monte USA—Tomato Sauce, Original Style Stewed Tomatoes, Tomato Paste

Contadina Foods—Tomato Paste and Tomato Puree

Pet—Progresso Tomato Paste and Tomato Puree

Beatrice/Hunt-Wesson, Inc.—Hunt's All Natural Tomato Paste, Hunt's All Natural Tomato Sauce, Hunt's Stewed Tomatoes

Pure & Simple—Johnson's Spaghetti Sauce, Trader Giotto's Italian Garden

Westbrae Natural Foods—Ci'Bella Pasta Sauce—no salt, no oil

Thompson Kitchens—Pritikin Spaghetti Sauce

H. J. Heinz Co.—Weight Watchers Spaghetti Sauce with Mushrooms

Sandoz Nutrition Corp.—Featherweight Healthy Recipes Spaghetti Sauce

RICE CAKES

Westbrae Natural Foods—Teriyaki Rice Cakes

H. J. Heinz Co.—Chico San (several varieties)

Hollywood Health Foods—Mini Rice Cakes (several varieties)

Pacific Rice Products—Mini Crispys (several varieties)

Lundberg Family Farms—Rice Cakes (several varieties), Brown Rice Chewies and Brown Rice

Hain Pure Food Co.—Hain Rice Cakes

Conrad Rice Mill, Inc.—Konriko Original Brown Rice Cakes, unsalted, no preservatives

CRACKERS

H. J. Heinz Co.—Weight Watchers Crispbread

Westbrae Natural Foods—Brown Rice Wafers

Ralston Purina Co.—Natural Ry-Krisp

O. Kavli A/S—Kavli Norwegian Crispbread

Barbara's Bakery—Crackle Snax, Lightbread

Sandoz Nutrition Corp.—Wasa Crispbread (several varieties)

Parco Foods—Hol-Grain brand (several varieties)

Edward & Sons Trading Co.—Baked Brown Rice Snaps

GMB Enterprises, Inc.—Horowitz Margareten Dietetic Matzos and Unsalted Matzos, Goodman's Unsalted Matzos

The B. Manischewitz Company—Manischewitz Dietetic, Unsalted, and Whole Wheat Matzos

Aron Streit, Inc.—Streit's Dietetic, Unsalted, and Lightly Salted Matzos

Jacobsen's Toast, Division of Log House Foods, Inc.—Jacobsen's Snack Toast, low sodium, cholesterol free

Stella D'Oro Biscuit Co., Inc.—Stella D'Oro Dietetic Bread Sticks

POPCORN

Nature's Best—Nature's Cuisine (natural popcorn)

H. J. Heinz Co.—Weight Watchers Microwave Popcorn

PRETZELS

Granny Goose Foods—Stick Pretzels 100% Natural Bavarian Pretzels (salted and unsalted varieties)

Laura Scudder's—Mini-Twist Pretzels, Bavarian Pretzels, Pretzel Sticks

Anderson Bakery Co.—Oat Bran Pretzels

Snyder's of Hanover—Sourdough Hard Pretzels (salted and unsalted varieties)

OTHER SNACKS AND CRACKERS

Fat, sodium, and cholesterol vary among the following brands, but these are acceptable supermarket brands:

Happy Heart Food Co.—Happy Heart Chips

Health Valley Foods—Golden Wheat Lites

New Generation Foods, Inc.—Spicer's for weight control

Procter & Gamble—Pringles Light Chips

Superior Protein Products Company—Lite Munchies

Crackin Good Bakers, Inc.—Crackin Good Unsalted Party Pretzels, Crackin Good low sodium crackers and unsalted tops

Quinlan Pretzels, Inc.—Quinlan Pretzels (no cholesterol)

Charles Pretzels, Inc.—Charles Pretzels No Salt

The Cape Cod Potato Chip Company—Cape Cod Potato Chips, all natural, cholesterol free

Frito-Lay, Inc.—Ruffles Light (cholesterol free, ⅓ less oil), Doritos Light (cholesterol free, ⅓ less oil), Chee•tos Light

General Mills, Inc.—Pop-Secret Light Popcorn

Beatric/Hunt-Wesson, Inc.—Orville Redenbacher's Gourmet Light

Keebler Company—Wheatables Low Salt crackers, Thin Bits, cholesterol free, low in saturated fat, Keebler Wheat Zesta Saltine Crackers, Unsalted Tops Zesta Crackers (cholesterol free, low in saturated fat), Keebler Town House Classic Crackers, cholesterol free and low in saturated fat; Keebler Town House Classic Crackers Low Salt

Interbake Foods, Inc.—Sesame Crackers and Stoned Wheat Crackers, no cholesterol, unsalted tops

Nabisco, Inc.—Low Salt Premium Saltine Crackers, Unsalted Tops Premium Crackers, Whole Wheat Premium Plus Saltine Crackers

Weight Watchers International, Inc.—Weight Watchers Snack Chips

Ralston Purina Company—Natural Ry-Krisp, no cholesterol

Venus Wafers, Inc.—Venus Oat Bran Wafers, salt free

Devonsheer Div. of Arnold Foods—Devonsheer Unsalted Melba

Wasa GmbH—Wasa Lite Rye Crispbread

Old London Div., CPC International, Inc.—Old London Unsalted Melba Toast and Crisp and Natural

Wheatabix of Canada—Krispen Light Natural Crispbread

COOKIES

Sunshine Biscuit, Inc.—Sunshine Country Style Oat Bran and Oatmeal Cookies, no cholesterol; Sunshine Country Style Chocolate Chip Low Cholesterol Cookies, Hydrox Cookies, no cholesterol

The Estee Corp.—Estee Cookies and Wafers (fructose sweetened, sodium free, cholesterol free)

Archway Cookies, Inc.—Archway Cookies, low cholesterol, low sodium, no palm oil

Keebler Company—Keebler Vanilla Wafers, Keebler Cinnamon Crisp, Keebler Graham Crackers, Keebler Honey Grahams (all cholesterol free and low in saturated fat)

BREADS

Interstate Brands—Pritikin Bread (several varieties—contain added raisin juice)

Garden of Eatin'—Bible Bread (salted and unsalted)

Breads for Life—Sprouted 7-Grain Bread, Sprouted Wheat with Raisins, Sprouted Rye Bread

International Baking Co.—Mr. Pita

Grainaissance—Mochi (several varieties)

Nature's Path Foods—Manna Bread

Lifestream Natural Foods—Essene Bread

OTHER BREADS

Pepperidge Farm, Inc.—Pepperidge Farm Very Thin White and Wheat, no cholesterol, low fat, low sodium; Pepperidge Farm Light Style no cholesterol, low fat, low sodium

Arnold Bakers Division of Arnold Foods Company—Arnold Melba Thin Bread, Arnold Bakery Light,

Flowers Family Bakeries, Inc.—Nature's Own Light

Interstate Brands—Roman Light

Holsum Bakeries—Holsum Light Natural

SOUPS

CANNED

Hain Pure Food Co.—Split Pea Soup

Real Fresh—Andersen's Soup (Split Pea)

Pritikin Systems, Inc.—Pritikin Lentil Soup (Strict vegetarians note: other Pritikin Soups may contain dairy product.)

Campbell Soup Company—Campbell's Low Sodium soups, Campbell's Special Request soups (condensed)
Note: Many soups by Health Valley and Progresso are low in fat (check labels).

DRY PACKAGED

Hain Pure Food Co.—Natural Classics Onion, Natural Classics Potato Leek

Westbrae Natural Foods—Ramen (several varieties)

Nile Spice Foods—Cous-Cous (several varieties)

Eden Foods—Buckwheat Ramen, Whole Wheat Ramen

Sokensha Co.—Soken Ramen

Romanoff Foods, Inc.—Romanoff MBT Instant Chicken Flavored Broth low sodium

LUNCHEON MEATS, FRANKS, AND BACON

Carl Buddig and Co.—Carl Buddig Lean meats, 93% Fat Free (7% Fat)

Hillshire Farm—Lean Classic Ham, Polska Kielbasa Lite, Deli Select 96% Fat Free Ham, 98% Fat Free Turkey, and 98% Fat Free Chicken

Galileo Salame—Galileo Pepperoni, 33½% less salt

Oscar Mayer Foods Corp.—Oscar Mayer Lower Salt Bacon (35% less), Oscar Mayer Thin Sliced (luncheon meats, 96% Fat Free), Oscar Mayer Light (luncheon meats)

Swift-Eckrich, Inc.—Sizzlean Cured Beef Breakfast Strips (turkey added, 50% leaner), Butterball (80–98% fat free turkey hot dogs and luncheon meats), Eckrich Lite Bunsize Franks

Louis Rich Co.—Louis Rich Bun-Length Turkey Franks (80% Fat Free)

Hebrew National Kosher Foods—Hebrew National Lite Beef Franks

Bilmar Foods, Inc.—Mr. Turkey Smoked Sausage

Armour Food Company—Armour Jumbo Beef Hot Dogs (90% fat free), Armour Lower Salt Bacon (40% less salt)

CANNED SEAFOOD

Bumble Bee Seafoods, Inc.—Bumble Bee Chunk Light Tuna in water, Bumble Bee Solid White Tuna in water, Bumble Bee Pink Salmon in water

The Monterey Canning Co.—Blue Bay Chunk Light Tuna in water, Blue Bay Solid White Tuna in water

Starkist Seafood Co.—Starkist Chunk Light Tuna in spring water, Starkist Solid White Tuna in spring water, Starkist Diet Chunk Light Tuna in pure distilled water, Starkist Diet Chunk White Tuna in water

Van Camp Seafood Company, Inc.—Chicken of the Sea Chunk Light Tuna in spring water, Chicken of the Sea Pink Salmon in water, Chicken of the Sea Solid White Tuna in spring water

Sandoz Nutrition Corp.—Featherweight Pink Salmon in water, Featherweight Chunk Light Tuna in water

Mitsubishi Foods (MC), Inc.—3 Diamonds Chunk Light Tuna in water

NO-YOLK NOODLES

Foulds, Inc.—No Yolks Cholesterol Free Egg Noodle Substitute

Borden, Inc.—Creamette No Egg Yolk Ribbons (no cholesterol low sodium)

CANNED FRUITS

Mott's U.S.A., a Div. of Cadbury-Schweppes, Inc.—Mott's Natural Applesauce no sugar added, no preservatives

The Monterey Canning Co.—Thrifty Maid Applesauce no sugar added

Musselman's, Div. of Knouse Foods—Musselman's Natural Applesauce sodium free, no preservatives, no sugar added

Del Monte Corp.—Del Monte Lite Fruit Cups

Tri Valley Growers—Libby's Lite Fruit Cocktail

Sandoz Nutrition Corp.—Featherweight Lite Fruits

The Monterey Canning Co.—Astor Lite Fruit Cocktail

CANNED VEGETABLES

The Pillsbury Company—Green Giant Niblets Corn, no salt or sugar added

Sandoz Nutrition Corp.—Featherweight green beans, whole kernel golden corn, no salt added

The Monterey Canning Co.—Astor whole crispy golden sweet corn no sugar added

Del Monte Foods—Del Monte whole kernel corn, green beans, stewed tomatoes, and tomato sauce, no salt added

FROZEN ENTRÉES

Pet Incorporated—Van de Kamp's Light Fillets

Mrs. Paul's Kitchens, Inc.—Mrs. Paul's Light Entree, Mrs. Paul's Light Fillets

Chef America—Lean Pockets

The Pillsbury Company—Green Giant Garden Gourmet–Perfect Light Entree

Stouffer's Foods—Lean Cuisine, Lean Cuisine Pasta Salads

Weight Watchers International, Inc.—Weight Watchers Entrees and Side Dishes

The All American Gourmet Co.—The Budget Gourmet Light

Kibun Corporation—Kibun Gold Low Calorie Meals

Conagra Frozen Foods—Light and Elegant

Conagra Frozen Foods—Healthy Choice Low Fat entrees

Stouffer's Foods—Stouffer's Right Course entrees

Tyson Foods, Inc.—Tyson Gourmet Selection Low Fat

Conagra Frozen Foods—Armour Classics Lite

MISCELLANEOUS FROZEN FOODS

Welch's—Welch's Frozen Juice no sugar added

The Quaker Oats Company—Aunt Jemima Lite Microwave Pancakes and Waffles

Nabisco Brands, Inc.—Egg Beaters

Worthington Foods, Inc.—Morning Star Farms Scramblers, Morning Star Farms Cholesterol Free Breakfast Patties, Morning Star Farms Cholesterol Free Breakfast Links, Morning Star Farms Grillers Cholesterol Free Patties (hamburger)

Egg Products, Inc.—Egg Supreme

YOGURTS AND CHEESES

Kraft, Inc.—Kraft Light Naturals, ⅓ less fat

Heinz Nutrition Products, Inc.—Weight Watchers Natural Mozzarella Cheese Flavor 40% less fat, Weight Watchers Natural Swiss Cheese Flavor 35% less fat, Weight Watchers Natural Sharp Cheddar Cheese 40% less fat

Dorman's Low Sodium Swiss Cheese, Low Sodium Lo-Chol Muenster Cheese, American Cheese, and Provolone Cheese

Galaxy Cheese Co.—Formagg Cheese Substitute no cholesterol, no lactose, low sodium

Borden, Inc.—Borden Lite-Line Cheese

Kraft, Inc.—Kraft Light n' Lively

Heinz Nutrition Products, Inc.—Weight Watchers Cheese, 75% less fat

Kraft, Inc.—Kraft Light Philadelphia Cream Cheese

Winn Dixie Stores, Inc.—Light Superbrand Cream Cheese

The Dannon Company, Inc.—Dannon Nonfat, Lowfat, and Light yogurt

Kraft, Inc.—Lightly n' Lively Yogurt no sugar added

Yoplait USA, Inc.—Yoplait Light

Winn Dixie Stores, Inc.—Superbrand lowfat yogurt, light yogurt

Pro-Mark Co., Inc.—Weight Watchers Ultimate 90 nonfat yogurt

Friendship Dairies, Inc.—Friendship lowfat cottage cheese, whipped lowfat cottage cheese, Lite Delite (light sour cream), Sour Treat

Sargento Cheese Co.—Sargento Natural Lite Ricotta Low Fat Cheese

Pollio Dairy Products Corp.—Polly-O Lite Ricotta

M. Maggio Co.—Maggio LoFat Part Skim Ricotta

Kraft, Inc.—Light n' Lively Lowfat Cottage Cheese

SWEETS

The Estee Corp.—Estee Candies

General Mills, Inc.—Betty Crocker Creamy Deluxe Frosting, no cholesterol

The Pillsbury Company—Pillsbury Ready to Spread Frosting Supreme, no cholesterol, no palm oil

General Mills, Inc.—Nature Valley Cholesterol Free Granola Bars

Entenmann's, Inc.—Entenmann's Cholesterol Free baked goods

Natural Nectar Products Corporation—Fi-Bar no cholesterol

General Foods Corp.—Jell-O Sugar Free gelatin, pudding, and pie filling desserts

Beatrice/Hunt-Wesson, Inc.—Hunt's Snack Pack Light Pudding

The Estee Corp.—Estee Reduced Calorie low sodium, no sugar pudding and gelatin

Sandoz Nutrition Corp.—Featherweight Sweet Pretenders Pudding and Pie Filling and Gelatin

H. Fox & Co., Inc.—NO-CAL Flavoring

Superbrand Dairy Products distr. by Winn Dixie, Inc.—Superbrand Ice Milk, Superbrand Sugar Free Fudge Pops, Superbrand Frozen Yogurt

General Foods Corp.—Crystal Light Cool 'n Creamy Frozen Dessert Bars

Eskimo Pie Corporation—Sugar Free Eskimo Pies

Isaly Klondike Company—Klondike Lite Sugar Free (97% fat free)

Popsicle Industries, Inc.—Sugar Free Popsicle, Sugar Free Fudgsicle

Weight Watchers International, Inc.—Weight Watchers Frozen Desserts

Tofulite Division—Loft's Tofulite cholesterol free, lactose free

Yoplait USA, Inc.—Yoplait 97% Fat Free Soft Frozen Yogurt

General Foods Corporation—Cool Whip

Pet Incorporated—La Creme

Pepperidge Farm, Inc.—Pepperidge Farm Cholesterol Free Pound Cake

Steve's Homemade Ice Cream, Inc.—Steve's Gourmet Light Ice Cream

The Simplesse Company—Simple Pleasures Frozen Dairy Desert

Weight Watchers International, Inc.—Weight Watchers Grand Collection Ice Milk

Kraft General Foods—Sealtest Fat Free Frozen Dessert

Crowley Foods, Inc.—Crowley Frozen Yogurt 97% Fat Free

Kraft, Inc.—Breyers Natural Light Ice Milk

HOW TO THROW A FOREVER FIT PARTY

Forever Fit is a lifestyle as much as it is a total health, fitness, and beauty regimen. We believe that a commitment to total health demands a commitment to a new lifestyle. An excellent way to enjoy leisure time with friends and relatives, yet still achieve your new health, fitness, and beauty goals, is to throw a *Forever Fit* party. It's simple and fun, and it may help to convince a few stubborn acquaintances or family members to change their life for the better.

Food that used to be creamed, buttered, and fried is now served grilled, broiled, lightly sautéed, toasted, and steamed. We want to show you how to put more vitamins, fiber, and complex carbs and less fat, cholesterol, and salt into your entertaining. Here's how to make *Forever Fit* substitutions at your next big bash:

Use	Instead of
All *Forever Fit* recipe entrées, dips, sauces, snacks, soups, beverages (see Appendix I):	conventional recipes
Twin Labs' Feelin' Fit Meal Replacer or another liquid meal replacer protein shakes	milk shakes
Sparkling cranberry or other fruit juice	wine spritzers
Grilled shrimp with lemon	cocktail franks in a blanket
Tomato salsa	French onion or other high-fat dip
Low-sodium Bavarian pretzels	potato chips
Unsweetened water or juice-packed fruits	syrup-packed fruits
Approved jams and jellies on pancakes	butter and syrup on pancakes
Approved crackers with approved jams	high-fat crackers with butter
Lower-fat cookies (fig bars, graham crackers, animal crackers)	high-fat chocolate chip or other fat-laden cookies
Air-popped popcorn	conventional popcorn popped in oil
Sugar-free natural-style applesauce	applesauce made with sugar
Angel food cake	other higher-fat cakes
Jell-O Sugar Free Cook 'n Serve Chocolate Pudding	puddings made with sugar and whole milk

Use	Instead of
All *Forever Fit* recipe desserts	all high-fat desserts such as ice cream, pastries, etc.
Mrs. Dash or Vegit low-sodium seasoning blends	salt
Low-sodium soy sauce (still limited)	regular soy sauce
Equal sweetener	sugar, honey, syrup
Pam vegetable spray for sautéing	vegetable oils

ADDITIONAL PARTY SNACKS

Here is a list of our favorite low-cal snacks, which we serve when we entertain:

- Liquid meal replacer Feelin' Fit (Twin Labs) or (choose your own favorite brand)
- Low-fat frozen yogurt (any flavor): up to 5 ounces
- Jell-O Sugar Free Cook 'n Serve Chocolate Pudding
- Dried fruit: up to 1 ounce
- 1 serving of any low-fat ice cream substitute or a dietetic-type dessert bar such as Weight Watchers frozen desserts or FrozFruit frozen fruit bars

ADDITIONAL PARTY SUGGESTIONS

- Use mustard as a condiment for sandwiches instead of high-fat spreads such as mayonnaise, vegetable oil, butter, or margarine.
- Use Body Quench (available in health-food stores) if you desire a low-calorie, sweet-tasting beverage (orange or lemon-lime flavor).
- Limit alcohol intake, including light beer, wine, and hard liquor, no more than twice a week. One type of alcoholic beverage and its corresponding permitted amount may be substituted for another type of alcoholic beverage; e.g., one light beer (12 ounces) equals one 3½-ounce glass of wine equals 1½ ounces hard liquor.

7

PRODUCTS THAT CAN HELP ROUND OUT YOUR FOREVER FIT LIFESTYLE

ACTIVITY DRINKS

For nearly one million years the best drink for active people, from cavemen to last year's Wimbledon champions, has been pure water. With such an unrivaled historical precedent and impressive record of success, one might assume that water would continue to enjoy the number-one spot as the drink of champions for at least another million years. Scientific progress, however, pays little attention to precedent; plain old water may soon become a nutritional dinosaur, at least for active people who want to achieve maximum physical performance.

The main problem with drinking water during and after physical activity is that *water replaces only water*. The energy and metabolic requirements of prolonged physical activity simply cannot be satisfied with plain water.

During the last few years food technologists and sports nutritionists have formulated a new breed of beverage called "high-tech water." Some are now available to the public, and several more will be marketed by the end of this year. Scientists have succeeded in transforming ordinary distilled water into a nutritionally enhanced beverage that can rapidly and effectively supply the body with several important energy nutrients that research has shown to be effective in increasing endurance and stamina.

High-tech water is much more than warmed-over Gatorade; it is in fact a truly scientific blend of salts, glucose polymers (long-chain molecules of the sugar glucose), fructose (natural fruit sugar that helps restore glycogen), and minerals such as calcium and magnesium that the body needs to sustain muscular activity. Formulas differ, according to manufacturer, and some will most likely be more effective than others in extending the limits of human endurance.

There is, however, one common attribute shared by all high-tech waters—glucose polymers. These are long-chain branched molecules of the ordinary sugar glucose. Research has shown that a drink containing about 3 to 5 percent glucose polymers and 2 percent fructose can leave the stomach and enter the bloodstream (and eventually the muscles) just as fast as water but with the additional benefits of energy and electrolyte (mineral) replacement.

Three primary factors affect physical performance, duration of activity, and recovery from activity during prolonged exercise: *dehydration* (loss of body water), *carbohydrate depletion* (glycogen exhaustion), and *hyperthermia* (elevation of body temperature). In the past, water has been the most effective nutrient in retarding the performance-robbing effects of dehydration and hyperthermia, while high-complex carbohydrate diets have helped slow glycogen depletion.

Some activity drinks don't leave the stomach soon enough due to their high osmolarity (concentration of salts and sugars) and may actually draw water into the stomach from exercising muscles. These drinks generally contain a high concentration of sucrose and/or glucose, which can delay stomach emptying.

Glucose polymers, however, exert a smaller osmotic pressure and are absorbed rapidly from the stomach and small intestine. Since the delivery of water and sugars to the body is controlled by stomach emptying, the polymerized form of glucose shortens the time and increases the amount of water and carbohydrate delivered to the muscles. Glucose polymer solutions can prolong exercise times and can increase the absorption of calcium in the small intestine.

THE ELECTROLYTES: MAGNESIUM, POTASSIUM, CHROMIUM, SODIUM, CALCIUM, AND CHLORIDE

Several electrolytes and minerals are important in physical activity—magnesium, potassium, chromium, sodium, calcium, and chloride. These electrolytes can affect water movement within the body and help regulate the delicate acid–base balance of the blood, which can affect endurance and performance.

Magnesium helps to convert carbohydrates to energy. It also aids in controlling heartbeat, activating enzyme systems, and controlling muscle contraction. Dr. Kenneth Cooper (Aerobics Institute, Dallas, Texas) has shown that runners experience a decrease in blood levels of magnesium during long-distance running. Dr. Roy J. Shepard (University of Toronto) has discovered that distance runners lose significant amounts of magnesium in their sweat.

Potassium is essential for stimulating nerve impulses, maintaining the delicate acid–base balance in the body, and converting glucose to glycogen (stored carbohydrate). Potassium also helps to widen blood vessels, increasing blood flow to help carry heat away from exercising muscles.

Chromium, long overlooked as an essential element in activity drinks, has finally received recognition as an important mineral in regulating carbohydrate metabolism during physical activity. As a part of rehydration and energy drinks, chromium can aid in the utilization and storage of carbohydrate to boost endurance.

Recently sports scientists discovered that very small amounts of sodium (up to 100 milligrams per cup), when added to water, actually improved the absorption of water from the stomach. This was an important finding for all endurance athletes, who constantly face the threat of dehydration. By increasing the rate of water absorption, sodium-containing activity drinks can help regulate blood plasma acid–base balance and actually help improve athletic performance. Chloride, a salt associated with sodium (as in sodium chloride—common table salt), is also an important electrolyte that helps regulate the acid–base balance of the blood plasma.

Calcium, the main mineral of the skeleton, also is vital to determining the excitability of nerve and muscle tissue, including heart muscle. Physically active people who consume high-protein diets and alcohol, and whose intake of calcium falls below recommended levels, may run the risk of forcing calcium out of their skeletons to replace lost calcium in the urine and sweat.

Proper fluid management before, during, and after exercise is essential to optimal health and peak performance. Improper fluid replacement will most certainly adversely affect exercise performance and endurance. The new high-tech waters can help satisfy the energy and fluid demands of physical activity better than plain water.

While water will remain the primary and most effective ingredient in the new high-tech waters, current research suggests that newer water-based activity drinks can boost energy and endurance while helping to prevent dehydration and fatigue. Two companies, Twin Laboratories (product: Body Quench) and Ross Laboratories (product: Exceed), have already developed high-tech drinks that contain effective rehydrating and energy-giving substances. In our opinion these are two of the best fluid and energy replacement activity drinks on the market today.

We predict that soon all active people will pass up old-fashioned water in favor of these new souped-up drinks. In fact the day may not be too far off when restaurant waiters routinely inquire, "How would you like your water, regular or high-tech?"

THE CALCIUM QUESTION

You can feel it in your bones.

You may be confused about osteoporosis, the bone-loss disease that can weaken and destroy your skeleton if you don't do something about it today. You're not alone.

We know that you share the concerns of millions of health-conscious dieters who want to take charge of their health but aren't really sure how to beat the aging clock and prevent osteoporosis. That's why we're going to show you how we use Mother Nature to help slow down Father Time and beat aging at its own game.

We're going to give you the straight facts about calcium—how much you need and which commercial brands are best.

THE HARD TRUTH

Tums brand antacid tablets for osteoporosis? High-fat, cholesterol-rich dairy products to build strong bones? Oyster shells for everyone? Are these the quackish ravings of nutritionists-gone-nuts or the safe and sound dietary recommendations of highly trusted public health-care organizations?

Oddly enough, they're advice from both groups!

Everyone's attention, it seems, has been captured by the current craze for calcium, including, of course, those who stand to gain the most financially from our frantic quest for health and vitality. And, as you might expect, each group with a vested interest in convincing you, the consumer, to gulp more calcium each day employs its own special logic in justifying the calcium craze. Such recommendations, even those issued by some of our most trusted health-care organizations, may not always be in your best interest. We're going to show you why. And we're going to reveal why we believe the *Forever Fit* Plan is the safest and most effective approach to preventing osteoporosis.

SLUGGISH SUPPLEMENTS

All calcium supplements are not manufactured to the same specifications. That's the surprising conclusion of researchers who recently studied the *bioavailability* (the ability of the body to absorb a measured dose) of the most widely used forms of calcium, *including pure milk*. What did the research show?

ALL CALCIUM SUPPLEMENTS ARE NOT THE SAME

It showed two important facts. The first, that the six most common forms of calcium, including calcium ingested through milk, are all absorbed, give or take a few points, *equally well*. The second, that calcium carbonate, the most common form of supplemental calcium, was actually absorbed better, by nine points, than the calcium in milk (calcium carbonate is the most widely used calcium supplement, mainly because it contains more elemental calcium per gram and therefore requires relatively smaller tablets or capsules).

Commercial calcium supplements do not contain solely the pure calcium salts used in the study, but rather a mixture of fillers, binders, and other ingredients that facilitate forming calcium into tablet form. These additives may inhibit the disintegration and dissolution of the calcium tablet as it passes through the stomach and intestines.

The investigators of this study concluded that all common forms of calcium, including calcium from milk, are equally absorbed by the body. The determining factor for bioavailability of calcium, however, was *how much calcium in commercial supplements dissolved in the stomach and intestines*. If the calcium supplement you rely on dissolves only partially or perhaps *not at all*, then its form is of little consequence.

CALCIUM SUPPLEMENTS: LET THE BUYER BEWARE

A study in 1987 undertook to discover the rates of dissolution and disintegration of commonly used commercial calcium supplements, and the results were nothing less than shocking. Investigators at the University of Maryland School of Pharmacy discovered that almost *half of the most popular commercial calcium supplements they tested pass out of the intestines before they can be dissolved.*

That's right. Nearly 50 percent of the over-the-counter calcium carbonate supplements tested did not disintegrate within 30 minutes—the standard set for calcium supplements by the United States Pharmacopeia (USP). Some of the biggest offenders were the so-called private-label companies—those that formulate supplements for supermarkets, drugstores, and department stores.

When we investigated how this deplorable situation could exist, we discovered another shocking fact. Nutritional supplements are not required by law to meet USP standards. The Food and Drug Administration (FDA) currently requires only calcium-containing prescription *drugs,* not over-the-counter supplements, to meet USP guidelines. Thus consumers enjoy little protection under current FDA regulations and have no assurance that their money isn't wasted or their health isn't jeopardized.

A DO-IT-YOURSELF HOME TEST

If you're not sure about your favorite brand of calcium supplement, we offer a practical test that you can use to test *any* supplement for dissolution and disintegration. Place the nutritional supplement to be tested in regular-strength vinegar (the kind you use on salads and in cooking) for 30 minutes. Stir occasionally and observe the results. If the supplement is completely dissolved and dispersed in the vinegar after 12 minutes, it gets a high mark. Under 30 minutes places it in the acceptable category, roughly meeting the same USP guidelines that researchers use in laboratory tests. If the supplement hasn't dissolved after 30 minutes, you may want to switch to a brand that does.

CALCIUM DOS AND DON'TS

We've compiled a set of guidelines designed to help you avoid potential problems with calcium supplements. These recommendations, based on the latest pharmaceutical research data, can help you get the most out of your calcium supplement:

- Do not take calcium supplements on an empty stomach; taking tablets with meals will help maximize absorption.
- Avoid taking calcium supplements at night, because stomach acid secretion is at a low.
- Do not take supplements if they contain *tricalcium phosphate,* because this calcium salt is relatively insoluble in the stomach (600 milligrams of calcium in the form of tricalcium phosphate supplies only about six milligrams of calcium because of poor dissolution).
- If you are achlorhydric (cannot produce enough stomach acid), you should consider using calcium lactate or citrate because of better dissolution under achlorhydric (high pH) conditions (check with your physician first).
- Avoid dolomite and bonemeal because of potential contamination with radioactive waste and lead.
- Avoid very-high-protein diets low in calcium and other minerals because they promote the loss of these nutrients in the urine.
- Don't rely on dairy products as your source of calcium. Use vegetable sources rich in calcium such as beans, peas, and lentils.
- Avoid alcoholic beverages if you are a high-risk candidate for osteoporosis, because alcohol has been shown to accelerate calcium loss.

ORAL-CARE PRODUCTS

Your mouth is a jungle. It sounds pretty scary, but it's the simple truth. At the very moment you are reading this sentence more than 300 species of *billions* of plant life forms are thriving in your mouth. Even washing your mouth out with soap won't help for very long. Minutes later, back come the bacteria, by the millions—eventually causing bad breath, tooth decay, gum disease, and tooth loss if left unchecked.

During the research of this book we learned enough about the "invisible" jungle in our mouths and the damage it can do to literally scare us enough to search for a way to prevent the apparently inevitable tooth decay and gum disease that cause over *half the people in this country to lose ALL their teeth by the end of middle age.* Superb oral health is central to getting the greatest enjoyment out of food and drink. Heaven knows, we love to do both, but without healthy mouths, gums, and teeth, proper nutrition becomes difficult or even impossible. Healthy teeth and gums are something we would not want to live without, and we're certain you feel the same. That is why we developed our plan for oral health.

WHY DENTISTS HAVEN'T STOPPED THE TOOTH LOSS EPIDEMIC

Dentists and oral hygienists have recommended for years that people follow a regular program of oral hygiene and professional care. Nearly every health-care professional recommends the following:

- Brushing twice every 24 hours with a fluoride-containing dentifrice (toothpaste)
- Flossing at least once every 24 hours
- Using mechanical or irrigation devices to remove plaque
- Getting regular dental checkups and cleanings

Despite the fact that dentists, hygienists, and health-care organizations have promoted this plan for decades, surveys have revealed that an alarming number of people refuse to follow this sound advice. The primary problem is and always has been plaque.

WHAT IS PLAQUE?

Plaque is a soft, clinging substance found on teeth, and it is the main culprit in the majority of cases of gum, tooth, and bone disease. Plaque is not a food residue, as many people believe (this is quite obvious since it forms more rapidly during sleep than following meals), but rather is composed primarily of bacteria and metabolic by-products from bacteria and your own cells. Dentists generally classify plaque as that occurring *above* the gum line (supragingival) and that occurring *below* the gum line (subgingival).

Dentists have traditionally considered plaque a plague; however, recent research has shown that not all plaque is bad. While some elements of plaque are highly destructive, good elements within the plaque can outweigh the bad. The challenge in fighting plaque, therefore, is to control the elements that are harmful while at the same time enhancing those elements that promote good oral health.

Dentists know that plaque must routinely and frequently be removed to prevent tooth and gum disease. Effective plaque removal requires at least two things: regular professional care and personal home care. Obviously your dentist and oral hygienist can do an excellent job at removing plaque from your teeth, but it's up to you to *keep removing plaque daily*. And that's where most of the problem lies. People simply don't follow their dentist's advice. Many people, it seems, are looking for an easy way to achieve oral health, and of course the manufacturers of oral health-care products would like us to believe that their products offer the best protection against everything from cavities to gum disease. But do any of these products really work?

SANGUINARIA

Medical history teaches us that many folk remedies based on ordinary plant extracts have been used for centuries with apparent success, despite the fact that modern science officially or formally fails to recognize the efficacy of these substances.

Sanguinaria, an ordinary plant extract, formerly used in cough and cold medications, has recently been marketed as a plaque reducer and decay preventative that may retard or prevent the onset of gum disease that causes most tooth loss, even in people who have already suffered serious gum and tooth disease.

Actually sanguinaria (it derives its name from the bloodroot plant, from which it is extracted) and related naturally occurring substances have been used in the U.S. since the early 1800s in a variety of medications, including cough syrups and cold remedies as an expectorant. The chemical structure of sanguinaria extract is similar to the active ingredient found in African chew sticks, which have been reported to be beneficial to the oral hygiene of African native cultures. It differs *chemically* from all other substances that have been used for plaque control to date. Research is still inconclusive as to the actual effectiveness of sanguinaria, and the FDA has not permitted the manufacturer of sanguinaria-containing mouthwash to make any unsubstantiated health claims (only one mouthwash, Listerine, has been granted the right to claim that it is effective against plaque).

Research reports indicate that sanguinaria works by stopping bacteria from causing tooth decay and gum disease. Theoretically, if you can kill the harmful bacteria in your mouth, you can help prevent tooth decay and related gum disease.

Sanguinaria supposedly works not only by reducing the numbers of harmful bacteria in your mouth but also by preventing the bacteria from turning the sugars and starches in your diet into corrosive acid that eats away at tooth enamel, gum tissue, and underlying bone.

Some studies have shown that use of sanguinaria-containing toothpaste and oral rinse (trade name: Viadent) can significantly reduce and even eliminate bleeding gums (which can signal impending gum disease) because these products stop the cause—the harmful bacteria that can irritate gums. If you suffer from bleeding gums, we recommend that you see your dentist immediately for a thorough examination.

For many people, keeping one's teeth as long as possible is not sufficient enough reward because it does not offer immediate gratification. The use of sanguinaria-containing toothpaste and oral rinse or the use of an over-the-counter product like Listerine or a prescription plaque fighter you can get from your dentist (note that some dentists and hygienists report that some prescription antiplaque agents such as Peridex can cause significant tooth staining that must be removed professionally) may help you achieve greater oral protection against harmful plaque even if you follow your dentist's advice less than perfectly. *We urge you to consult with your dentist before using these or any oral hygiene products.*

Everyone can benefit from using ancillary products such as a good-quality toothbrush (we especially like the Interplak brand electric toothbrush), mouthwash, and oral irrigation devices (such as the Water-Pik brand device). But the primary method of keeping teeth and gums healthy is still the daily *mechanical* removal (brushing and flossing) of plaque.

People who are accustomed to using an oral irrigation device will be happy to learn that they can use Listerine or other plaque fighters in their irrigation device. Many dentists now recommend that their patients use this type of system as part of their daily oral hygiene regimen. We recommend that you consult your dentist about the advisability of using an oral irrigation system for additional plaque protection.

We want to stress here that the easiest and most cost-effective way for anyone to prevent periodontal disease is the *daily* habit of removing plaque from the teeth. We believe that the use of Listerine mouthwash or dentist-prescribed plaque fighters can be a part of a total oral health-care program. We urge you to visit your dentist and oral hygienist for routine checkups and regular oral health care. *Always check with your dentist and oral hygienist before using any new products, including those mentioned in this chapter.*

THE VITAMINS WE TAKE

The question most people ask us most frequently is what vitamins we take. Well, our answer usually disappoints them because it is actually a very simple formula. We suspect that people generally believe we've concocted some secret and exotic blend of miracle nutrients that keeps us youthful and energetic.

The truth is, it is the ordinary foods we eat that form the foundation for our health and vitality, but we choose to supplement our healthy diet for the following reasons:

1. We don't always eat perfectly.
2. Exercise can boost the need for certain nutrients.
3. When we follow a reduced-calorie diet, it's difficult to obtain optimal amounts of all the nutrients we need.
4. We come in contact with environmental contaminants, such as air pollution, X rays, carcinogens in food and air, cigarette smoke, and radiation exposure from airline flights. All of these substances may increase our need for protective nutrients, such as beta-carotene, vitamin C, and vitamin E.
5. We know that daily stress may increase the need for extra nutrition.
6. Aging can reduce the absorption and assimilation of nutrients.

We take a multivitamin supplement called the Aerobic Pak (Twin Laboratories) as our basic vitamin "insurance" supplement. That's about as exotic as we get. With all of the nutritious foods we generally eat and our vitamin-fortified liquid meal replacer, we enjoy a nutrient-rich diet that we believe helps keep us youthful and energetic. Some health-care professionals frown at the suggestion of supplementing one's diet with vitamins or vitamin-fortified foods. While all the evidence is not yet in, we believe enough research has been published about the protective effect of certain nutrients against environmentally related cancer and other degen-

A NUTRIENT-RICH DIET KEEPS US YOUTHFUL AND ENERGETIC

erative diseases to suggest that it is prudent for us to take out some "vitamin/mineral insurance." We feel that the decision to supplement your diet with a multivitamin/mineral formula is a personal one. We've told you our personal decision, but we are not going to insist that you supplement your diet with additional nutrients beyond those you can obtain in ordinary foods. We strongly suggest that you consult with a physician trained in nutrition or a nutritionist or dietitian about the advisability of taking any type of nutritional supplements.

WHAT ABOUT FIBER?

Fiber is a hot nutritional topic these days because food manufacturers have made a variety of health claims that have stimulated a lot of controversy. We believe that the health benefits of fiber need to be brought into proper perspective.

Studies have shown that fiber does improve regularity, it does help reduce the risk of colon and bowel cancer, and it can be useful in the management of lower-gastrointestinal-tract diseases such as Crohn's disease and diverticulosis. It may help reduce blood cholesterol levels, and it may aid in imparting a sense of satiety and fullness after a meal. We believe that it is definitely essential for optimal health.

You can negate the healthful benefits of fiber by eating the ordinary high-fat/high-cholesterol American diet. People who enjoy two eggs fried in butter or margarine, bacon or sausage, and hash brown potatoes for breakfast will accomplish little by throwing wheat bran on their cereal. And people who wolf down most commercial brands of oat bran muffins and other fiber-containing baked goods may gain little in the way of intestinal health from these ordinarily high-fat/cholesterol-laden goodies.

Fiber is effective most when you observe two rules of healthful eating: you must eat a low-fat/low-cholesterol diet that contains a variety of high-fiber foods (such as whole grains, cereals, fruits, and vegetables), and you must eat a variety of fiber (soluble, such as wheat bran, which aids in intestinal regularity, and insoluble, such as fiber from fruit—apples, oranges, grapefruit, bananas—which helps control blood lipids).

During periods of reduced calorie intake, we rely on high-fiber foods and a product called Fiber Booster (Twin Laboratories) to ensure that we eat about 30 to 40 grams of total fiber (soluble and insoluble) each day. Fiber Booster contains both types from a variety of fiber-rich sources, including psyllium, oat bran, rice bran, and barley. Our demanding travel schedule used to play havoc with our regularity until we started using it. Now even the most rigorous schedule or dietary indiscretions no longer disrupt our regularity.

A number of popular fiber supplements are available in most health-food stores and supermarkets today, such as Metamucil and Senokot. And one product, a high-fiber candy bar we like—the Slim•Fast Dutch Chocolate Flavor Bar (Thompson Medical Company)—supplies six grams of fiber. However, since it contains four grams of fat, we use it in those rare moments when we crave a chocolate-flavored candy bar.

While we think most products that provide soluble and insoluble fiber from natural food sources are fine when used to supplement the diet while we are on a reduced-calorie weight-loss plan, *we strongly urge you to check with your physician if you have a chronic problem with regularity, and we urge you to check with your physician before taking any supplementary fiber product, including the ones mentioned in this book.*

8

KEEP YOUR SKIN
AND HAIR FOREVER FIT

B eauty will be ravaged by age, and the face that charmed will be ploughed by wrinkles. The time will come when it will vex you to look at a mirror, and grief will prove a second cause of wrinkles.

—Ovid

By the time you are 50, you have the face you deserve.

—George Orwell

ROBERT

We couldn't agree more. The scientific evidence to date confirms that many people, unfortunately, abuse their skin. And the results couldn't be any plainer than the nose (and skin) on your face!

Your skin is a mirror of your age. People will often judge your age and even sex appeal *solely* by its appearance. And judging by sales of skin-care products, many people are willing to spend a lot of money in their quest for younger-looking and beautiful skin.

We think that your first and foremost consideration should be to achieve *healthy* skin, because we've discovered a simple fact: *healthy skin leads to beautiful skin.* We're going to tell you how we keep our skin healthy, based on our own experiences with skin-care products and the latest research and information we've gathered from some of this country's leading dermatologists.

YOUR AMAZING SKIN

Since your skin is the largest organ of your body and covers 10 square feet in the average person, we thought you might be interested in some skin facts you may not know. For example:

1. *The skin is always filthy.* That's right. Try as you will to cleanse it, you can't. Every nook and cranny of your skin is literally teeming with bacteria. Within minutes of bathing and scrubbing, back come the bacteria to cover it again. But that's good, because these are good germs that help create an antiseptic mantle over the body, keeping out harmful germs.

2. *The skin excretes waste products.* Again, this is good. The skin can help overworked or diseased organs like the kidneys and the liver to do their job by helping rid the body of toxic waste products like urea, a by-product of protein metabolism.

3. *The skin breathes.* Remember what happened to the girl who was covered entirely in gold paint in the famous James Bond movie *Goldfinger*? She died (just in the movie) of suffocation because one of the most important ways her body breathed was through her skin. Just as our lungs exchange oxygen for carbon dioxide, our skin does the same.

4. *In just one square inch, the skin contains about 20,000 sensory cells to keep our brain and other organs "aware" of external changes in the environment, 1,300 nerve endings that register pain and pleasure, 650 sweat glands, 165 pressure complexes that sense a variety of types of touch, 100 sebaceous glands, 78 sensory systems for sensing cold temperatures, and 65 hairs!*

THE FOREVER FIT SKIN-CARE TIPS

The only scientifically sound approach to nourishing your skin is faithfully following a *total* diet, exercise, and skin-care plan. Eating the proper diet—we believe the *Forever Fit* Plan is the best—will lay the foundation for a healthy skin plan that can help you look your best.

Remember, though, that your skin will change throughout life much like an outdoor landscape, and many of the changes are similarly caused by environmental elements such as sun, wind, water, and air pollution. But with a little protective maintenance and care you can enjoy healthy skin your whole life.

One of the first things people notice about us is our healthy, smooth skin. And for good reason. We follow our own advice. We've learned, through trial, error, and research, the necessary steps to achieve beautiful skin. And now we want to share that information with you.

STEP ONE: HEALTHY SKIN STARTS FROM WITHIN

The first step in achieving healthy skin is to follow the *Forever Fit* dietary principles. We have designed our plan to provide ample quantities of the vital nutrition your skin needs to be its very best. Healthy and beautiful skin starts with a proper diet. Deficiencies of all kinds show up on the skin. For example, a protein deficiency, such as experienced by many people in third-world countries, cause skin lesions. Pellagra, dietary deficiency disease caused by lack of vitamin B_3 (niacin), also causes disfiguring skin lesions.

Some of the common nutritional factors for healthy skin include:

- The B vitamins in general are essential to promoting and maintaining healthy skin. Inadequate intakes of the B complex group of vitamins will result in rough, dry, cracked, and scaly skin.
- Vitamin C is essential for collagen formation (fibers that give skin its support), especially during wound healing.
- Vitamin A and beta-carotene (the plant form of vitamin A) are essential ingredients for skin growth and maintenance and help protect skin from environmental toxins such as pollution and cigarette smoke.
- Vitamin E seems to enhance the effectiveness of vitamin A and also offers protection from the same environmentally harmful substances.

- Of all the common skin-nourishing nutrients in our foods, however, there are two that we believe are often overlooked as being vital to achieving healthy, beautiful skin: *fiber* and *water*. These two quite ordinary and inexpensive substances work together in your digestive tract to help excrete waste products without placing a burden on already overworked skin. That's one important reason why the *Forever Fit* Plan includes plenty of water (four to eight glasses each day) and fiber.

STEP TWO: PROTECTING YOUR SKIN FROM THE ENVIRONMENT

The most important word in skin protection is *sunscreen*. Nothing helps keep your skin from premature aging better than a sunscreen.

Natural skin pigment, or melanin, which all of us possess in varying degrees, is nature's sunscreen. Blacks, who have the most melanin, show relatively fewer signs of skin aging and lower skin cancer rates than whites. Compared to white skin, black skin, on the average, permits only one fourth to one fifth of the ultraviolet (UV) radiation from the sun to penetrate the skin. "But even black people can damage their skin if they stay in the sun too long," says Dr. Madhu Pathak, pigment researcher for Harvard Medical School's dermatology department.

About 500,000 Americans develop skin cancer each year, and 90 percent of these cancers are on parts of the body most exposed to sunlight—the face, neck, shoulders, and arms. And skin cancer rates are much higher in the Sunbelt than in northern latitudes.

TYPES OF SUNSCREENS

Other than natural skin pigment, there are two basic types of sunscreens you can find in today's sun-blockers: physical reflectors and chemical absorbers.

Reflector-type sunscreens—the kind you often see on the skiers' and lifeguards' noses—usually contain zinc or iron oxides or titanium dioxide. Skin experts warn that if these sunscreens are not applied evenly and replaced as they wear off, UV rays can get through to skin.

Chemical absorber–type sunscreens can be found in a variety of suntan lotions, creams, and oils. The most common absorber-type sunscreens are derived from PABA (para-aminobenzoic acid) or benzophenone. Some sunscreens contain both. Both UV-A and UV-B are harmful. The sun showers us with both types, and tanning salons use UV-A almost exclusively. Most experts say both types can cause skin damage. A more complete formulation may also include other UV absorbers, such as salicylate or cinnamate, that offer broader wavelength absorption.

Two sunscreen cautions: PABA and its derivatives can stain fabrics and may cause skin irritation in susceptible people. If you decide to go for a tan in the south of France, beware of a European sunscreen called *5-methoxy-psoralen (5-MOP)*. According to U.S. researchers this compound has been linked to promoting skin cancer, and accordingly it has not received the approval of the FDA for use in American sun-blocking products.

HOW DOES YOUR SUNSCREEN RATE?

In 1978 the FDA recommended that companies that make sun-blocking products rate the efficacy of such products to provide protection against sunburn by listing a sun protection factor (abbreviated SPF) on the packaging of these products. Most firms now label their products with an SPF number starting at 1—providing the least protection—and up. Most skin experts now advise that you select a product with an SPF of 15. This, they say, affords adequate UV protection. We also learned that products that offer higher SPFs offer no more real protection than do products with an SPF rating of 15. The only real difference, the experts claim, is that the higher-SPF-rated products cost more. The professionals cautioned us against using sunscreens rated at less than SPF 15, especially since the rating system does not account for varying degrees of UV intensity in different parts of the world or for differences in humidity, heat, sweat rate, wind, and other factors, all of which tend to reduce the effectiveness of sunscreens. Some sunscreens such as Aloe-Gator, contain ingredients to help keep the product from washing off with sweat or in water.

A number of companies currently make products with ratings up to SPF 20, including Clinique, Sea and Ski, Coppertone, Bain de Soleil, and Aramis. Undoubtedly new ones will become available each year, as more people decide that a suntan is no longer the mark of a healthy, glowing complexion. Look at directions carefully; some products need to be reapplied frequently.

Here are a few more facts that may help shed some light on protecting your skin from premature aging due to overexposure to UV radiation:

1. Apply a sunscreen product. You'll need about four to five teaspoons when you're wearing only a swimsuit. Cover all exposed area—even the top of your head if bald (those with hair should wear a hat).
2. Skin that turns red on the Jersey shore in 20 minutes will take only 10 minutes to do so on Miami Beach. Skiers at high altitudes receive less protection than people who live at sea level, because the atmosphere thins out at higher altitudes and because snow and ice can reflect 90 percent of the sun's rays.
3. You may actually enjoy more UV protection from smog and air pollution in Los Angeles than you can on a cloudy day in Seattle. Smog and air pollution tend to block and absorb harmful UV radiation, while clouds tend to transmit UV radiation (of course it still may be healthier to breathe the air in Seattle).

THE PROTECTIVE ROLE OF ANTIOXIDANTS

Skin researchers have long contended that aging of the skin is due, in part, to harmful environmental products called *free radicals*. A free radical is an electrically charged atom or molecule that can damage cell membranes and genetic material, leading to premature aging, cancer, and/or cell death.

There is a class of compounds known as *antioxidants* that clearly prevent and minimize the damage that free radicals can cause. Ordinary antioxidants are produced by the body or taken in with the foods we normally eat. Vitamins A, C, and E; some B vitamins; enzymes that contain common minerals such as zinc, copper, iron, and manganese; bioflavonoids (commonly found in foods that contain vitamin C); and ordinary amino acids can and do serve the body as antiaging antioxidants.

In the middle of the 1980s, the cosmetic industry introduced a number of antioxidant-containing products that embrace the concept of using antioxidants to prevent skin aging. Leading companies such as Shiseido (Facial Concentrates, introduced in 1984), Estee Lauder (Line Preventor, introduced in 1985), Avon (Momentum with Daytime Defense Complex, introduced in 1985), and Guerlain (Evolution, introduced in 1986) contain conventional antioxidants. Since that time almost every major cosmetic company has jumped on the antioxidant bandwagon.

Skin experts seemed divided on the efficacy of topically applied antioxidants such as vitamin A and vitamin E in protecting the skin from the environment. We believe real evidence for their role will be a product of the 21st century, but the prevention of aging via sunscreens and antioxidants is nevertheless accessible *now*.

MOISTURIZERS

The ostensible purpose of all cosmetic moisturizer products is to penetrate the top layers of the skin to effect a smooth, soft feel. Regardless of various antiaging claims made by manufacturers of these products, such as "cell renewal," "improves microcirculation," "prevents wrinkles," etc., the one unifying concept is to keep the skin *hydrated*. Why? Because research conducted by the cosmetics industry has revealed that the number-one consumer skin problem is *dry skin*. Normally, dry skin occurs because some skin does not slough off (desquamate) at a rate to prevent cells from sticking for weeks at a time. This disrupts normal skin metabolism and interferes with the skin cells' ability to bind water.

Cosmetic chemists rely on a number of ingredients to give their products the ability to pull moisture from the air and/or to prevent moisture from escaping from the skin. Here are some of the most common substances to look for in a moisturizer that may help dry skin:

Na-PCA (Sodium-pyrollidone carboxylate): Na-PCA has been shown to draw water out of the air to the skin. It has also been shown to aid in restoring flexibility to skin. We believe that it is an important ingredient to look for in a moisturizer. Products such as Moistique (Twin Laboratories), available at health-food stores, and Skin Principle (Max Factor) have contained Na-PCA for years, even though most consumers were unaware of the importance of this ingredient.

Urea: This is a by-product of normal protein metabolism. Urea can partially diffuse into the top layer of the skin and may help "ease" the path of water into the skin's rough layer.

Hydroxy acids: These may aid in imparting elasticity to the skin to promote a soft, smooth feel. This class of compounds includes lactic, citric, malic, and pyruvic acids—all of which are commonly found in the cells.

Soluble collagen protein: This naturally occurring substance provides a foundation of support for the skin and contains moisturizing properties as well; with age (due mainly to exposure to UV radiation), soluble collagen protein becomes damaged, causing wrinkles.

Regardless of how or why they work, the main problem with all of these compounds is their transitory action. One newer approach, recently introduced by several companies, is to encapsulate one or more of these ingredients into microcapsules called *liposomes*. These entrap water-soluble moisturizers such as hydroxy acids in a sphere of fat-soluble substance such as lecithin. The overall result of using liposomes is to allow for the slow release of water and moisturizers out of the liposome and onto the skin. Niosomes (L'Oréal) and Capture (Christian Dior) are among the products that use this type of liposome technology.

WHICH MOISTURIZER IS BEST?

We've talked to a number of leading dermatologists to identify the ingredients they believe would be most effective in a skin moisturizer product.

One important thing we learned from the dermatologists with whom we spoke: moisturizers that use fancy names like *revitanol, liposomes, plastoderm, elasten, elasyn,* and *placental extracts* are probably no more age-retardant than a jar of old-fashioned petroleum jelly (which makes an excellent, though greasy, moisturizer). Some use ingredients familiar to you—such as eggs, milk, and honey, implying that they are "natural" or "organic" qualities but they may frequently cause allergic reactions.

Albert Kligman, M.D., noted dermatologist at the University of Pennsylvania, says all those expensive products are worthless for rejuvenating your skin. He is highly critical of advertising that claims scientific but unpublished breakthroughs. He says, "They are hiding under the 'capitalist doctrine that we don't tell our secrets to anyone.'"

Joel Kassimir, M.D., a New York dermatologist, explains why so many people like these products. "Many of these moisturizers are elegant to use and feel wonderful on the skin. The moisturizers don't penetrate any further than the upper layers of the dermis, so they can't enhance cell renewal. And certainly none of these ingredients can be absorbed and incorporated into the genetic material. The collagen molecule is too thick to be absorbed into the skin, but *collagen is a good ingredient in a moisturizer, because it holds in the natural dampness.*" "But," he emphasizes, "it won't replace the collagen that has been worn away from age and sun."

OUR MOISTURIZER RECOMMENDATION

Which moisturizer do we think is best?

Based on our research, the one moisturizer that contains most of the ingredients the experts agree *really* work is Moistique (Twin Laboratories). It contains Na-PCA (draws water from the air and holds it in the skin), lanolin (an emollient that helps the skin retain water), soluble collagen (holds in natural dampness), vitamins A and E (antioxidants), and octyl dimethyl PABA (sunscreen).

Currently Moistique is available only through health-food stores, but in our opinion it's worth the trouble to track it down.

Regardless of which moisturizer you decide to use, use it faithfully. It will not spray you with the fountain of youth—advertising promises notwithstanding—but it will hold your skin's moisture where it belongs. And that makes moisturizers the greatest ally your skin can have.

CHER

My skin was never horrendous as a teenager. I did, however, have the usual flare-ups. But I never had any *serious* skin problems until I was doing *The Sonny & Cher Show* and my face was in makeup for 18 hours at a time. I just about lived in makeup under hot lights and I developed a horrible allergy to the kind of makeup they were using. Basically what I got was makeup poisoning. My skin just went into complete insanity. It looked like a pizza—it was beyond comprehension. I looked like Freddie from *A Nightmare on Elm Street*. Talk about bringing down your confidence level. This was hard to take.

USE MOISTURIZER FAITHFULLY

I saw a few specialists. One of them put me under radiation and basically tried to nuke the problem away. This treatment was popular sometime around World War II and in the fifties. My face turned brown all over, like a hand-tooled Mexican wallet. It was so frightening I was hysterical. So now I have to have my thyroid checked periodically because people exposed to those levels of radiation have a much higher rate of thyroid cancer than anyone else.

Then I found Dr. Norman Orentreich in New York and he did a series of chemical peels on my face, not as some beauty treatment but to strip away the discolored skin until it got somewhere near real-looking. For a couple of years my skin was really a mess.

In the early seventies I developed what is called adult acne, which is very common in women nowadays. This was made worse by being in makeup constantly. I could barely shoot the show and stay under the lights for all those hours. The acne also came on due to bad food, stress, smog, and pollution, because your skin catches and shows everything. Adult acne is very tough to treat because you can have really dry skin and break out with oily cysts at the same time.

Then I met Dr. Arnold Klein in Beverly Hills. With Dr. Klein I began using Retin-A to treat chronic cystic acne, and I've been on a prescription for Retin-A for 10 years now. I'm like one of the world's experts on this drug, which was prescribed back then only for the treatment of serious acne problems. Back then, a popular acne treatment was Accutane. No more pimples. Both Retin-A and Accutane are in the family of drugs known as retinoids. But Accutane, which is taken internally, was recently linked to severe birth defects when used by pregnant women. Fortunately Retin-A has never been associated with birth defects, because as a topical treatment very little gets absorbed into the blood.

I know Retin-A works. It's unbelievable. I have used it to control my acne. But what I learned about Retin-A under the care of both Dr. Klein and Dr. Orentreich is what everyone else has discovered over the past couple years: Retin-A also acts as a deaging agent on your skin and has this incredible way of reversing the damage done by too much sun. I'm in my forties, and I have no wrinkles. Actually, I'm starting to see a couple under my eyes, but they're kind of minimal for my age. I know of girls much younger than I am who have crow's-feet. It didn't occur to me until I was in my early forties that it had to do with Retin-A. It makes your skin more resilient, stronger.

But you have to be careful and know exactly what you're doing to your face with it. I know a lot of women are going to get messed up because Retin-A has to be applied in a very careful way. It can really be harsh. For me, Dr. Klein mixes it with a mild moisturizing cream called hydrocortisone. What comes straight from the laboratory in the tube is pretty potent.

I do stop using it now and then, and when I get back on it, we go real gradually. He starts with an amount the size of a green pea, and I use it every third night for the first week. Then the second week I use it every other night, and the third week it's every night before sleep. As a result my skin looks smoother, younger, stronger than it ever has, and I can stay in makeup and under lights all I need to and not worry about my skin.

But, we'll warn you once again: Retin-A thins the outer layer of skin and makes you extremely photosensitive so you can't go in the sun. (Stage lights don't give off the kind of rays that make photosensitivity a problem.) If you absolutely have to spend time in the sun—and I'm too old to be spending time in the sun anyway—you should stop using it four days ahead of time.

You need to begin using a Retin-A cream in a certain way to get used to it. Another warning: I hate to say this, but most skin doctors don't know as much as we think they do. They worry a lot about cancers and skin diseases, but they're not too concerned with breaking out and how it can be treated. So if you just get a prescription for Retin-A full-strength (it comes in two strengths) and start on it without being on a doctor's program, you're going to be the unhappiest person in town because of the side effects. The side effects will be as bad as the problem you're trying to cure.

Here's the way Dr. Klein explained it to me: Retin-A's real name is *retinoic acid*. It was developed in the early seventies by Dr. Albert Kligman at the University of Pennsylvania and was shown to be effective against cystic acne by causing the skin's oil-producing glands to unclog and empty. Then, in 1987, a test was conducted to study the drug's usefulness for wrinkles and antiaging—since people like me were also discovering the drug's effectiveness with wrinkles. All the study subjects had Retin-A applied to their forearms; half had it used on their faces as well. Ninety-three percent of the "face" group showed improvement with wrinkles, and 100 percent showed improvement in forearm wrinkles.

But it's still the face that concerns most of us. Retin-A makes the facial skin dry and scaly, with a reddish glow. It makes your skin peel. That's why Dr. Klein starts me off with the weaker mixture that first week—and every time I start applying it again. Otherwise my skin would be red and irritated and peely and horrible. I really hate to start using it each time because you have to go through that stage where your skin is too dry. But this is good because that dryness sloughs and regenerates the skin all the time. And keeps it smooth. I mean, I'm making new skin constantly—that's why my skin looks so young. When you're younger, you slough your skin much faster and your skin stays smoother and healthier by itself.

This is no miracle drug and it won't work overnight. And it must be used under a dermatologist's care. Deep "smile" creases and "frown lines" will never totally disappear. Crow's-feet will soften but won't vanish. Dr. Klein usually recommends that treatments continue for six to 12 months before dropping to a maintenance program of two treatments a week. It does not lead to permanent improvement; it only works as long as you use it. But it definitely does improve your skin tone and is without question the most effective drug known to reverse sun damage.

One thing is for sure: it beats all the expensive creams and lotions at the cosmetic counters in department stores and boutiques. I can name very few products that did what they claimed to do. One I like is Lancôme's eye cream called Progrès. Mario Badescu and Kiehl's, both in New York City, put out a line of terrific skin-care products. In New York I go to Alla at Mario Badescu's for facials and in Los Angeles I go to The Face Place for facials from Scott Donnelly. But keep in mind that while most of the best skin creams will make your skin feel soft and smooth and less dry, they won't affect wrinkling and sun damage because they don't penetrate.

For the most part, women are willing to go out and buy just about anything. I once saw an ad on TV for a face-cleaning system and went right out and bought it and felt like the world's biggest sucker. But it is a reputable product called the Metrin System, and I do like it. And there is this great cream on the market called Buf Cream for women who have dry skin but break out. It's noncomedogenic, which means it won't give you blackheads or pimples but it will moisturize your skin. It's more of a humectant. Still, most beauty products offer empty promises. You could group them on your cosmetic counter and all of them together won't do anything for you, ever.

The cosmetics firms are trying to sell something, so they're going to tell you things that might stretch the truth. There are very few things that can really penetrate the skin. Retin-A is one of them. It's one of the few major breakthroughs in years and it was basically an accident. I happen to be one of the lucky women using it for one reason but who found it was really terrific for another. Now, of course, there are other products trying to get on the bandwagon. But Retin-A's the real thing and it makes a real difference.

Another radical skin treatment is collagen injections. The two most common uses these days are to smooth wrinkles or give you fuller lips. I found out I am among the less than 3 percent of the population who are allergic to collagen.

I went to Dr. Klein to get the standard test for allergies before my collagen shots. My arm blew up so huge he took pictures of it to demonstrate what a major allergic reaction looks like. There may soon be a version of nonallergenic collagen that I would use. But I don't think most doctors are smart enough to use it, so I can't recommend it.

Another method of getting rid of wrinkles is implanting tissue from another part of the body—but it's a hit-or-miss procedure that my skin doctor would not do. So if he won't do it, I don't believe it's a good method.

Another system of skin care he recommends against is washing your face. That's right. Washing your face—no matter what kind of skin you have—just doesn't make sense, especially if your skin is dry. I stopped washing my face a long time ago. I don't use soap or water on my face. I use a lotion called Stearyl, a lipid-free cleanser, which is made by Syosset Laboratories. I put it on a cotton pad, apply it all over my face, and then wipe it off. That's it.

Dr. Klein finally convinced me to stop washing with soap. He said, "I know you think you won't be clean but trust me." Not washing, not scrubbing my face with soap and water just didn't seem right to me. The problem is soap and water destroy your skin—they take all the moisture out of it.

I have really dry body skin and I use a product called Aqua Care that helps trap water inside the skin. It's not a very fancy product. It comes in a tube, and I put it on when I'm in the shower. I mix it with a product from JAFRA Cosmetics, Inc., called Jafra Royal Almond Body Oil. I always mix products. Jafra Royal is a clear pink oil and I make my own half-and-half mixture and rub it on when I'm in the shower.

When it comes to hair care I can only share my experiences as the ultimate consumer, because I am always looking to look better. When I do a photo session my hair has got to look not just okay but appealing and inviting because the product I'm selling is me. I think women should go to a beauty supply place and just experiment with products until they find something that feels good for their hair. You can tell what works by how your hair reacts.

I've done just about everything you can do to hair. When I was little my mother gave me my first permanent—one of those electric ones that burned my hair to a frizzle. I had this little Afro. I've bleached my hair, it's broken off, I've dyed it. And the funny part is I have pretty healthy hair. Usually you are blessed with good hair or you aren't. But I do know there are better, healthier things you can put on your hair than some of the stuff we buy at the cosmetic counter.

I once had a problem with chemical damage because of what this one hairdresser did to my hair. The effects were so awful I thought I was going to have to cut my hair off. I was really freaked. But my friend Michelle Pfeiffer told me not to cut it. She said that when she did *Scarface* her hair was bleached white every week and turned to straw. She mentioned a place, Jheri Redding, where you can cut off a piece of hair and take it to them and they'll give you treatments to fix your hair. "Just try this," she said, "because it really helps." I tried it and she was right. There was a significant difference.

My hair is naturally dark and straight. After my teenage years I didn't do anything to it for a really long time—till my mid-thirties. Then in the year I did *Mask* I had red hair, white hair, black and white hair; it fell out and broke off. I bleached it, permed it—did everything you can to it.

I always wore wigs for work through most of the seventies. The woman who did my wigs for *The Sonny & Cher Show*, Renate Leuschner, was unbelievable. I had a dozen or more wigs going at any one time. And I had my own waist-length hair tucked underneath. It was in great condition then, long and straight, because I wasn't doing anything to it. I have lots of volume but I have fine hair. That is, the strands themselves are fine but I have lots and lots of them.

Ever since *Mask* I don't like ruining my hair for work. I wore a wig in *Mask* but only after my hair was ruined. They didn't want me to wear a wig; they wanted me to make my own hair red. I thought this was really

I'VE DONE EVERYTHING YOU CAN DO TO HAIR

stupid. They took the color out of my dark hair and made it red and ruined it. Then I wore a wig. For *Come Back to the Five and Dime, Jimmy Dean, Jimmy Dean* that was my own hair but I teased it. Teasing's bad—it breaks your hair right off. On a set all day long they mess around with your hair. If I'm in a wig it doesn't bother me if they tease it or spray it or put hot rollers in it. But I don't want to kill my own hair with colors, perms, blow-drying, and hot rollers. For *Silkwood* I didn't wear a wig. But for *The Witches of Eastwick, Suspect, Moonstruck*, and *Mermaids* I did wear wigs.

I use one particular shampoo and conditioner a lot—both by Philip Kingsley. I like Kingsley products because when my hair was permed and totally abused those products were very gentle and I noticed it looked nicer after I used his shampoo. So I just continued using it. The line of natural products from Aveda is pretty good too, as are hair care products from Nexxus, Jheri Redding, Lori Davis, and a line call Sea Plasma. They make a difference, because most of the over-the-counter products can be too abrasive and too drying. You could wash your pots and pans with them. We put too much heat on our hair and we put too many chemicals in it. We're all guilty of that, especially now that we use so many mousses, shaping and styling gels, hair sprays, hot curlers, and blow dryers.

One exception is a mousse from José Eber, because it's designed for dry or damaged hair. It's not heavy, it's not alcohol-based, and it gives your hair body and volume without making it feel like cardboard is coming out of your head.

I do put a nonperoxide rinse on my hair because it has a natural reddish cast that I don't like. So I put a drabber in it that keeps the red from coming through.

Climate can really affect your hair and skin and there's not much you can do about that. My hair feels a lot better in summer. In New York through the winter you've got radiators on constantly and no moisture inside your apartment. But if you go to Aspen for skiing, that's maybe the worst place in the world for hair and skin—it's just horrible. I mean, you turn into a mummy up there in the mountains it's so dry and bright.

The truth is, if you want you hair to be and feel its very best you should probably go to Tahiti or the south of France. There's a lot of humidity and the water is soft. Unfortunately, most of us don't want to travel *that* far for soft water.

SOURCES OF SKIN INFORMATION

If you want more information about skin care, here are three sources of information:

American Academy of Dermatology
P.O.B. 3116
Evanston, IL 60204–3116
(708) 869-3954

American Society of Dermatologic Surgery
Toll-free hot line: (800) 441-ASDS

Skin Cancer Foundation
245 Fifth Avenue, Suite 2402
New York, NY 10016
(212) 725-5176

9

STAYING FOREVER FIT

ROBERT

The user-friendly walking plan and exercise suggestions that we make in this chapter is designed to work wonders in conjunction with the *Forever Fit* Permanent Weight-Loss Plan. Perhaps for the first time in your life, you'll see why and how it's the easy-to-do exercises that pay off in the long run—or, rather, the long walk. Indeed, if anyone tells you our program doesn't work—well, tell that person to take a hike. Or more specifically, gradually work up to a 60-minute, three mile-an-hour hike.

By following the Permanent Weight-Loss Plan you'll be able to exercise *longer* without fatigue. This is essential to our program, which combines aerobic walking and muscle-toning exercises.

The reason: the experts now agree that it's *how long* you exercise that determines how much fat you'll burn—*not* how strenuous the exercises are to perform. We see no point in devising a workout that quickly becomes so painful and intimidating that you are doomed to throwing in the towel. We've focused on an exercise strategy you can live with and maintain permanently.

We also realize many people have a problem even *starting* an exercise routine. That's nothing to be ashamed of. But if you let us help you, we will show you how to rev up your metabolism to burn 250 to 500-plus extra calories a day, so you can enjoy life at your ideal weight and boast a healthy cardiovascular system.

AEROBIC WALKING FOR PERMANENT WEIGHT LOSS

EASY-TO-DO EXERCISE WORKS BEST

The latest research studies have established that people who embrace a moderate and easy-to-follow exercise program—starting with a daily walk at about three miles per hour for about 30 minutes—*lose more weight, keep more weight off, and stay with their exercise routine longer* than people who engage in more vigorous, vein-popping routines. This means beginners should aim to complete about 1½ miles in the 30 minutes, working up to cover four miles in one hour.

There is simply no doubt about it: daily brisk walking is one of the best exercises you can do to burn off excess calories. Compared to more strenuous jogging, walking is orthopedically better and can burn about two-thirds as many fat calories. A 140-pound woman, for example, can burn about 600 calories during one hour of jogging at an 11-minute-per-mile pace and about 300 calories on a one-hour brisk walk at a four-mile-per-hour pace. This may appear to be a big difference until you realize that a jogger who burns 600 calories in an hour will have actually burned about 250 calories from fat, plus 350 calories from carbohydrate (glycogen). A walker may burn only 300 total calories an hour—but about 150 of those calories come from fat plus 150 more from glycogen.

And, as you learned in Chapter 4, the level of glycogen reserves in the body acts as a keen sensor for appetite stimulation: the more you burn, the hungrier you get. Thus an *easy-to-do exercise such as walking burns about two-thirds as much fat as more strenuous jogging but stimulates your appetite less.*

EAT THE RIGHT FOODS AFTER EXERCISE TO BURN FAT

If, after exercise, you enjoy a *Forever Fit* meal, low in fat and high in complex carbohydrates, you can easily replace all 200 calories of glycogen you burned during a one-hour walk and still remain in "negative

DAILY BRISK WALKING IS ONE OF THE BEST EXERCISES

fat balance." This means that the fat you lost during exercise will not be regained by eating. But you will replenish all of the glycogen you burned from the carbohydrate in your *Forever Fit* meal, which is what you want to take place. (Remember, if you deplete your glycogen stores, your appetite will increase.)

And if you happen to overeat on carbohydrate-rich foods such as breakfast cereal, bread, or fresh fruit (up to about 500 calories), you still won't gain much fat because the body will respond by storing most of the extra calories as additional glycogen and by cranking up the metabolic rate to burn the excess carbohydrate. That's why the *Forever Fit* Diet and a moderate workout, structured around walking, work so well together.

EXERCISE AFTER YOU ARISE

You can maximize the amount of fat you burn during your walk if you do it shortly after awakening in the morning, *before breakfast*. This is because after an overnight fast, glycogen levels will be at their lowest and walking will burn proportionately more fat than carbohydrate. The body tends to burn carbohydrates and fats in a mixture that is proportionate to the amounts stored. If, however, you walk after a high-carbohydrate/low-fat breakfast, you will minimize fat burning and maximize carbohydrate burning. This is due to the effect of insulin, liberated after a carbohydrate meal, which speeds up carbohydrate burning and shuts down fat burning.

WALK THIS WAY

Many diet books quote a familiar nutritional dictum: "For every 3,500 calories you burn, you will lose one pound of fat." Unfortunately, that's a pound of baloney.

Let's examine what really happens when someone burns 3,500 calories over the course of one week. Let's say that you're about 20 pounds heavier than you'd like to be.

The truth is that during much of the time that you are striving to lose those extra 20 pounds of fat your body will be burning roughly a 50/50 fuel mixture of carbohydrate/fat (some protein is also burned, but the amount is much smaller than carbohydrate and fat, so we'll ignore it for purposes of this discussion). If you burn 500 calories each day during your walk, about 250 calories will come from fat stores, and about 250 calories will come from glycogen; therefore, in one week you will burn *half* a pound of fat, or 1,750 calories. The other 1,750 calories you'll burn will come from glycogen, which will be replenished each day from your diet.

If you ordinarily consume 2,500 calories each day and on the *Forever Fit* Permanent Weight-Loss Plan you reduce your caloric intake to 1,000 calories, you will be reducing your consumption by 1,500 calories a day. About 20 percent of those calories—300—will be fat, so in one week you will eliminate about 2,100 fat calories from your diet. Add to that the 1,750 fat calories you'd burn off in one week by walking one hour each day, and you have a fat calorie deficit of 3,850, or a little over one pound of actual fat burned every week.

Fat loss will vary from individual to individual and will most likely be more impressive if you are considerably overweight at the start of a diet and have been regularly eating a high-fat diet. But over the long haul the figures we have presented here give you an accurate, realistic picture of real fat loss.

When you look at the number of calories you could burn during vigorous forms of activity, you might be tempted to do more than walking.

We certainly don't discourage vigorous exercise, but keep in mind the following points:

- Studies—and our own experiences—have shown convincingly that for most people it's generally easier to stay with an exercise plan if the exercise is not too vigorous or difficult.
- Vigorous exercise is generally tougher on the body; hence you'll stand a greater chance of suffering from an injury that could put a stop to your exercise regimen.

ACTIVITY BREAKDOWN FOR A 120-LB. WOMAN

	INTENSITY	CALORIES BURNED	TIME
Walking, 3.0 mph	Moderate	257	1 hour
Cycling, 10.0 mph	Moderate	357	1 hour
Running, 9:00-per-mile pace	High	585	1 hour
Tennis, competitive singles	Mod. High	516	1 hour
Basketball, full-court	High	641	1 hour
Skiing, cross-country, 5 mph	High	599	1 hour

ACTIVITY BREAKDOWN FOR A 160-LB. MAN

	INTENSITY	CALORIES BURNED	TIME
Walking, 3.0 mph	Moderate	317	1 hour
Cycling, 10.0 mph	Moderate	438	1 hour
Running, 9:00-per-mile pace	High	718	1 hour
Tennis, competitive singles	Mod. High	633	1 hour
Basketball, full-court	High	788	1 hour
Skiing, cross-country, 5 mph	High	737	1 hour

- Walking is low-impact, so it's something you can do every day with no lingering painful effect.
- Walking requires no special equipment, so pack your walking shoes and you can do it everywhere, even on out-of-town business trips and vacations.
- Carefully controlled studies have shown that walking does not appreciably increase appetite when compared to other, more strenuous exercises.

Above all, it is important to note that medical professionals who study weight-loss programs and treat obesity believe that regular exercise is not merely an auxiliary part of weight loss. They tell us it is a critical and necessary part of a permanent weight-loss plan. These clinicians have found over the years that those who enjoy regular, moderate, easy-to-do exercise have a real chance of making a permanent change in their weight, while those who do not exercise rarely enjoy long-term success.

STRENGTH TRAINING FOR OPTIMAL HEALTH

Aside from helping to prevent brittle, thinning bones, obesity, and a sluggish metabolic rate, strength training—we're talking about workouts with machines and light weights, not heavy powerlifting—has been shown to exert some additional health benefits.

There is evidence that strength training may be as effective as aerobic exercise in improving glucose tolerance, thereby reducing the risk of diabetes. A recent study at the University of Maryland revealed that a small group of men, none of whom were regular exercisers, who followed a moderate strength-training program three days a week enjoyed improved glucose tolerance (measured by monitoring blood glucose and insulin levels) to the same degree experienced by a similar group of men who followed a jogging program. Some of the men in both the strength-training and jogging groups suffered from high blood pressure, impaired glucose tolerance, and high cholesterol levels—all risk factors for heart disease.

Thus medically supervised exercise for people with a high cardiovascular disease risk profile or predisposition to diabetes (or diabetes itself) may stand to benefit greatly from a plan that includes moderate strength training and aerobic exercise.

ADDITIONAL BENEFITS OF STRENGTH TRAINING FOR WOMEN

STRENGTH TRAINING IS HIGH ON THE LIST

Most scientists now agree that regular aerobic activity such as walking can help you live longer, live better, and stay slimmer. But now, another form of exercise—strength training—is high on the list of many longevity experts. Recent research suggests that maintaining or building just a little muscle can help you lose excess body fat faster, take preventive measures against osteoporosis by building bone density, and actually help reduce some important risk factors for heart disease. A recent study of obese women (average weight, 240 pounds) on a low-calorie liquid diet (about 500 calories a day—a caloric intake that we believe is too low for most people) showed that the most effective exercise while dieting was either aerobic walking combined with weight training or strength training alone.

As an additional benefit, the women in the study who participated in strength training not only lost more fat than women who did just aerobics; they also lost less muscle and, just as importantly, *showed no decrease in resting metabolism*. This means that their bodies continued burning calories at a normal rate instead of slowing down calorie burning, which normally occurs during periods of caloric restriction.

A SPECIAL NOTE ABOUT WEIGHT LOSS

If you lose just one pound of pure fat each week, you have accomplished an amazing nutritional feat. We know of weight-loss schemes that promise 30 pounds in two weeks and we know that's a lie. Here's why:

1. *Even if you run five miles each day, your body will burn only about ½ to 1 pound of fat each week.* That means that if you run five miles *every day* without changing your diet, you will lose water, protein, carbohydrate, and fat each day, but at the end of the week your real fat loss will amount to about ½ to 1 pound.

2. *If you follow the* Forever Fit *Permanent Weight-Loss Plan without exercising, you will lose about ½ to 1 pound of fat each week.* Because of your new, lower intake of fat, higher intake of carbohydrate, and high-biologic-quality protein, your body will burn fat, replenish valuable glycogen, and minimize the loss of vital muscle. Even without exercise, you can still lose up to about one pound of fat every week.

3. *If you exercise each day* and *follow the* Forever Fit *Permanent Weight-Loss Plan, you can lose up to two pounds of fat each week until you reach your target weight.* This is only an estimate for actual fat loss. Your loss may be higher or lower, depending on a variety of elements such as body weight, muscle mass, duration and frequency of exercise, individual metabolism, and the climate you live in (you will tend to burn fat faster in warmer climates).

Now perhaps you can understand why a two-pound fat loss per week is about the maximum you can and should hope for while following a nutritionally balanced and sensible weight-loss diet. A one- to two-pound weight loss each week is generally considered safe by most health experts. Remember: your *weight* loss may actually appear on the scales as more than two pounds per week, at least during the first month of your new eating plan, due to changes in body composition, the fact that you'll be carrying less internal waste material, and other factors.

The only discouraging point in any weight-loss plan comes when you weigh yourself the day following a particularly long and strenuous workout. Here's the usual scenario:

You walk or jog or play twice as long as you ever did in the past. You're proud of yourself; you feel good about your accomplishment—and rightly so. You feel that *good* kind of tired, that exercise high that comes when you've pushed yourself to the peak of your performance. And of course that day you eat carefully and adhere strictly to the *Forever Fit* Diet guidelines. The following morning, you eagerly mount the nearest scale, and ... *you've gained a pound!*

Have you turned air into fat? Is life that cruel and unfair? No, it's nothing like that. Your body has simply *compensated* for the increase in exercise by turning more of the food (carbohydrate) you ate that day into your good friend glycogen. Remember that glycogen is *stored* carbohydrate. And for every ounce of glycogen stored, your body also stores three to four ounces of water with it for a net weight gain (but not fat gain) of four to five ounces. You actually got *thinner* the day you exercised so hard, because you burned off body fat.

The new glycogen you stored will not make you any fatter—your body will just weigh a little more until you lose more fat to compensate for the glycogen-plus-water gain. Our primitive 20th-century bathroom scales cannot yet discriminate between fat and glycogen plus water. The water stored with glycogen is good for you (it will help hydrate you during your next exercise bout), unlike the water your body retains when you eat too much salt, which causes edema (swelling) and can raise blood pressure and strain the heart.

Which brings us to another weight-gain warning: whenever you overeat salty foods (usually in restaurants, because *Forever Fit* followers don't usually salt their foods at home), the excess salt will cause your body to swell with water and—you guessed it—that shows up the next day on the scale as a weight (not fat) gain. So beware. The kosher dill or spicy chicken Parmesan you enjoy tonight can ruin your weigh-in tomorrow!

CHER

I don't think I will ever stop exercising. I can imagine not working out for two weeks. I can imagine taking a vacation from it or going through times when I am not so gung ho. But I can't imagine giving up exercise for as long as I live.

I think walking is the single most important exercise you can do. I was really shocked when I saw what it did to change the shape of my sister's body. I hadn't seen Georganne in a while, and she had gained a lot of weight in her butt and thighs. I got her a walking machine. She spent six weeks doing that and then visited me, put on some shorts, and I about dropped dead. I was amazed at how her body shape and muscle tone had improved.

The best thing about walking is that it's great for you and it's something you can do for the rest of your life. Unless you buy a treadmill, you don't need space for it in your home, and it doesn't cost anything beyond a good pair of walking shoes.

Find someplace beautiful outside and set your pace. For reasons that have to do with being a public figure, it's hard for me to get in a good outdoor walk. I can do the treadmill in snow or rain or 100-degree heat or zero-degree cold.

I tried running for years, and I always hated it no matter how long and fast I went or how strong I got. I usually did three-mile runs. It was always grueling. What's great about walking is that you don't have the constant pounding, which can lead to pain and injury in all your lower joints. Also, for a woman, your breasts are going everywhere when you run, your ovaries are going everywhere, you're jarring your shins. It's just not the greatest thing for your body.

I really work hard when I walk. I always feel I can push myself but not kill myself like I did with running. I can go as fast as many people run—four to five-plus miles an hour—and I sweat like you wouldn't believe. But it's something I can tolerate. Walking encourages me to go to my limit, but running pushed me over it. I just love walking and the way it makes me feel.

Robert has stressed one thing to me over and over: to control weight you need a minimum workout of at least 30 minutes of walking, at a speed of four miles per hour, at least four days per week. That's one mile in fifteen minutes. If you have never walked for speed before, you may want to set your very first goals lower than that—but advance toward a 15-minute mile.

Robert recommends that if you want to do more, start by increasing the *frequency* and *duration* rather than the speed. A 30-minute walk at four miles an hour covers two miles, so if you are walking outdoors, map out one or several different routes using a car odometer.

Set your own pace. Even if you're starting from zero and do only five minutes a day, then just add two minutes every few days—it's consistency that counts. Sometimes you can't even do 20 minutes in the beginning.

If you are able to, or would rather walk on a treadmill, use the digital readouts to gauge your pace, push your distance, and check your average speed. There are a lot of advantages to home treadmills. They aren't *that* expensive. You can get a real decent one for under $1,500, but if you spend more you get more features and sturdier equipment. Some excellent treadmills in the $2,500 to $4,000 range go faster and can tilt to simulate walking uphill.

I put soft one-pound weights around my wrists. They don't really build obvious muscle, but you'll see better toning for sure. This burns off fat, pushes up your heart rate, and gives you increased definition without thickening your arm with muscle. And it benefits your cardiovascular system. Most experts say that even without weights you should swing your arms vigorously as you walk.

I do not use ankle weights—anymore—and we don't recommend them. I tried ankle weights and got bad shinsplints and calf pains and had to lay off for a while. My doctor told me the weights put too much stress on my legs.

You will get the same "training effect" or "jogger's high" from cardiovascular exertion through walking as you would from jogging. You must first know your "target heart rate" and stay within that range for at least 20 minutes while walking. Then there are times I want to push myself to the upper limits of the range, going as hard as I can without doing myself in.

Usually target heart rates are computed like this: $(220 - \text{age}) \times .85$ for upper limit and $(220 - \text{age}) \times .75$ for lower limit. So for an otherwise healthy, normal 40-year-old man or woman, target range is between 153 and 135. (You should check with your doctor to determine what he or she recommends as a reasonable and safe target heart rate for you.)

I was surprised at how easy it was for me to get from 4.0 miles per hour to 4.5 while walking in just a couple of days. I'm real comfortable at 4.5 miles per hour and then go to 4.7 a day or two later. I hang there for a few days. Then I'll push to 4.8, 4.9, really going for that last break past 5.0. The max I can do is 5.2, which, believe me, is *moving*.

PUSH YOURSELF TOWARD A NEW SET OF GOALS

Hitting 5.0 uphill gets harder, as does maintaining 4.5 to 4.8 over a longer time. This is a tremendous workout. If I sustain 5.0 miles per hour for 20 or 30 minutes or more, I'll break into an unbelievable sweat and feel fabulous afterward. That's a mile every 12 minutes. In New York City that's almost two blocks a minute, which is faster (and cheaper) than cabs and buses in traffic.

Set your own pace and make it easy in the beginning to reach your goals for distance, duration, and speed. Then, if you're comfortable and ready, push yourself each week, or each month, toward a new set of goals—go a little farther, a little longer, a little faster, or until you reach your top pace and workout level. You'll know you're getting a great workout just by the way you feel.

I'm fortunate in that I can almost always arrange to have treadmills, small weights, and other workout equipment set up in my hotel when I'm on location. That was incredibly important for me the year I did three movies in a row—*Suspect*, *The Witches of Eastwick*, and *Moonstruck*. Still, it was nearly impossible to keep to a routine because of schedules and changing locations. But I can always find a treadmill, regardless of where I'm shooting.

Whatever effort it takes to get in my miles is worth it, even hitting the treadmill before a 6:00 A.M. call. It's rough starting at 5:00 or 5:30 A.M., but by the time I drag my ass back to the hotel after a long day of shooting I'm dead tired.

Making a movie demands almost every waking hour. It is really grueling. Each of my film experiences has been different, but I always tried to stick to my workout schedule. Yet I learned early on it doesn't always work that way.

For *Silkwood* I had to put on weight. Mike Nichols didn't want me to look angular and have cheekbones, because he said that I would look too much like a model, when, in fact, I was playing a nuclear plant worker. He even padded my pants. So I didn't work out. I ate instead. I just had a blast. I didn't pay attention to what I ate. I ate stuff I knew was fattening: ice cream, malts, potato chips, junk. No problem keeping the weight up on *that* diet.

I had these great little scenes and had very little responsibility. I didn't realize I was doing so well with the work. It was a very heavy film, and I was the comic relief. Most of my scenes were light except for the one with Meryl on the porch. So people were always glad to see me, because no matter how you try to get away from it on location you pretty much take on the personality of the character you're playing.

On *Mask* I didn't—and couldn't—really work out much and I lost a tremendous amount of weight. I was playing a drug addict. I did real light, gentle exercises and couldn't really kill myself because I was so thin.

Mask was the most emotionally demanding movie I've made. Nothing else I've done comes close to the scene where my son, Rocky, dies. They filmed his death scene for five days and I had to keep the emotional pitch up there the whole time—in the morning, before and after lunch, late into the evening. I had to pick it up exactly where we left it the next day or after a meal break or after that afternoon dip in your energy level—without deviation. Of course the whole idea is that the audience won't see it took five days to get five minutes on film.

Suspect wasn't always easy because my character—the wrongly accused homeless man's defense attorney—was always tired. Besides, it was cold in Washington in March and there were a lot of exteriors and I was freezing and in the rain all the time. Actually, I thought I'd hate night shoots, but they really helped me work out because I'd work from 7:00 P.M. to 7:00 A.M. and sleep until 3:00 P.M. and then have the whole afternoon to get up, be fresh, and work out right before going to the set. I much preferred that.

Then for *Moonstruck* I was in Toronto in January, and I got sick. By the time I finished those three movies I was exhausted, tired of being on the road and away from everybody I love and waking up in strange hotel rooms in the dark alone before dawn.

So far, the only real rough time I've had staying with workouts—when I could—was when I did *Mermaids* in and around Boston the last four months of 1989. I had exercise equipment—a Lifestep machine and a reclining stationary bicycle to go with the treadmill. But circumstances were against me. It was the coldest autumn on record for Boston, and we had to move the exercise machines down from the unheated attic into the warmer living room. I tried getting up at 4:00 to 4:30 A.M., but we were all freezing our butts off. And I was just exhausted from the moment I awoke.

It was the Epstein-Barr virus, the mysterious, recurring fatiguing condition also known as the Yuppie Flu. It comes and goes, gives me a slight fever, and makes me crabby. It leaves me drained and makes me want to sleep a lot at eight o'clock. I've never been hit with it that bad. I've worked with it, I've exercised and powered my way through it. I try not to pay much attention to it. Being sick like that just does not fit into my life.

The real problem from the onset was tension on the set. We switched directors midway through the shoot. Frank Oz was replaced by Richard Benjamin, who was really wonderful. But we were on a tight schedule, constantly under the gun. So for the first time, I just lost the motivation and didn't do well. But life doesn't always allow you to do exactly what you want. There was just too much stress: I was crying all the time and just dead tired.

I started eating out of nerves. Also the catering was so awful I was having salads and shrimp cocktails brought over from nearby diners. I got heavier than I have ever been as an adult. And then there were the M&Ms.

I put on 12 to 15 pounds and lost an awful lot of my overall muscle tone. I think that more than qualifies as a diet-fitness "lapse." I was bummed. Finally, by early December I asked my sister and two close friends to come out to Boston to be with me.

But I know myself. I knew this wasn't forever. I just had to kind of divorce myself from my body for the time being, focus on my work, and blow off the workouts until we finished the shoot. That was really painful for me to do because I work so hard at integrating mind and body.

I also work hard at integrating clothes and body. I couldn't fit into any of my clothes when I went away for the holidays. I put it on pretty much everywhere, with a little extra in the thighs and hips. I had never been known for dressing to hide my body, so it wasn't really much fun.

I knew I had a lot of hard work ahead of me. I had a concert tour coming up and gave myself three months to drop all the weight and get into shape for the Heart of Stone '90 tour. Knowing what kinds of outfits I had in mind, I knew I *had* to lose every ounce. There is no excess baggage allowed in those outfits.

So I threw myself into a disciplined diet and exercise schedule that is an extension of the *Forever Fit* Plan. At the start it was painful to look at my body and see how far I had let it slide. I worked out hard for a couple of months with no staggering, magnificent results. I couldn't let my willpower weaken so I kept thinking to myself, "The process is crucial, it makes me feel better, and if I don't see perfection taking shape right away, at least it'll be *something*." That's the kind of game you play with yourself to sustain motivation.

When it came to dieting, I made really strong food choices and followed the *Forever Fit* Plan. I threw away my M&Ms but allowed myself a treat once in a while. There was no point in starving myself because the body just responds by lowering its thermostat and burning much more slowly. When you start eating again you're screwed. Besides, denial on diets leaves me feeling so deprived it's like having to accept that food has literally gone off the face of the earth. I happen to like cherry Rondos, which are like miniature Dove Bars. So I allowed myself two of those a day. I kept working out like crazy—and, yes, I got results.

Four days before my first show on tour, I woke Paulette, my best friend, at about 6:00 A.M. and said, "Paul, you're not gonna believe this, but I'm in my opening-number jeans."

I had made it. But the maintenance was just beginning. I couldn't afford to let my body slide again once the tour started. The skintight outfits aside, I'd be running my ass off all over the stage while singing and dancing and running up and down stairs in high heels *and* changing nine times during the set *and* keeping up with the dancers in the show who were half my age. It's hard to do all that and make an audience think you're really having *fun* out there if you're out of breath.

So my cardiovascular health had to be way up there, or I couldn't have pulled off any of it. Another key to motivation was that I don't want to go out on a concert tour at 40-something before 10,000 to 20,000 fans every night with everyone judging me and I'm 12 pounds overweight. That possibility can really frighten me. I know my body is supposed to look a certain way.

So, to make sure it looked right, I brought my "gym"—and my eating discipline—on the road. As always, exercising saved my life. I had brought to my hotel suite in every city a Bally Lifestep machine, the reclining bicycle, and the Precor treadmill, along with some free weights, my two weighted bars, and one multifaceted upper-body machine.

This time around Paulette, Angela, my exercise partner, my sister Georganne, and I worked out together and watched all kinds of good stuff on TV and video so it wouldn't be hell. We watched *Oprah*, we watched MTV, we watched the miniseries on the Kennedy family. We watched *Gone With the Wind* for about a week. We called the producers of *The Golden Girls*, and they sent a bunch of episodes. I really love that show because I think the characters are inspirational—and, truthfully, when we're all working out together, we *are* the Golden Girls.

Later in this chapter I'll tell you more about the specific exercise program for strength training that works for me. But our goal in this book is to give as much information and help as possible to you. We feel the best way to recommend a strength-training program is through video-tape. Learning exercise routines isn't like following a recipe—where the measurements are precise and universal. You must make sure your place-ment and balance are correct. You must see someone *doing* it. After more than 15 years with trainers, I am still working on my placement and motion so I don't hurt myself.

Another thing: my own routine is advanced and beyond what beginners can or should do. You must be careful to develop a program for your own needs. I've designed an advanced-level workout that suits my particular fitness requirements. There's one class, almost entirely based on ballet positions and moves, that's great for me for my work but isn't what most people need.

So it makes no sense for us to recommend you do exactly what I do. Therefore, my exercise partner, Angela, and I have reviewed several workout videos and selected those few we feel present the safest and most effective toning and strengthening routines. We know which muscle groups and tricky little areas you want to work on and we picked videos that show exactly how to attack them.

What makes a tape great isn't necessarily a series of exercise move-ments that someone has just invented. Truthfully, there are just so many ways you can isolate your triceps or inner thigh muscles. So what we look for in videotapes is intelligent instruction, correct and precise body placement, and, above all, great motivation from the instructor. And you're not going to feel alone while working out to a tape showing a floor full of people. Remember, though, a tape will produce results for you only if you look forward to it and work out with it on a regular basis.

The truth is most women (and men) are concerned with four muscle groups—the ones that begin to go on you as you get through your thirties and early forties: the stomach, thighs, butt, and under the arms (triceps) and biceps and pecs for men (most women don't even know they have biceps). In addition to basic aerobics tied to a regular walking program,

I think everyone should look for videotape workouts that focus on some sort of spot work for those muscle groups or any other problem areas. For example, if you have a hip problem, there are hip and thigh tapes or you could join a class that's focused on hips and butt. Or for people with long-term weight problems or a bad back, there's an excellent beginner's tape—*Stretch for Life*, by Doreen Riveria—that focuses entirely on stretching the spine.

Our advice is to rent any of the following tapes and try them out in your living room. See how they feel; see how much you can learn from them. Shop around. These are only recommendations. They are all good but you may like one more than others. The important thing is to find one and get with it.

In a typical week, once you're into it, you should do your aerobic walking at least four times. If possible, add a 20- to 30-minute strength-training session for an all-around workout on those days. You might get that session in a gym. But if you don't belong to one, or can't find the time, use the videotape workout. If you don't have the time or find that that's too much in a day, alternate through the week between walking and strength training. And, if you have access to the equipment, alternate aerobic workouts. Aside from speed walking, most gyms offer Stairmaster, Biocycle, Lifecycle, and Lifestep machines.

EXERCISE VIDEO EVALUATIONS

Richard Simmons' Sweating to the Oldies: This is great fun for absolute beginners and people who are overweight and out of shape. It provides an introduction to movement, and Richard's motivation is excellent for people who have struggled with their weight and who need that little push to get their body moving. It will absolutely help them start firming up and losing weight. He does his tapes with a group of people anyone can identify with easily, and they all seem to enjoy these simple workouts to great old rock and roll songs.

Jane Fonda's Easy Going tape: Actually, all of Jane's tapes are very good. Jane is in her fifties and has an incredible body. She's a woman I really admire. The camera work in her tapes is excellent and Jane explains exercises and makes them fun. Jane's tapes are consistently good through the whole range of levels—right on through *Jane Fonda's Workout*. This 90-minute tape is the hardest one. Her tapes are geared to heavy or thin people seeking both aerobics and toning. You can't go wrong. It's a matter of deciding what's good for you.

Callanetics: This is a great all-around exercise tape if you don't want to sweat. It's very nonfrightening. The instructor, Callan Pinckney, is great at motivation. Her movements are very good and she knows how to isolate muscles. It could be a beginner's tape for someone who is just becoming aware of his or her body and muscles, who doesn't want to do aerobics but only wants to learn movement and toning. She discusses the exercises in a relaxing and reassuring way and she doesn't move you through the workouts too quickly. You're not huffing and puffing; you're not jumping all around. It's great for people who have never really used their body. I actually tried working out to it and did not love it for myself. But I could see it would be great for people who don't want to start off as rigorously as I do things.

Kathy Lee Crosby's Beautiful Body Workout: This is a very good 20-minute tape for beginners. If you're younger and don't know very much about weights but are eager to get into it, then this is a valuable introductory tape for those who wouldn't know how to start. It uses some hand weights but nothing difficult to find these days. It's good for beginners only because it goes very slowly and also she is very precise. A good one-on-one.

One of my favorite one-on-one tapes is Joanie Greggains' *Firm Fannies*. She is just fabulous, a terrific motivator. Joanie is particularly good with placement and input and very knowledgeable about movement. This tape is an intermediate workout.

Molly Fox Shape-Up: This is an excellent intermediate to advanced tape for abdominals, thighs, and butt. Molly teaches slow, precise movements, intense concentration on muscles, and very hard work. She gets you to really focus on the muscles you're working on, the way a dancer has to move slowly with tremendous concentration on movement, placement, and the muscles being used.

The Firm series of tapes are all excellent for the seriously motivated. They specialize in movement with weights and are somewhat aerobic, but they mostly stress toning. The equipment used is easy to find. Called *Aerobic Workout with Weights* volumes 1, 2, and 3, these tapes run an hour. Volume 4 runs about 40 minutes. Look over all of them and decide which you like. These classes are challenging and well done. They combine muscle toning and muscle strengthening with aerobics, which I think is an interesting concept. You're not completely out of breath, but you're breathing hard enough to feel the cardiovascular exertion you need for improved fitness. You're also using light weights through *The Firm* exercises. And using your upper body while doing aerobic exercise gives you far greater benefit. When I'm on the treadmill, I can swing my arms low by my sides, rest them on the bar, or carry very light Spenco weights and exercise my arms. When I do that, it brings my heart rate right up there in the target zone in a hurry.

Stretch For Life by Doreen Riveria: As I mentioned before, this is not a standard exercise tape but a workout for overweight or out of shape people with back problems who want to learn to stretch and move through a normal range of motion. It's a very good overall introduction to the body and movement.

WORDS OF ENCOURAGEMENT AND PRACTICAL ADVICE

No matter what exercise plan you choose for yourself, I've always felt a "philosophy" of fitness is as important as the actual routines. Whether you can keep to a program or not depends as much on your motivation and attitude as it does on your muscles and lungs. We know all the mental games and tricks you need to hang in there. So before you throw yourself into your exercise plan, we want to offer some suggestions that work for us.

Try to set up a buddy system. This is really the key. You can expect a new workout routine—at any age, any level—to feel tough at first. But it doesn't also have to be lonely. As social animals we stand a better shot at sticking to an exercise schedule when we work out with one or more friends. And it's better for you than going to lunch with the girls.

I can stay in the gym or on the treadmill forever if there is someone else around. My girlfriends and I watch movies, *Oprah Winfrey, Geraldo,* and videotaped episodes of *The Golden Girls.* We just B.S. and laugh and have a great time. Everyone goes at a different pace but gets the support they need to keep at it. And the videos take your mind off the work and give you something to watch other than a blank wall.

If either my workout partner, Angela, or I want to blow off a workout, the other one says we have to do it and we do it. As a result, we make it to the gym almost every day. It's the only way I've been able to stay with it all this time—more than 15 years. When I used to jog years ago with a group of girlfriends, we used peer pressure on whoever didn't want to do the run that day. That's the trick—find one or two friends you can connect with through exercise. When I started out, I never went alone. It's like trying to learn math alone or become a ballerina alone, with no one there to teach you. It's very difficult if not almost impossible. For example, you can make it social in any number of ways. Get together with a friend at a gym and find a trainer you're comfortable with; or do an aerobics class together with an instructor who jumps around with the class and creates the feeling that aerobics can be fun.

If you stay home, get some mothers or a homemakers' group together, have members take turns watching the kids, or work out to a tape when the kids nap. Make room for exercise because your whole day will go better afterward.

Or you can go walking outdoors with a neighbor and listen to a Walkman for background music as you walk and chat.

It can also be social at home with a group of friends, sharing tapes, doing different classes. If you're exercising alone at home, you can even make it social with your TV. Put on a videotape and make it as appealing as you possibly can and not lonely. Bouncing around alone in your living room is not that much fun.

If you're working out to an audiotape or your own routine, put on a TV show or tape, just to have something to look at.

If you have to get up early in the morning before work and do your exercise then, the best way to go is a videotape because the person on the tape always has the same upbeat gung ho attitude. *They* don't know it's six in the morning where you are. Plus, they're in a group of energetic people and they've brought the music, so it's not something you have to think up yourself. At the crack of dawn counting off exercises by yourself without music just doesn't seem to make it. There are also some terrific exercise shows on cable stations syndicated around the country, such as Joanie Greggains' *Morning Show* and Gilad's *Bodies in Motion* that can be taped and used at your own convenience.

Magazines like *Shape* and *Self* are always running pieces about women who have gone from 280 pounds to 125 pounds through exercise and dieting. Their case histories can be inspiring and make you feel less alone if you are just starting out and prone to feeling hopeless. You read those kinds of stories and nothing seems impossible anymore.

Vary the workout every day so it's never mindless and boring. Whatever exercise routine you follow, we suggest you work on different muscle groups each day and do something a little differently all the time to alleviate the boredom.

Keep an exercise and walking journal. Most treadmills have digital readouts, so I keep a detailed record of my miles each day and per week, my pace and duration. I know if I'm pushing hard enough or going too easy. You can learn a lot about yourself by tracking your rate of progress and what goes through your mind as you advance.

I put all kinds of stuff in my journal after my workouts—how I felt before I got in the gym, where resistance, if any, was coming from, how I felt after exercising.

My workout journal is a lot like a diary. It's either "My body's screwed," "Time to start over," or "I'm so exhausted today," etc. I just write

KEEP AN EXERCISE JOURNAL

everything down in there. One week's entries Monday through Sunday, when I had a bout of Epstein-Barr virus, went like this: "Temperature. Temperature. Temperature. Temperature. Temperature." The next two weeks' entries indicated I did 55 miles, then 61 miles.

In February 1987, here's what I wrote down on different days one week: "Very stressful time with *Witches*. Very trying." "Wake up! Muscle tone down." "Going through a rough time. Not sure what it's from. Maybe the accident on *Witches* or fact that I'm not working out like I should. All I know is I'm in a slump and must be strong enough to pull myself out." "Today is the day to change gears. Every day I feel like I'm falling back. If I keep trying, it's bound to kick." "This wasn't that bad. 17 miles this week."

I wrote these recent entries during one week: "Went out to movies with everybody. New day. Recommit." "Great show. I was so scared." One day on tour I wrote: "Not sure why I've been procrastinating but alas I have been, so there. Well tough. I'm quite motivated now so f— it. Love, Me."

Don't bother going to a gym for a workout if what you're really looking for is a boyfriend. For years I worked out in gyms without men or gyms with a women's section, like the Vertical Club in New York. The gym is the one place where I don't want to worry about my looks. I love to sweat like a pig. My hair sticks to me. I don't wear makeup. I don't wear jewelry. I don't wear fancy clothes. I don't want to go with clean hair. I want to go funky and concentrate on what I'm there for. It doesn't make any sense to dress up. I wear ripped-up old sweatshirts shredded with holes and disintegrating baggy old sweatpants, with my hair back in a knot or up with a rag around it. I don't want to care how I look in the gym because I'm in there kicking butt to make sure I look great *everywhere else*. I don't want to have to be Cher. I don't want to be looked at.

So I rarely go out anymore to gyms, because I enjoy the luxury of having my own gym at home. No one bothers me when I'm exercising, including my assistants, Debbie, Etsuko, and Paulette. They won't interrupt me because they know I get really freaked out. It's time for me to be private in there with my workout partner and friends.

Make sure you design the workout that best suits your own needs, not those of a trainer. If you're going to the gym, find an instructor who can help you through the routines that you've chosen. My sister once threw herself into a training program on Nautilus machines, figuring the more weight plates she could throw on there the better. After a month she was crying because she had gained an inch on her thighs from muscle mass and what she had wanted was to lose fat and get muscle tone. Sure, her thighs were more powerful, but she didn't like the way they looked. I personally never liked Nautilus equipment for myself. I don't even believe men and women should work out together. Their physiologies are so different. They shouldn't run together either, because their strides are also different. Besides, when you're working out with women you're not trying to impress anyone.

Most women don't want heavy muscle mass. They want longer, sleeker lines, more cut (definition), and better toning. They should focus on low weights and high repetitions. Men, to build muscle mass, should focus on high weight and low reps. I personally don't want to build bulky muscles. I want to define, tighten, and tone.

Another time, a dancer friend of mine and I were working out in a gym together, and she started off with 10-pound free weights for a triceps extension. And I said, "Are you out of your mind?" She said her trainer had told her to do that. I told her the most you should do with one arm is five pounds. I do three sets of 15 or 20 reps but with a maximum of five pounds, and that's good enough. But this male trainer told her she was, as she quoted him, "a pussy for not doing more weight." She could have really hurt herself.

It took me a long time to see that just because someone works in a gym doesn't mean he knows what he's talking about—or knows as much as I do. Not everyone who is good at something can teach it. I can act, but I sure can't teach acting. And some people who are physically fit are not emotionally fit to teach. They should gently encourage you, but instead they pressure you into "Come on, come on, you're a pussy, give me 10 more pounds."

The best trainers I've worked with are helpful and supportive and sympathetic to what you are trying to achieve.

We can't stress this enough: begin with a challenging but realistic routine—one you can finish. You'll begin to look forward to it more if it doesn't leave you feeling intimidated or defeated. Never set your goals so high that you fall short and beat yourself up about it. There is always that tendency to throw yourself into it for a few days, see no change, and go, "Screw this—who wants to be in this kind of pain? Time to get a pint of ice cream."

Be patient. As adults one problem about beginning a workout program is that we are not very excited about the prospect of learning to do something. In our minds we associate learning with not being grown up or mature or intelligent. We feel frightened of what's new, or insecure. There are other associations with school. When someone says calisthenics, to many people that means jumping jacks, which means the army or football practice in late summer. So they might resist. Aerobics classes are more fun than that. The word *workout* itself makes it seem like "work." But you make a certain peace with it and give in to it.

This is where the body and mind interconnect and help each other. You

BEGIN WITH A CHALLENGING BUT REALISTIC ROUTINE

can let yourself enjoy it, or you can think of it as drudgery, like going off to the dentist.

Give yourself, say, a month and tell yourself: "I'm going to be good and diligent about this for a month. Five days (or three) a week." But make that commitment for a month. Not longer. *Consistency* is the watchword. Go slowly. Don't set huge goals. Instead, appreciate the changes you will see after one week, after two weeks.

There is nobody whose body won't change through exercise. It's just not a possibility. I first learned that way back when Sonny and I were doing *The Sonny & Cher Show* and I had to learn all kinds of dance routines for our production numbers. I had been a skinny tomboy and athletic. I had an okay body as a teenager, but I didn't really do anything with it; it was nondescript, undefined.

So though I could pick up the steps easily enough, I was no dancer. I started going to dance classes with the dancers on their lunch breaks from rehearsals, and I saw actual progress with my body—I could lift my leg to *here* this week, and then to *here* the next. I watched my body actually change as I pressured it to go further. It was a real phenomenon, and I saw how much stronger your body could get.

Over the years I tried a series of gym classes around L.A. that were kind of trendy. One was where you worked out with this big boxlike thing with straps and pulleys and you built up your muscles that way. I tried running, as I said, which wasn't fun. Then, when I was pregnant with Elijah, I began working with my workout partner Angela. This was in late 1975, and Sonny and I were into our second TV series. Angela and I worked together every day through the pregnancy and I was just trying to keep my weight down and keep toned. I didn't get into strength training and weights until much later.

After Elijah was born Angela and I kept running with our buddy system and then did a 50-minute strength-training class every day. I saw lots of dramatic changes—particularly in the legs and butt—once she and I got our workouts in gear. I'm real strong from the waist up and real weak from the waist down. Legs and butt are the first to go and the last to get better. My arms and stomach come back in 10 days. My stomach gets like a washboard, and my arms get all kinds of definition. My lats come out unbelievably.

And so I developed this tendency to kind of blow off the lower parts so I could focus on where I saw changes right away—the upper body. I have small calves; I'm long in the body and real low-slung. I never liked working on the lower body. But over the years Angela and I put together our exercise classes so that I really work hard on all the muscle groups. When I began working with Robert, he put me on the walking program

START
A WALKING
PROGRAM

and changed the way I was eating. Since then I have continued to work with Angela for the advanced strength-training workouts and moved into alternate low-impact aerobic workouts on Lifestep, Biocycle, Precor, Cybex, and other kinds of equipment.

I've been working off two or three main "classes"—they're actually audiotapes we've put together—for ten years. These classes are indelibly printed into my mind so I don't need to see my instructors anymore, only hear them. But they are recorded at the classes so I just go right from one series of moves to the next without thinking.

My classes each go close to 45 minutes. There's a dance class, focused on ballet-type movements, balance, placement, and hips; there's a class for the stomach, butt, and hips, and there's a class with free weights and a weight bar for the upper body. A day's workout consists of an aerobic workout on one of the machines for 40 minutes at least, then two of the three 45-minute classes.

**TAKE A
CLASS FOR
STOMACH,
BUTT, AND HIPS**

USE
FREE WEIGHTS
FOR THE
UPPER BODY

BE SURE
TO COOL
DOWN AFTER
WORKING OUT

Instead of the usual stretching exercises, I begin with the ballet-type workout as a basic body-opening class that warms the muscles and loosens me up. It looks slow and casual but is really intense. As Angela always says, there is no muscle training like ballet, which requires perfect placement, balance, and intense mental focus on the muscles as they move.

Angela, a former ballet dancer herself, puts it this way: "Mental energy gets focused into the muscle. The mind is centered with the body. The most important thing is getting the brain in touch with the body."

Many of these moves are in ballet's first, second, and fifth positions and use pliés and rond de jambe motions. It forces me to be very precise with positioning and motion, which helps with my stage performances and acting work. Ballet movements are extremely controlled and, when done slowly, are wonderful for muscle warming and toning. When I'm "warmed-up," I move on.

My legs-stomach-butt routine is split up like this: 20 to 25 minutes on my back for various kinds of killer stomach crunches; 10 to 12 minutes on my side for inner-thigh lifts; 10 to 12 minutes on all fours for various reverse leg lifts; donkey kicks and stretches to strengthen and tighten the hamstrings, hips, and butt.

My workout class for the abdominal muscles is broken into exercises for lower, middle, and upper stomach muscles and for left and right sides. Many of them are "crunches" that are common to almost every workout class or videotape.

I do at least 10 separate exercises.

There's a series of leg raises, crunches, bicycle crunches, killer football crunches, etc. Technique and form are key with crunches, at any level of difficulty: it's important not to speed through them with jerky, sloppy movements. That doesn't isolate the muscles. I keep my stomach in, tuck in the pelvis, and keep the small of my back as flat on the floor as possible. I don't rely on shoulders, head, and neck to raise my upper body off the floor for crunches. I focus my mind and energy on the abdomen, tighten it, and lift my torso up gradually.

My final class is for upper body work, which uses both free weights and a weight bar, with each exercise series focusing on a specific muscle group, whether it's the pectorals, latissimus dorsil, biceps, deltoids, or triceps.

For instance, most women have trouble with their triceps; that's the underside of the arm that tends to get flabby and just kind of hang there if you aren't careful. So I do a range of triceps exercises.

A great exercise I do for the pecs is the flyes. For the lats, which give men in particular a great tapered look through the torso, we do lat pulldowns, front and behind. Gym equipment is needed for this one.

For the biceps there's nothing better than a weight bar and a dumbbell for free-weight curls.

Remember, I'm not explaining each of these exercises in detail because I don't believe you can learn to do an exercise *properly* from a description in a book. You need to *see* the exercise demonstrated, either in person or on a videotape.

These are just some of the routines I do. But don't con yourself. If you can move up, move up when you're ready. Be flexible and work up the exercise routine that works best for you. If you need to change your program or goals, stay at a level, or go backward, then change, stay, or go backward. It's your own honor system. There is no one here to watch you but yourself.

But it will pay off. Women who have never been able to show off their arms or wear short skirts or bathing suits are suddenly hooked on exercise and just out of their minds to keep at it because of the changes they see and the way those changes make them feel. Suddenly everybody's telling you how great you look, and it's much easier to just say no to all the bad and unhealthy foods you used to eat. The substituted comfort you got from food is now coming from your husband or boyfriend, your boss or your friends, but most importantly, *yourself.*

10

PERSONAL OBSERVATIONS

ROBERT

As you have now discovered, *Forever Fit* is as much a fitness plan as it is a new way of healthy living. But the words on the preceding pages should also encourage you to rethink the way you live your life.

Do not take the information presented in the preceding chapters lightly. This information is the result of my years of education, research, and success with counseling people from all walks of life—from Wimbledon champions to politicians to sedentary, overweight, high-risk candidates for heart disease. It is also the result of Cher's years of practical trial-and-error testing—valuable knowledge that no university can teach.

I want you to become a nutritional renegade. By that I mean that I want you to avoid the trap of believing everything you see, hear, and read about health and nutrition. This means questioning the advice of time-honored and well-respected national health organizations. For example, the recommended dietary cholesterol and fat intakes published several well-meaning health organizations are, in my opinion, too high for optimal health and maximum protection against coronary heart disease. As you learned in Chapter 3, the *Forever Fit* cholesterol recommendations are more consistent with the wealth of published medical research than those offered by some of these health organizations.

It is no easy task to try to change the eating habits of a nation, especially when you're bucking the system. I have fought battles against nutritional corruption and the political and economic forces that influence the way certain influential scientists "think." I have criticized several national health organizations. As you may guess, this kind of renegade behavior can make you a few enemies, but it can also make you many friends as well. I have had the pleasure of meeting and talking with physicians and dietitians who have discovered that my recommendations for safe cholesterol levels are consistent with published medical research. More importantly, many physicians now recommend the type of diet that I have championed for years—to their own families and patients. And recently several health organizations have radically changed their views on safe cholesterol levels and recommended intakes. But they still have a long way to go before they are in line with the *Forever Fit* recommendations for ideal blood cholesterol levels and daily cholesterol consumption (Chapter 3).

WHY I BECAME A NUTRITIONAL "RENEGADE"

The first nutrition course I ever took (I was an undergraduate at the time) was a biochemical nutrition course (Ph.D. level) offered in the nutrition department at Florida State University. Competing against doctoral candidates, I received the highest grade in the class. That was when I learned that I had a natural aptitude for the study of nutrition.

My intensive studies in organic chemistry, medical biochemistry, human physiology, histology (microscopic anatomy), biology, embryology, oncology (the study of cancer cells), and medical pharmacology had prepared me to critically evaluate the information that was being taught in the graduate school curricula not only at FSU but also at other departments of nutrition in colleges and universities across the country. And what I discovered, to put it bluntly, really pissed me off.

The then-prevailing nutritional dogma taught in American academia was fraught with faulty concepts and fundamentally incorrect information. I refused to let such teachings go unchallenged. I disputed and debated with my professors because many of their teachings and beliefs were inconsistent with published scientific findings. I thus became a nutritional renegade early on during my graduate education.

TAKING ON THE BIG GUYS

Someone once said that you have to break a few eggs to make an omelet, and that's precisely what I did when I challenged the American Heart Association for recommending too much fat and cholesterol in its dietary guidelines. I warned the AHA that it was far too permissive in its cholesterol and fat allowances for the general public. Too many eggs were being broken; too many omelets were being eaten by an unsuspecting public. I started my war against cholesterol in 1976, and the battle is not over yet. The AHA's cholesterol and fat recommendations are to this day, in my opinion, still far too generous for most people's own good. And so the battle goes on.

WINNING YOUR OWN PERSONAL BATTLE

You may have no wish to take on national health organizations as I have or to critically evaluate the volumes of nutritional and medical literature that flood my desk. Fair enough. You've got other things to do. Like staying fit and healthy.

When you bought *Forever Fit*, you purchased *expert knowledge*. I want you to use that knowledge to help conquer the modern plagues of obesity, heart disease, and other health problems. I want you to use this expert knowledge to help you in your personal, professional, and active life.

The rewards of your personal quest for fitness and health are just weeks away. Cher and I faithfully follow the *Forever Fit* dietary guidelines and principles because they pay off in a big way. Our program will work for you too. We designed it especially to help keep you forever fit.

CHER

I've been a peaks-and-valleys person ever since I was little. Much of my life has been about great heights. I don't know if there's anyplace to go from the heights but depths. I'd love it if you could go to medium heights, but I haven't been able to work it out like that. And yet even in rough times that were devastating—when I've been stressed out, had anxiety attacks, and felt practically suicidal, thinking life, as I know it, is over—I got on the treadmill for an hour, and the exercise just wore down the negative feelings and pulled me out of the valleys.

People who exercise, I think, are less hostile than those who don't. Some people have always made fun of bodybuilders for seeming dopey and stupid. But a lot of bodybuilders I've known have been really spiritual. It's as though they've found something beyond the physical world and to me they often seem kind of peaceful. They've pumped themselves up and released all their pent-up aggressions. I'm high-strung, I work in a high-stress field, and I've noticed that I'm much meaner when I don't get in a good workout that takes the edge off.

Maybe I won't feel 100 percent better, but I'll be considerably better. Once the endorphins get released in the brain, I'll feel more peaceful. As I exercise I might see more opportunities and options opening up and feel good knowing my body has accomplished something even though at the outset my mind didn't think it could.

It's like my body has always been my mind's best friend in those hard times. When my mind was really depressed, my body just took over and said, "Here, let me help you for a while." Training is so psychological, proving each day how closely the mind and body work together. I can't work on one and not on the other.

This is the only life I've got, so I'm going to do what I can to make it the best one I can. Because of my childhood, my whole life's history, because of the career I have chosen—because I'm probably not the most stable person in the world—I have to keep reminding myself to maintain a strong spiritual tie to the universe because I sometimes feel I might otherwise just float away.

This is something I wrestle with all the time—remembering that the spiritual aspect of life is the captain of the ship. That's why training is so important. I have a tendency to sink into a solemn, loner kind of behavior. I have always been pretty moody and introspective and gone through periods of real melancholy. There's a history of that in my family and probably a chemical basis for it too. People were high-strung, moody, with

MY WHOLE LIFE IS A WORK IN PROGRESS

lots of drug and alcohol abuse. I have managed not to get sucked into depressions for long periods of time. I think I've been strong about dealing with my life while continuing my search for inner stability.

My activity in the outside world is restricted. I like to go shopping, and when I do there are millions of people who are so shocked that I'm in their midst that they're overwhelmed and want to talk to me. I must say I do get a lot of fun out of that. Having just been all over America on my tour, I've had some great experiences with people who are really funny. They are for the most part extremely positive. But I have never liked crowds and there are places I can't go anymore.

I don't always feel connected to people. My whole life, even when I was little, was not what most people would call normal. I am not the normal actress or the normal singer. I have never exactly been the most normal mother. One time I remember Elijah and I were going to visit his school, and he asked me, "Mom, do you have any mother clothes?" I told him I might be able to dredge up something. I came out of my room with what was as close to mother clothes as possible, and he went, "Well, I guess that's better than I expected." The truth is, I don't even know what mother clothes are except that I know they're not what's hanging in *my* closet.

I've always felt separate, and sometimes, it's true, I achieved that feeling out of trying; but most of the time I achieved it just by being odd and then thinking, "Well, screw it, I might as well just be odd."

In my career I know magazine editors decide whether I am on this week's "in" list and "the best thing since sliced bread" in some new and improved version of myself or if it's time for me to be "stupid" and the "worst dressed" and the "most unhip" and "passé" with no one liking me. That's a difficult life for me to live with, constant approvals or disapprovals. That can take a heavy toll on the human being.

But I'm working on myself constantly. My whole life is a work in progress. I keep doing new things in my career; in my spiritual and mental life I keep trying to have new experiences. When I feel I'm stagnating, I change and move on. I'm sure I could find good things about most religions and spiritual paths and philosophies. People seek inner calm from many different sources and I have tried to find something worthwhile in a lot of them.

The search for stability began early. I had a difficult childhood. When I was six months old, my mother left me in the care of some Catholic nuns and then had a hard time getting me back several months later. She put me there because she had to work and didn't have enough money to pay for child care. My mother's father was an alcoholic, as were other family members. *My* father didn't drink, but even worse, he did heavy drugs off and on.

Once my sister was born a few years later, by a different father, things got a lot better. I felt more connected. I was crazy about my stepfather. My mother, sister, and stepfather—those are my three favorite people when I look back on my life. He lived with us on and off from the time I was six until I turned 11. But they were just fighting constantly and were together, apart, together, apart. He was an alcoholic too. I do have some great happy memories, but I know it was really rough.

My mother constantly moved my sister and me around and was kind of flighty. She lived out of her time frame, searching to be an independent woman at a time when there weren't a lot of role models and there wasn't a movement for women's rights. We didn't eat much meat, but we did eat lots of salads and vegetables and bran muffins and stuff like that 30 years ago. My friends and I actually thought my mother was kind of crazy.

We had a fun enough time, but we had no money. There were no new clothes, new cars, new anything. As I grew up, I realized a lot of people judged you on just those material things. I was really insecure, shy, introverted, and kind of skittish. But I had all kinds of fantasies that I was going to be famous—an actress or singer or something like that. Even today we always sit around and laugh about that. But the truth is: I believe that whatever I want I can get.

I never thought of myself as pretty. I still don't, but I do think I am very stylish and I think that's a lot better because you lose your looks eventually. Besides, you can't be too happy when you're not pretty anymore if you've always put too much emphasis on it. I was just a skinny tomboy and always wanted to be a blonde. I wasn't real popular, either. I was always into a different "head" from my peers. Plus, I had a learning disability called *dyslexia*, and I left school after tenth grade.

Ever since then my story's been that I've had to work really hard against all odds every time I decided to pursue something. It never seemed like I went with the flow, so after a while I just said, "Screw it. I'm not going with it anyway."

I've always been outrageous and, I think, very creative, in my appearance. I once got kicked out of school in ninth grade for wearing bizarre clothes. I saw *Breakfast at Tiffany's*, and I thought I was Holly Golightly, so I wore two ponytails and black sunglasses to all my classes. I just wanted to be her.

When I met Sonny, he was a weird dresser and we started wearing psychedelic clothes offstage before the late sixties. Onstage he wore a suit; I wore a dress. One night our stage clothes got lost and we went out in our street clothes. People thought we were English and everyone loved you back then if you were English.

Not everyone loved me when I decided to pursue acting. It took me five years to get a job. Film executives didn't think I was talented. No one did. Everybody thought I was this major dipshit, so nobody wanted to give me a chance.

It took a rebellious guy—director Robert Altman—to give me my first break. He cast me for *Come Back to the Five and Dime, Jimmy Dean, Jimmy Dean.* He wanted to prove everyone wrong—and I guess he did. I know the Academy thought of me as an outsider and a lot of actors were pissed off because I was working. Back then, if I had gone around saying, "I'm going to get an Academy Award in a couple years," people would have gone, "Yeah, right—get a life."

But when I got it, I thought, "If I can get this from where people thought I was coming from, than *anyone* can do *anything.*"

Then, after I did a few films, when I tried to get back into rock and roll, a lot of musicians thought I was some dipshit who didn't belong in music. Somehow, for me, it's always been like that.

My life has been very disjointed—very popular, very public, making mistakes in front of everybody in the world. If I wasn't as strong as I am, I don't know how well I'd have made it through. I never turned to drugs; I never turned to alcohol. I always turned into myself.

That's one reason why I believe women in particular admire or respect me. First they see me stumbling and picking myself up, moving forward and changing against the odds. They see I'm really honest. I know my faults and my strengths, and I try to do the best I possibly can. I can be stopped, for a minute, but I don't fail. I have succeeded in every line of business that you can go into as an entertainer. I've raised two children by myself. I think women can all relate to that too.

I'm also kind of rebellious and I don't care what the consequences are. It's in that sense mostly that I think of myself as an American. I remember not long ago I was with a friend who brought me to one of those preppy designer boutiques on Madison Avenue in New York to buy some boxer shorts or something. I was in my leather jacket. I was, like, "What is wrong with this picture?" People were gawking at me but in a way where they'd rather break their necks than admit it. The place reeked of pretension and that just makes me crabby.

I said, "Being here is really a mistake. It makes me want to be rude. Get me out of here before I insult everyone."

The shop girls were walking around like Princess Di in their ridiculous outfits and ridiculous attitudes, acting condescending, and the guys were talking about Muffy and Buffy and the ski weekend. They were all talking like they were in some TV ad. It was just unbelievable. And I thought: Please, this is going to make me puke.

So I got into an elevator with these three guys and one guy said, "Well, what do you think about me and Muffy for this weekend?" And the other guy said, "Oh, she's already gone skiing. You don't have a chance." I said to myself, "Don't say anything smartass." I feel the necessity in situations like that to beat these people up verbally. They just piss me off. I guess I'm just still really, really rebellious. But nothing makes me feel more American that that. I've always been that way, and I'm probably going to be that way until I'm 70 and I won't have anything to rebel against.

But for now, for the nineties anyway, there is plenty to change in our society—and I'd like to think I represent a new era for women. One thing that has to change is the way society deals with women and aging. Growing older in America is harder for women. We get negated so much by our age. This is very hard to fight against. Men have always made the rules. A lot of times you're afraid you're going to lose your body as a woman because you're older—you're not perfect, bubbly, and cute, and 20 and all that. Or you think you'll become devalued and that you haven't achieved all the things you wanted to.

Most of us are, to some degree, fixated with not wanting to be obsolete. We're given less and less value by society as we get older. If this were a culture where there were more benefits from aging itself, then people wouldn't be so frightened of getting older. But things are improving. So many women now have reached a certain age and remained so vital that it has helped change people's opinions of what aging means for a woman.

I'm sure a lot of people think I'm obsessed. Maybe I am. Maybe it's because I picked a career that unfortunately has a lot to do with face value. You not only have to be talented; you have to look great while you're being talented. Most people don't have to go out in front of 20,000 people every night and not only look good but *be* good and be funny and happy even if they have PMS and have a cold or sprained their ankle or had a fight with their boyfriend and their heart is broken.

This isn't just paranoia over something that doesn't exist. The pressures on a woman my age in the film business would make the healthiest person a little bit paranoid. Paul Newman can still do love scenes with 23-year-old girls. It's almost never the other way around.

In fact, it can be a lot worse than that. On the night of my fortieth birthday I was told by George Miller, the director of *The Witches of Eastwick*, that I wasn't sexy enough to work in the movie with Jack Nicholson. This was unbelievable to me. On your fortieth birthday you don't want to have someone tell you you're not attractive. George told me this came directly from Jack, and as I was listening to this on the phone, Chastity and my girlfriend Paulette were bringing me cake with the candles burning while I had tears streaming down my face. George hired and fired me four times for that project and I eventually found out Jack had never said he didn't want me in the film.

But that's the way it goes. No one said it was going to be easy or fair. Of course, on the other hand, later the same night we all went out dancing and I met Rob Camiletti, who was 18 years younger than me, and *he* sure had no problem with my being attractive because he became my boyfriend for three years.

But in my career you're always thinking, "If I put on some weight, I won't get a job." Even staying fit, the truth is I'm in an age category of actresses where it gets a little dicey, a little strange. I can tell myself, "I'm not getting older, I'm getting better," all I want, but the truth is: the great roles for women over 40 are few and far between, and there are lots of parts I can't play.

But there are plenty others I *can* and will play because I do look good—roles that other actresses my age can't play simply because they don't look good. I don't ever want to go, "Well, I can't wear this and show off this part of my body for this video or film part because I haven't kept up in the gym." So while I won't do something crazy to look my best, I will do whatever I need to do. And I feel working out is a small price to pay.

I've killed myself in the gym to have this body. It isn't like I've got some amazing secret that nobody else has. And when I don't want to exercise, I look like hell. It's not anything you'd want to see. I don't get obese, but I do get soft. When I pig out, I lose definition. I won't get in a bathing suit and I won't pose for pictures I want millions of people to see.

Then I'll bust my butt and get my body back under control. What's ironic is that the press wants to write off my body as the result of cosmetic surgery. It amazes me that people are choosing to bust my chops over this. This way they can dismiss me—and exercising—by saying, "Well, look at her, she just went out and *bought* that body."

Does one negate the other? If I have cosmetic surgery, does that mean I don't work out? My nose always bothered me since childhood. My teeth were crooked and pushed in too far. But they're mine and if I want to pull them out and wear them on my back, does that make any difference? It's my body to do with what I want.

Look, we're a visual society. I didn't make this society. I just live here. I adapted to it. I've been pretty open about the stuff I've had done and I feel it was the wrong choice. It's done nothing but come back to me in the most negative ways. I just don't understand people's preoccupation with the amount of surgery I've had done. I think it started in France, when a newspaper ran a picture with arrows pointing to my body and detailing all the things they claimed I had done, like having my ribs taken out to cinch my waist, liposuction on my hips and legs, having cheek and chin and butt implants, having my stomach tightened, whatever.

I just blew it all off. It amazes me that people can be so stupid not to realize I'd have big ugly scars in all these places. But are these cheek-bones any different from the ones I had back with Sonny? This rib cage is still my rib cage. I don't even know if you can lift your ass surgically. It would sure leave a thick scar in an area where I could never wear my kind of clothes. It just wouldn't be worth it. It would frighten me, like having ribs removed. As for liposuction, it works for women who are, say, nicely proportioned down to the waist and then have cellulite and hips from hell. For those women it would be worth the scarring so they wouldn't be embarrassed by huge saddlebags. And there's an operation for women with bad stretch marks from pregnancy, where they cut you open and pull the skin down over your stomach to tighten it.

I've had my bust done—and redone. This was one nasty plastic surgery nightmare. The first time, I got a bad infection and really bad scarring. My chest had gotten huge when I was pregnant, and my skin got stretched out real bad. So I had it tightened up. It's a fabulous procedure that really works. I had this done after both Chas and Elijah were born. And then I had to have it corrected a couple of times because of scarring.

Some people feel you must live with what you're born with, and that makes you a true spirit and a true beauty. It's not my concept. People should do what makes them happy.

Frankly, when I saw my face 10 feet tall in close-ups on a movie screen, it's a little bit different from just talking to somebody on the street. I wanted my nose done because it really bothered me. My teeth were straightened and brought out with braces and a retainer. It improved the shape of my mouth because it gave me more of a mouth. Maybe that's why people think I've had chin and cheek implants.

It wasn't like I ever tried hiding anything: the year I was nominated for *Silkwood* I showed up for the Academy Awards ceremonies wearing braces. That was real difficult. I didn't want to smile at all.

I never liked the way I looked much, but it's okay. I've done the best I can do with it. If I had been given a choice, I don't think I'd have picked this look. I might have gone more with Michelle Pfeiffer's look.

I'd like to look really great for as long as I can. If some people think that makes me terminally vain, then yes, I am that. I don't think feminists should get upset if women want to change their looks. This is the real world and we're going to get older no matter what. It's just that I'd rather get older looking like Loretta Young than get older looking like, say, Thelma Ritter even though she was one of my favorite actresses.

I think many women will buy surgery over exercise because they aren't aware that you can really change your body by working out. If that's their choice, then they must be extremely careful to find the right doctor and see the "before" and "after" pictures of his patients. Find a friend you trust who is absolutely thrilled to death with someone's work. Make sure the doctor is really a plastic surgeon, not just an M.D. who's got his own plastic surgery clinic. There's a difference, and you won't want to wear that difference on your face or body for the rest of your life. There's no residence training for plastic surgery like there is for brain surgery, psychiatry, and pediatrics.

The bottom line is: plastic surgery is no panacea. Nothing can change and maintain the shape of your body better than exercise and proper eating. My sister, who is like the most nonphysical person in the world, lost 20 pounds and she looks unbelievable. She was frightened by exercise and fought it. Maybe she was scared of failure, of looking incompetent, of not getting the grasp of it right away. Now, for the first time ever, she wears my skirts and looks a lot younger. And the shape and tone of my own body have changed dramatically over the years.

More to the point, by fixing your look entirely through plastic surgery, you miss the exhilarating highs of daily workouts and you don't learn how to use your body to help your mind and spirit stay healthy. I've seen incredible transformations when people reshape their bodies—and that can only change your mind and behavior in positive ways.

When I sink into negative attitudes, I feel it's as if my mind has been a traitor to my body. I know only two ways of handling depression, stress, and tension. One way is to be dramatic for a couple days, and then I get bored with that. Some people need to be in drama all the time. I can choose drama or not. If I do get caught up in it, I might deal with my problems by eating a whole pint of Häagen-Dazs in the middle of my bed. I mean, I pull all the stunts everyone else does.

The other way—exercise—is much smarter. I lie back, take big deep breaths, and hit the treadmill. I may still fight it all the way to the gym, going, "I don't want to do this, I really don't want to do this." But I get on the treadmill and make a deal: "If you don't want to be on the treadmill after five minutes, then you can get off."

And I never get off. It's the best way I know to work through an awful lot of my frustrations and tension. I admit I don't have the capability to handle stress without little tricks like the treadmill. I'll just slip in a movie on the VCR and a fast walk will dissipate the stress and anxiety.

There is no more dramatic proof of how exercise can be my major best friend than when I've got PMS. Some women get it terribly after 35, and I get it horribly—backache, stomachache, bloaty, crabby, uncomfortable in my own skin. My rings don't fit my fingers, I'm depressed, weepy—I mean, I'm not a fun person. There are days when I wake up crying hysterically. Those days I go through my workout and the change in 45 minutes is extraordinary. I feel leveled out.

One serious disappointment came when I didn't get the female lead for an MGM movie called *Road Show*—a film that I do not believe has ever been made. My film career had just started. It wasn't like things were pouring in.

Jack Nicholson and Timothy Hutton were supposed to be in it and Marty Ritt was the director. I had read for the part, and Marty had told me, "Cher, you're perfect. I haven't had this feeling since I met Sally Field and I immediately knew she was Norma Rae. Plus, I've just seen *Silkwood*, and it's perfect. *You're* perfect."

I had a deal memo with the studio. They were even asking me what size trailer I wanted for the location, and I said I just wanted the same size trailer Timothy Hutton has. I had gotten a T-shirt with the MGM logo on it and I was so excited I even had it rhinestoned. I *had* the job.

It was my 39th birthday, so I went off to New York. Meryl Streep and I had gone that night to see a play and we ran into a friend who's a cinematographer. He asked me what I was going to do next and I said, "Well, I'm in this great movie for MGM. Jack Nicholson's in it."

And he said, "Which movie is this with Jack Nicholson?"

"It's his next movie."

"Yeah, I know, but his next movie is *Road Show*."

"Yeah, right," I said. "That's the one."

"God, Cher, if I were you, I'd call someone."

So Meryl and I looked at each other funny. "Call someone?" I asked. I did try calling someone but couldn't get him on the phone for three days. And this was my agent. Everyone just suddenly disappeared. There was no one to get angry at, just nobody. I told Marty Ritt I was off the picture, and he quit. I found out Debra Winger and Mary Steenburgen were also told by people they had the same part. I was real depressed. In fact, I still have the MGM T-shirt, except I put MGM SUCKS on it in rhinestones.

I exercised my way out of that one too. I figured if I'm going to survive in a field where this happens all the time, I better find a way to handle the ups and downs.

I'm not alone. I know so many people who are seeking a spiritual path to help them cope with what goes on in their lives and the world around them. I don't know many of them who aren't also seeking a physical discipline in their lives. I don't understand how anyone can really believe the two can exist separately.

The spiritual aspect of my life has finally started coming more into focus. It's so easy for other worries to get in the way, but I'm giving my spiritual life more energy now. I could really get fried living the way I do, and sometimes I do. I also know there's a way to come back to myself. I love nothing more than to come home and sit by the ocean.

Talking about one's spiritual work sounds like mystical crap, but everything has had its place in my search. I tried est a long time ago, and while it was not a life-changing experience, it was interesting. Now I read a lot and I stay open to things that come across my path. I have had great Christian experiences and Jewish experiences and I once went to see Guru Mayi in Santa Monica. That was great. And as I've said, I'm open to the possibility that there are positive lessons to come out of all different books and religions and institutions.

I began practicing transcendental meditation in the mid-1980s. I get lazy and forget to do it until I get really crazed, and then I'll get back into it. I found TM almost impossible in the beginning. My mind just did not want to be quiet. I found it really frightening to be still. I don't know why. It just jumps in there with all kinds of stuff. It frightens me sometimes to achieve the complete stillness you can get through meditation. Maybe it's because the rational mind feels its job is to solve problems and it can't stop doing its job. To just let things go and be still is the most difficult thing to do, but it is the best thing for me and I do not achieve it easily. That's why I'm a work in progress: I'm always working on trying to get clearer.

"Being in the moment" is what you call it in acting, and it's what most people can't do in their lives—just be in the moment. There are just too many distractions and neon signs everywhere we go in this life. For me, when I have a great workout or when I've done a scene well in a film, I won't even be aware of the time. It'll end before I can step out of it and comment on it consciously or check my watch. Those are the moments when my mind and my body are as one.

MY MIND AND MY BODY ARE AS ONE

I've learned a lot about how that works from a healer friend of mine named Rosalyn Bruyere. She heals with her hands and, boy, if she puts her hands on you, you know you've been touched. Even *near* your body you feel it. It's simply unbelievable. I think many Americans are so frightened of any programs and rituals we did not grow up with because we assume they're wrong or devious or mysterious. But she is truly tuned in to some kind of higher power. The first time I went to her for something, she put her hands over my stomach and all of a sudden my stomach and skin started tingling and vibrating.

When I had a series of three operations, I refused to go under general anesthetic the last time. I had felt really sick for days afterward the first times and wanted to die. It was horrible. The doctor told me I was ridiculous, it couldn't be done that way. I said, "Let me bring this friend of mine into the operating room and let her help me, guide me through this."

"You're nuts," he said. I said I didn't care. Rosalyn sat beside me and held my hand, and I guess there were times I was in pain and she'd just talk to me and pass her hands over the site of the operation. The surgeon was absolutely amazed, and I went through it fine. I was like out of it—kind of—and don't remember feeling anything.

I try to do something "spiritual" every day. Just as I take my exercise equipment with me on the road, I always pack a bag full of books and audiotapes of books wherever I travel. When I was touring, I spent so many hours on the bus and being driven around that I sat and "listened" to these books if I was too tired to read.

Meditation was also a great way to rest after my shows, after giving everything I had onstage. I'd get in the bus, take off my makeup, put on one of the many self-help audiotapes I take with me, and start the meditation. Or I'd do my own words, my mantra. And then I'd get very peaceful, taking deep breaths, going within myself, being still and quiet.

Books have always given me comfort and inspiration. When I come across passages about certain emotions or states of mind I have experienced, it makes me feel I'm not so unusual, that someone else has shared that too. A close friend gave me an incredible book called *Each Day a New Beginning: Daily Meditations for Women*. It's one title in the Hazelden Meditation Series. The Hazelden Foundation is the drug and alcohol treatment center in Minnesota. This book is for women especially, and I know it's been used in Alcoholics Anonymous and other recovery programs for people with drug-addicted personalities. But their books are great for anyone.

MEDITATION IS A GREAT WAY TO REST

There's a passage for each day of the year, written by famous and nonfamous women. I start every morning with that day's reading. The series also has books geared to families, men, young adults, overeaters and dieters, and even one called *Meditations for Women Who Do Too Much*. I take them all with me wherever I travel and have given them away to women friends. These books make you stop and reflect on things, get a different slant on your day. I'll carry around in my mind and heart the theme in that day's reading. If I miss my reading, I'll go, "Gee, I could use that book again; it really helps me." It's just that little extra thing, a little inner pep talk.

On July 1, for example, I read, "Our lives are in process every moment, which means change is ever-present. As new information is sorted and acquired, old habits are discarded. We don't let go of some old behaviors easily.... Emotional development was stunted for most of us with the onset of our addicted behaviors."

I never had addicted behaviors, but I can really understand what they're saying. The Hazelden books are both totally spiritual but also practical.

My favorite book on the subject of inner growth—it's just about the best book I've ever read—is called *Healing the Child Within* by Charles Whitfield. It hit really close to home and gave so much insight into the problems I saw in myself. It also comes with a workbook, which made it easy for me to grasp, and helped by suggesting ways to change those problems. It's mostly about people who didn't have happy childhoods and what people do to compensate for that unhappiness.

I think most people have to kind of subjugate parts of their personalities when they're growing up in one way or another because adults are not always open to letting children express themselves freely. An dthe book also deals with the ordeal of having alcoholic parents or a really sick member in the family and how that affects us when we grow up. As I read through it, things started to crystallize for me so that I could discover ways to deal with them. Of course, there's Dr. Scott Peck's *The Road Less Traveled*, a book that offered real valuable insights. Robert Heinlein's *Stranger in a Strange Land* was also an inspirational book even though it's a novel.

Another really incredible book—and tape—for me is by Louise Hay: *You Can Heal Your Life*. She's done a lot of work with AIDS patients in L.A., and her book is unbelievable. She deals with being a lot gentler to yourself, not so critical and demanding of yourself, and having a much more loving attitude toward people and therefore toward yourself. It's about not having expectations no one can fulfill but that leave you constantly disappointed in people.

Then there's *A Course in Miracles* taught by Marion Williamson, which is long and demanding but worthwhile. She gives wonderful lectures and makes fabulous self-help cassettes. I haven't finished it, but I always take it with me on the road and I'm always working on it. It's more like having a Bible with you. (I also take one of them.)

And there's Gerald G. Jampolsky's book, *Love Is Letting Go of Fear*, although he is harder to get than some others because he is so unconditional. I'd also recommend for women seeking to change their lives *Codependent No More*. The subject of codependency comes up in *Healing the Child Within*, and at first I didn't catch on because the term isn't really what it is. They should have another word for it. It's about not being who you are in a relationship—building up a facade and pretending you're someone different.

I have a whole bunch of audiotapes by John Bradshaw, who is the big star nowadays in the self-help and recovery fields. I've gotten amazing help from his work. His *Healing the Shame That Binds You* is one title I always have with me. Bradshaw's about the best; he just kills me. He's so intelligent. He's developed great lectures and readings.

Of course, beyond books there's always therapy for anyone seeking change and self-improvement. But you have to find the right therapist and it may take one or two wrong ones before you connect. I was lucky. I found the absolutely greatest psychiatrist in the world. I had gone to a lot of different people over the years, and I always thought shrinks were a bunch of crap. I think everyone needs someone they can sit and talk with who has an overview and nothing to gain by your answers. Someone who is more intelligent than you are. I tried therapy a bunch of times through the years and never stayed with it. I just kept saying, "Therapy is horseshit. These people are either impressed with me or I'm smarter than they are or something."

But in the mid-eighties, I was going through an extremely painful time and I had personal, medical, and career reasons to seek help again. I had some bad medical problems and no one knew what they were. I ended up needing three different operations, one right on top of the other. Ironically, it was just a few months after I won the Academy Award for *Moonstruck* and all of a sudden things turned and got really rough for me. The surgeries alleviated but didn't completely rectify the situation.

So I took matters into my own hands and I called Scott Peck for a referral. I left a message and he called back. "I heard you needed me to talk to you," he said, in this rural, gentle, Will Rogers kind of way. I said, "Scott, I'm having a real hard time, and I need someone like you."

He said he'd work on it and when he called me back again he said, "As luck would have it, my wife has come up with the perfect person for you to see."

So he gave me Elaine and she's simply the greatest psychiatrist. I wanted a man, someone smarter than me and I didn't think a woman was going to be as smart as me, which is unbelievably sexist and stupid of me. But that was my experience. And then I met Elaine and I kept saying to myself, "Please be a lot smarter than me, please." She's blond with a southern accent and from Atlanta and totally Laura Ashley. God, she is great. I have learned so much from her and so much of what I've learned is exactly the opposite of what I was brought up with.

For starters, there's this: no one wants to go through life unloved, but if you don't love yourself as much as you possibly can, if you're not selfish about loving yourself first and foremost, then you can never be loving and helpful and giving and a lot of other things to people and feel truly fulfilled.

By selfish I mean really knowing what you need so you can satisfy yourself. A lot of women get sick because they subjugate their feelings and their whole lives. Then they're frustrated and angry and illness is their body's only way of getting their feelings out.

I was afraid of change for a long time. But as I changed, I found it more comfortable than I anticipated. And so it seemed more intelligent to keep changing. I was always really critical and demanding of myself and of other people—and got really angry when people didn't do what I wanted. I learned they can't always do what I want. That expectation is stupid and childish. I had to look at myself without condemning myself. I learned to observe without judging. I'm now a much nicer person. Everybody comments on that now. I used to go through life completely tough on the outside and never reveal my insides to anyone.

I always loved other people, but I could also be curt and critical and show my love by criticizing. I felt it was my job to fix everything all the time. That comes from being six years old and being the one in my family who came up with solutions. Everybody came to me with their problems.

But then I'd get overloaded and cranky, or I'd take on too much work and get drained. I'd try to hold all my feelings in and not tell anyone I was upset or overburdened. Nobody was allowed to see what I was really going through—I was just like this machine, like Robocop. Now I can show my real nature. I'm more open and, I hope, a lot easier to understand.

Can I tell you one last thing? I am really far away from physical perfection. I know that. For me, Bo Derek in *10* is a perfect body. But when I'm working out again after a layoff or a slide, I see my body making changes, and I'm real thrilled. I know I'm never going to achieve "perfection," but I'm going to get as close as my body can get, and that's going to make me feel happy about myself and what I can accomplish.

And I think that's all people really want—to know their body can be the best body it can be, to keep firm, toned, and slim and live at the best weight they desire to be. That would be enough. None of us can achieve perfection per se—and besides, it isn't important. We can still be the best people we can be, and any improvement that draws us closer to that lifelong goal is better than what we have today.

The point is not to focus on muscle groups or obsess about specific kinds of foods to deny yourself. It's to create a new attitude about health and fitness and about your self, your physical and spiritual selves, working together harmoniously, improving together.

To become the best we can be, a program for fitness can't be just a fad. It can't be part of your way of life. It should *be* your way of life, just as it's been for Robert and me. And now, we hope, you've discovered what we've known for years: that staying in shape and feeling your best isn't just for today—it can be forever.

CREATE A
NEW ATTITUDE
ABOUT YOURSELF

APPENDIX I
FOREVER FIT RECIPES

BREAKFAST

BAKED OMELET

SERVES 6

---

8 egg whites
1 cup evaporated skim milk
½ cup low-fat cottage cheese
½ cup Kraft Grated American Cheese Food, Sharp Cheddar Flavor
⅛ teaspoon pepper

---

1. Preheat oven to 350°. Spray a 9-inch cake pan with Butter Flavor Pam.
2. Place all ingredients in a food processor or blender. Mix until smooth.
3. Pour into prepared pan and bake for 30 to 35 minutes or until mixture is set. Cut into 1½- to 2-inch pie slices. Serve warm.

PER SERVING
CALORIES
90
PROTEIN
11 g
SODIUM
267 mg
CARBOHYDRATE
6.4 g
FAT
2 g
CHOLESTEROL
8 mg

POTATO SCRAMBLE

SERVES 4

PER SERVING
CALORIES
142
PROTEIN
11 g
SODIUM
451 mg
CARBOHYDRATE
20.3 g
FAT
1.9 g
CHOLESTEROL
5 mg

2 cups cubed potatoes (boiled, drained, and finely diced)
1 cup chopped onion
¼ cup grated Parmesan cheese
1 ½-ounce packet Butter Buds
⅛ teaspoon pepper
1¼ cups skim milk
8 egg whites

1. Put potatoes in a saucepan, cover with cold water, and bring to a boil. Reduce heat to low and simmer potatoes until just tender. Drain potatoes and finely dice them.
2. Spray a large nonstick frying pan with Pam. Brown onion in pan over medium-high heat. Add potatoes and cook 5 minutes more.
3. Place remaining ingredients in a food processor or blender. Mix until smooth.
4. Pour mixture over potatoes and onions. Cook until eggs are set, stirring occasionally.

BLUEBERRY PANCAKES

MAKES 10 PANCAKES
SERVING SIZE: 2 PANCAKES

PER SERVING
CALORIES
226
PROTEIN
8.3 g
SODIUM
380 mg
CARBOHYDRATE
46.8 g
FAT
0.8 g
CHOLESTEROL
3 mg

1 cup whole wheat pastry flour
¼ cup oat bran
2 tablespoons granulated fructose
2 teaspoons baking powder
1 teaspoon dried orange peel
1 ½-ounce packet Butter Buds
1 egg white
1⅓ cups evaporated skim milk
2 cups fresh or defrosted and drained frozen blueberries

1. Combine first 6 ingredients in a large bowl. Mix well.
2. Whisk together egg white and evaporated skim milk. Add to dry mixture and blend well. Fold in blueberries.
3. Spray a nonstick frying pan with Pam. Heat over medium-high heat.

4. Pour about ¼ cup batter into frying pan at a time, making several pancakes at once. When pancakes are bubbly and bubbles start to burst, turn with a spatula. Cook until golden brown.
5. Place pancakes on heated platter. Repeat cooking process until batter is used up, wiping the pan out and respraying with Pam as needed.
6. Sprinkle with Equal sweetener or serve with Blueberry Sauce (see below for recipe).

BLUEBERRY SAUCE

MAKES 1½ CUPS
SERVING SIZE: ¼ CUP

---

1 12-ounce package frozen blueberries, defrosted
3 to 4 packets Equal sweetener

---

1. Place blueberries and Equal to taste in a food processor or blender. Puree.
2. Warm sauce over medium heat before serving with pancakes.

PER SERVING
CALORIES
31
PROTEIN
0.3 g
SODIUM
0 mg
CARBOHYDRATE
6.9 g
FAT
0.3 g
CHOLESTEROL
0 mg

BRAN PANCAKES

MAKES 12 PANCAKES
SERVING SIZE: 2 PANCAKES

PER SERVING
CALORIES
250
PROTEIN
6.9 g
SODIUM
339 mg
CARBOHYDRATE
53.9 g
FAT
0.5 g
CHOLESTEROL
2 mg

1½ cups whole wheat pastry flour
½ cup bran
¼ cup oat bran
⅔ cup granulated fructose
2 teaspoons baking soda
1 teaspoon dried orange peel
1 cup evaporated skim milk
2 egg whites

1. Combine the first 6 ingredients in a large bowl. Mix well.
2. Whisk together the evaporated skim milk and the egg whites. Add to the dry ingredients and blend well.
3. Spray a nonstick frying pan with Pam. Heat to medium-high.
4. Pour about ¼ cup batter onto frying pan at a time, making several pancakes at once. When pancakes are bubbly and the bubbles start to burst, turn with a spatula. Cook until golden brown.
5. Place pancakes on heated platter. Repeat cooking process until batter is used up, wiping the pan out and respraying with Pam as needed.
6. Serve with Equal sweetener, unsweetened applesauce, unsweetened jelly, or Aunt Jemima or Log Cabin Lite Syrup or Strawberry Sauce (see page 175 for recipe).

STRAWBERRY SAUCE

MAKES 1 CUP
SERVING SIZE: ¼ CUP

1 16-ounce package frozen strawberries, defrosted and drained
3 to 4 packets Equal sweetener

1. Place strawberries and Equal in a bowl. Mash strawberries with a fork until thick and no whole strawberries remain.
2. Chill before serving on whole grain pancakes, toasted whole wheat bagels, or whole wheat English muffins. Chill leftovers.

PER SERVING
CALORIES
112
PROTEIN
0.6 g
SODIUM
3 mg
CARBOHYDRATE
29.4 g
FAT
0.1 g
CHOLESTEROL
0 mg

"NEED NO SYRUP" BANANA PANCAKES

MAKES 12 PANCAKES
SERVING SIZE: 2 PANCAKES

1¼ cups whole wheat flour
2 tablespoons granulated fructose
2 teaspoons low-sodium baking powder
1 cup skim milk
2 egg whites, lightly beaten
3 to 4 large diced bananas

1. Combine first 4 ingredients in a large bowl. Mix well.
2. Add egg whites and blend.
3. Spray a nonstick frying pan with Butter Flavor Pam. Heat to medium-high.
4. Add bananas to the mixture (batter should be full of diced bananas).
5. Pour the batter onto frying pan about ¼ cup at a time, making several pancakes at once.

PER SERVING
CALORIES
259
PROTEIN
7.2 g
SODIUM
39 mg
CARBOHYDRATE
59.4 g
FAT
1.5 g
CHOLESTEROL
1 mg

(continued)

6. With rubber spatula turn pancakes when they are bubbly and the bubbles burst. Cook until the underside is golden brown.

7. Place the pancakes on a heated platter. Repeat the cooking process. As needed, clean the pan and respray with Pam to avoid a burned look.

OATMEAL APPLE-RAISIN PANCAKES

MAKES 10 PANCAKES
SERVING SIZE: 2 PANCAKES

PER SERVING
CALORIES
267
PROTEIN
9.6 g
SODIUM
379 mg
CARBOHYDRATE
55.4 g
FAT
1.4 g
CHOLESTEROL
3 mg

¾ cup whole wheat pastry flour
½ cup oatmeal
¼ cup oat bran
2 tablespoons granulated fructose
2 teaspoons baking powder
¼ teaspoon ground cinnamon
1 ½-ounce packet Butter Buds
1 egg white
1⅓ cups evaporated skim milk
½ cup raisins
1 cup finely chopped peeled Red Delicious apple

1. Combine the first 7 ingredients in a large bowl.

2. Whisk together egg white and evaporated skim milk. Add to the dry ingredients and mix. Fold in raisins and apples.

3. Spray a nonstick frying pan with Pam. Heat over medium-high heat.

4. Pour about ¼ cup batter onto frying pan at a time, making several pancakes at once. When pancakes are bubbly and the bubbles start to burst, turn with a spatula. Cook until golden brown.

5. Place pancakes on a heated platter. Repeat cooking process until batter is used up, wiping the pan out and respraying with Pam as needed.

6. Sprinkle with Equal sweetener or serve with unsweetened jam or applesauce. They're great just plain!

PUMPKIN PANCAKES

M A K E S   1 0   P A N C A K E S
S E R V I N G   S I Z E :   A B O U T   2   P A N C A K E S

1 cup whole wheat pastry flour
2 teaspoons baking powder
¼ teaspoon baking soda
⅛ teaspoon ground nutmeg
1 ½-ounce packet Butter Buds
3 tablespoons granulated fructose
½ teaspoon dried orange rind
2 egg whites
¾ cup low-fat buttermilk
1 cup canned pumpkin puree

1. Combine the first 7 ingredients in a large bowl. Mix well.
2. Beat together egg whites and low-fat buttermilk. Stir in pumpkin. Add to dry ingredients and blend well.
3. Spray a nonstick frying pan with Pam. Heat over medium-high heat.
4. Pour about ¼ cup batter onto frying pan at a time, making several pancakes at once. When pancakes are bubbly and the bubbles start to burst, turn with a spatula. Cook until golden brown.
5. Place pancakes on heated platter. Repeat cooking process until batter is used up, wiping the pan out and respraying with Pam as needed.
6. Serve with Equal sweetener, unsweetened applesauce, unsweetened jelly, or Aunt Jemima or Log Cabin Lite Syrup.

PER SERVING
CALORIES
244
PROTEIN
6.3 g
SODIUM
606 mg
CARBOHYDRATE
52.4 g
FAT
0.9 g
CHOLESTEROL
2 mg

BROWN RICE–PINEAPPLE CEREAL

S E R V E S   4

PER SERVING
CALORIES
278
PROTEIN
8.6 g
SODIUM
330 mg
CARBOHYDRATE
60.5 g
FAT
1 g
CHOLESTEROL
3 mg

3 cups cooked brown rice
½ cup chopped dried pineapple
¼ cup raisins
1 cup evaporated skim milk
1 ½-ounce packet Butter Buds

1. Place all ingredients in a saucepan. Mix well.
2. Bring to a boil over medium-high heat, stirring constantly. Cook for 1 minute.
3. Reduce heat to low, cover, and simmer for 5 to 7 minutes.

OATMEAL AND PRUNES CEREAL

S E R V E S   2

PER SERVING
CALORIES
228
PROTEIN
7.2 g
SODIUM
536 mg
CARBOHYDRATE
47.1 g
FAT
1.9 g
CHOLESTEROL
3 mg

1 cup water
¼ cup chopped pitted prunes
⅔ cup oatmeal
1 ½-ounce packet Butter Buds
½ cup skim milk
Equal sweetener to taste

1. Place water and prunes in a saucepan. Bring to a boil.
2. Add oatmeal, Butter Buds, and skim milk. Cook over medium-high heat for 1 minute, stirring several times.
3. Let stand for a few minutes before serving. Add Equal as desired.

BAKED BREAKFAST TOAST

SERVES 8

½ teaspoon ground cinnamon
3 egg whites
½ cup (1 4-ounce can) apple juice concentrate (100 percent natural)
1 ½-ounce packet Butter Buds
8 thin slices whole wheat bread

---

1. Preheat oven to 400°. Spray a 9- by 13-inch pan with Pam.
2. Beat together cinnamon, egg whites, apple juice concentrate, and Butter Buds until the Butter Buds are dissolved.
3. Soak bread in egg white mixture. Do not leave bread in liquid too long or it may fall apart.
4. Arrange slices in prepared baking dish. Bake for 10 minutes. Turn slices over and bake for another 10 minutes or until golden brown. You may have to wipe out the baking dish and respray with Pam to avoid a burned look.
5. Sprinkle with Equal or serve with "Fried" Apples (page 199), Blueberry Sauce (page 173), or Strawberry Sauce (page 175).

PER SERVING	
CALORIES	88
PROTEIN	3.9 g
SODIUM	264 mg
CARBOHYDRATE	17.1 g
FAT	0.8 g
CHOLESTEROL	1 mg

APPETIZERS

DILL DIP

MAKES 1 CUP
SERVING SIZE: 2 TABLESPOONS

PER SERVING
CALORIES
26
PROTEIN
3.6 g
SODIUM
116 mg
CARBOHYDRATE
2.1 g
FAT
0.3 g
CHOLESTEROL
1 mg

1 cup low-fat cottage cheese
1 tablespoon dried minced onion
2 tablespoons lemon juice
¼ teaspoon dried dill weed

1. Place all ingredients in a food processor or blender. Mix until smooth.
2. Serve with fresh vegetables or whole wheat crackers or as a potato topping.

HUMMUS

MAKES 1¼ CUPS
SERVING SIZE: ¼ CUP

PER SERVING
CALORIES
132
PROTEIN
7 g
SODIUM
404 mg
CARBOHYDRATE
23.2 g
FAT
1.6 g
CHOLESTEROL
1 mg

1 19-ounce can chick-peas, drained
1 teaspoon dried minced garlic
1 ½-ounce packet Butter Buds
2 teaspoons lemon juice
1 teaspoon tamari soy sauce
1 teaspoon water

1. Place all ingredients in a food processor or blender. Mix until smooth.
2. Serve as a dip with raw vegetables or as a spread with whole wheat melba toast.

ONION DIP

MAKES 2 CUPS
SERVING SIZE: ½ CUP

1 16-ounce carton plain low-fat yogurt
1 1.2-ounce package dry Lipton Onion Recipe Soup Mix (package marked 20% less salt)
½ teaspoon curry powder

1. Mix ingredients well and chill for several hours.
2. Serve as a dip for raw vegetables or as a topping for baked potato or spread on whole wheat bread, bagels, or crackers.

PER SERVING	
CALORIES	65
PROTEIN	4.1 g
SODIUM	218 mg
CARBOHYDRATE	7.4 g
FAT	2.1 g
CHOLESTEROL	9 mg

PINTO BEAN DIP

MAKES 2 CUPS
SERVING SIZE: ¼ CUP

2 15-ounce cans pinto beans, drained and rinsed
¼ cup Kraft Grated American Cheese Food, Sharp Cheddar Flavor
¼ cup chopped onion
1 tablespoon chili powder

1. Place all ingredients in a food processor or blender. Mix until smooth.
2. Use as a dip for fresh vegetables or spread on whole wheat melba toast or crackers. This dip is also good for bean burritos. Serve with flour tortillas, chopped onion, and tomatoes.

PER SERVING	
CALORIES	96
PROTEIN	5.9 g
SODIUM	43 mg
CARBOHYDRATE	16.2 g
FAT	1.2 g
CHOLESTEROL	2 mg

QUICK PITA PIZZA APPETIZER

SERVES 8

PER SERVING
CALORIES
49
PROTEIN
2.4 g
SODIUM
99 mg
CARBOHYDRATE
7.9 g
FAT
1.2 g
CHOLESTEROL
2 mg

2 large whole wheat pita bread loaves
1 cup low-sodium spaghetti sauce
2 tablespoons dried minced onion
¼ cup grated Parmesan cheese

1. Preheat oven to 425°. Split each pita loaf into 2 rounds. Toast lightly in oven.
2. Spray a nonstick cookie sheet with Pam. Place the 4 pita rounds on cookie sheet. Spread each with ¼ cup spaghetti sauce, ½ tablespoon onion, and 1 tablespoon cheese.
3. Bake for 4 to 6 minutes or until hot and bubbly. Cut each round into quarters and serve immediately.

SOUPS AND STEWS

CHICKEN BROWN RICE SOUP

MAKES 8 CUPS
SERVING SIZE: ABOUT ¾ CUP

1 cup thinly sliced celery
2 cups coarsely chopped carrots
½ cup chopped onion
5½ cups defatted chicken broth
1 ½-ounce packet Butter Buds
½ teaspoon dried oregano
½ teaspoon pepper
½ teaspoon garlic powder
1 teaspoon dried dill weed
1 14½-ounce can whole tomatoes, drained and chopped
½ cup low-sodium tomato sauce
1 cup frozen corn kernels
1¼ cups cubed cooked chicken
1 cup brown rice
1 bay leaf

PER SERVING
CALORIES
119
PROTEIN
10.8 g
SODIUM
623 mg
CARBOHYDRATE
17.2 g
FAT
1.2 g
CHOLESTEROL
16 mg

1. Spray a Dutch oven with Pam. Place the celery, carrots, and onions in pot and cook over medium-high heat for 5 minutes, stirring constantly. Add a little water if necessary to prevent sticking.
2. Add chicken broth and bring to a boil. Reduce heat to low and simmer for 5 minutes.
3. Add remaining ingredients and simmer for 20 minutes, stirring frequently.

LENTIL PASTA SOUP

MAKES 8 CUPS
SERVING SIZE: ABOUT ¾ CUP

PER SERVING	
CALORIES	
143	
PROTEIN	
9.7 g	
SODIUM	
597 mg	
CARBOHYDRATE	
25.1 g	
FAT	
0.5 g	
CHOLESTEROL	
0 mg	

½ cup finely chopped onion
½ cup finely chopped carrot
½ cup finely chopped celery
1 cup finely chopped tomato
1 cup lentils, washed and picked over
1½ quarts defatted chicken broth
dash of pepper
1 ½-ounce packet Butter Buds
1 cup ditalini pasta

1. Spray a Dutch oven with Pam. Place onion, carrots, and celery in pot and cook over medium-high heat for 5 to 7 minutes, stirring constantly.
2. Add tomatoes and cook for 3 minutes more.
3. Add lentils, chicken broth, pepper, and Butter Buds. Bring to a boil. Reduce heat to low, cover, and simmer for 30 minutes, stirring frequently.
4. Add ditalini. Cook for 10 minutes more or until pasta is tender.

LIMA BEAN CHOWDER

MAKES 8 CUPS
SERVING SIZE: ABOUT ¾ CUP

PER SERVING	
CALORIES	
169	
PROTEIN	
8.6 g	
SODIUM	
451 mg	
CARBOHYDRATE	
32.6 g	
FAT	
1.4 g	
CHOLESTEROL	
3 mg	

2 cups chopped onion
2 cups cubed peeled potato
3 cups defatted chicken broth
3 cups frozen lima beans
1 ½-ounce packet Butter Buds
¼ teaspoon pepper
2 cups frozen corn kernels
⅓ cup Kraft Grated American Cheese Food, Sharp Cheddar Flavor

1. Spray a 3-quart saucepan with Butter Flavor Pam. Add onion and cook over medium-high heat until tender. Add potatoes, chicken broth, lima beans, Butter Buds, and pepper.
2. Bring to a boil. Reduce heat to low, cover, and simmer for 10 minutes.

3. Add corn and cook for 10 minutes more, stirring occasionally. While stirring, mash some of the potatoes against the side of the pan with the back of spoon.
4. Stir in cheese and cook for 5 minutes more.

QUICK CORN SOUP

SERVES 6

3 cups evaporated skim milk
1 ½-ounce packet Butter Buds
2 tablespoons chopped onion
⅛ teaspoon white pepper
2 cups cooked corn kernels
1 cup defatted chicken broth

1. Place the evaporated skim milk, Butter Buds, onion, pepper, and 1¼ cups of the corn in a food processor or blender. Mix until smooth.
2. Place pureed ingredients in a saucepan. Add the chicken broth and remaining corn. Cook over medium-high heat, stirring constantly, until heated through. Be careful not to curdle milk by overheating.

PER SERVING	
CALORIES	
172	
PROTEIN	
12.6 g	
SODIUM	
449 mg	
CARBOHYDRATE	
31 g	
FAT	
0.7 g	
CHOLESTEROL	
5 mg	

THICK MINESTRONE

MAKE 8 CUPS
SERVING SIZE: ABOUT 1¾ CUPS

PER SERVING
CALORIES
162
PROTEIN
9.2 g
SODIUM
491 mg
CARBOHYDRATE
29.9 g
FAT
1.3 g
CHOLESTEROL
1 mg

½ cup sliced carrot
½ cup sliced celery
½ cup chopped onion
1 14½-ounce can chicken broth, defatted
1½ cups water
1 teaspoon dried parsley
1 teaspoon tamari soy sauce
⅛ teaspoon pepper
¾ teaspoon garlic powder
1 28-ounce can Italian plum tomatoes, drained and chopped
1 8-ounce can low-sodium tomato sauce
1 16-ounce can red kidney beans, drained
½ cup ditalini pasta
grated Parmesan cheese

1. Place the first 11 ingredients in a large saucepan. Bring to a boil. Reduce heat to medium and cook for 10 to 15 minutes or until carrots and celery are tender.
2. Add kidney beans and ditalini. Cook for 10 to 15 minutes more or until ditalini is al dente.
3. Serve with a sprinkle (no more than 1 teaspoon) of Parmesan cheese on top of the soup if desired.

WHITE BEAN AND TURKEY STEW

MAKES 4 CUPS
SERVING SIZE: 1 CUP

1 cup chopped onion
1 teaspoon dried minced garlic
½ cup sliced celery
½ teaspoon dried thyme
¼ teaspoon pepper
1 ½-ounce packet Butter Buds
1 tablespoon tomato paste
1¾ cups defatted chicken broth
2 cups chopped cooked turkey
2 19-ounce cans white kidney beans (cannellini), drained
1 bay leaf

PER SERVING	
CALORIES	
386	
PROTEIN	
38.3 g	
SODIUM	
717 mg	
CARBOHYDRATE	
47.3 g	
FAT	
5 g	
CHOLESTEROL	
57 mg	

1. Spray a Dutch oven with Pam. Place onion, garlic, and celery in pan and cook over medium heat until onion is lightly browned.
2. Add remaining ingredients and simmer for 20 to 25 minutes, stirring often.

ZUCCHINI SOUP

MAKES 6 CUPS
SERVING SIZE: 1½ CUPS

4 cups quartered and sliced (¼-inch thick) zucchini
1 14½-ounce can low-sodium tomato sauce
1 cup chopped onion
1½ cups defatted chicken broth
1 tablespoon dried parsley
¼ teaspoon dried oregano
¼ teaspoon garlic powder
⅛ teaspoon pepper
1 teaspoon tamari soy sauce
½ teaspoon dried dill weed
¼ teaspoon dried basil

PER SERVING	
CALORIES	
86	
PROTEIN	
5.4 g	
SODIUM	
367 mg	
CARBOHYDRATE	
17.6 g	
FAT	
0.5 g	
CHOLESTEROL	
0 mg	

1. Place all ingredients in a large saucepan and bring to a boil.
2. Reduce heat to low, cover, and simmer for 10 to 15 minutes or until zucchini is tender.

SALAD DRESSINGS AND SPREADS

BLUE CHEESE DRESSING

MAKES 1⅓ CUPS

SERVING SIZE: ABOUT 2 TABLESPOONS

PER SERVING
CALORIES
16
PROTEIN
2.1 g
SODIUM
100 mg
CARBOHYDRATE
1.1 g
FAT
0.4 g
CHOLESTEROL
2 mg

1 cup low-fat cottage cheese
½ cup skim milk
3 tablespoons reduced-calorie blue cheese dressing (any brand)

1. Place low-fat cottage cheese and skim milk in a food processor or blender. Mix until smooth.
2. Pour into a bowl and add lite blue cheese dressing. Stir to mix. Serve over a fresh garden salad.

BUTTERMILK GARDEN DRESSING

MAKES ½ CUP
SERVING SIZE: UP TO ¼ CUP

½ cup low-fat buttermilk
½ cup chopped fresh parsley
¼ teaspoon dried thyme
½ teaspoon dry mustard

1. Place all ingredients in a food processor or blender. Mix until smooth.
2. Chill to blend flavors and serve over a fresh vegetable salad.

PER SERVING
CALORIES
20
PROTEIN
1.6 g
SODIUM
33 mg
CARBOHYDRATE
2.8 g
FAT
0.6 g
CHOLESTEROL
1 mg

CHEESE SPREAD

MAKES 1 CUP
SERVING SIZE: 2 TABLESPOONS

1 cup low-fat cottage cheese
½ cup Kraft Grated American Cheese Food, Sharp Cheddar Flavor

1. Place ingredients in a food processor or blender. Mix until smooth.

Note: Try a toasted cheese sandwich. Spread 1 tablespoon cheese spread on a whole wheat English muffin. Place in a preheated 350° oven. Cook until top is bubbly and lightly browned.

PER SERVING
CALORIES
37
PROTEIN
4.5 g
SODIUM
174 mg
CARBOHYDRATE
1.1 g
FAT
1.5 g
CHOLESTEROL
6 mg

DELUXE THOUSAND ISLAND DRESSING

MAKES 2 CUPS
SERVING SIZE: 2 TABLESPOONS

PER SERVING
CALORIES
28
PROTEIN
1.9 g
SODIUM
105 mg
CARBOHYDRATE
4.7 g
FAT
0.2 g
CHOLESTEROL
1 mg

¾ cup low-fat cottage cheese
¾ cup skim milk
⅓ cup chili sauce
2 tablespoons instant minced onion
½ cup sweet pickle relish, drained and rinsed

1. Place first 4 ingredients in a food processor or blender. Mix until smooth.
2. Pour into a bowl and add relish. Mix well.
3. Chill to blend flavors and serve over a fresh garden salad.

GARLIC ITALIAN DRESSING

MAKES 1⅔ CUPS
SERVING SIZE: ABOUT 1½ TABLESPOONS

PER SERVING
CALORIES
23
PROTEIN
2.9 g
SODIUM
84 mg
CARBOHYDRATE
2.3 g
FAT
0.3 g
CHOLESTEROL
1 mg

¾ cup low-fat cottage cheese
¾ cup skim milk
1½ teaspoons garlic powder
3 tablespoons chopped onion
1 teaspoon Worcestershire sauce
½ teaspoon dry mustard
1 teaspoon dried oregano
1 tablespoon chopped fresh parsley
1 tablespoon wine vinegar

1. Place all ingredients in a food processor or blender. Mix until smooth.
2. Chill to blend flavors and serve over a fresh garden salad.

HAAS MAYONNAISE SPREAD

MAKES ¾ CUP
SERVING SIZE: 2 TABLESPOONS

1 cup low-fat cottage cheese
2 teaspoons lemon juice
½ teaspoon tamari soy sauce
1 teaspoon prepared mustard

1. Combine all ingredients in a food processor or blender. Mix until completely smooth.
2. Chill.

PER SERVING
CALORIES
28.4
PROTEIN
4.7 g
SODIUM
176 mg
CARBOHYDRATE
1.2 g
FAT
0.4 g
CHOLESTEROL
0.2 mg

SCALLION SALAD DRESSING

MAKES 1 CUP
SERVING SIZE: 2 TABLESPOONS

½ cup chopped scallions
½ cup no-oil Italian dressing*
1 tablespoon lemon juice
1 teaspoon tamari soy sauce
¼ cup water
⅛ teaspoon pepper

1. Place all ingredients in a food processor or blender. Mix with 4 to 5 quick pulses.
2. Chill and serve over a fresh vegetable salad.

*Supermarkets now carry several brands of no-oil dressings. Check the salad dressing or diet food section of your local stores.

PER SERVING
CALORIES
8
PROTEIN
0.1 g
SODIUM
140 mg
CARBOHYDRATE
1.9 g
FAT
0 g
CHOLESTEROL
0 mg

TARRAGON DRESSING

MAKES ¾ CUP
SERVING SIZE: 2 TABLESPOONS

½ cup low-fat cottage cheese
¼ cup no-oil Italian dressing
1 tablespoon lemon juice
1 tablespoon red wine vinegar
1½ teaspoons Worcestershire sauce
1½ teaspoons tamari soy sauce
1 teaspoon dried tarragon

1. Place all ingredients in a blender or food processor. Mix until smooth.
2. Serve over a fresh vegetable salad.

PER SERVING	
CALORIES	19
PROTEIN	2.5 g
SODIUM	206 mg
CARBOHYDRATE	1.9 g
FAT	0.2 g
CHOLESTEROL	1 mg

THICK AND CREAMY HERB DRESSING

MAKES ¾ CUP
SERVING SIZE: 2 TABLESPOONS

¼ cup no-oil Italian dressing
¼ cup low-fat cottage cheese
¼ cup plain low-fat yogurt
¼ cup grated Parmesan cheese
1 teaspoon dried minced garlic
½ teaspoon Italian seasoning

1. Place all ingredients in a food processor or blender. Mix until smooth.
2. Serve over a fresh vegetable salad or serve as a dip. If dressing thickens too much in the refrigerator overnight, add a little skim milk to thin it out.

PER SERVING	
CALORIES	30
PROTEIN	2.9 g
SODIUM	187 mg
CARBOHYDRATE	1.7 g
FAT	1.3 g
CHOLESTEROL	4 mg

ZESTY CHILI DRESSING

MAKES 2 CUPS
SERVING SIZE: 2 TABLESPOONS

½ cup evaporated skim milk
½ cup chili sauce
¼ cup no-oil Italian salad dressing
3 tablespoons chopped onion
3 tablespoons red wine vinegar
1 teaspoon tamari soy sauce
½ teaspoon dried basil
¼ teaspoon hot red pepper flakes

1. Place all ingredients in a blender or food processor. Mix until smooth.
2. Serve over a fresh vegetable salad.

PER SERVING
CALORIES
10
PROTEIN
0.7 g
SODIUM
51 mg
CARBOHYDRATE
2 g
FAT
0 g
CHOLESTEROL
0 mg

SALADS

APPLE-CELERY SALAD

SERVES 4

PER SERVING
CALORIES
154
PROTEIN
5.4 g
SODIUM
133 mg
CARBOHYDRATE
23.3 g
FAT
5.9 g
CHOLESTEROL
1 mg

3 cups cubed (unpeeled) Red Delicious apples
1 cup sliced celery
3 tablespoons toasted sesame seeds
¼ cup Haas Mayonnaise Spread (page 191)
lettuce leaves

1. Place first 3 ingredients in a large bowl.
2. Add Haas Mayonnaise Spread and toss to coat.
3. Chill and divide evenly among 4 bowls lined with lettuce.

BIANCHI'S SHRIMP AND MACARONI SALAD

SERVES 10

PER SERVING
CALORIES
245
PROTEIN
18.2 g
SODIUM
246 mg
CARBOHYDRATE
38.6 g
FAT
1.5 g
CHOLESTEROL
47 mg

2 cups (10½ ounces) cooked, peeled and deveined, and chopped shrimp
1 cup finely chopped carrots
1 cup finely chopped celery
½ cup finely chopped onion
1 pound macaroni, cooked according to package directions
1 tablespoon celery seed
¼ teaspoon pepper
1¼ cups Haas Mayonnaise Spread (page 191)
2 tablespoons skim milk
3 tablespoons lemon juice

1. Place first 5 ingredients in a large bowl. Mix well.
2. Place remaining ingredients in a small bowl. Mix well. Pour over shrimp mixture and toss to coat.
3. Chill to blend flavors.

CREAMY POTATO SALAD

M A K E S   5   C U P S
S E R V I N G   S I Z E :   ¾   T O   1   C U P

¾ cup low-fat cottage cheese
¼ cup plain low-fat yogurt
2 tablespoons white vinegar
1 ½-ounce packet Butter Buds
¼ teaspoon pepper
1 cup sliced celery
¼ cup coarsely chopped onion
4 cups peeled and cubed cooked potatoes

1. Combine the first 5 ingredients in a food processor or blender. Mix until smooth.
2. Place remaining ingredients in a large bowl. Mix. Pour cottage cheese mixture over vegetables and toss to coat.
3. Chill before serving.

PER SERVING	
CALORIES	113
PROTEIN	6.3 g
SODIUM	316 mg
CARBOHYDRATE	21.3 g
FAT	0.6 g
CHOLESTEROL	3 mg

CUCUMBER POTATO SALAD

M A K E S   8   T O   1 0   C U P S
S E R V I N G   S I Z E :   A B O U T   ¾   C U P

¾ cup plain low-fat yogurt
½ cup low-fat cottage cheese
2 teaspoons dried dill weed
3 teaspoons Butter Buds
⅛ teaspoon pepper
3½ cups peeled, seeded, and chopped cucumbers
½ cup chopped scallions, including some of the green
7 cups cooked and quartered (unpeeled) red-skinned potatoes

1. Place the first 5 ingredients in a food processor or blender. Mix until smooth.
2. Combine remaining ingredients in a large bowl. Pour yogurt mixture over the vegetables and toss to coat.
3. Chill before serving.

PER SERVING	
CALORIES	102
PROTEIN	4.4 g
SODIUM	98 mg
CARBOHYDRATE	20.5 g
FAT	0.6 g
CHOLESTEROL	2 mg

CURRIED COLESLAW

MAKES 9 CUPS
SERVING SIZE: ¾ CUP

PER SERVING	
CALORIES	66
PROTEIN	1.7 g
SODIUM	114 mg
CARBOHYDRATE	15 g
FAT	0.6 g
CHOLESTEROL	2 mg

6 cups shredded green cabbage
¾ cup sliced celery
2 cups chopped Red Delicious apples
¼ cup raisins
1 cup plain low-fat yogurt
1 tablespoon lemon juice
4 packets Equal sweetener
1 ½-ounce packet Butter Buds
½ teaspoon curry powder

1. Place cabbage, celery, apples, and raisins in a large bowl. Toss to mix.
2. Combine remaining ingredients in a small bowl and mix well.
3. Pour over cabbage mixture and toss to coat.
4. Chilll before serving.

SWEET POTATO SALAD

SERVES 10

PER SERVING	
CALORIES	112
PROTEIN	1.7 g
SODIUM	13 mg
CARBOHYDRATE	26.5 g
FAT	0.8 g
CHOLESTEROL	1 mg

3 cups cooked, peeled, and cubed sweet potatoes
2 cups chopped Red Delicious apples
2 cups seedless green grapes
2 cups sliced bananas
¾ cup plain low-fat yogurt
1 tablespoon lemon juice
3 packets Equal sweetener
¼ teaspoon dried orange peel

1. Place the first 4 ingredients in a large bowl. Mix.
2. Mix remaining ingredients in a small bowl. Pour over the sweet potatoes and fruit and toss to coat.
3. Chill before serving.

MACARONI SALAD

SERVES 8

½ pound macaroni, cooked according to package directions
1 cup peeled and chopped cucumber
½ cup thinly sliced radishes
1 cup shredded carrot
1 cup chopped tomato
½ cup evaporated skim milk
½ cup no-oil Italian salad dressing
½ cup low-fat cottage cheese
1 teaspoon dried dill weed
1 ½-ounce packet Butter Buds
½ teaspoon onion powder
1 teaspoon instant minced onion
pinch of pepper

PER SERVING	
CALORIES	
160	
PROTEIN	
7.3 g	
SODIUM	
340 mg	
CARBOHYDRATE	
31 g	
FAT	
0.7 g	
CHOLESTEROL	
2 mg	

1. Combine macaroni with the vegetables.
2. Place remaining ingredients in a food processor or blender. Mix until smooth.
3. Pour dressing over macaroni and vegetables and toss to coat. Chill before serving.

TUNA CHICK-PEA SALAD

SERVES 6

1 cup finely chopped onion
½ teaspoon garlic powder
¼ cup no-oil Italian dressing
2 tablespoons lemon juice
1½ tablespoons wine vinegar
2 cups cooked chick-peas *or* 1 15-ounce can, drained
¼ cup finely chopped fresh parsley
¼ teaspoon pepper
1 6½-ounce can water-packed solid white tuna, drained and flaked

PER SERVING	
CALORIES	
175	
PROTEIN	
16 g	
SODIUM	
528 mg	
CARBOHYDRATE	
24.3 g	
FAT	
1.9 g	
CHOLESTEROL	
19 mg	

1. Place all ingredients in a large bowl and mix well.
2. Chill to blend flavors.

ZUCCHINI-CARROT SALAD

SERVES 4

PER SERVING	
CALORIES	
128	
PROTEIN	
4 g	
SODIUM	
169 mg	
CARBOHYDRATE	
15.6 g	
FAT	
6.5 g	
CHOLESTEROL	
0 mg	

1½ cups zucchini in julienne strips (⅓ by 1½ inches)
2 cups carrots in julienne strips (⅓ by 1½ inches)
1 tablespoon frozen orange juice concentrate
1½ teaspoons Dijon mustard
1 teaspoon red wine vinegar
2 tablespoons no-oil Italian dressing
1 teaspoon tamari soy sauce
pinch of dried thyme
pinch of pepper
⅓ cup coarsely chopped walnuts

1. Place zucchini and carrots in a large bowl. Mix.
2. Place remaining ingredients except walnuts in a food processor or blender. Mix until smooth. Add walnuts and pulse until walnuts are coarsely ground.
3. Pour mixture over carrots and zucchini. Toss to coat.

SIDE DISHES

DILLED CORN AND SNOW PEAS

SERVES 6 AS A SIDE DISH

2 17-ounce cans corn, drained
2 6-ounce packages frozen snow peas
¾ cup water
1 ½-ounce packet Butter Buds
½ teaspoon dried dill weed
⅛ teaspoon pepper

1. Place all ingredients in a saucepan and bring to a boil.
2. Reduce heat to low and simmer, covered, for 2 to 3 minutes or until snow peas are tender-crisp. Serve as a side dish or as a meal over hot cooked brown rice.

PER SERVING	
CALORIES	130
PROTEIN	5.6 g
SODIUM	225 mg
CARBOHYDRATE	28 g
FAT	1 g
CHOLESTEROL	0 mg

"FRIED" APPLES

MAKES 1½ CUPS
SERVING SIZE: ¼ CUP

1 6-ounce can pure apple juice concentrate
2 ½-ounce packets Butter Buds
4 cups peeled sliced apples
1 packet Equal sweetener

1. Pour apple juice concentrate into a nonstick frying pan. Heat over medium-high heat.
2. Gradually add Butter Buds. Stir until dissolved.
3. Add apples and raise heat to high. Cook until liquid has evaporated, stirring constantly. Add Equal sweetener and stir.
4. Serve with whole wheat pancakes, English muffins, or toasted bagels or as a side dish with an egg white omelet. Serve warm or chilled.

PER SERVING	
CALORIES	119
PROTEIN	0.6 g
SODIUM	335 mg
CARBOHYDRATE	29.7 g
FAT	0.4 g
CHOLESTEROL	1 mg

MACARONI AND CHEESE

SERVES 6

PER SERVING	
CALORIES	220
PROTEIN	12.3 g
SODIUM	245 mg
CARBOHYDRATE	34.5 g
FAT	3.4 g
CHOLESTEROL	11 mg

¼ teaspoon dry mustard
⅛ teaspoon pepper
1 cup evaporated skim milk
½ cup low-fat cottage cheese
¾ cup Kraft Grated American Cheese Food, Sharp Cheddar Flavor
½ pound macaroni, cooked according to package directions

1. Preheat oven to 350°. Spray a 2-quart casserole dish with Butter Flavor Pam.
2. Place the first 5 ingredients in a food processor or blender. Mix until smooth.
3. Place macaroni in the prepared casserole dish. Pour cheese mixture over macaroni. Bake for 20 to 25 minutes or until top is bubbly.

MASHED POTATO PIE

SERVES 8

PER SERVING	
CALORIES	106
PROTEIN	6 g
SODIUM	479 mg
CARBOHYDRATE	19.6 g
FAT	0.6 g
CHOLESTEROL	3 mg

4 cups peeled and cubed potatoes
1 cup chopped onion
½ cup skim milk
3 ½-ounce packets Butter Buds
½ cup low-fat cottage cheese
¼ teaspoon garlic powder
1 tablespoon grated Parmesan cheese
⅛ teaspoon pepper
4 egg whites

1. Preheat oven to 350°. Spray a 9-inch deep-dish pie pan with Butter Flavor Pam.
2. Place potatoes in a saucepan and cover with water. Bring to a boil. Boil for 20 to 25 minutes or until tender. Drain.
3. While potatoes are cooking, spray a nonstick frying pan with Pam. Add onion and cook over medium heat for 5 to 8 minutes or until browned. Set aside.
4. Place potatoes and skim milk in a bowl. Mix with an electric mixer or hand masher until smooth. Stir in onions.

(continued)

5. Place remaining ingredients in a food processor or blender. Mix until smooth. Fold into potatoes.

6. Spoon mixture into prepared pie pan. Spread evenly. Cook for 45 to 50 minutes or until golden brown on top.

OVEN "FRENCH FRIES"

SERVES 2

1 large potato, peeled and cut into ½-inch-thick strips
3 egg whites
1½ tablespoons grated Parmesan cheese
pinch of pepper

1. Preheat oven to 400°. Spray a cookie sheet with Pam.

2. Whisk together egg whites, Parmesan cheese, and pepper.

3. Dip potato strips in egg white mixture to coat.

4. Arrange potatoes on prepared cookie sheet. Bake for 15 minutes. Turn and cook for 15 minutes more or until golden brown.

5. Serve with ketchup on the side.

PER SERVING	
CALORIES	325
PROTEIN	19.4 g
SODIUM	289 mg
CARBOHYDRATE	54.6 g
FAT	3.4 g
CHOLESTEROL	6 mg

POTATOES AU GRATIN

SERVES 8

7 cups cooked, peeled, and sliced potatoes (preferably baked)
1 ½-ounce packet Butter Buds
1½ cups low-fat cottage cheese
½ cup low-fat yogurt
⅛ teaspoon pepper
½ cup Kraft Grated American Cheese Food, Sharp Cheddar Flavor
½ cup skim milk

1. Preheat oven to 350°. Spray a 2-quart casserole dish with Pam.

2. Place potatoes in a large bowl. Place rest of ingredients in a food processor or blender. Mix until smooth.

3. Pour over potatoes. Toss to coat. Spoon into prepared casserole dish. Bake for 30 to 35 minutes or until hot and bubbly.

PER SERVING	
CALORIES	185
PROTEIN	10.5 g
SODIUM	376 mg
CARBOHYDRATE	30.9 g
FAT	2.2 g
CHOLESTEROL	8 mg

ENTRÉES

BAKED GARLIC SNAPPER

SERVES 4

PER SERVING	
CALORIES	
475	
PROTEIN	
99.2 g	
SODIUM	
385 mg	
CARBOHYDRATE	
1.5 g	
FAT	
5 g	
CHOLESTEROL	
171 mg	

3 egg whites
1½ teaspoons garlic powder
1 tablespoon grated Parmesan cheese
4 snapper fillets
lemon wedges

1. Preheat oven to 350°. Spray a 12- by 8-inch baking dish with Pam.
2. Whisk together the first 3 ingredients. Dip each fillet in the mixture to coat. Arrange fillets in baking dish.
3. Bake for 10 minutes. Turn fillets and bake for 20 minutes more. Serve with lemon wedges.

BAKED ORANGE CHICKEN

SERVES 4

PER SERVING	
CALORIES	
207	
PROTEIN	
24.6 g	
SODIUM	
302 mg	
CARBOHYDRATE	
21.4 g	
FAT	
2.2 g	
CHOLESTEROL	
79 mg	

4 skinned chicken breast halves (2 pounds total)
1 ½-ounce packet Butter Buds
¾ cup frozen orange juice concentrate
¼ teaspoon dried orange peel
¼ cup water
1 teaspoon ground ginger
½ teaspoon ground allspice

1. Preheat oven to 350°. Spray a 12- by 8-inch baking dish with Butter Flavor Pam.
2. Arrange chicken in baking dish.
3. Whisk together remaining ingredients until Butter Buds are dissolved. Pour over chicken.
4. Bake for 50 to 60 minutes or until chicken is no longer pink in the middle, basting often with orange juice in baking dish.

CHICKEN CACCIATORE

SERVES 4

4 skinned chicken breast halves (2 pounds total)
pepper to taste
1 medium-size onion, sliced into 1/2-inch rings
1 teaspoon dried minced garlic
1 28-ounce can tomatoes, drained and chopped
1 14 1/2-ounce can low-sodium tomato sauce
1/2 teaspoon dried basil
1/2 teaspoon dried oregano
1 teaspoon tamari soy sauce
1 pound linguine, cooked according to package directions

PER SERVING
CALORIES
606
PROTEIN
40.6 g
SODIUM
279 mg
CARBOHYDRATE
100.6 g
FAT
4.1 g
CHOLESTEROL
78 mg

1. Spray a large nonstick frying pan with Olive Oil Pam. Sprinkle chicken breasts with pepper and brown in frying pan over medium heat. Remove from pan and set aside.
2. Respray pan with Pam. Add onion and garlic and cook until browned. Add remaining ingredients except linguine. Cook for 5 to 7 minutes.
3. Return chicken to pan, cover, and simmer for 20 to 30 minutes or until chicken is no longer pink in center.
4. Arrange linguine on a serving platter. Spoon chicken breasts and sauce over spaghetti.

CREAMY CHICKEN CASSEROLE

SERVES 8

PER SERVING	
CALORIES	253
PROTEIN	27.9 g
SODIUM	499 mg
CARBOHYDRATE	25.2 g
FAT	4.1 g
CHOLESTEROL	56 mg

1 cup chopped onion
2 cups sliced celery
¾ cup sliced mushrooms
¾ cup defatted chicken broth
1¼ cups evaporated skim milk
¼ teaspoon garlic powder
1 ½-ounce packet Butter Buds
¼ teaspoon pepper
1 cup low-fat cottage cheese
½ cup Kraft Grated American Cheese Food, Sharp Cheddar Flavor
3 cups cubed cooked chicken
3 cups cooked brown rice

1. Preheat oven to 350°. Spray a 12- by 8-inch baking dish with Butter Flavor Pam.
2. Spray a nonstick frying pan with Butter Flavor Pam. Add onion and celery and cook over medium heat 5 to 8 minutes until tender, adding a little water to the pan during cooking. Add mushrooms and cook for 2 to 3 minutes more.
3. Place chicken broth, evaporated skim milk, garlic powder, Butter Buds, pepper, low-fat cottage cheese, and Kraft cheese in a food processor or blender. Mix until smooth.
4. Place chicken, brown rice, onion, celery, and mushrooms in a large bowl. Pour cheese mixture over the chicken and mix well.
5. Pour into prepared baking dish. Bake 35 to 40 minutes or until hot and bubbly.

TERIYAKI CHICKEN KABOBS

SERVES 8

1 cup dry sherry
½ cup tamari soy sauce
½ cup water
2 teaspoons ground ginger
½ teaspoon garlic powder
2 teaspoons dry mustard
2 pounds skinned and boned chicken breast, cut into 1-inch cubes
1 medium-size onion, peeled, quartered, and separated into sections

1. Place first 6 ingredients in a bowl. Mix until blended.
2. Using 4 pieces of chicken and 4 pieces of onion for each skewer, alternate chicken and onion on 8 wooden skewers.
3. Arrange skewers in baking dish. Pour marinade over skewers, turning to coat. Marinate for at least 2 hours in refrigerator.
4. Broil for 10 to 15 minutes, turning skewers every 5 minutes and basting with marinade. Serve with steamed brown rice.

PER SERVING
CALORIES
122
PROTEIN
14.5 g
SODIUM
460 mg
CARBOHYDRATE
4.4 g
FAT
1.4 g
CHOLESTEROL
45 mg

EGGPLANT LASAGNE

SERVES 10

PER SERVING
CALORIES
316
PROTEIN
19.5 g
SODIUM
627 mg
CARBOHYDRATE
53 g
FAT
3.5 g
CHOLESTEROL
8 mg

1 large (about 1 pound) eggplant, peeled and cut into ½-inch slices
1 recipe Tomato-Mushroom Spaghetti Sauce (page 210)
1 pound lasagne noodles
1½ pounds low-fat cottage cheese
grated Parmesan cheese

1. Preheat oven to 375°. Spray a 13- by 9-inch baking dish with Olive Oil Pam.
2. Over medium-high heat, cook eggplant slices in a small amount of water in a nonstick frying pan until slices are browned and tender. Add water as needed (it will evaporate quickly).
3. Spread a small amount of sauce on the bottom of the prepared baking dish. Arrange *uncooked* noodles in the bottom of the pan. Spread one third of the low-fat cottage cheese over noodles, sprinkle with 2 tablespoons Parmesan cheese, and top with a few of the eggplant slices. Repeat layers, ending with noodles, sauce, and Parmesan cheese.
4. Bake, covered, for 45 minutes. Remove cover and cook for 10 minutes more. Let cool for 10 minutes before slicing.

LINGUINE ALFREDO

SERVES 4

PER SERVING
CALORIES
292
PROTEIN
13.7 g
SODIUM
474 mg
CARBOHYDRATE
49.7 g
FAT
3.8 g
CHOLESTEROL
10 mg

½ pound linguine, cooked according to package directions
1 ½-ounce packet Butter Buds
½ cup evaporated skim milk
½ cup grated Parmesan cheese
⅛ teaspoon white pepper
pinch of ground nutmeg

1. While linguine is cooking, mix remaining ingredients in a saucepan over medium heat. Heat through, stirring constantly.
2. Add cooked linguine to pan and toss to coat.

PASTA PIE

SERVES 6

1 cup chopped onion
1 teaspoon dried minced garlic
1 14½-ounce can tomatoes, drained and chopped
2 teaspoons dried basil
1 teaspoon tamari soy sauce
pinch of hot red pepper flakes
1 tablespoon dried parsley
1 cup low-sodium tomato sauce
5 egg whites, lightly beaten
½ pound spaghetti, cooked according to package directions
7 tablespoons grated Parmesan cheese

1. Preheat oven to 350°. Spray a 9-inch pie pan with Olive Oil Flavor Pam.
2. Spray a nonstick frying pan with Olive Oil Pam, add onion, and cook over medium heat until brown.
3. Place all the ingredients in a large bowl except 3 tablespoons of the Parmesan cheese. Mix well.
4. Pour mixture into prepared pie pan. Spread evenly. Sprinkle top with remaining Parmesan cheese.
5. Bake for 45 minutes. Let stand for 10 minutes before cutting into 2-inch pie slices.

PER SERVING	
CALORIES	218
PROTEIN	11.3 g
SODIUM	449 mg
CARBOHYDRATE	36.9 g
FAT	2.6 g
CHOLESTEROL	5 mg

VEGETABLE PASTA CASSEROLE

SERVES 8

PER SERVING
CALORIES
177
PROTEIN
11.2 g
SODIUM
167 mg
CARBOHYDRATE
29.3 g
FAT
2 g
CHOLESTEROL
5 mg

½ pound pasta shells, cooked according to package directions
½ cup sliced fresh mushrooms
1 10-ounce package frozen chopped broccoli, defrosted and squeezed dry
1 10-ounce package frozen chopped cauliflower, defrosted and squeezed dry
½ cup low-fat cottage cheese
¾ cup evaporated skim milk
¼ cup plus 2 tablespoons grated Parmesan cheese
1 tablespoon dried parsley
½ teaspoon dried oregano
½ teaspoon dried basil
½ teaspoon garlic powder
⅛ teaspoon dried marjoram

1. Preheat oven to 350°. Spray a 12- by 8-inch baking dish with Pam.
2. Toss pasta, mushrooms, broccoli, and cauliflower in a large bowl.
3. Place remaining ingredients except 2 tablespoons Parmesan cheese in a food processor or blender. Mix until smooth.
4. Pour over pasta mixture and toss to coat. Spoon into prepared baking dish. Sprinkle top with remaining Parmesan cheese.
5. Bake for 30 minutes or until hot and bubbly.

BASIL AND TOMATO SAUCE

SERVES 4

1 teaspoon dried minced garlic
½ cup finely chopped onion
3 28-ounce cans peeled Italian tomatoes, drained and finely chopped (reserve liquid)
1 teaspoon dried basil
½ teaspoon hot red pepper flakes

1. Spray a large nonstick frying pan with Olive Oil Pam. Brown garlic and onion in pan.
2. Add rest of ingredients. Simmer for 30 minutes. Add 2 to 3 tablespoons of the reserved tomato liquid if needed.
3. Serve over freshly cooked spaghetti.

PER SERVING
CALORIES
31
PROTEIN
1.4 g
SODIUM
122 mg
CARBOHYDRATE
6.7 g
FAT
0.2 g
CHOLESTEROL
0 mg

TURKEY MEATBALLS

SERVES 8

1 pound ground turkey
¾ cup whole wheat bread crumbs
2 egg whites
½ teaspoon garlic powder
1 tablespoon grated Parmesan cheese
2 tablespoons finely chopped onion
½ teaspoon dried oregano
⅛ teaspoon pepper
1 recipe Spaghetti Sauce (recipe follows)
1 16-ounce package spaghetti, cooked according to package directions

1. Preheat oven to 350°. Spray a cookie sheet with Pam.
2. Combine first 8 ingredients in a large bowl. Mix well. Form mixture into 1-inch balls (makes approximately 18 to 20).
3. Place on cookie sheet. Bake for 10 minutes. Turn and bake for 10 minutes more.
4. Place meatballs in spaghetti sauce. Bring to a boil. Reduce heat and simmer for 10 minutes.
5. Serve over freshly cooked spaghetti.

PER SERVING
CALORIES
351
PROTEIN
26.4 g
SODIUM
139 mg
CARBOHYDRATE
50.8 g
FAT
4.1 g
CHOLESTEROL
44 mg

SPAGHETTI SAUCE

SERVES 4

PER SERVING	
CALORIES	101
PROTEIN	4.2 g
SODIUM	185 mg
CARBOHYDRATE	23.1 g
FAT	0.9 g
CHOLESTEROL	0 mg

¾ cup chopped onion
1½ teaspoons dried minced garlic
2 15-ounce cans low-sodium tomato sauce
1 15-ounce can tomatoes, drained and chopped
1 teaspoon granulated fructose
2 tablespoons chopped fresh parsley
1 teaspoon dried oregano
⅛ teaspoon pepper
pinch of ground cinnamon
1 bay leaf

1. Place all ingredients in a large saucepan and bring to a boil.
2. Reduce heat to medium-low and simmer for 30 minutes. Serve over hot cooked spaghetti.

TOMATO-MUSHROOM SPAGHETTI SAUCE

SERVES 10

PER SERVING	
CALORIES	66
PROTEIN	2.8 g
SODIUM	255 mg
CARBOHYDRATE	14.5 g
FAT	0.6 g
CHOLESTEROL	0 mg

2 15-ounce cans low-sodium tomato sauce
2 28-ounce cans tomatoes, drained and chopped
1½ cups sliced fresh mushrooms
1 cup finely chopped onion
1 teaspoon dried minced garlic
1 teaspoon dried parsley
1 teaspoon dried oregano
½ teaspoon dried basil
1 packet Butter Buds
¼ teaspoon hot red pepper flakes
1 teaspoon granulated fructose
1 bay leaf

1. Place all ingredients in a large saucepan and bring to a boil.
2. Reduce heat to medium-low and simmer for 30 minutes. Remove bay leaf and serve over hot cooked spaghetti.

HOT BEAN CHILI WITH BROWN RICE

MAKES 4 CUPS
SERVING SIZE: 1 CUP

1 cup chopped onion
½ cup dried minced garlic
1 16-ounce can red kidney beans, drained and rinsed
1 28-ounce can tomatoes, drained and chopped
1 4-ounce can green chilies, drained and chopped
1 teaspoon chili powder
1 cup low-sodium tomato sauce
3 cups hot cooked brown rice

1. Spray a 2-quart saucepan with Pam. Place onion and garlic in saucepan and cook over medium-high heat until onions are tender.
2. Add remaining ingredients, cover, and simmer for 15 minutes.

PER SERVING	
CALORIES	275
PROTEIN	10.1 g
SODIUM	199 mg
CARBOHYDRATE	57.1 g
FAT	1.8 g
CHOLESTEROL	0 mg

TWO-BEAN BAKE

SERVES 10

1 cup chopped onion
1 teaspoon dried minced garlic
1 19-ounce can red kidney beans, drained and rinsed
1 19-ounce can white kidney beans (cannellini), drained and rinsed
1 16-ounce bag frozen corn kernels, cooked according to package directions
1 28-ounce can crushed tomatoes
1 teaspoon dried oregano
1 teaspoon dried dill weed
¼ teaspoon hot red pepper flakes

1. Preheat oven to 350°. Spray a 2-quart casserole dish with Pam.
2. Spray a nonstick frying pan with Pam. Add onion and cook over medium heat until browned. Add garlic and cook for 2 to 3 minutes more.
3. Place remaining ingredients in a large bowl. Add onion and garlic and mix well.
4. Pour into prepared casserole dish and bake for 45 minutes or until hot and bubbly.

PER SERVING	
CALORIES	147
PROTEIN	7.8 g
SODIUM	109 mg
CARBOHYDRATE	29.6 g
FAT	1 g
CHOLESTEROL	0 mg

EGGPLANT PROIETTO

SERVES 4

PER SERVING
CALORIES
117
PROTEIN
11.2 g
SODIUM
416 mg
CARBOHYDRATE
16.3 g
FAT
1.7 g
CHOLESTEROL
4 mg

1 medium-size (about 3/4 pound) eggplant, peeled and cut into 1/2-inch slices
1 cup low-fat cottage cheese
1 egg white
1/2 teaspoon garlic powder
1 tablespoon grated Parmesan cheese
1 tablespoon finely chopped fresh parsley
1/8 teaspoon pepper
2 cups Tomato-Mushroom Spaghetti Sauce (page 210)

1. Preheat oven to 350°. Spray a 12- by 8-inch baking dish with Olive Oil Pam.

2. Over medium-high heat, cook eggplant slices in a small amount of water in a nonstick frying pan until slices are browned and tender. Add water as needed (it will evaporate quickly).

3. Combine remaining ingredients except sauce in a bowl. Mix well.

4. Place 4 slices of the eggplant in the baking dish. Top each slice with 1/4 cup of the cottage cheese mixture. Cover with 4 more slices of eggplant. Pour sauce over eggplant. Use rest of eggplant in another recipe.

5. Bake for 30 to 35 minutes or until hot and bubbly.

EGGPLANT PARMESAN

SERVES 4

1 large (about 1 pound) eggplant, peeled and cut into ½-inch slices
2 cups Spaghetti Sauce (page 210)
4 to 5 tablespoons grated Parmesan cheese

1. Preheat oven to 350°. Spray a 1½-quart baking dish with Olive Oil Pam.
2. Over medium-high heat, cook eggplant slices in a small amount of water in a nonstick frying pan until slices are browned and tender. Add water as needed (it will evaporate quickly).
3. Spoon a small amount of sauce into the bottom of the baking dish. Arrange eggplant slices in dish, top with sauce, and sprinkle with 1 tablespoon Parmesan cheese. Repeat layers, ending with sauce and Parmesan cheese on top.
4. Bake for 30 to 35 minutes or until hot and bubbly.

PER SERVING	
CALORIES	94
PROTEIN	5.1 g
SODIUM	178 mg
CARBOHYDRATE	16.3 g
FAT	2.3 g
CHOLESTEROL	4 mg

STUFFED RED PEPPERS

SERVES 4

½ cup plain low-fat yogurt
1 large egg white, lightly beaten
6 tablespoons Parmesan cheese
½ teaspoon garlic powder
1 teaspoon dried basil
⅛ teaspoon pepper
1 ½-ounce packet Butter Buds
1 10-ounce package frozen chopped broccoli, defrosted and squeezed dry
2 medium-size red bell peppers, halved lengthwise, seeded, and
   membranes removed

1. Preheat oven to 350°. Spray an 8-inch square baking dish with Pam.
2. Combine the first 7 ingredients in a large bowl. Mix well. Add broccoli and toss to coat.
3. Spoon mixture into prepared peppers. Arrange in prepared baking dish.
4. Bake for 30 to 40 minutes or until peppers are fork-tender and filling is hot and bubbly.

PER SERVING	
CALORIES	97
PROTEIN	8.1 g
SODIUM	435 mg
CARBOHYDRATE	10.5 g
FAT	3.2 g
CHOLESTEROL	9 mg

VEGGIE-STUFFED PEPPERS

SERVES 4

PER SERVING	
CALORIES	
231	
PROTEIN	
8.6 g	
SODIUM	
336 mg	
CARBOHYDRATE	
29.6 g	
FAT	
11.1 g	
CHOLESTEROL	
3 mg	

4 medium-size red bell peppers
¾ cup shredded carrot
1½ cups cooked corn kernels
⅓ cup coarsely chopped walnuts
1 ½-ounce packet Butter Buds
2 tablespoons whole wheat bread crumbs
2 tablespoons sesame seeds
2 tablespoons finely chopped onion
2 tablespoons Kraft Grated American Cheese Food, Sharp Cheddar Flavor
1 egg white, lightly beaten

1. Cut off tops of peppers and remove seeds and membranes. Place peppers in a large saucepan of boiling water and boil for 5 minutes. Remove and drain. Preheat oven to 350°.

2. Combine remaining ingredients in a large bowl and blend well.

3. Spoon mixture into prepared peppers. Arrange peppers in a baking dish and bake for 30 minutes or until heated through.

ZUCCHINI FRITTATA

SERVES 8

2 cups shredded zucchini
6 jumbo egg whites
3/4 teaspoon Italian seasoning
1 cup low-fat cottage cheese
1/2 cup Kraft Grated American Cheese Food, Sharp Cheddar Flavor
3/4 teaspoon dried minced garlic
1 1/2-ounce packet Butter Buds
1/8 teaspoon pepper

1. Preheat oven to 350°. Spray a 9-inch pie plate with Pam. Place zucchini in a large bowl and set aside.
2. Place remaining ingredients in a food processor or blender. Mix until smooth.
3. Pour over zucchini and blend. Spoon zucchini mixture into prepared pie dish.
4. Bake for 35 to 40 minutes or until golden and bubbly on top.

PER SERVING	
CALORIES	68
PROTEIN	8.4 g
SODIUM	352 mg
CARBOHYDRATE	4.6 g
FAT	1.7 g
CHOLESTEROL	6 mg

ZUCCHINI ITALIANO

SERVES 6

4 cups sliced (1/4-inch thick) zucchini
2 teaspoons dried minced garlic
1 28-ounce can tomatoes, drained and chopped
3/4 cup low-sodium tomato sauce
1/4 teaspoon pepper
1 teaspoon dried oregano
2 tablespoons finely chopped fresh parsley
3 tablespoons grated Parmesan cheese

1. Preheat oven to 350°. Spray a 13- by 9-inch baking dish with Olive Oil Pam. Arrange zucchini in dish.
2. Spray a nonstick frying pan with Pam. Place remaining ingredients except Parmesan in pan. Cook over medium-high heat for 20 minutes, stirring occasionally.
3. Pour sauce over zucchini. Sprinkle with Parmesan cheese. Bake for 30 minutes or until zucchini is tender.

PER SERVING	
CALORIES	58
PROTEIN	3.3 g
SODIUM	163 mg
CARBOHYDRATE	10.1 g
FAT	1.3 g
CHOLESTEROL	2 mg

BREADS AND MUFFINS

APPLESAUCE BRAN MUFFINS

MAKES 12 MUFFINS
SERVING SIZE: 1 MUFFIN

PER SERVING
CALORIES
118
PROTEIN
2 g
SODIUM
65 mg
CARBOHYDRATE
27.6 g
FAT
0.3 g
CHOLESTEROL
0 mg

1½ cups whole wheat pastry flour
½ cup bran
⅓ cup granulated fructose
1 tablespoon baking powder
½ teaspoon ground cinnamon
⅔ cup raisins
½ cup tightly packed shredded peeled apple
1 cup unsweetened applesauce
2 egg whites
3 tablespoons skim milk

1. Preheat oven to 425°. Spray a 12-cup muffin tin with Pam.
2. Combine all dry ingredients in a large bowl. Add raisins, apples, and applesauce. Blend.
3. Whisk together egg whites and skim milk. Add to dry ingredients and fruit. Mix well.
4. Fill muffin cups ¾ full with batter. Bake for 20 minutes or until golden brown on top.

LIME MUFFINS

MAKES 12 MUFFINS
SERVING SIZE: 1 MUFFIN

2 cups whole wheat pastry flour
1 cup granulated fructose
3 teaspoons baking powder
1 cup tightly packed shredded peeled Red Delicious apple
1 teaspoon grated lime zest
¼ cup evaporated skim milk
2 egg whites
¼ cup lime juice

1. Preheat oven to 375°. Spray a 12-cup muffin tin with Butter Flavor Pam.
2. Combine the first 3 ingredients in a large bowl. Add the apple and lime zest.
3. Beat together evaporated skim milk, egg whites, and lime juice. Pour into dry ingredients. Mix well.
4. Fill muffin cups ¾ full with batter. Bake for 20 to 25 minutes or until a wooden pick inserted into one of the muffins comes out clean. The muffins should be golden brown on top.

PER SERVING	
CALORIES	153
PROTEIN	2.4 g
SODIUM	69 mg
CARBOHYDRATE	35 g
FAT	0.3 g
CHOLESTEROL	0 mg

OATMEAL-PINEAPPLE MUFFINS

MAKES 12 MUFFINS
SERVING SIZE: 1 MUFFIN

PER SERVING	
CALORIES	124
PROTEIN	4 g
SODIUM	169 mg
CARBOHYDRATE	26.1 g
FAT	0.7 g
CHOLESTEROL	1 mg

1 cup whole wheat pastry flour
¾ cup oats
¼ cup oat bran
1 ½-ounce packet Butter Buds
2 tablespoons granulated fructose
3 teaspoons baking powder
⅔ cup chopped dried pineapple
1 cup tightly packed shredded peeled Red Delicious apple
1 cup evaporated skim milk
1 egg white

1. Preheat oven to 375°. Spray a 12-cup muffin tin with Butter Flavor Pam.
2. Combine first 6 ingredients in a large bowl. Add dried pineapple and apple and mix well.
3. Whisk together evaporated skim milk and egg white. Add to dry mixture. Blend well.
4. Fill each muffin tin ¾ full with batter. Bake for 20 to 25 minutes or until a wooden pick inserted into the middle of one of the muffins comes out clean. The tops should be golden brown.

LEMON BREAD

MAKES 1 LOAF
SERVING SIZE: 1½-INCH SLICE

2 cups whole wheat pastry flour
¾ cup granulated fructose
1 tablespoon baking powder
1 ½-ounce packet Butter Buds
½ cup coarsely chopped pecans
2 tablespoons grated lemon zest
1¼ cups tightly packed shredded peeled Red Delicious apple
2 egg whites
½ cup evaporated skim milk
2 tablespoons lemon juice

1. Preheat oven to 350°. Spray a 9- by 5-inch loaf pan with Butter Flavor Pam.
2. Combine first 4 ingredients in a large bowl. Mix well.
3. Add pecans, lemon zest, and apple. Mix.
4. Beat together egg whites, evaporated skim milk, and lemon juice. Pour into dry mixture. Blend well.
5. Pour into prepared loaf pan. Bake for 40 to 50 minutes or until a wooden pick inserted into the middle of the pan comes out clean.
6. Let cool before slicing.

PER SERVING	
CALORIES	119
PROTEIN	2.1 g
SODIUM	69 mg
CARBOHYDRATE	22.5 g
FAT	2.3 g
CHOLESTEROL	0 mg

PRUNE BREAD

MAKES 1 LOAF
SERVING SIZE: 1½-INCH SLICE

PER SERVING	
CALORIES	
138	
PROTEIN	
1.9 g	
SODIUM	
109 mg	
CARBOHYDRATE	
26.5 g	
FAT	
3.0 g	
CHOLESTEROL	
0 mg	

2 cups whole wheat pastry flour
2 teaspoons baking powder
½ teaspoon baking soda
⅔ cup granulated fructose
1 ½-ounce packet Butter Buds
1 tablespoon grated lemon zest
⅔ cup coarsely chopped pecans
1 cup coarsely chopped prunes
¾ cup tightly packed shredded peeled Red Delicious apple
2 egg whites
¼ cup prune juice
⅓ cup frozen orange juice concentrate

1. Preheat oven to 350°. Spray a 9- by 5-inch loaf pan with Pam.
2. Combine the first 5 ingredients in a large bowl. Add the lemon zest, pecans, prunes, and apple. Blend.
3. Beat together egg whites, prune juice, and orange juice concentrate. Pour into dry ingredients and mix well.
4. Pour mixture into prepared loaf pan. Bake for 50 to 60 minutes or until a wooden pick inserted into the middle of the loaf comes out clean. Let cool before slicing.

SWEET CHEESE BREAD

MAKES 1 LOAF
SERVING SIZE: 1½-INCH SLICE

2 cups whole wheat pastry flour
1 teaspoon baking powder
½ teaspoon baking soda
1 ½-ounce packet Butter Buds
⅔ cup granulated fructose
¾ cup Kraft Grated American Cheese Food, Sharp Cheddar Flavor
2 cups shredded peeled apples
⅓ cup finely chopped walnuts
3 egg whites
¼ cup evaporated skim milk

PER SERVING
CALORIES
127
PROTEIN
3.1 g
SODIUM
142 mg
CARBOHYDRATE
22.2 g
FAT
3.1 g
CHOLESTEROL
3 mg

1. Preheat oven to 350°. Spray a 9- by 5-inch loaf pan with Pam.
2. Combine all dry ingredients in a large bowl. Add cheese, apples, and walnuts. Mix.
3. Beat together egg whites and evaporated skim milk. Pour into dry ingredients. Blend well.
4. Pour into prepared loaf pan. Bake for 50 to 60 minutes or until a wooden pick inserted into the middle of the loaf comes out clean. Let cool before slicing.

ZUCCHINI BREAD

M A K E S   1   L O A F
S E R V I N G   S I Z E : 1½-I N C H   S L I C E

PER SERVING
CALORIES
114
PROTEIN
2.2 g
SODIUM
109 mg
CARBOHYDRATE
21.6 g
FAT
2.2 g
CHOLESTEROL
0 mg

1¾ cups whole wheat pastry flour
1 cup granulated fructose
1 ½-ounce packet Butter Buds
1 teaspoon baking soda
½ teaspoon ground nutmeg
½ cup finely chopped walnuts
1½ cups tightly packed shredded peeled zucchini
3 egg whites
1 teaspoon vanilla extract

1. Preheat oven to 350°. Spray a 9- by 5-inch loaf pan with Butter Flavor Pam.
2. Combine the first 5 ingredients in a large bowl. Mix well.
3. Add walnuts and zucchini. Blend well.
4. Beat together egg whites and vanilla extract. Add to dry mixture. Blend well.
5. Pour batter into the prepared loaf pan. Bake for 50 to 60 minutes or until a wooden pick inserted into the center of the loaf comes out clean.

DESSERTS

BROWNIES

MAKES 16 BARS
SERVING SIZE: 1 BAR

1½ cups whole wheat pastry flour
½ teaspoon baking powder
1 cup shredded peeled apple
1 cup granulated fructose
3 egg whites
⅓ cup evaporated skim milk
3 tablespoons unsweetened cocoa powder
1 teaspoon vanilla extract
1 cup carob chips
½ cup chopped pecans

1. Preheat oven to 350°. Spray an 8-inch square pan with Butter Flavor Pam.
2. Combine all ingredients except carob chips and pecans in a bowl. Mix well.
3. Fold in chips and nuts. Pour batter into prepared baking pan. Bake for 30 to 35 minutes or until a wooden pick inserted into the middle of the pan comes out clean.
4. Cool on rack for 10 to 15 minutes before cutting into 2-inch squares.

PER SERVING	
CALORIES	182
PROTEIN	2.9 g
SODIUM	24 mg
CARBOHYDRATE	30.6 g
FAT	5.7 g
CHOLESTEROL	0 mg

RAISIN BROWNIE CUPCAKES

M A K E S   1 2   C U P C A K E S
S E R V I N G   S I Z E :   1   C U P C A K E

1 cup whole wheat pastry flour
⅔ cup granulated fructose
⅛ cup carob powder
⅛ cup unsweetened cocoa powder
2 teaspoons baking powder
½ cup skim milk
1 egg white
1 teaspoon vanilla extract
⅔ cup shredded peeled Red Delicious apple
1 cup raisins
½ cup chopped pecans

1. Preheat oven to 350°. Spray a 12-cup muffin tin with Butter Flavor Pam.
2. Combine the first 5 ingredients in a large bowl. Set aside.
3. Mix skim milk, egg white, and vanilla extract in a separate bowl. Add to the dry ingredients and blend.
4. Add apple, raisins, and pecans. Mix.
5. Fill muffin tins ¾ full with batter. Bake for 20 to 25 minutes or until a wooden pick inserted into the middle of one of the cupcakes comes out clean.

OATMEAL APPLE SQUARES

MAKES 24 SQUARES
SERVING SIZE: 1 2-INCH SQUARE

1½ cups oatmeal
½ cup whole wheat pastry flour
1 teaspoon baking powder
1¼ cups tightly packed shredded peeled apple
2 cups granulated fructose
3 egg whites
1 tablespoon vanilla extract
1½ cups raisins
1 cup finely ground pecans
3 ½-ounce packet Butter Buds
¼ teaspoon ground cinnamon

1. Preheat oven to 350°. Spray a 13- by 9-inch pan with Butter Flavor Pam.
2. Combine all ingredients in a bowl and mix well. Pour into prepared baking pan.
3. Bake for 45 to 50 minutes or until a wooden pick inserted into the middle of the pan comes out dry. Let cool before cutting into 2-inch squares.

PER SERVING	
CALORIES	187
PROTEIN	2.4 g
SODIUM	142 mg
CARBOHYDRATE	34.1 g
FAT	5.2 g
CHOLESTEROL	0 mg

FRENCH APPLE PIE

SERVES 8

PER SERVING	
CALORIES	
373	
PROTEIN	
2.6 g	
SODIUM	
265 mg	
CARBOHYDRATE	
76.8 g	
FAT	
7.9 g	
CHOLESTEROL	
1 mg	

Filling
6½ cups sliced peeled apples
¾ cup granulated fructose
3 tablespoons whole wheat pastry flour
¾ teaspoon ground cinnamon
1 ½-ounce packet Butter Buds
½ cup raisins
1 tablespoon lemon juice

Topping
¾ cup finely chopped pecans
¾ cup granulated fructose
¼ cup whole wheat pastry flour
1 ½-ounce packet Butter Buds
2 to 3 tablespoons lightly beaten egg whites

1. Preheat oven to 350°. Spray a 9-inch pie plate with Butter Flavor Pam.
2. Combine all filling ingredients in a large bowl. Mix well. Spoon into prepared pie plate.
3. Combine first 4 topping ingredients in a small bowl. Add egg whites 1 tablespoon at a time, mixing with a fork. Mixture should be crumbly.
4. Cover top of pie with mixture. Press lightly with back of fork.
5. Bake for 40 to 50 minutes or until top is golden and pie is bubbly.

LEMON PIE

SERVES 8

8 egg whites
2 tablespoons grated lemon zest
½ cup low-fat cottage cheese
1 cup evaporated skim milk
¾ cup granulated fructose
1 ½-ounce packet Butter Buds

1. Preheat oven to 350°. Spray a 9-inch cake pan with Pam.
2. Place all ingredients in a food processor or blender. Mix until smooth.
3. Pour into prepared cake pan. Bake for 35 to 45 minutes or until golden on top. Chill.

PER SERVING	
CALORIES	135
PROTEIN	7.3 g
SODIUM	266 mg
CARBOHYDRATE	25.1 g
FAT	0.3 g
CHOLESTEROL	2 mg

"CHOCOLATE" PUDDING

SERVES 6

⅔ cup granulated fructose
3 tablespoons unsweetened carob powder
2 tablespoons dry form, low-medium fat, plain cocoa powder
3 tablespoons cornstarch
1¾ cups skim milk

1. Combine all ingredients in a saucepan. Mix until all ingredients have dissolved.
2. Turn heat on medium-high. Stir constantly until the mixture starts to boil. Continue to cook and stir for approximately 1 minute or until the mixture thickens and changes color.
3. Pour the mixture into six small custard cups. Chill.

PER SERVING	
CALORIES	149.3
PROTEIN	2.9 g
SODIUM	37 mg
CARBOHYDRATE	34.2 g
FAT	0.4 g
CHOLESTEROL	1 mg

CHOCOLATE CHERRY CAKE

SERVES 12

PER SERVING	
CALORIES	
244	
PROTEIN	
4 g	
SODIUM	
13 mg	
CARBOHYDRATE	
39.5 g	
FAT	
8.7 g	
CHOLESTEROL	
0 mg	

Filling
16 ounces frozen whole dark sweet pitted cherries, defrosted
¼ cup water
3 tablespoons granulated fructose
1½ tablespoons cornstarch
1½ teaspoons almond flavoring

1. Drain the juice from the cherries into a saucepan. Set cherries aside.
2. Add water, fructose, and cornstarch to the cherry juice. Stir until fructose and cornstarch have dissolved. Turn heat on medium-high. Stir constantly until the sauce thickens and turns clear.
3. Remove from heat. Add cherries and almond flavor. Blend well. Place in refrigerator to cool.

Cake
⅔ cup whole wheat pastry flour
¼ cup unsweetened cocoa powder
¼ cup carob powder
1½ cups chopped walnuts
¾ cup tightly packed shredded peeled apple
1 cup granulated fructose
3 egg whites
3 teaspoons vanilla extract

1. Preheat oven to 350°. Spray an 8-inch cake pan with Butter Flavor Pam.
2. Combine all ingredients except egg whites and vanilla in a large bowl. Set aside.
3. Beat egg whites and vanilla together lightly. Add to the dry ingredients and blend.
4. Pour half of the mixture into a cake pan. Spoon the cherry mixture over the cake mixture. Pour the rest of the cake mixture on top of the cherries. Spread to cover the cherries.
5. Bake for 45 to 50 minutes or until a wooden pick inserted into the middle of the cake comes out clean.

CHERRY FREEZE

SERVES 4

1 16-ounce package frozen unsweetened cherries
4 to 5 packets Equal sweetener
½ teaspoon almond extract
½ cup evaporated skim milk, chilled

1. Place frozen cherries, Equal, and almond extract in a food processor or blender. Mix until consistency is like coarsely chopped ice.
2. With motor running, gradually add evaporated skim milk. Blend until consistency is smooth (2 to 3 seconds). Serve immediately.

PER SERVING	
CALORIES	87
PROTEIN	3.6 g
SODIUM	40 mg
CARBOHYDRATE	17.6 g
FAT	0.4 g
CHOLESTEROL	1 mg

STRAWBERRY FREEZE

SERVES 4

1 20-ounce package frozen strawberries
6 packets Equal sweetener
½ cup evaporated skim milk, chilled

1. Place frozen strawberries and Equal in a food processor or blender. Mix until coarsely chopped.
2. With motor running, gradually add evaporated skim milk. Mix until smooth. Serve immediately.

PER SERVING	
CALORIES	167
PROTEIN	3.3 g
SODIUM	41 mg
CARBOHYDRATE	40.3 g
FAT	0.2 g
CHOLESTEROL	1 mg

APPENDIX II
FOREVER FIT
COMPUTER SOFTWARE

How would you like the luxury of letting your home or office computer analyze your diet and customize any of your favorite recipes to meet the nutritional standards of your new *Forever Fit* Diet?

How would you like the convenience of keeping track of your daily food intake (as well as that of all members of your family) and being able to see an automatically drawn graph of your intake of such nutrients as cholesterol, protein, fat, and sodium each week, as well as chart the daily, weekly, and monthly changes in your body weight?

Would you like a quick way to create a new food recipe, instantly analyze its nutritional content, automatically determine how to prepare it for any number of people, and then get a shopping list of the foods (and amounts of those foods) you need to purchase at the store?

If you would like an easy-to-use computer program that would do all this and much more, then I've created just the computer program for you. It's the new *Forever Fit* Computer Program, and it can help improve the quality of your life and boost your nutrition knowledge daily.

The *Forever Fit* Computer Program contains all of the recipes in this book (as well as 1,350 foods, including many of your favorite brands of fast foods) that you can modify in any way you wish to get an instant nutrition analysis and shopping list. You can also create your own favorite recipes and modify them to meet the nutritional standards of the *Forever Fit* Plan or any other special diet (this is especially useful for people with diabetes, heart disease, and high blood pressure).

Want to know how many calories you burn during any activity, from sex (whether you are the active or passive partner) to swimming? You can instantly find out by using the *Forever Fit* Computer Program's unique Calorie Burner module.

In addition, the *Forever Fit* Computer Program will:

- compare nutrition in foods, recipes, and daily menus;

- determine the percentage of calories from carbohydrate, protein, and fat;

- adjust any recipe to meet individual needs;

- list all recipes that contain a specific food;

- convert food quantities from one measure to another; and

- select food quantities based on nutritional value. For example, request that a food provide 15 grams of protein and the *Forever Fit* Computer Program will determine the proper amount of that food.

The Calorie Burner module will:

- monitor the daily activity and body weight of your entire family;

- compare the number of calories burned by various activities; and

- determine how much time various activities require to burn a desired number of calories. For example, you wish to know how much time you must spend walking at three miles per hour to burn 300 calories; the program will determine the necessary amount of time based on your current body weight.

The *Forever Fit* Computer Program and its Calorie Burner module will work with all IBM™ and IBM™-compatible and Apple™ Macintosh™ computers and are available from:

Small Planet Systems, Inc.
P.O. Box 4011
Tallahassee, FL 32315–4011
(800) 852-6007(toll-free)
(904) 224-9004

APPENDIX III
FOOD COMPOSITION TABLES

The food composition information in the following tables contains values for the six most important nutrients in the *Forever Fit* Diet— calories, fat, cholesterol, sodium, protein, and carbohydrate. For your convenience these tables contain the nutritional breakdown for every recipe in this book and in Robert Haas's bestselling nutrition books, *Eat to Win* and *Eat to Succeed*.

These tables will help you decide how to incorporate any food, *Forever Fit* recipe, or other recipe into your diet without risk of "eating blindly." For example, by simply noting the cholesterol value for the foods and/or recipes you eat each day, you can quickly and easily determine the portion sizes that will keep your cholesterol intake at healthy levels. The information in these tables can even help you decide which and how much of your favorite brand of fast food you can enjoy without overdoing the calories, fat, cholesterol, and sodium.

If you would like to construct, analyze, track, and graph your individual/family diet with a personal computer, consult Appendix II for details concerning the *Forever Fit* Computer Diet Program and the *Forever Fit* Calorie Burner, a computer program that will calculate and graph your daily caloric expenditure and link it to your daily food intake as calculated by the *Forever Fit* Computer Diet Program.

APPETIZERS

	Weight (oz)	Calories	Carbo. (g)	Protein (g)	Fat (g)	Choles. (mg)	Sodium (mg)
Crabmeat Dip, *ETS Recipe: 1 serving*	3.0	81.5	2.3	11.1	1.6	58.2	617.9
Cucumber and Onion Dip, *ETS Recipe: 1 serving*	0.9	17.9	2.2	2.0	0.2	0.7	61.5
Garden Dip, *ETS Recipe: 1 serving*	3.0	38.4	3.5	5.2	0.4	1.8	182.9
Onion Dip, *ETS Recipe: 1 serving*	4.3	65.4	7.4	4.1	2.1	9.1	217.8
Quick Pita Pizza Appetizer, *FF Recipe: 1 serving*	1.6	48.7	7.9	2.4	1.2	2.3	99.5
Salmon Spread, *ETS Recipe: 1 serving*	5.9	193.7	3.6	25.9	7.8	32.4	5018.0
Shrimp Cocktail, *ETS Recipe: 1 serving*	4.4	79.4	3.6	14.3	0.7	85.0	95.6
Stuffed Mushrooms, *ETS Recipe: 1 serving*	3.5	157.6	12.4	7.3	10.1	0.6	198.5

BEVERAGES

	Weight (oz)	Calories	Carbo. (g)	Protein (g)	Fat (g)	Choles. (mg)	Sodium (mg)
Banana Frothy, *ETS Recipe: 8 fluid ounces*	11.6	291.8	46.1	8.8	4.0	4.3	118.7
Beer, *light: 12 fluid ounces*	12.7	100.0	6.0	0.4	0	0	25.0
Beer, *3.6% alcohol by weight: 12 fluid ounces*	12.7	151.2	13.7	1.1	0	0	25.2
Brandy: *1 fluid ounce*	1.0	42.9	2.3	0+	0	0	1.1
Burgundy: *4 fluid ounces*	4.0	97.1	4.8	0.1	0	0	5.7
Chocolate Drink, *commercial, w/skim milk: 12 fluid ounces*	13.0	264.6	38.2	11.8	7.4	25.7	221.2
Chocolate Drink, *commercial, w/whole milk: 12 fluid ounces*	12.9	303.8	37.7	11.7	12.4	43.9	218.1
Chocolate Frothy, *ETS Recipe: 12 fluid ounces*	10.3	136.0	23.3	8.5	1.0	4.6	119.3
Chocolate Malted, *ETS Recipe: 8 fluid ounces*	8.3	199.5	44.6	7.2	0.8	3.0	100.1

	Weight (oz)	Calories	Carbo. (g)	Protein (g)	Fat (g)	Choles. (mg)	Sodium (mg)
Club Soda, *unsweetened: 12 fluid ounces*	12.7	0	0	0	0	0	88.5
Coca-Cola: *12 fluid ounces*	12.7	144.0	36.0	0	0	0	1.0
Cocoa Powder, dry form, low–medium fat, plain: *1 tablespoon*	0.2	11.0	2.7	1.0	0.6	0	0.3
Coconut Milk: *8 fluid ounces*	4.5	322.7	6.7	4.1	31.9	0	32.0
Coffee, *beverage, ground: 8 fluid ounces*	8.3	2.0	0.5	0	0	0	26.0
Coffee, *beverage, instant: 8 fluid ounces*	8.5	2.0	1.2	0	0	0	2.0
Coffee, *instant, decaf., dry form: ½ tablespoon*	0.1	6.0	1.6	0.4	0.1	0	3.0
Coffee, *Sanka, beverage, instant, decaf.: 8 fluid ounces*	8.3	5.0	1.2	0	0	0	0
Cream Soda: *12 fluid ounces*	12.7	154.8	39.6	0	0	0	0
Eggnog, nonalcoholic: *4 fluid ounces*	4.3	176.0	12.6	5.7	11.6	173.6	117.9
Eggnog, w/alcohol: *4 fluid ounces*	4.3	212.0	11.6	5.0	10.9	170.6	107.3
Gatorade, citrus: *12 fluid ounces*	12.2	58.5	15.8	0	0	0	184.5
Gatorade, cola: *12 fluid ounces*	12.2	58.5	13.8	0	0	0	162.0
Gin, 80 proof, 33.4% alcohol by weight: *1 fluid ounce*	1.1	69.3	0	0	0	0	0.3
Ginger Ale, pale dry, golden: *12 fluid ounces*	12.7	111.6	28.8	0	0	0	4.0
Ginger Ale, sugar free: *12 fluid ounces*	12.7	4.0	1.5	0	0	0	32.0
Hawaiian Punch: *12 fluid ounces*	13.2	180.0	43.9	0.1	0	0	75.0
Hot Cocoa, homemade: *8 fluid ounces*	8.5	208.8	24.7	8.6	8.6	31.2	117.8
Kool-Aid, all flavors: *12 fluid ounces*	12.7	150.0	37.5	0	0	0	1.5

Beverages (continued)	Weight (oz)	Calories	Carbo. (g)	Protein (g)	Fat (g)	Choles. (mg)	Sodium (mg)
Mocha Frothy, *ETS Recipe: 8 fluid ounces*	9.4	115.8	20.1	7.7	0.7	4.4	113.7
Mountain Dew: *12 fluid ounces*	12.7	171.0	42.8	0	0	0	31.0
Mr. Pibb: *12 fluid ounces*	12.7	140.0	37.5	0	0	0	17.0
Nog Frothy, *ETS Recipe: 8 fluid ounces*	10.4	134.0	23.6	8.0	0.8	4.6	119.1
Orange Dream, *ETS Recipe: 8 fluid ounces*	9.1	106.3	21.8	3.8	0.4	2.0	52.5
Orange Soda: *12 fluid ounces*	12.7	167.0	45.4	0.1	0	0	18.0
Pepsi-Cola: *12 fluid ounces*	12.7	156.0	39.4	0	0	0	18.0
Pepsi-Cola, sugar free: *12 fluid ounces*	12.7	1.0	0.2	0	0	0	63.0
Pepsi Light: *12 fluid ounces*	12.7	71.0	17.6	0	0	0	12.0
Postum, instant powder: *½ tablespoon*	0.2	15.0	3.7	0.3	0	0	3.0
Quinine Soda, sweetened: *12 fluid ounces*	12.7	111.6	28.8	0	0	0	0
Root Beer, Hires: *12 fluid ounces*	12.7	146.0	39.8	0	0	0	4.0
Root Beer, Hires, sugar free: *12 fluid ounces*	12.7	2.0	0.4	0	0	0	53.0
Royal Crown Cola: *12 fluid ounces*	12.7	156.0	39.0	0	0	0	1.0
Rum, 80 proof, 33.4% alcohol by weight: *1 fluid ounce*	1.1	69.3	0	0	0	0	0
Seven-Up: *12 fluid ounces*	12.7	144.0	36.0	0	0	0	4.0
Sherry, dry: *4 fluid ounces*	4.2	168.0	9.6	0.4	0	0	4.0
Sprite: *12 fluid ounces*	12.7	144.0	62.3	0	0	0	47.0
Sprite, sugar free: *12 fluid ounces*	12.7	5.0	0	0	0	0	48.0

	Weight (oz)	Calories	Carbo. (g)	Protein (g)	Fat (g)	Choles. (mg)	Sodium (mg)
Strawberry Frothy, *ETS Recipe: 8 fluid ounces*	11.6	232.5	29.7	8.5	3.9	4.3	118.4
Tab, sugar-free: *12 fluid ounces*	12.7	1.0	0.1	0	0	0	27.0
Tang, orange, beverage: *12 fluid ounces*	12.7	202.5	50.7	0	0.1	0	25.5
Tang, orange, dry powder: *½ ounce*	0.5	51.5	12.6	0	0+	0	6.5
Tea, instant, beverage: *8 fluid ounces*	8.5	4.8	1.0	0	0	0	1.6
Tea, instant, dry powder: *½ tablespoon*	0.1	8.8	2.4	0	0	0	1.5
Tom Collins Mixer, 10–13% sugar: *4 fluid ounces*	4.4	57.5	15.0	0	0	0	0
Vodka, 80 proof, 33.4% alcohol by weight: *1 fluid ounce*	1.1	69.3	0	0	0	0	0.3
Water: *12 fluid ounces*	12.5	0	0	0	0	0	4.5
Whiskey Sour Mix: *4 fluid ounces*	4.2	47.6	11.8	0	0	0	8.0
Whiskey, 80 proof, 36.4% alcohol by weight: *1 fluid ounce*	1.1	69.3	0	0	0	0	0.3
Wine, dessert, 15.3% alcohol by weight: *4 fluid ounces*	4.2	164.4	9.2	0.1	0	0	4.8
Wine, table, 9.9% alcohol by weight: *4 fluid ounces*	4.2	102.0	5.0	0.1	0	0	6.0

BREADS/ROLLS/CRACKERS

	Weight (oz)	Calories	Carbo. (g)	Protein (g)	Fat (g)	Choles. (mg)	Sodium (mg)
Apple Bread, *ETW Recipe: 1 slice*	1.6	110.4	23.1	3.9	1.0	0	58.3
Apple Muffins, *ETW Recipe: 1 average*	2.6	178.8	40.3	5.0	1.0	0.3	69.3
Applesauce Bran Muffins, *FF Recipe: 1 average*	2.4	117.6	27.6	2.0	0.3	0	64.6
Bagel, whole wheat: *1 average*	1.6	102.0	22.0	4.8	1.4	0	242.0

Breads/Rolls/Crackers (*continued*)	Weight (oz)	Calories	Carbo. (g)	Protein (g)	Fat (g)	Choles. (mg)	Sodium (mg)
Baked Breakfast Toast, *FF Recipe: 1 slice*	1.8	87.6	17.1	3.9	0.8	1.0	264.2
Banana Bread, *ETW Recipe: 1 slice*	2.2	153.8	35.0	4.4	1.1	0	59.5
Banana Date Muffins, *ETS Recipe: 1 average*	2.2	105.4	25.1	1.8	0.3	0.1	9.6
Biscuit, from mix, w/milk: *1 average*	1.0	92.1	14.8	2.0	2.6	0.3	275.8
Blueberry Bran Muffins, *ETW Recipe: 1 average*	1.7	97.3	20.2	3.5	0.8	0.3	68.6
Boston Brown Bread: *1 serving*	1.0	59.8	12.9	1.6	0.4	0.3	71.2
Bran Date Bread, *ETS Recipe: 1 average*	2.3	177.9	31.5	4.5	4.4	0.6	48.0
Bread Crumbs, dry, grated: *3½ ounces*	3.5	389.0	72.8	12.5	4.6	5.0	730.3
Bread Crumbs, whole wheat: *3½ ounces*	3.5	287.1	56.4	12.5	3.7	5.0	621.3
Bun, hamburger or hot dog: *1 average*	1.4	119.0	21.2	3.3	2.2	0	202.0
Cherry-Almond Muffin, *ETS Recipe: 1 average*	1.9	146.1	26.7	3.3	3.1	0.6	19.9
Corn Fritter: *1 average*	3.5	377.0	39.7	7.8	21.5	88.0	477.0
Corn Muffin, *ETW Recipe: 1 average*	2.9	116.9	24.1	4.8	0.9	0.6	113.6
Corn Bread, from mix, w/egg, milk: *1 slice*	1.6	104.9	14.8	2.7	3.8	31.1	334.8
Cracked Wheat Bread: *1 slice*	0.8	60.5	12.0	2.0	0.5	0.5	121.7
Crackers, sandwich type, peanut-cheese: *3½ ounces*	3.5	487.2	55.7	15.1	23.7	15.9	984.3
Earth Bread, *ETW Recipe: 2 slices*	2.5	160.1	32.9	6.3	1.4	0	73.7
French or Vienna Bread: *2 slices*	1.4	116.0	22.2	3.6	1.2	1.2	232.0
Graham Crackers, plain: *2 average*	0.5	53.8	10.3	1.1	1.3	0	93.8

	Weight (oz)	Calories	Carbo. (g)	Protein (g)	Fat (g)	Choles. (mg)	Sodium (mg)
Italian Bread: *2 slices*	1.4	110.4	22.6	3.6	0.3	0.4	234.0
Lemon Bread, *FF Recipe: 1 slice*	1.8	118.6	22.5	2.1	2.3	0.4	69.5
Lime Muffins, *FF Recipe: 1 average*	2.4	152.6	35.0	2.4	0.3	0.2	69.3
Matzo, unsalted: *1 slice*	1.1	117.0	25.4	3.0	0.3	0	1.0
Muffin, blueberry, home recipe: *1 average*	1.6	126.5	18.9	3.3	4.2	37.3	284.4
Muffin, bran, home recipe: *1 average*	1.4	104.4	17.2	3.1	3.9	41.2	179.2
Muffin, corn, w/whole ground meal, vegetable shortening: *1 average*	1.6	129.6	19.1	3.2	4.6	24.8	222.8
Muffin, plain, home recipe: *1 average*	1.6	132.3	19.0	3.5	4.5	23.9	198.5
Oatmeal-Pineapple Muffins, *FF Recipe: 1 average*	2.4	124.2	26.1	4.0	0.7	1.1	168.6
Orange Muffin, *ETW Recipe: 1 average*	1.7	127.6	26.2	5.3	1.0	0.4	114.4
Pecan Cranberry Bread, *ETS Recipe: 1 slice*	1.5	148.3	29.6	1.8	2.6	0	80.6
Prune Bread, *FF Recipe: 1 slice*	1.8	138.0	26.5	1.9	3.0	0.2	109.1
Pumpernickel Bread: *2 slices*	2.3	157.4	34.0	5.8	0.8	0.6	364.2
Pumpkin-Apple Bread, *ETS Recipe: 1 slice*	1.6	92.4	21.3	3.0	0.4	0.3	63.9
Raisin Bread: *2 slices*	1.6	120.5	24.7	3.0	1.3	1.4	167.9
Raisin Bread, toasted: *1 slice*	0.7	60.0	12.3	1.5	0.6	0.6	83.6
Rice Cake: *1 average*	0.3	35.0	7.6	0.7	0.2	0	14.1
Rice Crackers: *3 average*	0.4	31.0	6.7	0.8	0	0	8.0
Roll, baked from mix: *1 average*	1.2	104.6	19.1	3.1	1.6	1.4	109.5

Breads/Rolls/Crackers (continued)	Weight (oz)	Calories	Carbo. (g)	Protein (g)	Fat (g)	Choles. (mg)	Sodium (mg)
Roll, Brown-and-Serve, browned: 1 average	1.4	131.2	21.9	3.5	3.1	3.2	224.8
Roll, Danish Pastry, commercial, ready-to-serve: 1 average	1.4	164.6	17.8	2.9	9.2	25.4	142.7
Roll, hard, commercial: 1 average	1.2	109.2	20.8	3.4	1.1	1.1	218.8
Roll, sweet: 1 small	1.2	110.6	17.3	3.0	3.2	3.1	136.1
Roll, whole wheat: 1 average	1.2	89.9	18.3	3.5	1.0	1.1	197.4
Rusk: 1 slice	0.4	41.9	7.1	1.4	0.9	0.9	24.6
Rye Bread, American: 2 slices	1.6	112.0	24.0	4.2	0.6	1.0	256.0
Saltines: 2 average	0.2	26.0	4.3	0.5	0.7	0	66.0
Sesame Sweet Bread, ETS Recipe: 1 slice	1.7	110.0	20.5	2.7	2.1	0.9	13.2
Soda Crackers: 2 average	0.5	61.5	9.9	1.3	1.8	0	154.0
Sweet Cheese Bread, FF Recipe: 1 slice	2.0	127.5	22.2	3.1	3.1	3.2	142.5
Sweet Potato Muffin, ETS Recipe: 1 average	2.1	140.5	30.7	2.1	1.3	0.3	13.9
Tortilla: 1 average	0.8	60.5	12.0	2.0	0.5	0.5	121.7
White Bread: 2 slices	1.6	124.2	23.2	4.0	1.5	1.4	233.2
Whole Wheat Bread: 2 slices	1.6	111.8	21.9	4.8	1.4	1.4	242.4
Whole Wheat Bread, ETW Recipe: 1 slice	1.6	107.8	23.2	4.0	0.6	0.1	3.1
Whole Wheat Raisin Bread, ETW Recipe: 1 slice	1.2	110.4	22.4	4.7	1.0	0.5	73.0
Zucchini Bread, FF Recipe: 1 slice	1.5	114.2	21.6	2.2	2.2	0.2	109.4
Zwieback: 3½ ounces	3.5	419.7	73.7	10.6	8.7	8.9	248.1

CASSEROLES/COMBINATIONS

	Weight (oz)	Calories	Carbo. (g)	Protein (g)	Fat (g)	Choles. (mg)	Sodium (mg)
Baked Cannellini, *ETS Recipe: 1 serving*	8.7	235.4	41.0	14.3	2.5	3.4	262.9
Baked Lentils, *ETS Recipe: 1 serving*	8.3	251.7	39.6	16.1	3.5	7.0	573.4
Basic Brown Rice and Chicken, *ETW Recipe: 1 serving*	7.8	305.1	39.0	24.0	5.2	53.1	276.4
Beans and Frankfurters, canned: *1 serving*	9.0	367.3	32.1	19.4	18.1	33.2	1375.0
Beef Pot Pie, commercial, frozen, unheated: *1 average*	8.0	435.8	40.9	16.6	22.5	40.9	830.8
Black Bean and Rice Casserole, *ETS Recipe: 1 serving*	6.1	178.7	25.2	13.9	2.7	9.8	295.7
Broccoli Brown Rice Hollandaise, *ETW Recipe: 1 serving*	7.7	140.6	20.3	10.8	2.4	4.8	180.3
Broccoli Macaroni Bake, *ETS Recipe: 1 serving*	8.5	311.3	50.1	19.3	3.8	6.7	403.4
Brown Rice and Cottage Cheese, *ETW Recipe: 1 serving*	6.7	181.8	24.7	12.9	3.2	9.7	370.0
Cannellini-Stuffed Zucchini, *ETW Recipe: 1 serving*	10.8	358.3	64.4	20.4	3.3	4.5	196.6
Carrot Casserole, *ETS Recipe: 1 serving*	4.5	124.6	22.9	4.6	1.8	3.8	180.4
Chicken and Broccoli Stir Fry, *ETS Recipe: 1 serving*	8.7	225.4	34.0	17.1	2.4	32.2	180.9
Chicken and Brown Rice Pie, *ETS Recipe: 1 serving*	6.3	192.1	21.8	17.8	3.3	29.5	270.8
Chicken Brown Rice Pie, *ETS Recipe: 1 serving*	6.8	192.1	21.8	17.8	3.3	29.5	270.8
Chicken Cacciatore, *FF Recipe: 1 serving*	16.3	606.1	100.6	40.6	4.1	78.0	278.5
Chicken Casserole, *ETW Recipe: 1 serving*	6.7	340.7	42.8	26.4	6.0	42.4	300.8
Chicken Chow Mein, w/o noodles, canned: *1 serving*	8.0	86.4	16.1	5.9	0.2	6.8	659.1
Chicken Curry, *ETW Recipe: 1 serving*	13.7	464.8	80.1	28.6	4.5	53.6	582.9

Casseroles/Combinations (*continued*)	Weight (oz)	Calories	Carbo. (g)	Protein (g)	Fat (g)	Choles. (mg)	Sodium (mg)
Chicken Curry Muffin, *ETS Recipe: 1 average*	4.7	130.4	15.9	12.0	1.9	23.8	116.8
Chicken Fried Rice, *ETS Recipe: 1 serving*	7.2	188.8	33.6	9.6	1.6	16.1	208.3
Chicken Pot Pie, commercial, frozen: *1 average*	8.0	497.1	50.4	15.2	26.1	29.5	933.0
Chik 'n' Chili, *ETW Recipe: 1 serving*	7.2	148.5	26.4	9.2	1.8	12.5	444.5
Chili Pie, *ETW Recipe: 1 serving*	8.1	247.1	48.4	12.9	1.6	0.3	305.4
Chop Suey, w/meat, canned: *1 serving*	8.8	155.0	10.5	11.0	8.0	30.0	1377.5
Coq au Vin Casserole, *ETW Recipe: 1 serving*	7.2	257.2	29.1	17.4	3.0	25.9	180.7
Corn and Brown Rice Stir Fry, *ETS Recipe: 1 serving*	8.7	234.0	51.8	6.1	1.7	0	112.7
Corn and Chicken Frittata, *ETW Recipe: 1 serving*	5.7	160.6	13.8	20.9	2.7	35.3	179.6
Corned Beef Hash with Potato, canned: *1 serving*	7.8	398.7	23.6	19.4	24.9	72.7	1189.4
Crabmeat au Gratin, *ETW Recipe: 1 serving*	13.5	439.7	45.2	35.8	10.1	108.2	812.9
Creamy Chicken Casserole, *FF Recipe: 1 serving*	9.4	253.2	25.2	27.9	4.1	56.0	499.2
Creamy Lasagna, *ETS Recipe: 1 serving*	9.7	404.7	43.8	32.3	10.2	54.6	442.0
Eggplant Lasagne, *FF Recipe: 1 serving*	13.3	315.7	53.0	19.5	3.5	7.6	626.5
Eggplant Moussaka, *ETW Recipe: 1 serving*	13.7	380.9	53.6	27.9	4.5	15.0	692.7
Eggplant Parmesan, *FF Recipe: 1 serving*	8.7	94.4	16.3	5.1	2.3	3.9	177.6
Eggplant Proietto, *FF Recipe: 1 serving*	10.4	117.1	16.3	11.2	1.7	3.9	416.3
Frozen Dinner, beef pot roast, w/potatoes, peas, corn: *1 average*	11.0	330.7	19.0	40.9	10.0	156.0	808.1
Frozen Dinner, fried chicken, w/potatoes, vegetables: *1 average*	11.0	539.8	35.3	39.9	26.5	152.9	1073.3

	Weight (oz)	Calories	Carbo. (g)	Protein (g)	Fat (g)	Choles. (mg)	Sodium (mg)
Frozen Dinner, meat loaf, w/tomato sauce, vegetables: *1 average*	11.0	407.4	30.5	24.9	20.8	96.4	1222.2
Frozen Dinner, sliced turkey, w/potatoes, peas: *1 average*	11.0	349.4	39.6	26.2	9.4	99.8	1248.0
Glazed Ratatouille, *ETW Recipe: 1 serving*	6.5	109.0	17.6	5.5	2.1	5.2	153.8
Hot Bean Chili with Brown Rice, *FF Recipe: 1 serving*	15.4	275.2	57.1	10.1	1.8	0	198.9
Imam Bayeldi, *ETW Recipe: 1 serving*	5.7	121.7	22.4	4.2	1.3	2.0	388.8
Indian Rice Casserole, *ETS Recipe: 1 serving*	7.5	157.7	29.6	5.1	2.5	8.1	55.0
Indian Vegetable and Rice Casserole, *ETW Recipe: 1 serving*	9.2	206.6	34.7	10.9	3.3	8.8	464.2
Italian Macaroni and Beans, *ETW Recipe: 1 serving*	7.0	112.9	19.9	5.3	1.6	2.6	324.0
Italian Stuffed Peppers, *ETW Recipe: 1 large*	15.0	420.1	76.4	22.8	3.3	3.9	910.0
Italian Vegetable Bake, *ETW Recipe: 1 serving*	7.5	94.9	14.9	5.1	2.1	3.9	658.6
Italian White Beans, *ETW Recipe: 1 serving*	7.0	112.9	19.9	5.3	1.6	2.6	324.0
Macaroni and Cheese, *FF Recipe: 1 serving*	3.9	220.5	34.5	12.3	3.4	11.4	244.5
Macaroni and Cheese, canned: *1 serving*	7.1	190.0	21.4	7.8	8.0	20.0	608.0
Mashed Potato Pie, *FF Recipe: 1 serving*	5.4	106.1	19.6	6.0	0.6	2.5	479.3
Melanzane Al Forno (Baked Eggplant), *ETW Recipe: 1 serving*	9.7	131.2	24.7	7.6	1.9	3.0	355.5
Mexican Rice, *ETS Recipe: 1 serving*	8.2	192.5	32.3	11.8	1.8	21.5	214.4
Onion Potato Pie, *ETS Recipe: 1 serving*	6.3	143.6	17.1	12.2	3.0	8.6	465.5
Oven "French Fries," *FF Recipe: 1 serving*	16.4	324.2	54.5	19.4	3.4	5.9	288.6
Pasta Pie, *FF Recipe: 1 serving*	6.5	217.9	36.9	11.3	2.6	4.6	449.0

Casseroles/Combinations (*continued*)	Weight (oz)	Calories	Carbo. (g)	Protein (g)	Fat (g)	Choles. (mg)	Sodium (mg)
Potato Casserole, *ETW Recipe: 1 serving*	12.0	283.1	55.4	13.2	1.5	5.5	208.3
Potato Cheese Bake, *ETS Recipe: 1 serving*	7.1	146.4	19.6	12.9	1.7	5.7	288.7
Potato Scramble, *FF Recipe: 1 serving*	7.4	141.5	20.3	11.0	1.9	5.0	451.3
Potatoes au Gratin, *FF Recipe: 1 serving*	7.2	185.0	30.9	10.5	2.2	8.3	376.4
Rice-Stuffed Green Pepper, *ETS Recipe: 1 large*	8.3	252.8	33.7	11.4	8.7	5.6	230.7
Rolled Stuffed Eggplant, *ETS Recipe: 1 serving*	10.0	202.1	31.5	13.3	3.2	9.0	950.2
Salmon Rice Loaf: *1 serving*	3.5	122.0	7.3	12.0	4.5	21.0	275.0
Spaghetti in Tomato Sauce, w/cheese, canned: *1 serving*	15.6	336.0	68.2	9.8	2.6	14.0	1690.0
Spaghetti with Meatballs in Tomato Sauce, canned: *1 serving*	7.8	227.9	25.2	10.8	9.1	19.9	1079.6
Spinach Cheese Pie, *ETS Recipe: 1 serving*	7.3	132.8	7.7	19.3	2.8	8.6	582.4
Spinach Cheese Pie, *ETW Recipe: 1 serving*	7.5	132.8	7.7	19.3	2.8	8.6	582.4
Spinach Noodle Casserole, *ETW Recipe: 1 serving*	6.8	234.3	33.4	17.4	3.3	7.1	520.8
Stuffed Cabbage, *ETW Recipe: 1 serving*	9.4	163.6	31.8	5.7	1.8	3.0	697.3
Stuffed Green Pepper, w/beef and bread crumbs: *1 average*	6.7	324.7	32.1	24.8	10.5	72.6	599.7
Stuffed Red Peppers, *FF Recipe: 1 serving*	4.9	97.1	10.5	8.1	3.2	8.9	434.7
Stuffed Tomatoes, *ETW Recipe: 1 serving*	11.0	276.0	56.5	12.2	3.5	3.5	380.9
Sweet Potato Casserole, *ETS Recipe: 1 serving*	7.6	227.5	54.5	3.1	0.8	0.3	32.8
Sweet Potato–Cranberry Bake, *FF Recipe: 1 serving*	3.5	152.7	26.3	1.9	5.2	0.6	135.3
Sweet Potato Stuffing, *ETS Recipe: 1 serving*	5.8	235.3	28.1	6.3	12.5	0.8	239.2

	Weight (oz)	Calories	Carbo. (g)	Protein (g)	Fat (g)	Choles. (mg)	Sodium (mg)
Tabbouleh, *ETS Recipe: 1 serving*	9.7	204.0	44.1	7.3	0.8	0	357.5
Tomato Broccoli Pie, *ETS Recipe: 1 slice*	6.5	124.5	11.8	12.7	3.3	9.7	386.6
Tomato Salmon Casserole, *ETW Recipe: 1 serving*	6.0	206.4	29.7	14.3	3.7	13.8	348.0
Tuna Casserole Supreme, *ETW Recipe: 1 serving*	7.0	253.7	30.9	20.1	4.6	31.6	207.2
Tuna Muffin, *ETW Recipe: 1 average*	4.2	129.4	14.8	13.4	1.5	22.8	147.0
Turkey Pot Pie, commercial, frozen: *1 average*	8.0	227.0	23.2	6.7	12.0	10.4	425.2
Turkey Stuffed Potato, *ETS Recipe: 1 average*	14.5	465.7	54.9	41.6	8.7	77.4	465.3
Veal Stuffed Eggplant, *ETS Recipe: 1 serving*	8.1	187.6	21.6	12.4	6.9	28.8	128.9
Veal-Stuffed Peppers, *FF Recipe: 1 serving*	13.9	340.3	29.3	27.2	13.2	81.6	342.6
Vegetable Pasta Casserole, *FF Recipe: 1 serving*	5.2	176.6	29.3	11.2	2.0	4.6	166.6
Vegetable Rice Casserole, *ETS Recipe: 1 serving*	7.7	190.2	36.1	8.4	2.1	4.5	430.3
Veggie-Stuffed Peppers, *FF Recipe: 1 serving*	7.2	230.5	29.6	8.6	11.1	3.0	335.7
Welsh Rarebit: *1 serving*	8.2	415.3	14.6	18.8	31.6	99.8	770.3
Ziti Casserole, *ETS Recipe: 1 serving*	9.7	320.4	48.0	20.9	5.1	8.0	682.7
Zucchini Corn Casserole, *ETS Recipe: 1 serving*	16.2	328.4	57.6	20.6	5.4	12.7	431.7
Zucchini Frittata, *FF Recipe: 1 serving*	3.6	67.8	4.6	8.4	1.7	6.1	352.5
Zucchini Italiano, *FF Recipe: 1 serving*	7.2	58.5	10.1	3.3	1.3	2.0	163.2
Zucchini Squares, *ETW Recipe: 1 average*	1.0	28.7	3.9	2.2	0.6	1.1	84.3

CEREALS/GRAINS

	Weight (oz)	Calories	Carbo. (g)	Protein (g)	Fat (g)	Choles. (mg)	Sodium (mg)
Apples and Brown Rice Cereal, *ETS Recipe: 1 serving*	10.4	298.6	57.3	5.8	5.8	0	5.1
Baked Barley, *ETS Recipe: 1 serving*	6.7	148.6	31.0	6.1	0.5	0	417.5
Barley, pearled, light, dry: *3½ ounces*	3.5	346.3	78.2	8.1	1.0	0	3.0
Barley, pearled, pot or Scotch: *3½ ounces*	3.5	345.3	76.6	9.5	1.1	0	4.0
Bran Buds Cereal: *1 serving*	1.0	73.1	21.5	3.9	0.7	0	174.1
Bran Cereal, 100% Bran: *1 serving*	1.0	76.3	20.7	3.5	1.4	0	196.5
Bran Cereal, 40% Bran Flakes: *1 serving*	1.0	92.4	22.2	3.6	0.5	0	263.9
Bran Flakes with Raisins: *1 serving*	1.0	88.5	21.4	3.1	0.6	0	207.0
Bran, wheat: *1 serving*	0.3	1.7	0.5	0.1	0+	0	0.1
Brown Rice, cooked, w/o salt: *1 serving*	5.3	178.5	38.3	3.8	0.9	0	3.0
Brown Rice, cooked, w/salt: *1 serving*	5.3	178.5	38.3	3.8	0.9	0	423.0
Brown Rice–Pineapple Cereal, *FF Recipe: 1 serving*	7.4	277.8	60.5	8.6	1.0	3.2	330.2
Brown Rice, raw: *1 serving*	1.7	176.4	37.9	3.7	0.9	0	4.4
Buckwheat, whole grain: *3½ ounces*	3.5	332.4	72.3	11.6	2.4	0	2.0
Bulgur, dry, commercial from club wheat: *3½ ounces*	3.5	356.2	78.9	8.6	1.4	0	4.0
Corn Chex, shredded corn cereal: *1 serving*	1.0	111.1	24.9	2.0	0.1	0	271.0
Cornflakes: *1 serving*	1.0	110.3	24.4	2.3	0.1	0	351.0
Cornflakes, low-sodium: *1 serving*	1.0	113.1	25.2	2.2	0.1	0	2.8

	Weight (oz)	Calories	Carbo. (g)	Protein (g)	Fat (g)	Choles. (mg)	Sodium (mg)
Cornflakes, sugar-covered: *1 serving*	1.0	108.0	25.7	1.4	0.1	0	229.6
Corn Grits, cooked w/o salt: *1 serving*	8.5	145.3	31.5	3.4	0.5	0	0
Corn Grits, cooked w/salt: *1 serving*	8.5	145.3	31.5	3.4	0.5	0	540.0
Corn Grits, dry form: *1 serving*	1.4	148.4	31.8	3.5	0.5	0	0.4
Cream of Wheat, cooked: *1 serving*	7.1	108.0	22.4	3.0	0.4	0	116.0
Cream of Wheat, instant, dry form: *1 serving*	1.3	139.1	28.7	4.0	0.5	0	5.7
Farina, quick-cooking, cooked w/o salt: *1 serving*	8.6	122.5	26.0	3.4	0.2	0	0
Farina, quick-cooking, dry form: *1 serving*	1.3	140.2	29.6	4.0	0.2	0	1.1
Grape Nuts Cereal: *1 serving*	1.0	100.0	23.0	3.7	0.3	0	174.0
Hot Brown Rice Cereal, *ETS Recipe: 1 serving*	10.0	253.7	52.6	8.3	1.2	2.4	67.3
Millet, whole grain: *1 serving*	1.8	163.5	36.4	4.9	1.4	0	0.5
Oat Cereal, plain: *1 serving*	1.5	155.0	30.1	7.7	0.8	0	218.9
Oat Cereal, puffed: *1 serving*	0.9	97.7	17.3	3.8	1.6	0	270.8
Oat Cereal, puffed, sugar-coated: *1 serving*	0.9	98.0	21.6	1.9	0.6	0	193.0
Oat Flakes: *1 serving*	1.6	166.2	32.6	8.4	0.7	0	402.7
Oatmeal and Prunes Cereal, *FF Recipe: 1 serving*	8.6	228.3	47.1	7.2	1.9	2.6	536.3
Oatmeal Royale, *ETW Recipe: 1 serving*	13.3	281.1	63.5	6.5	2.5	0	7.8
Oats, rolled, cooked w/o salt: *1 serving*	8.3	146.6	25.5	6.1	2.4	0	2.4
Oats, rolled, dry form: *1 serving*	1.0	108.7	19.0	4.5	1.8	0	1.1

Cereals/Grains (continued)	Weight (oz)	Calories	Carbo. (g)	Protein (g)	Fat (g)	Choles. (mg)	Sodium (mg)
Rice Bran: 1 serving	0.4	27.6	5.1	1.3	1.6	0	0
Rice Cereal, Cream of, cooked w/o salt: 1 serving	8.6	127.5	28.2	2.2	0.2	0	2.5
Rice Cereal, Cream of, dry form: 3½ ounces	3.5	367.1	81.8	6.3	0.5	0	6.0
Rice Cereal, puffed: 1 serving	0.5	56.3	12.6	0.9	0.1	0	0.4
Rice Chex Cereal: 1 serving	1.0	112.0	25.3	1.5	0.1	0	237.0
Rice Krispies Cereal: 1 serving	1.0	110.9	24.8	1.8	0.1	0	205.6
Rice Krispies Cereal, low-sodium: 1 serving	1.0	112.6	25.5	1.5	0.1	0	2.8
Rice, Polish: 3½ ounces	3.5	262.9	57.3	12.0	12.7	0	0
Rye, whole-grain, raw: 3½ ounces	3.5	331.4	72.8	12.0	1.7	0	1.0
Sorghum Grain, all types: 3½ ounces	3.5	329.4	72.4	10.9	3.3	0	1.0
Tapioca, dry: 1 serving	0.4	35.2	8.6	0.1	0+	0	0.3
Wheat Chex Cereal, w/malt, salt, sugar: 1 serving	1.4	146.8	32.9	4.0	1.0	0	268.0
Wheat Flakes Cereal: 1 serving	1.0	97.8	22.3	2.7	0.5	0	350.1
Wheat Germ Cereal, toasted: 3½ ounces	3.5	379.0	49.2	28.9	10.6	0	4.0
Wheat Germ, crude, commercially milled: 1 serving	0.4	36.3	4.7	2.7	1.1	0	0.3
Wheat, Malted Barley Cereal, cooked w/o salt: 1 serving	7.1	144.0	31.8	4.6	0.8	0	8.0
Wheat, Malted Barley Cereal, dry form: 1 serving	1.8	176.0	38.6	5.6	1.0	0	8.5
Wheat, Malted Barley Flakes Cereal: 1 serving	1.0	101.5	23.2	3.0	0.3	0	217.7

	Weight (oz)	Calories	Carbo. (g)	Protein (g)	Fat (g)	Choles. (mg)	Sodium (mg)
Wheat, Malted Barley Granules Cereal: *1 serving*	1.0	101.2	23.2	3.3	0.1	0	197.0
Wheat Meal Cereal, cooked w/o salt: *3½ ounces*	3.5	52.6	11.1	2.2	0.3	0	2.0
Wheat Meal Cereal, dry: *1 serving*	1.0	96.7	20.4	4.0	0.6	0	3.1
Wheat, Puffed Cereal, w/o sugar, salt: *1 serving*	1.0	103.2	22.6	4.2	0.3	0	1.1
Wheat, Shredded Wheat Cereal, w/o salt: *1 serving*	1.6	158.4	35.9	4.9	0.6	0	0.9
Wheat, whole grain, dry: *3½ ounces*	3.5	329.4	69.6	12.6	2.5	0	3.0
White Rice, cooked w/o salt: *1 serving*	5.3	163.4	36.3	3.0	0.1	0	0
White Rice, raw: *1 serving*	1.1	112.6	24.9	2.1	0.1	0	1.6
Whole Wheat Cereal, cooked w/o salt: *1 serving*	4.0	69.5	15.4	2.2	0.4	0	0
Whole Wheat Cereal, dry form: *1 serving*	1.0	97.0	21.3	3.2	0.6	0	0.6
Wild Rice, raw: *1 serving*	1.0	100.1	21.3	4.0	0.2	0	2.0

CHEESE

	Weight (oz)	Calories	Carbo. (g)	Protein (g)	Fat (g)	Choles. (mg)	Sodium (mg)
American Cheese Food, grated: *1 ounce*	1.0	93.0	2.1	5.6	7.0	25.0	337.0
American Cheese Food, past. process: *1 ounce*	1.0	93.0	2.1	5.6	7.0	18.1	452.5
American Cheese, past. process: *1 ounce*	1.0	106.3	0.5	6.3	8.9	26.6	405.4
American Cheese Spread, past. process: *1 ounce*	1.0	82.2	2.5	4.6	6.0	15.6	460.7
Blue Cheese: *1 ounce*	1.0	100.1	0.7	6.1	8.1	21.3	395.6
Brick Cheese: *1 ounce*	1.0	105.2	0.8	6.6	8.4	26.6	158.6

Cheese (continued)	Weight (oz)	Calories	Carbo. (g)	Protein (g)	Fat (g)	Choles. (mg)	Sodium (mg)
Camembert Cheese, domestic: 1 ounce	1.0	85.0	0.1	5.6	6.9	20.4	238.4
Cheddar Cheese: 1 ounce	1.0	114.2	0.4	7.1	9.4	29.8	175.9
Cottage Cheese, creamed: 1 ounce	1.0	29.2	0.8	3.5	1.3	4.3	114.8
Cottage Cheese, dry curd: 1 ounce	1.0	24.1	0.5	4.9	0.1	2.0	3.6
Cottage Cheese, 1% fat: 1 ounce	1.0	20.4	0.8	3.5	0.3	1.4	115.2
Cottage Cheese, 2% fat: 1 ounce	1.0	25.5	1.0	3.9	0.5	2.4	115.2
Cream Cheese: 1 ounce	1.0	98.9	0.8	2.2	9.9	31.2	83.8
Cream Cheese, light: 1 ounce	1.0	60.0	2.0	3.0	5.0	15.0	160.0
Limburger Cheese: 1 ounce	1.0	92.7	0.1	5.7	7.7	25.5	226.8
Mozzarella Cheese, part skim, low moisture: 1 ounce	1.0	79.0	0.9	7.8	4.8	15.0	150.0
Parmesan Cheese, grated: 1 ounce	1.0	129.3	1.0	11.8	8.5	22.4	527.7
Parmesan Cheese, hard: 1 ounce	1.0	111.1	0.9	10.1	7.3	19.3	454.0
Romano Cheese, grated: 1 ounce	1.0	110.0	1.0	9.0	7.6	22.4	340.0
Roquefort Cheese: 1 ounce	1.0	100.1	0.7	6.1	8.1	21.3	395.6
Swiss Cheese, domestic: 1 ounce	1.0	106.6	1.0	8.1	7.8	26.1	73.7
Swiss Cheese, past. process, w/o AD2 phosphate: 1 ounce	1.0	94.7	0.6	7.0	7.1	24.1	193.1
Swiss Cheese, past. process, w/1.5% AD2 phosphate: 1 ounce	1.0	94.7	0.6	7.0	7.1	24.1	388.5

COOKIES/CANDY/SNACKS

	Weight (oz)	Calories	Carbo. (g)	Protein (g)	Fat (g)	Choles. (mg)	Sodium (mg)
Animal Crackers: 3½ ounces	3.5	425.7	79.3	6.5	9.3	29.8	300.6
Apricots, candied: 3½ ounces	3.5	335.4	85.8	0.6	0.2	0	1.0
Butter Cookies, thin, rich: 4 average	0.8	100.5	15.6	1.3	3.7	16.7	92.0
Butterscotch Candy: 3½ ounces	3.5	393.9	94.1	0	3.4	9.9	65.5
Caramels, chocolate-flavored roll: 3½ ounces	3.5	392.9	82.1	2.2	8.1	1.0	195.5
Caramels, plain or chocolate: 3½ ounces	3.5	395.9	76.0	4.0	10.1	2.0	224.2
Caramels, plain or chocolate, w/nuts: 3½ ounces	3.5	424.7	70.0	4.5	16.2	2.0	201.4
Cheese Crackers: 3½ ounces	3.5	475.3	59.9	11.1	21.1	31.8	1030.9
Cheese Straws, w/lard: 3½ ounces	3.5	449.5	34.2	11.1	29.7	53.6	715.4
Cheese Straws, w/veg. shortening: 3½ ounces	3.5	449.5	34.2	11.1	29.7	31.8	715.4
Cherries, candied: 3½ ounces	3.5	336.4	86.0	0.5	0.2	0	2.0
Chewing Gum: 3½ ounces	3.5	314.5	94.5	0	0	0	0
Chocolate Candy, bittersweet: 3½ ounces	3.5	473.3	46.4	7.8	39.4	0	3.0
Chocolate Candy, semisweet: 3½ ounces	3.5	503.1	56.6	4.2	35.4	0	2.0
Chocolate Candy, sweet: 3½ ounces	3.5	523.9	57.5	4.4	34.8	1.0	32.7
Chocolate Chip Cookies, commercial: 1 serving	0.8	103.6	15.3	1.2	4.6	8.6	88.2
Chocolate-Coated Almonds: 3½ ounces	3.5	564.6	39.3	12.2	43.4	1.0	58.5
Chocolate-Coated Chocolate Fudge Candy: 3½ ounces	3.5	426.7	72.5	3.8	15.9	2.0	226.2

Cookies/Candy/Snacks (*continued*)	Weight (oz)	Calories	Carbo. (g)	Protein (g)	Fat (g)	Choles. (mg)	Sodium (mg)
Chocolate-Coated Chocolate Fudge Candy, w/nuts: *3½ ounces*	3.5	448.5	66.8	4.9	20.6	2.0	203.4
Chocolate-Coated Coconut Center Candy: *3½ ounces*	3.5	434.6	71.4	2.8	17.5	1.0	195.5
Chocolate-Coated Fondant: *3½ ounces*	3.5	406.8	80.4	1.7	10.4	1.0	183.6
Chocolate-Coated Fudge, Caramel, and Peanuts Candy: *3½ ounces*	3.5	429.6	63.6	7.6	18.0	3.0	202.4
Chocolate-Coated Honeycombed Candy, w/peanut butter: *3½ ounces*	3.5	459.4	70.1	6.5	19.3	1.0	161.7
Chocolate-Coated Nougat and Caramel Candy: *3½ ounces*	3.5	412.8	72.2	4.0	13.8	5.0	171.7
Chocolate-Coated Peanuts: *3½ ounces*	3.5	556.6	38.8	16.3	41.0	1.0	59.5
Chocolate-Coated Raisins: *3½ ounces*	3.5	421.7	70.0	5.4	17.0	9.9	63.5
Chocolate-Coated Vanilla Creams: *3½ ounces*	3.5	431.6	69.8	3.8	17.0	2.0	180.6
Chocolate Fudge Candy: *3½ ounces*	3.5	396.9	74.4	2.7	12.1	1.0	188.5
Chocolate Fudge Candy, w/nuts: *3½ ounces*	3.5	422.7	68.5	3.9	17.3	1.0	169.7
Citron, candied: *3½ ounces*	3.5	311.6	79.6	0.2	0.3	0	287.7
Cookies, from dough chilled in roll: *2 average*	0.8	119.0	15.6	0.9	6.0	9.4	131.5
Crackers, w/whole wheat: *4 average*	0.5	56.4	9.5	1.2	1.9	0	76.6
Fig Bars: *2 average*	1.0	100.2	21.1	1.1	1.6	10.9	70.6
Figs, candied: *3½ ounces*	3.5	296.7	73.1	3.5	0.2	0	33.7
Fondant Candy: *3½ ounces*	3.5	361.2	88.9	0.1	2.0	0	210.4
Gingerroot, crystallized, candied: *3½ ounces*	3.5	337.4	86.4	0.3	0.2	0	59.5
Gingersnap Cookies: *6 small*	0.8	100.8	19.2	1.3	2.1	9.4	137.0

	Weight (oz)	Calories	Carbo. (g)	Protein (g)	Fat (g)	Choles. (mg)	Sodium (mg)
Graham Crackers, chocolate-coated: 2 average	0.9	123.5	17.7	1.3	6.1	0	105.8
Graham Crackers, sugar-honey-coated: 2 average	0.9	106.9	19.9	1.7	3.0	0	131.0
Grapefruit Peel, candied: 3½ ounces	3.5	313.5	80.0	0.4	0.3	0	0
Gum Drops, starch jelly pieces: 3½ ounces	3.5	344.3	86.7	0.1	0.7	0	34.7
Hard Candy: 3½ ounces	3.5	383.0	96.4	0	1.1	0	31.8
Jelly Beans: 3½ ounces	3.5	364.1	92.4	0	0.5	0	11.9
Ladyfingers: 2 large	1.0	100.8	18.1	2.2	2.2	99.7	19.9
Lemon Peel, candied: 3½ ounces	3.5	313.5	80.0	0.4	0.3	0	0
Macaroons: 2 average	1.0	133.0	18.5	1.5	6.5	30.5	9.5
Marshmallow Cookie: 1 average	1.0	114.5	20.2	1.1	3.7	21.3	58.5
Marshmallows: 3½ ounces	3.5	316.5	79.8	2.0	0	1.0	38.7
Milk Chocolate Candy, plain: 3½ ounces	3.5	516.0	56.5	7.6	32.0	19.8	93.3
Milk Chocolate Candy, w/almonds: 3½ ounces	3.5	527.9	50.9	9.2	35.3	16.9	79.4
Milk Chocolate Candy, w/peanuts: 3½ ounces	3.5	538.8	44.3	14.0	37.8	12.9	65.5
Molasses Cookies: 2 average	1.1	126.6	22.8	1.9	3.2	11.7	115.8
Oatmeal Cookies, w/raisins: 2 average	1.0	126.3	20.6	1.7	4.3	10.9	45.4
Oatmeal Fruit Bars, ETW Recipe: 2 average	8.0	628.6	141.6	14.6	3.8	2.9	72.6
Orange Peel, candied: 3½ ounces	3.5	313.5	80.0	0.4	0.3	0	0
Peanut Bar: 3½ ounces	3.5	511.0	46.8	17.4	31.9	0	9.9

Cookies/Candy/Snacks (continued)	Weight (oz)	Calories	Carbo. (g)	Protein (g)	Fat (g)	Choles. (mg)	Sodium (mg)
Peanut Brittle: *3½ ounces*	3.5	417.7	80.4	5.7	10.3	0	30.8
Peanut Cookies: *2 average*	0.8	113.5	16.1	2.4	4.6	9.4	41.5
Pears, candied: *3½ ounces*	3.5	300.6	75.3	1.3	0.6	0	6.9
Pineapple, candied: *3½ slices*	1	90	22.7	0.2	0.1	0	2
Popcorn, popped, plain: *1 serving*	0.5	54.1	10.7	1.8	0.7	0	0.4
Popcorn, popped, w/butter, salt: *1 serving*	0.5	63.9	8.3	1.4	3.1	6.3	271.7
Popcorn, sugar-coated: *3½ ounces*	3.5	380.0	84.3	6.1	3.5	0	1.0
Popcorn, unpopped: *3½ ounces*	3.5	359.2	71.5	11.8	4.7	0	3.0
Potato Chips: *50 average*	3.5	568.0	50.0	5.3	39.8	0	340.0
Potato Sticks: *1 serving*	3.5	544.0	50.8	6.4	36.4	0	340.0
Pretzels, salted: *10 average*	4.8	526.5	102.5	13.2	6.1	0	2268.0
Pretzels, unsalted: *2 average*	1.0	110.0	22.0	4.0	1.0	0	10.0
Raisin Cookies: *2 average*	1.1	113.7	24.2	1.3	1.6	11.7	15.6
Salt Sticks, regular type, w/o salt coating: *3½ ounces*	3.5	381.0	74.7	11.9	2.9	3.0	694.6
Salt Sticks, regular type, w/salt coating: *3½ ounces*	3.5	381.0	74.7	11.9	2.9	3.0	1661.0
Shortbread Cookies: *4 average*	1.0	139.4	18.2	2.0	6.5	10.9	16.8
Sugar-Coated Almonds: *3½ ounces*	3.5	452.5	69.7	7.7	18.5	0	19.8
Sugar-Coated Chocolate Discs: *3½ ounces*	3.5	462.4	72.1	5.2	19.5	11.9	71.4
Sugar Cookie, thick, home recipe, w/butter: *1 average*	0.7	85.2	13.4	1.2	3.0	15.2	93.8

	Weight (oz)	Calories	Carbo. (g)	Protein (g)	Fat (g)	Choles. (mg)	Sodium (mg)
Sugar Cookie, thick, home recipe, w/vegetable shortening: *1 average*	0.7	88.8	13.6	1.2	3.4	7.8	63.6
Sugar Wafers: *4 average*	0.8	106.7	16.1	1.1	4.3	8.6	41.6
Vanilla Fudge Candy: *3½ ounces*	3.5	394.9	74.2	3.0	11.0	2.0	206.4
Vanilla Fudge Candy, w/nuts: *3½ ounces*	3.5	420.7	68.3	4.2	16.3	2.0	185.5
Vanilla Wafers: *4 average*	0.8	101.6	16.4	1.2	3.5	8.6	55.4

DESSERTS/DESSERT SAUCES

	Weight (oz)	Calories	Carbo. (g)	Protein (g)	Fat (g)	Choles. (mg)	Sodium (mg)
All in One Apple Pie, *ETS Recipe: 1 slice*	8.1	225.9	51.7	5.4	0.8	1.8	118.3
Angel Food Cake: *1 slice*	1.6	116.5	26.7	2.6	0.1	0	65.7
Apple Brown Betty: *1 serving*	7.6	324.7	63.9	3.4	7.5	17.2	329.0
Apple Cake, *ETS Recipe: 1 slice*	2.4	141.8	27.1	2.3	3.3	0	74.0
Apple Pie, w/lard: *1 slice*	5.6	409.6	61.0	3.5	17.8	17.6	481.6
Apple Pie, w/vegetable shortening: *1 slice*	5.6	409.6	61.0	3.5	17.8	0	481.6
Baked Apple, *ETW Recipe: 1 average*	10.5	302.6	77.3	2.5	1.1	0	9.2
Baked Plantain, *ETW Recipe: 1 serving*	5.2	155.0	39.7	1.4	0.6	0	5.2
Banana Custard Pie, w/lard, no salt in filling: *1 slice*	5.6	353.6	49.1	7.2	14.9	102.4	310.4
Banana Custard Pie, w/vegetable shortening, no salt in filling: *1 slice*	5.6	353.6	49.1	7.2	14.9	92.8	310.4
Banana Noodle Custard, *ETW Recipe: 1 slice*	9.1	324.0	65.9	14.5	1.5	4.0	154.7
Banana Nut Loaf Cake, *ETS Recipe: ½ slice*	1.8	101.0	18.7	1.4	2.6	0	30.6

Desserts/Dessert Sauces (*continued*)	Weight (oz)	Calories	Carbo. (g)	Protein (g)	Fat (g)	Choles. (mg)	Sodium (mg)
Blackberry Pie, w/lard, no salt in filling: 1 slice	5.6	388.8	55.0	4.2	17.6	17.6	428.8
Blackberry Pie, w/vegetable shortening, no salt in filling: 1 slice	5.6	388.8	55.0	4.2	17.6	0	428.8
Blueberry Pie, w/lard, no salt in filling: 1 slice	5.6	387.2	55.8	3.8	17.3	17.6	428.8
Blueberry Pie, w/vegetable shortening, no salt in filling: 1 slice	5.6	387.2	55.8	3.8	17.3	0	428.8
Blueberry Sauce, FF Recipe: 1 serving	2.0	30.9	6.9	0.3	0.3	0	0.5
Boston Cream Pie, w/butter: 1 slice	3.5	294.0	49.4	5.0	8.8	101.0	315.0
Boston Cream Pie, w/vegetable shortening: 1 slice	3.5	302.0	49.9	5.0	9.4	86.0	186.0
Bread Pudding, w/raisins: 1 serving	5.8	308.6	46.9	9.2	10.1	112.2	331.6
Brown Rice Fruit Custard, ETW Recipe: 1 serving	8.7	258.2	51.9	12.0	0.8	4.1	157.2
Brownie, from mix, made w/water, nuts: 1 large	1.8	201.5	29.9	2.4	9.3	32.0	109.0
Brownie, from mix, w/nuts, eggs, water: 1 large	1.8	214.0	31.5	2.5	10.0	21.5	83.0
Brownie, w/nuts, chocolate icing, commercial: 1 serving	1.8	209.5	30.3	2.4	10.3	19.5	100.0
Brownies, FF Recipe: 1 average	2.1	182.0	30.6	2.9	5.7	0.2	24.0
Butterscotch Pie, w/lard, no salt in filling: 1 slice	3.5	267.0	38.3	4.4	11.0	57.0	321.0
Butterscotch Pie, w/vegetable shortening, no salt in filling: 1 slice	3.5	267.0	38.3	4.4	11.0	52.0	214.0
Cane Syrup: 3½ ounces	3.5	260.7	67.4	0	0	0	5.0
Caramel Cake, no icing, w/butter: 1 slice	1.6	162.9	23.3	2.0	7.1	51.7	207.0
Caramel Cake, w/caramel icing, butter: 1 slice	1.9	198.6	31.6	2.0	7.5	51.2	204.1

	Weight (oz)	Calories	Carbo. (g)	Protein (g)	Fat (g)	Choles. (mg)	Sodium (mg)
Carob Chips: *3½ ounces*	3.5	511.0	60.2	5.9	28.7	0	17.5
Carob Nut Loaf, *ETS Recipe: 1 slice*	3.0	297.8	42.5	6.2	12.5	0.4	64.3
Cherry Freeze, *FF Recipe: 1 serving*	5.2	87.3	17.6	3.6	0.4	1.2	40.2
Cherry Pie, w/lard: *1 slice*	5.6	417.6	61.4	4.2	18.1	17.6	486.4
Cherry Pie, w/vegetable shortening: *1 slice*	5.6	417.6	61.4	4.2	18.1	0	486.4
Chocolate, bitter or baking: *3½ ounces*	3.5	501.1	28.7	10.6	52.6	0	4.0
Chocolate Cake Icing: *1 serving*	0.4	36.0	7.7	0.1	0.7	2.2	8.3
Chocolate Cake, no icing, w/butter: *1 slice*	1.8	174.5	25.3	2.4	8.0	41.5	201.0
Chocolate Cake, no icing, w/vegetable shortening: *1 slice*	1.8	183.0	26.0	2.4	8.6	29.0	147.0
Chocolate Cake, w/chocolate icing, butter: *1 slice*	1.8	179.5	27.7	2.2	7.7	33.0	158.0
Chocolate Cake, w/chocolate icing, vegetable shortening: *1 slice*	1.8	184.5	27.9	2.2	8.2	24.0	117.5
Chocolate Cherry Cake, *FF Recipe: 1 serving*	3.7	244.0	39.5	4.0	8.7	0	13.0
Chocolate Chiffon Pie, w/lard, no salt in filling: *1 slice*	2.8	262.4	35.0	5.4	12.2	112.0	201.6
Chocolate Chiffon Pie, w/vegetable shortening, no salt in filling: *1 slice*	2.8	262.4	35.0	5.4	12.2	105.6	201.6
Chocolate Cookies: *1 average*	0.8	97.9	15.7	1.6	3.5	8.6	30.1
Chocolate Meringue Pie, w/lard: *1 slice*	3.5	252.0	33.5	4.8	12.0	62.0	256.0
Chocolate Meringue Pie, w/vegetable shortening: *1 slice*	3.5	250.0	33.2	4.8	11.9	55.6	254.0
"Chocolate" Pudding, *FF Recipe: 1 serving*	3.7	149.3	34.2	2.9	0.4	1.4	37.1
Chocolate Pudding, from mix, w/milk, cooked: *1 serving*	4.6	161.2	29.6	4.4	3.9	15.6	167.7

Desserts/Dessert Sauces (*continued*)	Weight (oz)	Calories	Carbo. (g)	Protein (g)	Fat (g)	Choles. (mg)	Sodium (mg)
Chocolate Syrup, fudge type: *3½ slices*	0.8	66	10.8	1.0	2.7	0	18
Coffee Cake, from mix, w/eggs, milk: *1 slice*	2.1	193.2	31.4	3.8	5.8	37.2	258.6
Cone, for ice cream: *1 average*	0.4	45.2	9.3	1.2	0.3	0	27.8
Cookie Dough, plain, chilled in roll: *3½ ounces*	3.5	445.5	58.3	3.5	22.4	32.7	492.1
Cranberry Relish, *ETW Recipe: 1 serving*	1.5	51.4	13.1	0.3	0.1	0	1.1
Cream Puff, w/custard filling: *1 average*	3.7	244.7	21.5	6.8	14.6	151.2	87.2
Crustless Pumpkin Pie, *ETW Recipe: 1 slice*	5.0	163.0	34.0	6.2	0.5	1.8	104.3
Cupcake, no icing, from mix, w/eggs, milk: *1 average*	0.9	87.5	13.9	1.2	3.0	15.0	113.2
Cupcake, w/chocolate icing, from mix, w/eggs, milk: *1 average*	1.4	143.2	23.7	1.8	5.0	18.8	134.0
Custard, baked: *1 serving*	4.6	149.5	14.4	7.0	7.2	136.5	102.7
Custard Pie: *1 slice*	5.3	327.0	35.1	9.1	16.6	162.0	430.5
Devil's Food Cake, w/chocolate icing, cream filled: *1 slice*	3.0	315.3	37.2	3.0	18.6	44.2	161.5
Doughnut, cake type: *1 average*	1.1	125.1	16.4	1.5	6.0	19.2	160.3
Doughnut, glazed: *1 average*	1.3	149.9	16.5	2.0	8.5	9.3	74.0
Doughnut, plain: *1 average*	1.1	132.5	12.1	2.0	8.5	8.0	74.9
Eclair, w/custard filling, chocolate icing: *1 average*	3.9	262.9	25.5	6.8	15.0	149.6	90.2
French Apple Bake, *ETW Recipe: 1 serving*	7.0	261.5	58.2	6.3	1.5	0.5	43.7
French Apple Pie, *FF Recipe: 1 slice*	7.9	372.9	76.8	2.6	7.9	0.7	264.9
Frozen Yogurt, soft-serve: *1 serving*	4.0	149.9	30.8	4.4	1.7	11.3	117.2

	Weight (oz)	Calories	Carbo. (g)	Protein (g)	Fat (g)	Choles. (mg)	Sodium (mg)
Fruitcake, dark, w/butter: *1 slice*	1.4	145.2	23.9	1.9	5.5	26.4	94.0
Fruitcake, dark, w/vegetable shortening: *1 slice*	1.4	151.6	23.9	1.9	6.1	18.0	63.2
Fruitcake, *ETS Recipe: 1 slice*	2.0	203.4	37.8	2.8	6.0	0	29.2
Gelatin Dessert, plain, from powder, w/water: *1 serving*	4.2	70.9	16.9	1.8	0	0	61.3
Gelatin Dessert, w/fruit, from powder, w/water: *1 serving*	4.4	83.7	20.5	1.6	0.1	0	42.5
Gingerbread Cake, w/butter: *1 slice*	1.8	148.5	25.7	1.9	4.9	33.0	169.5
Gingerbread Cake, w/vegetable shortening: *1 slice*	1.8	158.5	26.0	1.9	5.3	21.5	118.5
Holiday Cake, *ETW Recipe: 1 slice*	5.8	385.7	81.8	11.5	3.1	0.4	197.1
Honey Spice Cake, from mix, w/caramel icing, eggs: *1 slice*	1.8	176.0	30.4	2.0	5.4	29.0	122.5
Honey, strained or extracted: *1 serving*	0.7	60.8	16.5	0.1	0	0	1.0
Ice Cream, regular, 10% fat: *1 serving*	2.3	134.3	15.9	2.4	7.2	29.9	58.1
Ice Cream, regular, 12% fat: *1 serving*	2.3	137.7	13.7	2.7	8.3	30.6	26.6
Ice Cream, rich, 16% fat: *1 serving*	2.6	174.7	16.0	2.1	11.8	43.7	54.1
Ice Milk, vanilla: *1 serving*	2.4	94.6	14.9	2.6	2.9	9.5	53.9
Lemon Chiffon Pie, w/lard, no salt in filling: *1 slice*	3.9	344.3	48.2	7.7	13.9	195.8	287.1
Lemon Chiffon Pie, w/vegetable shortening, no salt in filling: *1 slice*	3.9	344.3	48.2	7.7	13.9	185.9	287.1
Lemon Meringue Pie, w/lard: *1 slice*	4.9	354.2	52.4	5.1	14.2	138.9	391.7
Lemon Meringue Pie, w/vegetable shortening: *1 slice*	4.9	354.2	52.4	5.1	14.2	129.2	391.7
Lemon Pie, *FF Recipe: 1 slice*	3.6	134.5	25.1	7.3	0.3	2.3	266.4

Desserts/Dessert Sauces (*continued*)	Weight (oz)	Calories	Carbo. (g)	Protein (g)	Fat (g)	Choles. (mg)	Sodium (mg)
Maple Syrup: 3½ ounces	3.5	249.8	64.4	0	0	0	9.9
Marble Cake, w/boiled white icing, from mix, w/eggs: *1 slice*	1.8	165.5	31.0	2.2	4.3	25.5	129.5
Merv's Favorite Chocolate-Covered Cherry Cake, *ETS Recipe: 1 slice*	3.4	244.2	39.5	4.0	8.7	0	13.3
Mince Pie, w/lard: 1 slice	5.6	433.6	65.9	4.0	18.4	17.6	716.8
Mince Pie, w/vegetable shortening: 1 slice	5.6	433.6	65.9	4.0	18.4	1.6	716.8
Molasses, cane, light: 1 serving	0.7	50.4	13.0	0	0	0	3.0
Noodle Pudding, *ETW Recipe: 1 serving*	4.0	207.2	46.3	6.0	0.9	0.6	40.5
Oatmeal Apple Squares, *FF Recipe: 1 average*	2.0	187.2	34.1	2.4	5.2	0.3	141.6
Peach Pie, w/lard, no salt in filling: 1 slice	5.6	408.0	61.1	4.0	17.1	17.6	428.8
Peach Pie, w/vegetable shortening, no salt in filling: *1 slice*	5.6	408.0	61.1	4.0	17.1	0	428.8
Pecan Pie, w/lard, no salt in filling: 1 slice	3.5	418.0	51.3	5.1	22.9	70.0	221.0
Pecan Pie, w/vegetable shortening, no salt in filling: *1 slice*	3.5	418.0	51.3	5.1	22.9	63.0	221.0
Piecrust, from mix, w/water, baked: 3½ ounces	3.5	460.4	43.7	6.4	28.9	0	806.7
Piecrust, w/lard, baked: 3½ ounces	3.5	496.1	43.5	6.1	33.1	30.8	606.3
Piecrust, w/vegetable shortening, baked: 3½ ounces	3.5	496.1	43.5	6.1	33.1	0	606.3
Pineapple Chiffon Pie, w/lard, no salt in filling: *1 slice*	3.9	316.8	43.0	7.3	13.3	174.9	281.6
Pineapple Chiffon Pie, w/vegetable shortening, no salt in filling: *1 slice*	3.9	316.8	43.0	7.3	13.3	167.2	281.6
Pineapple Custard Pie, w/lard, no salt in filling: *1 slice*	5.3	330.0	48.1	6.0	13.0	91.5	279.0
Pineapple Custard Pie, w/vegetable shortening, no salt in filling: *1 slice*	5.3	330.0	48.1	6.0	13.0	82.5	279.0

	Weight (oz)	Calories	Carbo. (g)	Protein (g)	Fat (g)	Choles. (mg)	Sodium (mg)
Pineapple Pie, w/lard, no salt in filling: *1 slice*	5.6	404.8	61.0	3.5	17.1	17.6	433.6
Pineapple Pie, w/vegetable shortening, no salt in filling: *1 serving*	5.6	404.8	61.0	3.5	17.1	0	433.6
Pineapple-Pumpkin Upside Down Cake, *ETS Recipe: 1 slice*	3.7	191.0	46.2	2.4	0.4	0	79.0
Plain Cake, no icing, w/butter: *1 slice*	1.8	175.0	27.6	2.3	6.3	46.5	210.0
Plain Cake, no icing, w/vegetable shortening: *1 slice*	1.8	182.0	27.9	2.2	6.9	32.5	150.0
Plain Cake, w/chocolate icing, butter: *1 slice*	1.8	179.0	29.4	2.1	6.5	35.0	156.5
Plain Cake, w/chocolate icing, vegetable shortening: *1 slice*	1.8	184.0	29.7	2.1	6.9	25.0	114.5
Pound Cake, w/butter: *1 slice*	1.1	131.1	14.5	1.7	7.5	60.9	109.8
Pound Cake, w/vegetable shortening: *1 slice*	1.1	144.6	14.5	1.7	9.0	40.5	30.6
Prune Whip: *1 serving*	2.8	124.8	29.5	3.5	0.2	0	131.2
Pumpkin–Brown Rice Pudding, *ETS Recipe: 1 serving*	6.5	178.7	36.6	7.4	0.7	1.7	76.7
Pumpkin Pie, w/lard, no salt in filling: *1 slice*	5.3	316.5	36.7	6.0	16.8	97.5	321.0
Pumpkin Pie, w/vegetable shortening, no salt in filling: *1 slice*	5.3	316.5	36.7	6.0	16.8	91.5	321.0
Raisin Brownie Cupcakes, *FF Recipe: 1 average*	2.3	168.5	33.5	2.4	3.6	0.2	47.7
Raisin Pie, w/lard: *1 slice*	4.2	324.0	51.6	3.1	12.8	12.0	342.0
Raisin Pie, w/vegetable shortening: *1 serving*	4.2	324.0	51.6	3.1	12.8	0	342.0
Raspberry Preserve Bar, *ETS Recipe: 1 average*	1.7	162.1	21.2	4.0	7.6	0	7.9
Rennin Chocolate Dessert, from mix, w/milk: *1 serving*	4.6	129.5	17.9	4.3	4.8	15.3	66.0
Rennin Dessert, home prepared w/tablet: *1 serving*	4.5	113.0	14.7	3.9	4.4	15.2	104.1

Desserts/Dessert Sauces (*continued*)	Weight (oz)	Calories	Carbo. (g)	Protein (g)	Fat (g)	Choles. (mg)	Sodium (mg)
Rennin Dessert, vanilla, caramel, or fruit-flavored: *1 serving*	4.5	120.7	16.3	4.1	4.6	16.5	58.4
Rhubarb Pie, w/lard, no salt in filling: *1 slice*	5.6	404.8	61.1	4.0	17.1	17.6	432.0
Rhubarb Pie, w/vegetable shortening, no salt in filling: *1 serving*	5.6	404.8	61.1	4.0	17.1	0	432.0
Rice Pudding, w/raisins: *1 serving*	3.4	141.1	25.8	3.5	3.0	10.6	68.6
Sherbert, orange-flavored: *1 serving*	3.4	134.6	29.2	1.1	1.9	6.7	44.0
Sponge Cake: *1 slice*	1.8	148.5	27.0	3.8	2.8	123.0	83.5
Strawberry Freeze, *FF Recipe: 1 serving*	6.2	166.8	40.3	3.3	0.2	1.2	41.0
Strawberry Pie, w/lard, no salt in filling: *1 slice*	3.5	198.0	30.9	1.9	7.9	8.0	194.0
Strawberry Pie, w/vegetable shortening, no salt in filling: *1 slice*	3.5	100.0	15.6	1.0	4.0	0	98.0
Strawberry Sauce, *FF Recipe: 1 serving*	4.0	111.9	29.4	0.6	0.1	0	3.4
Sweet Potato Pie, w/lard, no salt in filling: *1 slice*	5.6	340.8	37.9	7.2	18.1	96.0	348.8
Sweet Potato Pie, w/vegetable shortening, no salt in filling: *1 slice*	5.6	340.8	37.9	7.2	18.1	86.4	348.8
Tapioca Cream Pudding: *1 serving*	4.6	174.5	22.3	6.5	6.6	126.3	203.1
Tapioca Dessert, apple: *1 serving*	4.3	142.8	35.9	0.2	0.1	0	62.2
Vanilla Pudding, home recipe, starch base: *1 serving*	4.3	135.4	19.4	4.3	4.8	17.1	79.3
White Cake, no icing, w/butter: *1 slice*	1.8	174.5	26.5	2.3	7.2	20.0	240.5
White Cake, no icing, w/vegetable shortening: *1 slice*	1.8	187.5	27.0	2.3	8.0	1.5	161.5
White Cake, w/chocolate icing, from mix, w/eggs: *1 slice*	1.8	175.5	31.4	1.9	5.3	1.0	113.5
Yellow Cake, no icing, w/butter: *1 slice*	1.8	172.5	28.8	2.3	5.8	40.0	184.0

	Weight (oz)	Calories	Carbo. (g)	Protein (g)	Fat (g)	Choles. (mg)	Sodium (mg)
Yellow Cake, no icing, w/vegetable shortening: *1 slice*	1.8	181.5	29.1	2.2	6.3	27.0	129.0
Yellow Cake, w/chocolate icing, butter: *1 slice*	1.8	176.0	29.9	2.1	6.1	32.0	145.0
Yellow Cake, w/chocolate icing, vegetable shortening: *1 slice*	1.8	182.5	30.2	2.1	6.5	22.0	104.0

EGGS

	Weight (oz)	Calories	Carbo. (g)	Protein (g)	Fat (g)	Choles. (mg)	Sodium (mg)
Baked Omelet, *FF Recipe: 1 serving*	3.9	89.9	6.4	11.0	2.0	8.4	267.3
Cheddar Scramble, *ETS Recipe: 1 serving*	4.5	98.4	4.0	12.7	3.2	10.8	344.8
Duck Egg, whole, fresh, raw: *1 average*	2.6	136.9	1.0	9.5	10.2	654.2	108.0
Egg, fried: *1 average*	1.8	90.0	0.5	5.8	6.9	267.0	156.5
Egg, hard-cooked: *1 average*	1.7	75.8	0.6	5.8	5.3	263.0	66.4
Egg, omelet: *1 average*	2.2	91.8	1.3	5.8	6.9	240.6	150.4
Egg, poached: *1 average*	1.7	75.4	0.6	5.8	5.3	261.6	140.5
Egg, scrambled: *1 average*	2.6	111.0	1.6	7.0	8.3	291.0	181.9
Egg White, flakes, dried: *3½ ounces*	3.5	348.3	4.2	76.3	0	0	1147.0
Egg White, powder, dried: *3½ ounces*	3.5	373.1	4.5	81.8	0	0	1228.8
Egg White, raw: *1 average*	1.1	15.2	0.4	3.1	0	0	47.2
Egg, whole, dried: *1 serving*	0.2	41.6	0.3	3.2	2.9	134.3	36.5
Egg, whole, dried, stabilized, glucose-reduced: *1 serving*	0.2	43.1	0.2	3.4	3.1	141.2	38.4
Egg, whole, raw: *1 average*	1.7	76.1	0.6	5.8	5.3	264.1	66.7

Eggs *(continued)*	Weight (oz)	Calories	Carbo. (g)	Protein (g)	Fat (g)	Choles. (mg)	Sodium (mg)
Egg Yolk, dried: *3½ ounces*	3.5	681.7	0.4	30.3	60.8	2905.3	89.9
Egg Yolk, fresh, raw: *1 serving*	0.6	54.9	0.1	2.5	4.9	221.2	10.7
Goose Egg, whole, fresh, raw: *1 average*	3.2	166.5	1.3	12.5	12.0	766.8	124.1
Haas "Scrambled Eggs and Bacon," *ETW Recipe: 1 serving*	4.5	239.3	33.9	16.4	4.4	4.6	824.6
Mushroom-Onion Scramble, *ETS Recipe: 1 serving*	5.0	97.6	5.4	13.7	2.1	5.9	322.9
Nova Scramble, *ETS Recipe: 1 serving*	3.5	64.4	3.1	8.9	1.6	6.0	970.9
Turkey Egg, whole, fresh, raw: *1 average*	2.8	136.8	0.9	11.0	9.5	746.4	121.0

FAST FOODS

	Weight (oz)	Calories	Carbo. (g)	Protein (g)	Fat (g)	Choles. (mg)	Sodium (mg)
Apple Pie, McDonald's: *1 serving*	3.2	295.0	30.5	2.2	18.3	15.0	408.0
Bean Burrito, Taco Bell: *1 serving*	5.9	343.0	48.0	11.0	12.0	25.1	272.0
Bean Burrito, w/o cheese, Taco Bell: *1 serving*	4.1	257.3	47.7	5.7	5.0	2.8	140.1
Beef Burrito, Taco Bell: *1 serving*	6.5	466.0	37.0	30.0	21.0	110.0	327.0
Beef Taco, Taco Bell: *1 serving*	2.9	186.0	14.0	15.0	8.0	90.0	175.0
Beefy Tostada, Taco Bell: *1 serving*	6.5	291.0	21.0	19.0	15.0	65.0	138.0
Bellbeefer, Taco Bell: *1 serving*	4.3	221.0	23.0	15.0	7.0	90.0	231.0
Bellbeefer, w/cheese, Taco Bell: *1 serving*	4.8	278.0	23.0	19.0	12.0	104.9	330.0
Big Mac, McDonald's: *1 serving*	6.6	541.0	39.0	25.6	31.4	75.0	963.0
Burrito, combination, Taco Bell: *1 serving*	6.2	404.0	43.0	21.0	16.0	110.1	300.0

	Weight (oz)	Calories	Carbo. (g)	Protein (g)	Fat (g)	Choles. (mg)	Sodium (mg)
Burrito Supreme, Taco Bell: *1 serving*	7.9	457.0	43.0	21.0	22.0	150.1	245.0
Cheeseburger, Burger King: *1 serving*	4.6	305.0	29.0	17.0	13.0	41.0	823.0
Cheeseburger, McDonald's: *1 serving*	4.0	306.0	30.4	15.6	13.3	41.0	724.0
Cherry Pie, McDonald's: *1 serving*	3.2	296.0	32.4	2.2	17.6	15.0	454.0
Chicken Dinner, Original Recipe, Kentucky Fried Chicken: *1 serving*	15.0	830.0	56.0	52.0	46.0	285.2	472.0
Chicken Drumstick, Kentucky Fried Chicken: *1 serving*	1.9	136.0	2.0	14.0	8.0	73.0	60.0
Chicken Thigh, Kentucky Fried Chicken: *1 serving*	3.4	276.0	12.0	20.0	19.0	147.0	88.0
Chicken Wing, Kentucky Fried Chicken: *1 serving*	1.6	151.0	4.0	11.0	10.0	70.0	60.0
Chili, Wendy's: *1 serving*	8.8	250.0	23.0	22.0	7.0	70.0	1190.0
Egg McMuffin, McDonald's: *1 serving*	4.7	352.0	26.0	18.0	20.0	192.1	911.0
Eggs, scrambled, McDonald's: *1 serving*	2.7	161.0	1.9	11.6	11.9	301.0	206.0
Enchirito, Taco Bell: *1 serving*	7.3	454.0	42.0	25.0	21.0	109.9	338.0
English Muffin, buttered, McDonald's: *1 serving*	2.2	186.0	28.0	5.6	5.6	10.0	446.0
Filet o' Fish, McDonald's: *1 serving*	4.6	402.0	34.0	15.0	22.7	43.0	707.0
French Fries, McDonald's: *1 serving*	2.4	211.0	25.0	3.1	10.6	10.0	112.0
Hamburger, Burger King: *1 serving*	3.2	252.0	29.0	14.0	9.0	26.0	372.0
Hamburger, McDonald's: *1 serving*	3.5	257.0	30.1	13.3	9.4	26.0	525.0
Hamburger, single, Wendy's: *1 serving*	7.1	440.0	33.0	25.0	25.0	75.0	708.0
Hot Cakes, w/butter and syrup, McDonald's: *1 serving*	7.3	472.0	89.0	8.0	9.0	35.0	1071.0

Fast Foods (continued)	Weight (oz)	Calories	Carbo. (g)	Protein (g)	Fat (g)	Choles. (mg)	Sodium (mg)
McDLT, McDonald's: *1 serving*	9.0	680.0	40.0	30.0	44.0	97.0	1030.0
Milk Shake, chocolate, McDonald's: *1 serving*	10.2	324.0	51.7	10.7	8.4	28.9	329.0
Milk Shake, strawberry, McDonald's: *1 serving*	10.3	346.0	57.5	10.3	8.5	29.8	257.0
Milk Shake, vanilla, Burger King: *1 serving*	11.1	331.0	48.5	13.2	9.5	31.5	306.0
Milk Shake, vanilla, McDonald's: *1 serving*	10.2	324.0	51.7	10.7	7.8	28.9	250.0
Pintos 'n' Cheese, Taco Bell: *1 serving*	5.6	168.0	21.0	11.0	5.0	25.1	210.0
Quarter Pounder, McDonald's: *1 serving*	5.8	418.0	33.0	25.6	20.5	69.0	278.0
Quarter Pounder w/cheese, McDonald's: *1 serving*	6.8	518.0	33.0	30.9	28.6	95.9	1206.0
Sausage, pork, McDonald's: *1 serving*	1.8	191.0	0	8.9	17.2	43.0	487.0
Taco, Taco Bell: *1 serving*	2.9	186.0	14.0	15.0	8.0	89.6	175.0
Tostada, Taco Bell: *1 serving*	3.0	179.0	25.0	9.0	6.0	22.0	186.0

FISH/SEAFOOD

	Weight (oz)	Calories	Carbo. (g)	Protein (g)	Fat (g)	Choles. (mg)	Sodium (mg)
Anchovy Paste: *3½ ounces*	3.5	198.4	4.3	19.8	11.3	70.8	7229.1
Anchovy, pickled, no added oil, not heavily salted: *3½ ounces*	3.5	174.6	0.3	19.1	10.2	54.6	816.6
Baked Garlic Snapper, *FF Recipe: 1 serving*	18.1	475.2	1.5	99.2	5.0	171.0	384.5
Barracuda, Pacific, raw: *1 serving*	3.5	112.1	0	20.8	2.6	54.6	39.7
Bass, Black Sea, raw: *3½ ounces*	3.5	92.3	0	19.1	1.2	54.6	67.5
Bluefish, baked or broiled: *1 serving*	3.5	157.8	0	26.0	5.2	69.5	103.2

	Weight (oz)	Calories	Carbo. (g)	Protein (g)	Fat (g)	Choles. (mg)	Sodium (mg)
Bluefish, raw: *3½ ounces*	3.5	116.1	0	20.3	3.3	54.6	73.4
Bonito, raw: *3½ ounces*	3.5	166.7	0	23.8	7.2	54.6	39.7
Broiled Shrimp, *ETS Recipe: 1 serving*	6.0	229.7	17.9	30.0	3.6	153.8	390.4
Butterfish, from Gulf waters, raw: *1 serving*	3.5	94.3	0	16.1	2.9	54.6	53.6
Carp, raw: *3½ ounces*	3.5	114.1	0	17.9	4.2	54.6	49.6
Catfish, freshwater, raw: *1 serving*	3.5	102.2	0	17.5	3.1	54.6	59.5
Caviar, sturgeon, granular: *1 serving*	0.7	52.4	0.7	5.4	3.0	60.0	440.0
Caviar, sturgeon, pressed: *1 serving*	0.7	63.2	1.0	6.9	3.3	76.8	440.0
Clam Fritters: *1 serving*	3.5	308.6	30.7	11.3	14.9	128.0	119.1
Clams, canned, drained solids: *1 serving*	3.5	97.2	1.9	15.7	2.5	62.5	119.1
Clams, canned, solids and liquid: *1 serving*	3.5	51.6	2.8	7.8	0.7	31.8	565.6
Cod, broiled: *1 serving*	3.5	168.7	0	28.3	5.3	80.4	109.1
Cod, raw: *3½ ounces*	3.5	77.4	0	17.5	0.3	49.6	69.5
Crab, canned: *1 serving*	3.5	100.2	1.1	17.3	2.5	100.2	992.2
Crab, steamed: *1 serving*	3.5	92.3	0.5	17.2	1.9	99.2	208.4
Fish and Mushroom Marinade, *ETW Recipe: 1 serving*	6.0	270.8	5.4	32.9	6.9	90.7	264.7
Fish Sticks, frozen, cooked: *4½ average*	3.5	174.6	6.4	16.5	8.8	46.6	175.6
Flounder, baked: *1 serving*	3.5	200.4	0	29.8	8.1	89.3	235.2
Frog Legs, raw: *4 large*	3.5	72.4	0	16.3	0.3	49.6	57.5

Fish/Seafood (continued)	Weight (oz)	Calories	Carbo. (g)	Protein (g)	Fat (g)	Choles. (mg)	Sodium (mg)
Grouper, raw: *3½ ounces*	3.5	86.3	0	19.2	0.5	54.6	60.5
Haddock, fried: *1 serving*	3.5	163.7	5.8	19.4	6.4	63.5	175.6
Haddock, raw: *3½ ounces*	3.5	78.4	0	18.2	0.1	59.5	60.5
Haddock, smoked: *1 serving*	3.5	102.2	0	23.0	0.4	75.4	6182.6
Halibut, broiled: *1 serving*	3.5	169.7	0	25.0	6.9	59.5	133.0
Herring, Bismarck type, pickled: *1 serving*	3.5	231.2	0	20.2	15.0	99.2	6182.6
Herring, bloaters, smoked: *1 serving*	3.5	194.5	0	19.4	12.3	95.3	6182.6
Herring, canned in tomato sauce, solids and liquid: *1 serving*	3.5	174.6	3.7	15.7	10.4	77.4	73.4
Herring, kippered, smoked: *1 serving*	3.5	209.4	0	22.0	12.8	108.2	6182.6
Herring, plain, canned, solids and liquid: *1 serving*	3.5	206.4	0	19.7	13.5	96.2	73.4
Lobster Paste, canned: *3½ ounces*	3.5	178.6	1.5	20.6	9.3	170.7	138.9
Lobster, steamed: *1 serving*	1.0	25.8	0.1	4.8	0.5	23.8	60.1
Mackerel, Atlantic, broiled w/butter: *1 serving*	3.5	234.2	0	21.6	15.7	100.2	73.4
Mackerel, Atlantic, canned, solids and liquid: *1 serving*	3.5	181.6	0	19.2	11.0	93.3	73.4
Mackerel, Pacific, canned, solids and liquid: *1 serving*	3.5	178.6	0	20.9	9.9	93.3	73.4
Mackerel, Pacific, raw: *3½ ounces*	3.5	157.8	0	21.7	7.2	94.3	73.4
Mussels, Pacific, canned, drained solids: *1 serving*	3.5	113.1	1.5	18.1	3.3	44.7	286.8
Ocean Perch, Atlantic, fried: *1 serving*	3.5	225.2	6.7	18.9	13.2	57.5	151.8
Ocean Perch, Atlantic, raw: *3½ ounces*	3.5	87.3	0	17.9	1.2	54.6	78.4

	Weight (oz)	Calories	Carbo. (g)	Protein (g)	Fat (g)	Choles. (mg)	Sodium (mg)
Oysters, canned, solids and liquid: 1 serving	3.5	75.4	4.9	8.4	2.2	44.7	377.0
Oysters, Eastern, meat only, raw: 3½ ounces	3.5	65.5	3.4	8.3	1.8	49.6	72.4
Oysters, Pacific and Western, Olympia, meat only, raw: 3½ ounces	3.5	90.3	6.4	10.5	2.2	49.6	72.4
Perch, white, raw: 3½ ounces	3.5	117.1	0	19.2	4.0	54.6	49.6
Pike, blue, raw: 3½ ounces	3.5	89.3	0	19.0	0.9	54.6	50.6
Poached Salmon, ETS Recipe: 1 serving	7.5	247.1	8.9	27.7	7.7	46.6	189.8
Red Snapper, raw: 1 serving	3.5	93.0	0	19.8	0.9	35.0	67.0
Roe, from salmon, sturgeon, or turbot, raw: 3½ ounces	3.5	205.4	1.4	25.0	10.3	357.2	72.4
Salmon, Atlantic, canned, solids and liquid: 3½ ounces	3.5	201.4	0	21.5	12.1	36.7	73.4
Salmon, Atlantic, raw: 3½ ounces	3.5	215.3	0	22.3	13.3	38.7	73.4
Salmon, broiled or baked: 1 serving	3.5	180.6	0	26.8	7.3	46.6	115.1
Salmon, pink, canned, solids and liquid, w/o salt: 1 serving	3.5	139.9	0	20.3	5.9	34.7	63.5
Salmon, pink, canned, solids and liquid, w/salt: 1 serving	3.5	139.9	0	20.3	5.9	34.7	384.0
Salmon, smoked: 3½ ounces	3.5	174.6	0	21.4	9.2	37.7	6182.6
Sardines, Atlantic, canned in oil, drained solids: 3½ ounces	3.5	201.4	0	23.8	11.0	138.9	816.6
Sardines, Pacific, canned in mustard, solid and liquid: 3½ ounces	3.5	194.5	1.7	18.7	11.9	109.1	754.1
Sardines, Pacific, canned in oil, drained solids: 3½ ounces	3.5	201.4	0	23.8	11.0	119.1	816.6
Scallops, frozen, fried: 1 serving	3.5	192.5	10.4	17.9	8.3	40.7	119.1
Scallops, steamed: 3½ ounces	3.5	112.0	4.5	23.2	1.4	35.0	262.0

Fish/Seafood (*continued*)	Weight (oz)	Calories	Carbo. (g)	Protein (g)	Fat (g)	Choles. (mg)	Sodium (mg)
Shad, American, baked: 1 serving	3.5	199.4	0	23.0	11.2	68.5	78.4
Shrimp, canned, wet pack, drained solids: 3½ ounces	3.5	115.1	0.7	24.0	1.1	148.8	138.9
Shrimp, canned, wet pack, solids and liquid: 3½ ounces	3.5	79.4	0.8	16.1	0.8	133.0	138.9
Shrimp, fried: 1 serving	3.5	223.3	9.9	20.1	10.7	148.8	184.6
Swordfish, broiled: 1 serving	3.5	172.6	0	27.8	6.0	79.4	133.0
Trout, brook, raw: 3½ ounces	3.5	100.2	0	19.1	2.1	48.6	46.6
Tuna, canned in water, solids and liquid, w/o salt: 1 serving	3.5	126.0	0	27.8	0.8	62.5	40.7
Tuna, canned in water, solids and liquid, w/salt: 1 serving	3.5	126.0	0	27.8	0.8	62.5	868.2
Turbot, raw: 3½ ounces	3.5	81.4	0	17.3	0.9	54.6	60.5
Whitefish, smoked: 1 serving	3.5	153.8	0	20.7	7.2	60.5	6182.6

FLOURS/FLOUR MIXES/DOUGH

	Weight (oz)	Calories	Carbo. (g)	Protein (g)	Fat (g)	Choles. (mg)	Sodium (mg)
Buckwheat Flour, light: 3½ ounces	3.5	344.3	78.9	6.4	1.2	0	2.0
Cornmeal, unrefined: 3½ ounces	3.5	359.2	73.9	8.9	3.4	0	1.0
Cornmeal, white, degermed, cooked w/o salt: 1 serving	8.5	120.0	25.7	2.6	0.5	0	0
Lima Bean Flour: 3½ ounces	3.5	340.3	62.5	21.3	1.4	0	4.0
Muffin Mix, corn, w/nonfat dry milk: 3½ ounces	3.5	405.8	71.0	6.2	10.6	6.0	804.7
Pancake Mix, buckwheat, dry form: 3½ ounces	3.5	325.5	69.8	10.4	1.9	0	1323.6
Roll Dough, frozen, unraised: 3½ ounces	3.5	265.9	47.0	7.4	5.0	5.0	478.3

	Weight (oz)	Calories	Carbo. (g)	Protein (g)	Fat (g)	Choles. (mg)	Sodium (mg)
Rye Flour, medium: *3½ ounces*	3.5	347.3	74.2	11.3	1.7	0	1.0
Soybean Flour, defatted: *3½ ounces*	3.5	323.5	37.8	46.6	0.9	0	1.0
Soybean Flour, high fat: *3½ ounces*	3.5	377.0	33.0	40.9	12.0	0	1.0
Waffle Mix, dry form: *3½ ounces*	3.5	454.4	64.9	6.4	19.1	0	1019.0
Wheat Flour, all-purpose: *3½ ounces*	3.5	361.2	75.5	10.4	1.0	0	2.0
Wheat Flour, bread type: *3½ ounces*	3.5	362.2	74.1	11.7	1.1	0	2.0
Wheat Flour, cake or pastry type: *3½ ounces*	3.5	361.2	78.8	7.4	0.8	0	2.0
Wheat Flour, gluten, 45% gluten, 55% patent: *3½ ounces*	3.5	375.1	46.8	41.1	1.9	0	2.0
Wheat Flour, self-rising, w/anhydrous monocal phosphate: *3½ ounces*	3.5	349.3	73.6	9.2	1.0	0	1070.6
Wheat Flour, self-rising, w/sodium acid pyrophosphate: *3½ ounces*	3.5	349.3	73.6	9.2	1.0	0	1349.4
Wheat Flour, whole wheat: *3½ ounces*	3.5	330.4	70.4	13.2	2.0	0	3.0

FRUIT

	Weight (oz)	Calories	Carbo. (g)	Protein (g)	Fat (g)	Choles. (mg)	Sodium (mg)
Acerola, raw: *3½ ounces*	3.5	31.8	7.6	0.4	0.3	0	6.9
Amaranth, raw: *3½ ounces*	3.5	35.7	6.4	3.5	0.5	0	70.4
Apple, dried, cooked w/o sugar: *3½ ounces*	3.5	56.6	15.2	0.2	0.1	0	19.8
Apple, dried, sulfured: *3½ ounces*	3.5	241.1	65.4	0.9	0.3	0	86.3
Apple, raw, w/o skin: *1 average*	5.3	85.5	22.2	0.1	0.4	0	1.7
Apple, raw, w/skin: *1 average*	5.3	88.5	22.9	0.3	0.6	0	1.7

Fruit Fish/Seafood (*continued*)	Weight (oz)	Calories	Carbo. (g)	Protein (g)	Fat (g)	Choles. (mg)	Sodium (mg)
Applesauce, canned, w/o sugar: 1 serving	4.3	50.0	13.2	0.2	0.2	0	2.5
Applesauce, ETS Recipe: 1 serving	7.5	140.9	35.4	0.7	0.6	0	2.9
Apricot Nectar, canned, 40% fruit: 1 serving	8.9	143.0	36.6	0.8	0.3	0	7.5
Apricots, canned, solids and liquid, juice-packed: 1 serving	9.1	123.8	31.7	1.5	0	0	10.3
Apricots, dried: 3½ ounces	3.5	236.2	61.3	3.6	0.5	0	9.9
Apricots, raw: 3½ ounces	3.5	47.6	11.0	1.4	0.4	0	0.9
Avocado, raw, pitted: 1 serving	5.3	241.5	11.1	3.0	22.9	0	15.0
Banana, common, raw: 1 average	5.3	138.0	35.1	1.5	0.8	0	2.0
Banana Puree: 3½ ounces	3.5	84.0	21.8	1.1	0.2	0	1.3
Blackberries, raw: 3½ ounces	3.5	51.6	12.7	0.7	0.4	0	0.7
Blueberries, frozen, w/o sugar: 3½ ounces	3.5	50.6	12.1	0.4	0.6	0	0.9
Blueberries, raw: 3½ ounces	3.5	55.6	14.0	0.7	0.4	0	6.0
Boysenberries, raw: 3½ ounces	3.5	51.6	12.7	0.7	0.4	0	0.8
Cantaloupe, raw: ¼ average	3.5	34.7	8.3	0.9	0.3	0	8.9
Casaba Melon, raw: 1 slice	3.5	26.0	6.2	0.9	0.1	0	12.0
Cherries, maraschino, bottled, solids and liquid: 3½ ounces	3.5	115.1	29.2	0.2	0.2	0	1.0
Cherries, sour, red, raw: 3½ ounces	3.5	49.6	12.1	1.0	0.3	0	3.0
Cherries, sweet, canned, water-packed, solids and liquid: 3½ ounces	3.5	45.6	11.7	0.8	0.1	0	1.0
Cherries, sweet, raw: 3½ ounces	3.5	71.4	16.5	1.2	1.0	0	1.5

	Weight (oz)	Calories	Carbo. (g)	Protein (g)	Fat (g)	Choles. (mg)	Sodium (mg)
Crabapple, raw: *3½ ounces*	3.5	75.4	19.7	0.4	0.3	0	1.0
Cranberries, raw: *3½ ounces*	3.5	48.6	12.6	0.4	0.2	0	1.0
Currants, black, European, raw: *3½ ounces*	3.5	62.5	15.3	1.4	0.4	0	2.0
Dates, domestic, natural, dry: *3½ ounces*	3.5	272.9	72.9	2.0	0.4	0	3.0
Elderberries, raw: *3½ ounces*	3.5	72.4	18.3	0.7	0.5	0	0
Figs, dried, uncooked: *3½ ounces*	3.5	253.0	64.9	3.1	1.2	0	10.9
"Fried" Apples, *FF Recipe: 1 serving*	5.4	119.1	29.7	0.6	0.4	0.9	335.1
Fruit Bits: *1 serving*	5.6	480.0	126.6	5.1	0.8	0	19.2
Fruit Cocktail, canned, water-packed, solids and liquid: *1 serving*	3.9	35.6	9.4	0.4	0.1	0	4.4
Gooseberries, raw: *3½ ounces*	3.5	43.7	10.1	0.9	0.6	0	1.0
Grapefruit, canned segments, water-packed, solids and liquid: *1 serving*	3.5	36.0	9.1	0.6	0.1	0	2.0
Grapefruit, raw: *½ average*	3.5	32.0	8.1	0.6	0.1	0	1.0
Grapes, American type, slip skin, raw: *33 average*	5.3	94.5	25.6	0.9	0.6	0	3.0
Grapes, European type, adherent skin, raw: *36 average*	5.6	113.6	28.5	1.1	1.0	0	3.2
Grapes, seedless, canned, water-packed, solids and liquid: *3½ ounces*	3.5	39.7	10.2	0.5	0.1	0	6.0
Guava, common, whole, raw: *1 average*	3.5	51.0	11.9	0.8	0.6	0	3.0
Honeydew Melon, raw: *¼ average*	5.3	52.5	13.8	0.8	0.1	0	15.0
Kumquats, raw: *5 average*	3.5	63.0	16.4	0.9	0.1	0	6.0
Lemon, raw, peeled: *1 average*	3.5	29.0	9.3	1.1	0.3	0	2.0

Fruit (*continued*)	Weight (oz)	Calories	Carbo. (g)	Protein (g)	Fat (g)	Choles. (mg)	Sodium (mg)
Lemon Rind, grated: *1 serving*	7.1	160.0	32.0	3.2	0.8	0	8.0
Lime Rind, grated: *1 serving*	7.1	160.0	32.0	3.2	0.8	0	8.0
Longans, raw: *3½ ounces*	3.5	59.5	15.0	1.3	0.1	0	0
Loquat, raw: *1 serving*	3.5	47.0	12.1	0.4	0.2	0	1.0
Litchi, raw: *3½ ounces*	3.5	65.5	16.4	0.8	0.4	0	1.0
Mango, raw: *½ average*	3.5	65.0	17.0	0.5	0.3	0	2.0
Nectarines, raw: *2 average*	3.5	49.0	11.8	0.9	0.5	0	0
Olives, Greek, salt-cured: *3½ ounces*	3.5	332.2	8.5	1.9	35.2	0	3267.2
Olives, green: *3½ ounces*	3.5	114.5	1.5	1.5	12.2	0	2381.4
Orange, California Navel, winter, peeled, raw: *1 small*	5.3	69.0	17.4	1.5	0.1	0	1.5
Orange, California Valencia, summer, peeled, raw: *1 average*	5.6	78.4	19.0	1.6	0.5	0	0
Orange, Florida, all commercial varieties, peeled, raw: *1 average*	7.1	92.0	23.0	1.4	0.4	0	0
Orange Rind, grated: *3½ ounces*	3.5	79.4	15.9	1.6	0.4	0	4.0
Papaya, dried: *3½ ounces*	3.5	260.0	67.8	3.1	0.7	0	15.9
Papaya, raw: *⅓ average*	3.5	39.0	9.8	0.6	0.1	0	3.0
Peaches, canned, juice-packed, solids and liquid: *1 serving*	3.5	44.0	11.6	0.6	0	0	4.0
Peaches, dried, sulfured, uncooked: *3½ ounces*	3.5	237.1	60.8	3.6	0.8	0	6.9
Peaches, raw: *1 average*	3.5	43.0	11.1	0.7	0.1	0	0.9
Pears, canned, juice-packed, solids and liquid: *1 small*	3.5	50.0	12.9	0.3	0.1	0	4.0

	Weight (oz)	Calories	Carbo. (g)	Protein (g)	Fat (g)	Choles. (mg)	Sodium (mg)
Pears, raw, w/skin: *1 average*	7.1	118.0	30.2	0.8	0.8	0	0
Persimmon, native, raw: *1 average*	3.5	127.0	33.5	0.8	0.4	0	1.0
Pineapple, canned, juice-packed, solids and liquid: *1 slice*	4.7	79.9	20.9	0.5	0.1	0	1.3
Pineapple, dried: *3½ ounces*	3.5	260.0	67.8	3.1	0.7	0	15.9
Pineapple, raw: *1 slice*	3.5	49.0	12.4	0.4	0.4	0	1.0
Pitanga, raw: *1 serving*	3.5	33.0	7.5	0.8	0.4	0	3.0
Plantain, raw: *1 small*	3.5	122.0	31.9	1.3	0.4	0	4.0
Plums, Damson, raw: *2 average*	3.5	66.0	17.8	0.5	0	0	2.0
Plums, purple, canned, water-packed, solids and liquid: *2 average*	3.5	41.0	11.0	0.4	0	0	1.0
Pomegranate, raw, pulp: *1 average*	3.5	68.0	17.2	0.9	0.3	0	3.0
Prunes, dried, cooked fruit and liquid, w/o sugar: *5 average*	3.9	137.8	36.6	1.2	0.2	0	2.2
Prunes, dried, uncooked: *1 large*	0.4	25.5	6.7	0.2	0	0	0.8
Quinces, raw: *1 serving*	3.5	57.0	15.3	0.4	0.1	0	4.0
Raisins, seedless, natural, unbleached, uncooked: *3½ ounces*	3.5	297.7	78.5	3.2	0.5	0	11.9
Raspberries, red, raw: *3½ ounces*	3.5	72.6	15.5	1.5	1.4	0	0.7
Sapodilla, raw, pulp: *1 serving*	3.5	83.0	20.0	0.4	1.1	0	12.0
Sapotes, raw: *1 serving*	3.5	134.0	33.8	2.1	0.6	0	10.0
Strawberries, raw: *3½ ounces*	3.5	29.8	6.9	0.6	0.4	0	1.0
Strawberries, sliced, frozen, sweetened: *1 serving*	4.4	120.0	32.4	0.6	0.1	0	3.7

Fruit (*continued*)	Weight (oz)	Calories	Carbo. (g)	Protein (g)	Fat (g)	Choles. (mg)	Sodium (mg)
Tangerine, fancy variety, raw: 2 small	3.5	44.0	11.2	0.6	0.2	0	1.0
Watermelon, raw: 1 slice	21.2	192.0	43.2	3.6	2.4	0	12.0

INFANT FOOD

	Weight (oz)	Calories	Carbo. (g)	Protein (g)	Fat (g)	Choles. (mg)	Sodium (mg)
Apples and Apricots, canned, strained, jr.: 3½ ounces	3.5	44.7	11.5	0.2	0.2	0	3.0
Applesauce, canned, strained, jr.: 3½ ounces	3.5	40.7	10.8	0.2	0.2	0	2.0
Bananas with Tapioca, canned, strained, jr.: 3½ ounces	3.5	56.6	15.2	0.4	0.1	0	8.9
Beans, green, canned, strained, jr.: 3½ ounces	3.5	24.8	5.9	1.3	0.1	0	2.0
Beef, canned, strained, jr.: 3½ ounces	3.5	106.2	0	13.5	5.4	93.3	80.4
Beef, w/beef heart, canned, strained, jr.: 3½ ounces	3.5	93.3	0	12.6	4.4	271.9	62.5
Beets, canned, strained, jr.: 3½ ounces	3.5	33.7	7.6	1.3	0.1	0	82.4
Carrots, canned, strained, jr.: 3½ ounces	3.5	26.8	6.0	0.8	0.1	0	36.7
Cereal, mixed grain, cooked, dry, jr.: 3½ ounces	3.5	369.1	70.5	13.0	4.0	0	466.3
Cereal, oatmeal, cooked, dry, jr.: 3½ ounces	3.5	394.9	68.7	13.5	7.7	0	433.6
Cereal, rice, cooked, dry, jr.: 3½ ounces	3.5	379.0	75.8	6.8	4.5	0	525.9
Chicken, canned, strained, jr.: 3½ ounces	3.5	129.0	0.1	13.6	7.8	86.3	46.6
Chocolate Pudding, strained, jr.: 3½ ounces	3.5	83.3	16.0	1.9	1.7	88.3	22.8
Dinner, chicken and noodles, strained, jr.: 3½ ounces	3.5	51.6	7.4	2.1	1.5	7.9	15.9
Dinner, canned, beef and egg noodle, strained, jr.: 3½ ounces	3.5	52.6	6.9	2.3	1.7	10.9	28.8

	Weight (oz)	Calories	Carbo. (g)	Protein (g)	Fat (g)	Choles. (mg)	Sodium (mg)
Dinner, beef and vegetables, strained, jr.: *3½ ounces*	3.5	74.4	4.2	5.7	4.2	27.8	35.7
Dinner, chicken and vegetables, strained, jr.: *3½ ounces*	3.5	77.4	5.9	6.2	3.6	27.8	26.8
Dinner, turkey and vegetables, strained, jr.: *3½ ounces*	3.5	86.3	6.0	5.6	4.8	24.8	29.8
Dinner, veal and vegetables, strained, jr.: *3½ ounces*	3.5	68.5	6.1	5.9	2.7	26.8	23.8
Dinner, macaroni, tomatoes, beef, strained, jr.: *3½ ounces*	3.5	54.6	8.7	2.2	1.1	9.9	16.9
Dinner, split peas, vegetables, ham or bacon, jr.: *3½ ounces*	3.5	70.4	11.2	3.3	1.3	10.9	13.9
Dinner, vegetables and beef, strained, jr.: *3½ ounces*	3.5	52.6	6.9	2.0	2.0	9.9	20.8
Dinner, vegetables and chicken, strained, jr.: *3½ ounces*	3.5	42.7	6.5	1.9	1.1	7.9	10.9
Dinner, vegetables and ham, strained, jr.: *3½ ounces*	3.5	47.6	6.8	1.8	1.7	10.9	11.9
Dinner, vegetables and lamb, strained, jr.: *3½ ounces*	3.5	51.6	6.8	2.0	2.0	7.9	19.8
Dinner, vegetables and liver, strained, jr.: *3½ ounces*	3.5	38.7	6.8	2.2	0.4	11.9	17.9
Dinner, vegetables and turkey, strained, jr.: *3½ ounces*	3.5	41.7	6.5	1.7	1.2	7.9	12.9
Dinner, vegetables, noodles, chicken, strained, jr.: *3½ ounces*	3.5	62.5	7.8	2.0	2.5	7.9	19.8
Egg Yolks, canned, strained, jr.: *3½ ounces*	3.5	201.4	1.0	9.9	17.2	779.9	38.7
Lamb, canned, strained, jr.: *3½ ounces*	3.5	102.2	0.1	14.0	4.7	97.2	61.5
Liver and Bacon, canned, strained, jr.: *3½ ounces*	3.5	122.0	1.3	13.6	6.5	261.9	299.7
Liver, canned, strained, jr.: *3½ ounces*	3.5	100.2	1.4	14.2	3.8	181.6	73.4
Peaches, canned, w/sugar, strained, jr.: *3½ ounces*	3.5	70.4	18.8	0.5	0.2	0	6.0
Pears and Pineapple, canned, strained, jr.: *3½ ounces*	3.5	40.7	10.8	0.3	0.1	0	4.0

Infant Food (*continued*)	Weight (oz)	Calories	Carbo. (g)	Protein (g)	Fat (g)	Choles. (mg)	Sodium (mg)
Pears, canned, strained, jr.: 3½ ounces	3.5	40.7	10.7	0.3	0.2	0	2.0
Plums with Tapioca, canned, strained, jr.: 3½ ounces	3.5	70.4	19.5	0.1	0	0	6.0
Pork, canned, strained, jr.: 3½ ounces	3.5	123.0	0	13.9	7.0	88.3	41.7
Prunes with Tapioca, canned, strained, jr.: 3½ ounces	3.5	69.5	18.4	0.6	0.1	0	5.0
Spinach, creamed, canned, strained, jr.: 3½ ounces	3.5	36.7	5.7	2.5	1.3	0	48.6
Squash, canned, strained, jr.: 3½ ounces	3.5	23.8	5.6	0.8	0.2	0	2.0
Sweet Potatoes, canned, strained, jr.: 3½ ounces	3.5	56.6	13.1	1.1	0.1	0	19.8
Teething Biscuit, jr.: 3½ ounces	3.5	389.0	75.8	10.6	4.2	0	359.2
Tomato Soup, canned, strained, jr.: 3½ ounces	3.5	53.6	13.4	1.9	0.1	0	291.7
Vanilla Pudding, strained, jr.: 3½ ounces	3.5	84.3	16.0	1.6	2.0	88.3	27.8
Veal, canned, strained, jr.: 3½ ounces	3.5	100.2	0	13.4	4.8	100.2	63.5
Vegetables, mixed, canned, strained, jr.: 3½ ounces	3.5	40.7	7.9	1.2	0.5	0	12.9

JUICES (FRUIT/VEGETABLE)

	Weight (oz)	Calories	Carbo. (g)	Protein (g)	Fat (g)	Choles. (mg)	Sodium (mg)
Acerola Juice, raw: 1 cup	8.7	52.1	11.9	1.0	0.7	0	7.4
Apple Juice Concentrate, undiluted, unsweetened: 1 cup	8.8	300.0	70.0	4.3	0.4	0	3.7
Apple Juice, unsweetened: 1 cup	8.7	116.6	29.0	0.2	0.2	0	7.4
Blackberry Juice, canned, w/o sugar: 1 cup	8.6	90.7	19.1	0.7	1.5	0	2.5
Cranberry Juice Cocktail, 33% juice, bottled: 1 cup	8.5	139.2	35.8	0	0.2	0	9.6

	Weight (oz)	Calories	Carbo. (g)	Protein (g)	Fat (g)	Choles. (mg)	Sodium (mg)
Grape Juice, canned or bottled: *1 cup*	9.0	155.8	38.3	1.5	0.3	0	7.7
Grape Juice Concentrate, undiluted, w/sugar: *1 cup*	8.8	447.5	111.0	1.5	0.7	0	17.5
Grapefruit Juice, canned, unsweetened: *1 cup*	9.0	97.1	23.0	1.3	0.3	0	2.6
Grapefruit Juice Concentrate, undiluted, w/o sugar: *1 cup*	8.8	365.0	86.5	5.0	1.3	0	7.5
Grapefruit Juice, fresh: *1 cup*	9.0	99.6	23.5	1.3	0.3	0	2.6
Lemon Juice, canned or bottled, unsweetened: *1 cup*	8.5	50.4	15.6	1.0	0.7	0	50.4
Lemon Juice, frozen, concentrate, unsweetened: *1 cup*	8.8	290.0	93.5	5.7	2.2	0	12.5
Lemon Juice, raw: *1 cup*	8.5	60.0	20.6	1.0	0	0	2.4
Lemonade, from concentrate, diluted 4⅓ parts water: *1 cup*	8.8	110.0	28.5	0.3	0	0	0
Lime Juice, canned or bottled, unsweetened: *1 cup*	8.5	50.4	16.1	0.7	0.5	0	38.4
Lime Juice, raw: *1 cup*	8.5	64.8	21.6	1.0	0.2	0	2.4
Limeade Concentrate, frozen, undiluted: *1 cup*	8.8	467.5	123.7	0.5	0.2	0	0
Limeade, from concentrate, diluted 4⅓ parts water: *1 cup*	8.8	102.3	27.5	0	0	0	0
Orange Juice Concentrate, undiluted, unsweetened: *1 cup*	8.8	397.5	95.5	6.0	0.5	0	7.5
Orange Juice, fresh: *1 cup*	9.0	114.9	26.6	1.8	0.5	0	2.6
Pineapple Juice, canned, unsweetened: *1 cup*	9.0	143.0	35.2	0.8	0.3	0	2.6
Pineapple Juice Concentrate, undiluted, unsweetened: *1 cup*	8.8	447.5	110.7	3.2	0.2	0	7.5
Prune Juice, canned or bottled: *1 cup*	8.5	170.4	41.8	1.4	0	0	9.6
Sauerkraut Juice, canned: *1 cup*	8.8	25.0	5.7	1.7	0	0	1967.5

Juices (Fruit/Vegetable) (*continued*)	Weight (oz)	Calories	Carbo. (g)	Protein (g)	Fat (g)	Choles. (mg)	Sodium (mg)
Tangelo Juice, raw: *1 cup*	9.0	104.7	24.8	1.3	0.3	0	2.6
Tangerine Juice, fancy variety, raw: *1 cup*	9.0	109.8	25.8	1.3	0.5	0	2.6
Tomato Juice: *1 cup*	8.6	46.0	10.4	2.2	0.2	0	486.0
Tomato Juice, canned or bottled, low-sodium: *1 cup*	8.5	45.6	10.3	1.9	0.2	0	7.2
Tomato Juice, canned or bottled, regular pack: *1 cup*	8.5	45.6	10.3	2.2	0.2	0	480.5
Tomato Juice Cocktail, canned or bottled: *1 cup*	8.5	50.5	12.0	1.7	0.2	0	480.5
Vegetable Juice Cocktail, canned: *1 cup*	8.5	40.8	8.6	2.2	0.2	0	480.5
Vegetable Juice, V-8, no salt added: *1 cup*	8.6	53.3	12.0	1.3	0	0	66.7

MEATS

	Weight (oz)	Calories	Carbo. (g)	Protein (g)	Fat (g)	Choles. (mg)	Sodium (mg)
Bacon, Canadian, broiled or fried, drained: *1 serving*	3.5	271.9	0.3	26.8	17.4	82.4	2535.2
Bacon, cured, broiled or fried, drained: *1 serving*	3.5	594.0	3.2	26.3	52.0	89.0	1021.0
Beef Chuck, lean, choice grade, braised: *1 serving*	3.5	212.3	0	29.8	9.4	90.3	52.1
Beef Club Steak, lean, choice grade, broiled: *1 serving*	3.5	242.1	0	29.4	12.9	90.3	71.9
Beef Double-Bone Sirloin, lean, choice grade, broiled: *1 serving*	3.5	214.3	0	30.4	9.4	90.3	74.4
Beef Flank Steak, total edible, lean, choice, braised: *1 serving*	3.5	194.5	0	30.3	7.2	93.3	53.0
Beef Heart, lean, braised: *1 serving*	3.5	186.5	0.7	31.1	5.7	271.9	103.2
Beef Liver, fried: *1 serving*	3.5	227.2	5.3	26.2	10.5	434.6	182.6
Beef Porterhouse, lean, choice grade, broiled: *1 serving*	3.5	222.3	0	30.0	10.4	90.3	73.4

	Weight (oz)	Calories	Carbo. (g)	Protein (g)	Fat (g)	Choles. (mg)	Sodium (mg)
Beef Rump, lean, choice grade, roasted: 1 serving	3.5	206.4	0	28.9	9.2	90.3	70.7
Beef Sirloin Steak, lean, choice grade, broiled: 1 serving	3.5	205.4	0	31.9	7.6	90.3	78.3
Beef T-Bone, lean, choice grade, broiled: 1 serving	3.5	221.3	0	30.2	10.2	90.3	73.9
Beef Tongue, medium-fat, braised: 1 serving	3.5	242.1	0.4	21.3	16.6	93.3	60.5
Bologna, all meat, w/beef, pork: 1 serving	3.5	313.5	2.8	11.6	28.1	54.6	1011.1
Brains, all kinds, raw: 1 serving	3.5	124.0	0.8	10.3	8.5	1984.5	124.0
Calf Liver, fried: 1 serving	3.5	259.0	4.0	29.3	13.1	434.6	117.1
Calf Sweetbread, braised: 1 serving	3.5	166.7	0	32.3	3.2	462.4	115.1
Corned Beef, medium-fat, cooked: 1 serving	3.5	290.7	0	15.7	24.8	67.5	1289.9
Dried Chipped Beef, cooked, creamed: 1 serving	3.5	152.8	7.0	8.1	10.2	39.7	710.4
Frankfurter, cooked: 1 serving	3.5	301.6	1.6	12.3	27.0	61.5	1091.5
Ground Beef, lean, 21% fat, cooked medium-rare: 1 serving	3.5	283.8	0	24.0	20.1	93.3	58.8
Ham, deviled, canned: 1 serving	3.5	348.3	0	13.8	32.0	64.5	1224.4
Ham, luncheon meat, sliced, regular, boiled: 1 serving	3.5	180.6	3.1	17.5	10.5	56.6	1306.8
Hog Liver, fried: 1 serving	3.5	239.1	2.5	29.7	11.4	434.6	110.1
Hog Tongue, braised: 1 serving	3.5	251.0	0.5	21.8	17.3	87.3	60.5
Knockwurst, w/pork, beef: 1 serving	3.5	305.6	1.8	11.8	27.6	57.5	1002.2
Lamb Leg, lean, choice grade, roasted: 1 serving	3.5	184.6	0	28.5	6.9	99.2	69.8
Lamb Loin, lean, prime grade, broiled: 1 serving	3.5	195.5	0	27.8	8.5	99.2	68.1

Meats (continued)	Weight (oz)	Calories	Carbo. (g)	Protein (g)	Fat (g)	Choles. (mg)	Sodium (mg)
Lamb Rib, lean, choice grade, broiled: 1 serving	3.5	209.4	0	27.0	10.4	99.2	66.1
Liverwurst, pork, fresh: 1 serving	3.5	323.5	2.2	14.0	28.3	156.8	853.3
Lunch meat, w/pork, beef, chopped together: 1 serving	3.5	350.3	2.3	12.5	31.9	54.6	1283.0
Pig's Feet, pickled: 1 serving	3.5	197.5	0	16.6	14.7	88.3	69.5
Pork, Boston Butt, lean, medium-fat, roasted: 1 serving	3.5	242.1	0	26.8	14.2	87.3	65.7
Pork, Ham, lean, light cure, medium-fat, roasted: 1 serving	3.5	185.5	0	25.1	8.7	87.3	898.7
Pork, lean cuts, medium-fat, roasted: 1 serving	3.5	234.2	0	27.8	12.8	87.3	68.1
Pork Loin, lean, retail, medium-fat, broiled: 1 serving	3.5	267.9	0	30.4	15.3	87.3	74.4
Pork Sausage, links or bulk, cooked: 1 serving	3.5	366.1	1.0	19.4	31.0	82.4	1283.9
Pork Spareribs, total edible, medium-fat, braised: 1 serving	3.5	436.6	0	20.6	38.6	88.3	36.1
Salami, w/pork, beef, cooked: 1 serving	3.5	248.1	2.3	13.8	19.9	64.5	1056.7
Sausage, Brown-and-Serve, browned: 1 serving	3.5	392.9	2.7	13.7	36.0	70.4	798.7
Veal Loin, total edible, medium-fat, broiled: 1 serving	3.5	232.2	0	26.2	13.3	100.2	64.2
Veal Scallopini, ETW Recipe: 1 serving	12.5	477.0	33.4	43.3	14.1	107.7	744.3
Venison, lean, raw: 1 serving	3.5	125.0	0	20.8	4.0	64.5	89.3
Vienna Sausage, w/beef, pork, canned: 1 serving	3.5	267.9	2.0	10.2	25.0	51.6	945.6

MILK/MILK MIXES

	Weight (oz)	Calories	Carbo. (g)	Protein (g)	Fat (g)	Choles. (mg)	Sodium (mg)
Buttermilk, cultured, from skim milk: 1 cup	3.4	38.4	4.6	3.2	0.9	3.8	100.7

	Weight (oz)	Calories	Carbo. (g)	Protein (g)	Fat (g)	Choles. (mg)	Sodium (mg)
Condensed Milk, sweetened, canned: 1 cup	10.5	963.0	163.2	23.7	26.1	101.2	381.0
Dry Milk, whole: 1 cup	3.5	496.0	38.4	26.3	26.7	96.2	371.3
Evaporated Milk, whole, unsweetened: 1 cup	8.9	338.0	25.3	17.2	19.1	74.2	266.0
Evaporated Skim Milk, unsweetened: 1 cup	9.0	198.0	28.9	19.3	0.5	10.0	294.0
Goat Milk, fluid: 1 cup	8.6	168.4	10.7	8.8	10.0	26.8	121.5
Human Milk, U.S. samples: 1 cup	8.5	168.0	16.6	2.4	10.6	33.6	40.6
Malted Milk, beverage: 1 cup	9.4	236.1	26.5	10.9	10.1	37.3	215.6
Malted Milk, dry powder: 1 cup	8.8	1027.5	181.3	32.7	21.3	49.9	1141.7
Nonfat Dry Milk, skim solids, instant: 1 cup	2.1	214.8	31.3	21.1	0.4	10.7	329.2
Nonfat Dry Milk, skim solids, regular: 1 cup	2.5	253.5	36.4	25.4	0.6	14.2	374.9
Reindeer Milk: 1 cup	8.6	571.0	10.0	26.4	47.8	34.2	383.1
Skim Milk: 1 cup	8.6	85.4	12.0	8.3	0.5	4.9	125.7
Skim Milk, 2% nonfat milk solids: 1 cup	8.6	136.7	13.4	9.5	4.9	19.5	143.5
Soybean Milk, fluid: 1 cup	9.3	86.8	5.8	8.9	3.9	0	0
Soybean Milk, powder, dry form: 3½ ounces	3.5	425.7	27.8	41.5	20.1	0	1.0
Whole Milk, 3.5% fat: 1 cup	8.6	148.9	11.5	8.1	8.1	34.2	119.6
Yogurt, plain, from partially skimmed milk: 1 cup	8.0	113.5	11.8	7.7	3.9	18.2	115.8
Yogurt, plain, from whole milk: 1 cup	8.0	138.5	10.7	7.9	7.5	29.5	105.3

MISCELLANEOUS

	Weight (oz)	Calories	Carbo. (g)	Protein (g)	Fat (g)	Choles. (mg)	Sodium (mg)
Almond Flavoring: *3½ ounces*	3.5	297.7	29.8	0	0	0	0
Arrowroot Powder: *3½ ounces*	3.5	359.7	86.8	0	0	0	49.6
Bacon Chips, imitation: *1 serving*	0.3	38.0	2.7	3.2	1.6	0	473.0
Baking Powder, home use, low-sodium: *3½ ounces*	3.5	82.4	19.9	0.1	0	0	6.0
Baking Powder, home use, tartrate: *3½ ounces*	3.5	77.1	18.7	0.1	0	0	7214.1
Baking Powder, w/calcium carbonate: *3½ ounces*	3.5	77.4	18.8	0.1	0	0	11527.8
Baking Soda: *3½ ounces*	3.5	0	0	0	0	0	27154.1
Banana Flavoring: *1 serving*	0.2	15.0	1.5	0	0	0	0
Butter Buds, mixed w/water: *1 serving*	1.0	12.0	3.0	0	0	0.7	250.0
Butter Buds, packages, dry: *1 serving*	0.5	48.0	12.0	0	0	2.8	1000.0
Carob Powder: *3½ ounces*	3.5	385.0	91.0	3.5	0	0	10.5
Cointreau: *3½ ounces*	3.5	347.3	32.7	0	0	0	0
Cornstarch: *3½ ounces*	3.5	359.2	86.9	0.3	0	0	0
Dextrose, anhydrous: *3½ ounces*	3.5	363.2	98.7	0	0	0	0
Equal: *3½ ounces*	3.5	396.9	0	9.9	0	0	0
Fructose, granulated: *3½ ounces*	3.5	396.9	99.2	0	0	0	0
Fructose, liquid: *3½ ounces*	3.5	396.9	99.2	0	0	0	0
Gelatin, dry: *1 serving*	0.2	23.5	0	6.0	0+	0	6.3

	Weight (oz)	Calories	Carbo. (g)	Protein (g)	Fat (g)	Choles. (mg)	Sodium (mg)
Liquor, almond-flavored: *1 serving*	5.6	560.0	52.8	0	0	0	0
Malt, dry: *1 serving*	1.0	103.1	21.7	3.7	0.5	0	22.4
Malt, extract, dried: *1 serving*	0.4	36.7	8.9	0.6	0	0	8.0
Meat Tenderizer, Adolph's: *1 serving*	0.2	2.0	0.5	0	0	0	1745.0
Pam: *1 serving*	0+	7.0	0	0	0.8	0	0
Rice Syrup: *3½ ounces*	3.5	396.9	99.2	0	0	0	0
Soybean Protein: *3½ ounces*	3.5	319.5	15.0	74.3	0.1	0	208.4
Sugar, brown: *3½ ounces*	3.5	370.1	95.7	0	0	0	29.8
Sugar, granulated: *3½ ounces*	3.5	382.0	98.7	0	0	0	1.0
Sugar, powdered: *3½ ounces*	3.5	382.0	98.7	0	0	0	1.0
TwinSport Quick Fix: *1 serving*	0.3	23.0	6.0	0	0	0	0
TwinSport Weight Control Powder: *1 serving*	1.0	90.0	18.0	5.0	0.5	3.0	75.0
TwinSport Weight Gain Powder: *1 serving*	1.5	249.0	28.0	7.4	5.0	4.0	111.0
Vanilla Flavoring: *3½ ounces*	3.5	297.7	29.8	0	0	0	0
Vegex, vegetable bouillon cube: *1 average*	0.1	8.0	1.0	1.0	0	0	900.0
Vinegar, cider: *1 serving*	0.5	2.1	0.9	0	0	0	0.1
Vinegar, distilled: *3½ ounces*	3.5	13.2	5.3	0	0	0	0
Vinegar, red wine: *1 serving*	0.5	1.8	0.7	0	0	0	0.1
Whey, sweet, dried: *3½ ounces*	3.5	350.3	73.9	12.8	1.1	6.0	10.7
Whey, sweet, fluid: *3½ ounces*	3.5	26.8	5.1	0.9	0.4	2.0	53.1

Miscellaneous (continued)	Weight (oz)	Calories	Carbo. (g)	Protein (g)	Fat (g)	Choles. (mg)	Sodium (mg)
Yeast, baker's, compressed: 3½ ounces	3.5	85.3	10.9	12.0	0.4	0	15.9
Yeast, baker's, dry active: 3½ ounces	0	0	0	0	0	0	0
Yeast, brewer's, debittered: 1 serving	0.3	22.6	3.1	3.1	0.1	0	9.7
Yeast, torula: 1 serving	0.3	22.2	3.0	3.1	0.1	0	1.2

NUTS/SEEDS

	Weight (oz)	Calories	Carbo. (g)	Protein (g)	Fat (g)	Choles. (mg)	Sodium (mg)
Almonds, raw: 3½ ounces	3.5	593.2	19.4	18.4	53.8	0	4.2
Almonds, roasted, w/salt: 3½ ounces	3.5	622.1	19.3	18.5	57.3	0	196.5
Brazil nuts, raw: 3½ ounces	3.5	649.2	10.8	14.2	66.4	0	0.7
Cashews, roasted, w/o salt: 3½ ounces	3.5	556.6	29.1	17.1	45.3	0	14.9
Cashews, roasted, w/salt: 3½ ounces	3.5	556.6	29.1	17.1	45.3	0	198.4
Chestnuts, dried: 3½ ounces	3.5	374.1	78.0	6.6	4.1	0	11.9
Chestnuts, fresh: 3½ ounces	3.5	192.5	41.8	2.9	1.5	0	6.0
Coconut Meat, dry, shredded, unsweetened: 3½ ounces	3.5	656.9	22.8	7.1	64.4	0	19.8
Coconut Meat, fresh: 3½ ounces	3.5	343.3	9.3	3.5	35.0	0	22.8
Filberts: 3½ ounces	3.5	629.1	16.6	12.5	61.9	0	2.0
Hickory nuts: 3½ ounces	3.5	667.8	12.7	13.1	68.2	0	1.0
Macadamia Nuts: 3½ ounces	3.5	685.6	15.8	7.7	71.0	0	1.0
Peanuts, roasted, w/skins, salted: 3½ ounces	3.5	577.5	20.4	26.0	48.3	0	414.8
Pecans, halves, raw: 3½ ounces	3.5	681.7	14.5	9.1	70.6	0	0

	Weight (oz)	Calories	Carbo. (g)	Protein (g)	Fat (g)	Choles. (mg)	Sodium (mg)
Pine Nuts: *3½ ounces*	3.5	628.4	16.5	15.2	60.9	0	19.8
Pistachio Nuts, w/o added salt: *3½ ounces*	3.5	589.4	18.9	19.2	53.3	0	1.0
Pumpkin Seeds, kernels, dry: *3½ ounces*	3.5	548.7	14.9	28.8	46.3	0	0
Sesame Seeds, decorticated, dry: *3½ ounces*	3.5	583.5	9.3	26.2	54.3	0	39.0
Squash Seeds, kernels, dry: *3½ ounces*	3.5	548.7	14.9	28.8	46.3	0	0
Sunflower Seeds, kernels, dry: *3½ ounces*	3.5	555.7	19.7	23.8	46.9	0	29.8
Walnuts, black, chopped, raw: *3½ ounces*	3.5	623.1	14.7	20.3	58.8	0	3.2
Walnuts, English, halves, raw: *3½ ounces*	3.5	645.9	15.7	14.7	63.5	0	2.0

OILS/FATS

	Weight (oz)	Calories	Carbo. (g)	Protein (g)	Fat (g)	Choles. (mg)	Sodium (mg)
Butter, salted: *1 tablespoon*	0.5	107.6	0+	0.1	12.2	32.9	124.0
Butter, unsalted: *1 tablespoon*	0.5	107.6	0+	0.1	12.2	32.9	1.7
Lard: *1 tablespoon*	0.5	117.0	0	0	13.0	12.0	0+
Margarine, regular, w/o salt: *1 tablespoon*	0.5	107.1	0.1	0.1	12.0	0	0.3
Margarine, regular, w/salt: *1 tablespoon*	0.5	107.9	0.1	0.1	12.1	0	141.5
Margarine, soft, w/o salt: *1 tablespoon*	0.4	85.9	0.1	0.1	9.6	0	3.3
Margarine, soft, w/salt: *1 tablespoon*	0.4	85.9	0.1	0.1	9.6	0	129.4
Olive Oil: *1 tablespoon*	0.5	123.8	0	0	14.0	0	0
Peanut Oil: *1 tablespoon*	0.5	123.8	0	0	14.0	0	0+

Oils/Fats (continued)	Weight (oz)	Calories	Carbo. (g)	Protein (g)	Fat (g)	Choles. (mg)	Sodium (mg)
Safflower Oil: *1 tablespoon*	0.5	123.8	0	0	14.0	0	0
Sesame Oil: *1 tablespoon*	0.5	123.8	0	0	14.0	0	0
Soybean Oil: *1 tablespoon*	0.5	123.8	0	0	14.0	0	0
Vegetable Shortening, cooking: *1 tablespoon*	0.5	123.8	0	0	14.0	0	0

PANCAKES/WAFFLES/CREPES

	Weight (oz)	Calories	Carbo. (g)	Protein (g)	Fat (g)	Choles. (mg)	Sodium (mg)
Blueberry Pancakes, *FF Recipe: 2 average*	6.2	226.2	46.8	8.3	0.8	3.2	379.9
Bran Pancakes, *FF Recipe: 2 average*	4.3	249.9	53.9	6.9	0.5	1.7	339.2
Buckwheat Pancakes, *ETW Recipe: 6 average*	7.0	244.1	41.9	15.6	2.0	2.4	824.2
Cinnamon French Toast, *ETS Recipe: 2 slices*	3.5	150.2	26.4	9.4	1.5	2.6	310.8
Corn Cakes, *ETS Recipe: 2 average*	8.6	264.8	57.1	10.0	1.5	1.7	68.6
Hawaiian Pancakes, *ETS Recipe: 2 large*	6.6	242.4	42.3	5.2	6.6	0.8	39.9
"Need No Syrup" Banana Pancakes, *ETS Recipe: 2 average*	8.2	259.2	59.4	7.2	1.5	0.8	39.5
Oatmeal Apple-Raisin Pancakes, *FF Recipe: 2 average*	5.8	266.6	55.4	9.6	1.4	3.2	378.7
Pancakes, buckwheat, w/egg, milk: *3 average*	4.8	270.0	32.1	9.2	12.3	89.1	626.4
Pancakes, from mix, w/egg, milk: *3 average*	4.8	303.8	43.7	9.7	9.9	99.9	761.4
Potato Pancakes, *ETS Recipe: 1 average*	6.0	124.8	24.0	6.0	0.7	1.3	130.3
Pumpkin Pancakes, *FF Recipe: 2 average*	6.0	243.9	52.4	6.3	0.9	1.9	605.8
Waffle, from mix, w/egg, milk: *1 average*	2.6	206.3	27.1	6.6	7.9	45.0	514.5

	Weight (oz)	Calories	Carbo. (g)	Protein (g)	Fat (g)	Choles. (mg)	Sodium (mg)
Waffle, from mix, w/water: *1 average*	2.6	228.8	30.1	3.6	10.5	0	420.0
Waffle, frozen: *1 average*	1.3	93.6	15.5	2.6	2.3	22.2	238.3

PASTA

	Weight (oz)	Calories	Carbo. (g)	Protein (g)	Fat (g)	Choles. (mg)	Sodium (mg)
Ditalini, dry form: *1 serving*	1.9	203.0	41.4	6.9	0.7	0	1.1
Linguine Alfredo, *FF Recipe: 1 serving*	3.6	292.2	49.7	13.7	3.8	9.8	474.0
Macaroni and Cheese Lombardo, *ETW Recipe: 1 serving*	5.2	234.3	29.3	19.9	3.8	26.0	396.7
Macaroni, cooked, firm: *1 serving*	4.9	207.3	42.2	7.0	0.7	0	1.4
Macaroni, cooked, tender: *1 serving*	4.9	155.5	32.2	4.8	0.6	0	1.4
Macaroni, dry form: *1 serving*	1.8	184.5	37.6	6.2	0.6	0	1.0
Macaroni, whole wheat, dry: *1 serving*	3.9	405.9	82.7	13.8	1.3	0	2.2
Noodles, Chow Mein, canned: *1 serving*	1.8	244.5	29.0	6.6	11.8	6.0	500.0
Noodles, Egg, cooked: *1 serving*	5.6	200.0	37.3	6.6	2.4	49.6	3.2
Noodles, Egg, dry: *1 serving*	2.6	283.4	52.6	9.3	3.4	68.7	3.7
Noodles, "No Yolk" thin, cooked: *3½ ounces*	3.5	52.5	10.0	2.0	0.5	0	0.5
Noodles, "No Yolk" thin, dry: *3½ ounces*	3.5	367.5	70.0	14.0	3.5	0	3.5
Noodles Romanoff, *ETS Recipe: 1 serving*	12.0	263.0	37.1	19.4	3.6	10.1	931.0
Noodles, spinach, w/o egg, dry: *3½ ounces*	3.5	367.5	70.0	14.0	3.5	0	3.5
Pasta and Garlic Sauce, *ETW Recipe: 1 serving*	8.2	311.8	49.4	22.8	1.9	6.2	553.0

Pasta (continued)	Weight (oz)	Calories	Carbo. (g)	Protein (g)	Fat (g)	Choles. (mg)	Sodium (mg)
Pasta e Fagioli, ETS Recipe: 1 serving	15.0	353.4	62.4	21.0	3.1	3.9	354.3
Spaghetti, cooked firm, 8–10 minutes: 1 serving	5.2	217.6	44.3	7.4	0.7	0	1.5
Spaghetti, cooked tender, 14–20 minutes: 1 serving	5.3	166.5	34.5	5.1	0.6	0	1.5
Spaghetti, dry form: 1 serving	1.3	140.4	28.6	4.8	0.5	0	0.8
Stuffed Shells, ETS Recipe: 1 serving	13.7	461.5	72.4	30.0	5.6	15.4	1658.1
Tini Linguini, ETW Recipe: 1 serving	6.9	380.3	47.2	31.6	6.3	45.8	745.3
Veal Lasagna, ETS Recipe: 1 serving	10.5	330.1	38.7	27.2	7.1	41.9	1229.8

PICKLES/RELISHES

	Weight (oz)	Calories	Carbo. (g)	Protein (g)	Fat (g)	Choles. (mg)	Sodium (mg)
Pickle Relish, sour: 1 tablespoon	0.5	2.9	0.4	0.1	0.1	0	203.0
Pickle Relish, sweet: 1 tablespoon	0.5	20.7	5.1	0.1	0.1	0	106.8
Pickles, bread-and-butter, fresh: 1 tablespoon	0.4	9.1	2.2	0.1	0+	0	84.1
Pickles, dill: 1 tablespoon	0.4	1.4	0.3	0.1	0+	0	178.5
Pickles, sour: 1 tablespoon	0.4	1.3	0.3	0.1	0+	0	169.1
Pickles, sweet: 1 tablespoon	0.4	18.3	4.6	0.1	0+	0	89.0

POULTRY

	Weight (oz)	Calories	Carbo. (g)	Protein (g)	Fat (g)	Choles. (mg)	Sodium (mg)
Baked Orange Chicken, FF Recipe: 1 serving	5.8	207.4	21.4	24.6	2.2	78.7	302.0
Capon, flesh and skin, raw: 1 serving	3.5	232.2	0	18.7	17.0	74.4	44.7

	Weight (oz)	Calories	Carbo. (g)	Protein (g)	Fat (g)	Choles. (mg)	Sodium (mg)
Chicken, all classes, dark meat, w/o skin, roasted: *1 serving*	3.5	174.6	0	27.8	6.3	85.9	85.3
Chicken, all classes, light meat, roasted: *1 serving*	3.5	164.7	0	31.4	3.4	85.9	63.5
Chicken, broiler, flesh only, broiled: *1 serving*	3.5	134.9	0	23.6	3.8	86.3	65.5
Chicken, fryer, breast, w/skin, fried: *1 serving*	3.5	220.3	1.6	31.6	8.8	88.3	75.4
Chicken, fryer, flesh only, fried: *1 serving*	3.5	217.3	1.7	30.4	9.0	93.3	90.3
Chicken Gizzard, simmered: *1 serving*	3.5	151.8	1.1	26.9	3.7	192.5	66.5
Chicken Heart, simmered: *1 serving*	3.5	183.6	0.1	26.2	7.8	240.1	47.6
Chicken, light meat, w/o skin, raw: *3½ ounces*	3.5	117.0	0	23.4	1.9	78.0	50.0
Chicken Liver, simmered: *1 serving*	3.5	155.8	0.9	24.2	5.4	626.1	50.6
Chicken, roaster, flesh and skin, roasted: *1 serving*	3.5	221.3	0	23.8	13.3	75.4	72.4
Chicken, roaster, flesh only, roasted: *1 serving*	3.5	165.7	0	24.8	6.5	74.4	74.4
Chicken, roaster, giblets only, raw: *1 serving*	3.5	126.0	1.1	18.0	5.0	234.2	76.4
Chicken Tetrazzini, *ETS Recipe: 1 serving*	6.4	208.5	26.6	18.9	1.9	45.9	117.8
Cornish Hen, flesh, w/o skin, roasted: *3½ ounces*	3.5	183.0	0	29.5	6.3	71.0	77.0
Cornish Hens, *ETS Recipe: 1 serving*	11.5	487.6	44.2	45.5	14.4	101.4	242.5
Duck, domesticated, flesh only, raw: *1 serving*	3.5	131.0	0	18.2	5.9	76.4	73.4
Duck, domesticated, total edible, raw: *1 serving*	3.5	323.5	0	15.9	28.4	97.2	73.4
Duck, wild, flesh only, raw: *1 serving*	3.5	136.9	0	21.1	5.2	80.4	73.4
Duck, wild, total edible, raw: *1 serving*	3.5	231.2	0	20.9	15.7	97.2	73.4

Poultry (continued)	Weight (oz)	Calories	Carbo. (g)	Protein (g)	Fat (g)	Choles. (mg)	Sodium (mg)
Goose, domesticated, flesh and skin, roasted: 1 serving	3.5	302.6	0	25.0	21.7	90.3	69.5
Goose, domesticated, flesh only, roasted: 1 serving	3.5	236.2	0	28.8	12.6	95.3	75.4
Pâté de Foie Gras, canned: 1 serving	0.5	69.3	0.7	1.7	6.6	22.5	104.6
Pheasant, flesh and skin, raw: 1 serving	3.5	179.6	0	22.5	9.2	70.4	39.7
Pheasant, flesh only, raw: 1 serving	3.5	132.0	0	23.4	3.6	65.5	36.7
Sweet and Sour Chicken, ETW Recipe: 1 serving	14.0	491.1	76.6	37.5	4.3	98.2	405.4
Teriyaki Chicken Kabobs, FF Recipe: 1 serving	4.5	122.3	4.4	14.5	1.4	44.6	460.0
Turkey, flesh and skin, roasted: 1 serving	3.5	206.4	0	27.9	9.6	81.4	67.5
Turkey, flesh only, roasted: 1 serving	3.5	168.7	0	29.1	5.0	75.4	69.5
Turkey Gizzard, simmered: 1 serving	3.5	175.6	2.1	26.6	6.1	224.2	54.6
Turkey Liver, simmered: 1 serving	3.5	167.7	3.4	23.8	5.9	621.1	63.5
Turkey Meatballs, FF Recipe: 1 serving	10	426	59.4	26.3	9.3	58	206

PRESERVES/JAMS/JELLIES

	Weight (oz)	Calories	Carbo. (g)	Protein (g)	Fat (g)	Choles. (mg)	Sodium (mg)
Apple Butter: 1 tablespoon	0.7	37.2	9.4	0.1	0.2	0	0.4
Grape Jam: 1 tablespoon	0.7	54.4	14.0	0.1	0 +	0	2.4
Guava Jelly: 1 tablespoon	0.7	54.6	14.1	0 +	0 +	0	3.4
Orange Marmalade: 1 tablespoon	0.7	54.4	14.1	0.1	0 +	0	2.5
Raspberry Preserves: 1 tablespoon	0.7	54.4	14.0	0.1	0 +	0	2.4

	Weight (oz)	Calories	Carbo. (g)	Protein (g)	Fat (g)	Choles. (mg)	Sodium (mg)
Red Cherry Preserves: *1 tablespoon*	0.7	54.4	14.0	0.1	0+	0	2.4
Strawberry Preserves: *1 tablespoon*	0.7	54.4	14.0	0.1	0+	0	2.4

SALADS

	Weight (oz)	Calories	Carbo. (g)	Protein (g)	Fat (g)	Choles. (mg)	Sodium (mg)
Apple-Celery Salad, *FF Recipe: 1 serving*	6.7	153.8	23.3	5.4	5.9	0.9	132.6
Apple Raisin Salad, *ETS Recipe: 1 serving*	5.1	224.8	33.2	6.1	9.8	0.7	50.7
Bean and Vegetable Salad, *ETW Recipe: 1 serving*	11.8	274.8	55.2	14.6	1.6	0	157.2
Bean Salad, *ETS Recipe: 1 serving*	7.0	210.1	40.3	10.7	1.9	0	274.2
Bianchi's Shrimp and Macaroni Salad, *FF Recipe: 1 serving*	5.4	245.1	38.7	18.2	1.5	46.6	245.6
Broccoli and Onion Salad, *ETW Recipe: 1 serving*	5.3	46.3	9.2	4.3	0.4	0	100.7
Carrot Salad Waldorf, *ETS Recipe: 1 serving*	11.1	250.0	50.8	5.0	5.1	1.7	108.2
Cauliflower-Broccoli Salad, *ETS Recipe: 1 serving*	5.4	51.8	7.2	6.3	0.6	1.4	130.7
Chickpea and Pasta Salad, *ETS Recipe: 1 serving*	8.1	197.0	33.3	11.7	3.0	3.0	414.0
Chicken Salad, *ETW Recipe: 1 serving*	6.4	181.0	9.3	27.8	3.3	66.4	227.0
Chicken Salad Supreme, *ETS Recipe: 1 serving*	9.9	251.5	25.5	19.3	9.3	44.9	129.5
Coleslaw, w/commercial French dressing: *1 serving*	4.2	114.0	9.1	1.4	8.8	13.2	321.6
Coleslaw, w/mayonnaise: *1 serving*	4.2	172.8	5.8	1.6	16.8	10.8	144.0
Coleslaw, w/mayonnaise-type salad dressing: *1 serving*	4.2	118.8	8.5	1.4	9.5	10.8	148.8
Corn Salad, *ETS Recipe: 1 serving*	7.3	138.5	31.2	5.6	1.3	0.5	75.3

Salads (*continued*)	Weight (oz)	Calories	Carbo. (g)	Protein (g)	Fat (g)	Choles. (mg)	Sodium (mg)
Creamy Potato Salad, *FF Recipe: 1 serving*	6.7	113.1	21.3	6.3	0.6	2.6	316.1
Cucumber Potato Salad, *FF Recipe: 1 serving*	6.1	102.2	20.5	4.4	0.6	2.0	98.4
Cucumber Salad, *ETW Recipe: 1 serving*	3.5	13.4	3.5	0.4	0+	0	21.0
Curried Coleslaw, *FF Recipe: 1 serving*	4.0	66.4	15.0	1.7	0.6	1.7	114.0
Grape and Chicken Salad, *ETS Recipe: 1 serving*	8.4	249.8	27.7	27.3	3.3	65.4	112.4
Lobster Salad, *ETS Recipe: 1 serving*	6.7	109.0	5.1	17.7	1.9	50.4	409.7
Macaroni Salad, *FF Recipe: 1 serving*	5.4	159.6	31.0	7.3	0.7	1.7	339.6
Oriental Salad, *ETS Recipe: 1 serving*	8.7	234.5	10.7	23.0	11.9	48.3	282.8
Potato Salad, w/cooked salad dressing, butter: *1 serving*	8.8	247.5	40.7	6.7	7.0	65.0	1320.0
Potato Salad, w/cooked salad dressing, magarine: *1 serving*	8.8	247.5	40.7	6.7	7.0	0	1320.0
Potato Salad, w/hard-cooked eggs, mayonnaise dressing: *1 serving*	8.8	362.5	33.5	7.5	23.0	162.5	1200.0
Red Cabbage and Apple Slaw, *ETS Recipe: 1 serving*	7.8	125.3	31.1	2.4	0.6	0	80.5
Red Potato Salad, *ETS Recipe: 1 serving*	9.1	145.8	28.4	6.9	1.0	3.2	211.4
Salad, w/lettuce, tomato: *1 large*	6.0	40.0	8.2	2.2	0.5	0	9.0
Shrimp Salad, *ETS Recipe: 1 serving*	7.5	274.3	34.0	28.9	1.8	115.7	319.9
Spinach Salad, *ETS Recipe: 1 serving*	5.7	140.2	7.5	10.9	8.0	5.8	308.7
Sweet Potato Salad, *FF Recipe: 1 serving*	5.5	111.8	26.5	1.7	0.8	1.4	13.0
Sweet Slaw, *ETS Recipe: 1 serving*	4.3	145.1	18.4	5.3	6.6	2.2	97.0
Tuna Bean Salad, *ETS Recipe: 1 serving*	7.7	196.7	24.9	18.3	2.3	22.3	305.5

	Weight (oz)	Calories	Carbo. (g)	Protein (g)	Fat (g)	Choles. (mg)	Sodium (mg)
Tuna Chickpea Salad, *FF Recipe: 1 serving*	5.1	175.4	24.3	16.0	1.9	19.3	527.7
Vegetable Potato Salad, *ETS Recipe: 1 serving*	11.6	192.8	36.5	11.6	1.0	2.3	455.5
Waldorf Salad Deluxe, *ETW Recipe: 1 serving*	10.3	257.7	59.9	6.4	1.9	4.9	172.0
Zucchini-Carrot Salad, *FF Recipe: 1 serving*	6.2	127.5	15.6	4.0	6.5	0	169.2

SANDWICHES/PIZZA

	Weight (oz)	Calories	Carbo. (g)	Protein (g)	Fat (g)	Choles. (mg)	Sodium (mg)
Pizza, w/cheese: *1 slice*	3.5	245.0	36.3	9.2	6.8	18.0	633.0
Pizza, w/sausage, cheese: *1 slice*	3.5	282.0	27.4	12.9	13.3	29.0	668.0
Pizza, w/sausage, w/o cheese: *1 slice*	3.5	234.0	29.6	7.8	9.3	19.0	729.0

SAUCES/SPREADS/CREAMS

	Weight (oz)	Calories	Carbo. (g)	Protein (g)	Fat (g)	Choles. (mg)	Sodium (mg)
Apple Butter, *ETW Recipe: 1 tablespoon*	0.6	8.8	2.3	0+	0+	0	0.3
Apple-Cranberry Sauce, *ETS Recipe: 1 tablespoon*	0.6	10.0	2.1	0.1	0+	0	0.2
Barbecue Sauce: *1 tablespoon*	0.5	11.3	1.9	0.3	0.3	0	122.3
Basil and Tomato Sauce, *FF Recipe: 3½ ounces*	3.5	99.8	20.3	3.6	0.5	0	95.1
Catsup, bottled, w/o salt: *1 tablespoon*	0.5	15.9	3.8	0.3	0.1	0	3.0
Catsup, bottled, w/salt: *1 tablespoon*	0.5	15.9	3.8	0.3	0.1	0	156.3
Cheese Spread, *FF Recipe: 1 tablespoon*	0.6	18.3	0.6	2.2	0.8	2.9	86.9
Chili Sauce, hot, green, canned: *1 tablespoon*	0.6	3.4	0.9	0.1	0+	0	4.3

Sauces/Spreads/Creams (continued)	Weight (oz)	Calories	Carbo. (g)	Protein (g)	Fat (g)	Choles. (mg)	Sodium (mg)
Cream, Half-and-Half: 1 tablespoon	0.5	19.5	0.6	0.5	1.7	5.6	6.1
Cream, heavy whipping: 1 tablespoon	0.5	51.8	0.4	0.3	5.6	20.6	5.6
Cream, light, coffee or table: 1 tablespoon	0.5	29.3	0.6	0.4	2.9	9.9	5.9
Cream, light whipping: 1 tablespoon	0.5	43.8	0.5	0.3	4.6	16.7	5.1
Cream, substitute, w/skim milk, lactose: 1 tablespoon	0.5	76.2	9.2	1.3	4.0	0	86.3
Dill Sauce Deluxe, ETW Recipe: 1 tablespoon	0.6	12.9	0.8	1.7	0.3	1.0	59.7
Eggplant Sauce, ETS Recipe: 3½ ounces	3.5	52.3	8.5	1.7	1.6	0	349.9
Fruit Spread, ETS Recipe: 1 tablespoon	0.6	28.2	3.3	1.7	1.1	0.6	46.6
Haas Mayonnaise Spread, ETW/FF Recipe: 1 tablespoon	0.7	14.2	0.6	2.4	0.2	0.9	87.7
Haas Peanut Butter, ETW Recipe: 1 tablespoon	0.9	45.9	8.1	2.4	0.9	0	0.5
Horseradish Sauce, prepared: 1 tablespoon	0.5	5.7	1.4	0.2	0+	0	14.4
Hot Sauce: 1 tablespoon	0.5	2.4	0.3	0.3	0	0	66.0
Hummus, FF Recipe: 1 tablespoon	0.7	33.0	5.8	1.7	0.4	0.1	101.0
Marinara Sauce, ETW Recipe: 3½ ounces	3.5	25.5	5.1	1.2	0.3	0	175.6
Mayonnaise, w/soybean oil, salt: 1 tablespoon	0.5	100.4	0.4	0.2	11.1	8.3	79.6
Mustard, brown, prepared: 1 tablespoon	0.5	13.7	0.8	0.9	0.9	0	196.0
Mustard, yellow, prepared: 1 tablespoon	0.5	11.3	1.0	0.7	0.7	0	187.8
Onion Dip, FF Recipe: 1 tablespoon	0.5	8.3	0.9	0.5	0.3	1.1	27.2
Peanut Butter: 1 tablespoon	0.5	86.0	3.2	3.9	7.2	0	18.0

	Weight (oz)	Calories	Carbo. (g)	Protein (g)	Fat (g)	Choles. (mg)	Sodium (mg)
Pesto, *ETS Recipe: 1 tablespoon*	0.5	19.3	1.4	0.7	1.4	0.5	74.0
Pimiento Cheese Spread, past. process: *3½ ounces*	3.5	372.1	1.7	21.9	31.0	93.3	1416.4
Pinto Bean Dip, *FF Recipe: 1 tablespoon*	0.7	24.0	4.1	1.5	0.3	0.5	10.7
Quick Tomato Sauce, *ETS Recipe: 1 tablespoon*	0.9	14.3	3.0	0.5	0.1	0.2	125.2
Spaghetti Sauce, *FF Recipe: 3½ ounces*	3.5	31.4	7.2	1.3	0.3	0	57.8
Tabasco Sauce: *1 tablespoon*	0.5	2.4	0.3	0.3	0	0	66.0
Tamari: *1 tablespoon*	0.5	9.6	1.2	1.3	0	0	857.9
Tamari, diluted ½ part water: *1 tablespoon*	0.5	4.8	0.6	0.7	0	0	428.9
Tartar Sauce, low-cal.: *1 tablespoon*	0.7	44.8	1.3	0.1	4.5	10.2	141.4
Tartar Sauce, regular: *1 tablespoon*	0.5	74.3	0.6	0.2	8.1	7.1	99.0
Tomato-Mushroom Spaghetti Sauce, *FF Recipe: 3½ ounces*	3.5	29.9	6.6	1.3	0.3	0.1	116.0
Tuna Haas, *ETW Recipe: 3½ ounces*	3.5	72.4	2.7	13.4	0.7	22.0	171.3
White Sauce, medium: *1 tablespoon*	0.6	25.9	1.4	0.6	2.0	6.6	60.6
Worcestershire Sauce: *1 tablespoon*	0.5	12.0	2.7	0.3	0	0	147.0

SOUPS/STEWS

	Weight (oz)	Calories	Carbo. (g)	Protein (g)	Fat (g)	Choles. (mg)	Sodium (mg)
Bean Soup, canned, w/equal volume of water: *1 cup*	8.5	169.0	21.7	7.2	4.8	0	831.0
Bean with Pork Soup, canned, w/equal volume of water: *1 cup*	8.8	170.0	22.5	7.7	6.0	2.5	940.0
Beef and Vegetable Stew, canned: *1 cup*	8.3	185.9	16.7	13.6	7.3	32.9	967.1

Soups/Stews (continued)	Weight (oz)	Calories	Carbo. (g)	Protein (g)	Fat (g)	Choles. (mg)	Sodium (mg)
Beef Noodle Soup, canned, w/equal volume of water: 1 cup	8.6	83.3	9.1	4.9	3.2	4.9	955.5
Black Bean Soup, ETS Recipe: 1 cup	8.3	236.3	43.0	15.4	1.0	0	164.9
Black-Eyed Pea Soup, ETW Recipe: 1 cup	8.0	175.8	34.2	9.7	0.7	0	163.1
Chicken Broth, defatted: 1 cup	8.8	27.0	1.0	4.9	0	0	795.0
Chicken Brown Rice Soup, FF Recipe: 1 cup	13.6	159.2	23.0	14.4	1.5	21.9	830.0
Chicken Consommé, canned, w/equal volume of water: 1 cup	8.8	40.0	1.0	5.0	1.5	7.5	795.0
Chicken Noodle Soup, canned, w/equal volume of water: 1 cup	8.5	74.4	9.4	4.1	2.4	7.2	1101.6
Chicken Vegetable Soup, canned, w/equal volume of water: 1 cup	8.6	76.0	8.8	3.7	2.9	9.8	960.4
Chicken with Rice Soup, canned, w/equal volume of water: 1 cup	8.5	60.0	7.2	3.6	1.9	7.2	811.2
Chili Bean and Rice Soup, ETW Recipe: 1 cup	10.5	213.5	41.6	10.9	1.1	0	347.0
Chili con Carne, canned, w/beans: 1 cup	8.1	306.0	28.1	17.3	14.0	39.1	1221.5
Chili con Carne, canned, w/o beans: 1 cup	8.1	460.1	13.3	23.7	34.0	59.8	1221.5
Chili, ETS Recipe: 1 cup	10.4	343.2	34.7	28.2	10.5	68.7	576.6
Chunky Chicken Noodle Soup, ETS Recipe: 1 cup	10.8	266.2	28.2	29.9	2.8	59.4	1171.0
Corn Chowder, ETS Recipe: 1 cup	8.0	153.5	33.2	6.0	1.2	1.5	41.8
Cream of Asparagus Soup, canned, w/equal volume of milk: 1 cup	8.5	156.0	15.8	6.2	7.9	21.6	1008.0
Cream of Celery Soup, canned, w/equal volume of milk: 1 cup	8.5	158.4	14.2	5.5	9.4	31.2	976.8
Cream of Chicken Soup, canned, w/equal volume of milk: 1 cup	8.5	184.8	14.4	7.2	11.0	26.4	1012.8
Cream of Mushroom Soup, canned, w/equal volume of milk: 1 cup	8.5	196.8	14.6	5.8	13.2	19.2	1041.6

	Weight (oz)	Calories	Carbo. (g)	Protein (g)	Fat (g)	Choles. (mg)	Sodium (mg)
Cream of Potato Soup, canned, w/equal volume of milk: *1 cup*	8.5	182.4	18.0	7.7	9.4	31.2	1238.4
Green Pea Soup, canned, w/equal volume of milk: *1 cup*	8.5	225.6	30.5	12.0	6.7	16.8	988.8
Hearty Vegetable Soup, *ETS Recipe: 1 cup*	8.7	314.1	63.6	16.4	1.7	0	373.4
Howard's Onion Soup, *ETW Recipe: 1 cup*	9.2	147.9	25.9	6.8	1.8	3.0	389.6
Kidney Bean Soup, *ETW Recipe: 1 cup*	10.2	110.6	21.3	6.1	0.5	0	399.4
Lentil Barley Soup, *ETS Recipe: 1 cup*	12.5	240.9	43.8	15.9	0.7	0	1214.0
Lentil Pasta Soup, *FF Recipe: 1 cup*	10.3	190.4	33.4	13.0	0.6	0.4	796.1
Lentil Soup: *1 cup*	8.5	169.0	21.7	7.2	4.8	0	831.0
Lima Bean Chowder, *FF Recipe: 1 serving*	8.6	168.7	32.6	8.6	1.4	2.6	450.8
Manhattan Clam Chowder, w/tomatoes, canned, w/equal volume of water: *1 cup*	8.6	78.4	12.3	4.2	2.2	2.5	1815.5
Minestrone Soup, canned, w/equal volume of water: *1 cup*	8.6	83.3	11.5	4.4	2.5	2.5	926.1
Navy Bean Soup, *ETS Recipe: 1 cup*	13.1	170.8	32.0	10.5	0.8	0	158.8
New England Clam Chowder, frozen, w/equal volume of water: *1 cup*	8.5	129.6	10.6	4.3	7.7	24.0	1044.0
Onion Soup, canned, w/equal volume of water: *1 cup*	8.5	58.0	8.2	3.8	1.7	12.0	1049.0
Onion Soup, dehydrated, dry: *1 serving*	0.4	32.3	5.9	1.3	0.7	0.6	985.3
Onion Soup, Lipton 20% less salt, dry: *1 serving*	1.2	35.0	6.0	1.0	0.5	0	640.0
Oyster Stew, commercial, w/equal volume of milk: *1 cup*	8.5	202.4	14.2	10.1	11.8	50.6	881.9
Oyster Stew, commercial, w/equal volume of water: *1 cup*	8.5	122.9	8.2	5.5	7.7	26.5	819.3
Potato Soup, *ETW Recipe: 1 cup*	8.0	166.7	33.2	8.6	0.4	2.5	278.9

Soups/Stews (continued)	Weight (oz)	Calories	Carbo. (g)	Protein (g)	Fat (g)	Choles. (mg)	Sodium (mg)
Quick Corn Soup, FF Recipe: 1 serving	8.5	171.7	31.0	12.6	0.7	5.4	449.2
Ranchero Chili, ETW Recipe: 1 cup	8.3	182.9	34.9	10.9	0.9	0	185.1
Split Pea Soup, canned, w/equal volume of water: 1 cup	8.6	183.8	27.2	10.0	4.2	7.4	975.1
Split Pea Soup, ETS Recipe: 1 cup	8.7	204.2	38.0	13.6	0.6	0	232.9
Sweet Potato Soup, ETW Recipe: 1 cup	8.3	239.7	35.4	4.6	1.9	4.3	320.4
Thick Minestrone, FF Recipe: 1 serving	14.7	162.0	29.9	9.2	1.3	1.3	490.7
Tomato Rice Soup, ETS Recipe: 1 cup	10.3	108.9	20.0	6.4	0.6	0	868.9
Tomato Soup, canned, w/equal volume of water: 1 cup	8.6	85.8	16.7	2.0	2.0	0	874.7
Turkey Noodle Soup, canned, w/equal volume of water: 1 cup	8.5	67.2	8.4	3.8	1.9	4.8	801.6
Vegetable Beef Soup, canned, w/equal volume of water: 1 cup	8.6	78.4	10.3	5.6	2.0	4.9	960.4
Vegetarian Vegetable Soup, canned, w/equal volume of water: 1 cup	8.6	73.5	12.3	2.2	2.0	0	835.5
White Bean and Turkey Stew, FF Recipe: 1 cup	14.7	386.4	47.3	38.3	5.0	57.3	717.2
Zucchini Soup, FF Recipe: 1 serving	13.1	85.7	17.6	5.4	0.5	0	367.3

SPICES

	Weight (oz)	Calories	Carbo. (g)	Protein (g)	Fat (g)	Choles. (mg)	Sodium (mg)
Allspice, ground: 1 teaspoon	0.1	5.0	1.4	0.1	0.2	0	1.0
Basil, ground: 1 teaspoon	0.1	6.0	1.3	0.3	0.1	0	0
Bay Leaf, crumbled: 1 teaspoon	0+	2.0	0.5	0+	0+	0	0
Celery Seed: 1 teaspoon	0.1	8.0	0.8	0.4	0.5	0	3.0

	Weight (oz)	Calories	Carbo. (g)	Protein (g)	Fat (g)	Choles. (mg)	Sodium (mg)
Chervil, dried: 1 teaspoon	0+	1.0	0.3	0.1	0+	0	0
Chili Powder: 1 teaspoon	0.1	8.2	1.4	0.3	0.4	0	26.3
Cinnamon, ground: 1 teaspoon	0.1	6.0	1.8	0.1	0.1	0	1.0
Coriander Seed: 1 teaspoon	0.1	5.0	1.0	0.2	0.3	0	1.0
Cumin Seed: 1 teaspoon	0.1	8.0	0.9	0.4	0.5	0	4.0
Curry Powder: 1 teaspoon	0.1	6.0	1.2	0.3	0.3	0	1.0
Dill Weed, dried: 1 teaspoon	0+	3.0	0.6	0.2	0	0	2.0
Fennel Seed: 1 teaspoon	0.1	7.0	1.0	0.3	0.3	0	2.0
Garlic Clove, raw: 1 ounce	1.0	37.8	8.5	1.9	0	0	9.4
Garlic Powder: 1 teaspoon	0.1	9.0	2.0	0.5	0+	0	1.0
Ginger, ground: 1 teaspoon	0.1	6.0	1.3	0.2	0.1	0	1.0
Italian Seasoning: 1 teaspoon	0+	3.0	0.6	0.1	0.1	0	1.0
Marjoram, dried: 1 teaspoon	0+	2.0	0.4	0.1	0+	0	0
Mint: 1 teaspoon	0+	3.0	0.6	0.2	0	0	2.0
Mrs. Dash: 1 teaspoon	0.1	7.0	1.7	0.2	0+	0	5.0
Mustard, dried: 1 teaspoon	0.1	12.0	0.4	0.6	0.9	0	0
Nutmeg, ground: 1 teaspoon	0.1	12.0	1.1	0.1	0.8	0	0
Onion Powder: 1 teaspoon	0.1	7.0	1.7	0.2	0+	0	1.0
Oregano, ground: 1 teaspoon	0.1	5.0	1.0	0.2	0.2	0	0

Spices (continued)	Weight (oz)	Calories	Carbo. (g)	Protein (g)	Fat (g)	Choles. (mg)	Sodium (mg)
Paprika: 1 teaspoon	0.1	6.0	1.2	0.3	0.3	0	1.0
Parsley, dried: 1 teaspoon	0+	1.0	0.2	0.1	0+	0	1.0
Pepper, black: 1 teaspoon	0.1	5.0	1.4	0.2	0.1	0	1.0
Pepper, red or cayenne: 1 teaspoon	0.1	6.0	1.0	0.2	0.3	0	1.0
Pepper, white: 1 teaspoon	0.1	7.0	1.7	0.3	0+	0	0
Poppy Seed: 1 teaspoon	0.1	15.0	0.7	0.5	1.3	0	1.0
Rosemary, dried: 1 teaspoon	0+	4.0	0.8	0.1	0.2	0	1.0
Sage: 1 teaspoon	0+	3.0	0.6	0.1	0.1	0	0
Salt, Morton Lite: 1 teaspoon	0.2	0	0	0	0	0	975.0
Salt, table: 1 teaspoon	0.2	0	0	0	0	0	1937.9
Tarragon, ground: 1 teaspoon	0.1	5.0	0.8	0.4	0.1	0	1.0
Thyme, ground: 1 teaspoon	0+	4.0	0.9	0.1	0.1	0	1.0
Turmeric, ground: 1 teaspoon	0.1	8.0	1.4	0.2	0.2	0	1.0
Vanilla: 1 teaspoon	0.2	6.0	1.5	0	0	0	0

TOPPINGS/SALAD DRESSINGS

	Weight (oz)	Calories	Carbo. (g)	Protein (g)	Fat (g)	Choles. (mg)	Sodium (mg)
Bacon, Onion, and Chive Topping, ETW Recipe: 2 tablespoons	1.0	24.9	2.1	2.4	0.7	2.1	126.0
Barbecue Chicken Topping, ETW Recipe: 3½ ounces	3.5	112.6	10.3	12.0	1.7	28.1	320.1
Blue Cheese Dressing, FF Recipe: 2 tablespoons	1.0	16.4	1.1	2.1	0.4	2.0	100.2

	Weight (oz)	Calories	Carbo. (g)	Protein (g)	Fat (g)	Choles. (mg)	Sodium (mg)
Blue Cheese Dressing, low-calorie: *2 tablespoons*	1.0	22.0	1.2	0.8	1.6	8.0	310.0
Blue Cheese Dressing, regular, w/salt: *2 tablespoons*	1.1	151.2	2.2	1.4	15.7	5.1	328.2
Bread Stuffing, from mix, w/egg, table fat, moist: *3½ ounces*	3.5	206.4	19.5	4.4	12.7	65.5	500.1
Bread Stuffing Mix, dry: *3½ ounces*	3.5	368.1	71.8	12.8	3.8	4.0	1320.7
Buttermilk Garden Dressing, *FF Recipe: 2 tablespoons*	0.7	10.2	1.4	0.8	0.3	0.5	16.4
Caesar Salad Dressing, *ETW Recipe: 3½ ounces*	3.5	52.5	3.7	7.5	0.9	3.1	347.2
Celery Seed Dressing, *ETS Recipe: 2 tablespoons*	1.0	16.6	1.4	1.9	0.4	1.4	70.1
Chicken in Wine Sauce Topping, *ETW Recipe: 2 tablespoons*	0.8	20.3	0.8	2.9	0.5	5.3	52.5
Creamy Italian Dressing, *ETW Recipe: 2 tablespoons*	1.2	21.9	1.6	2.8	0.5	1.7	102.2
Creamy Russian Dressing, *ETS Recipe: 2 tablespoons*	1.3	24.0	2.6	2.4	0.5	1.8	70.6
Deluxe Thousand Island Dressing, *FF Recipe: 2 tablespoons*	1.3	27.5	4.7	1.9	0.2	0.7	104.8
Dill Dip, *FF Recipe: 2 tablespoons*	1.2	25.8	2.1	3.6	0.3	1.4	115.9
French Dressing, regular, w/salt: *2 tablespoons*	1.2	138.0	5.6	0.2	13.2	18.0	438.0
Garlic Dressing, *ETS Recipe: 2 tablespoons*	1.6	31.4	1.8	4.8	0.5	2.3	174.7
Garlic-French Dressing, *ETS Recipe: 2 tablespoons*	1.3	6.0	1.9	0.1	0+	0	30.9
Garlic Italian Dressing, *FF Recipe: 2 tablespoons*	1.0	16.5	1.6	2.1	0.2	0.9	59.9
Green Goddess Dressing, *ETW Recipe: 2 tablespoons*	1.3	19.7	2.0	2.3	0.3	1.3	123.9
Herb Magic Italian Dressing: *2 tablespoons*	1.2	8.0	2.0	0	0	0	244.0
Horseradish Topping, *ETW Recipe: 2 tablespoons*	1.1	20.4	1.3	2.9	0.3	1.6	97.6

Toppings/Salad Dressings (*continued*)	Weight (oz)	Calories	Carbo. (g)	Protein (g)	Fat (g)	Choles. (mg)	Sodium (mg)
Italian Dressing, regular, w/salt: 2 tablespoons	1.0	140.0	3.0	0.2	14.4	20.0	236.0
Jeff's "Cream" Dressing, *ETW Recipe: 2 tablespoons*	1.1	18.8	1.0	3.1	0.3	1.2	101.0
Mushroom Topping, *ETW Recipe: 2 tablespoons*	1.5	23.0	1.6	3.2	0.4	1.6	100.6
Parsley Parmesan Dressing, *ETS Recipe: 2 tablespoons*	1.1	25.3	1.6	2.7	1.0	3.1	87.9
Roquefort Cheese Dressing, regular, w/salt: 2 tablespoons	1.0	152.0	2.2	1.4	15.6	6.0	328.0
Russian Dressing, w/salt: 2 tablespoons	1.0	148.0	3.2	0.4	15.2	6.0	260.0
Scallion Salad Dressing, *FF Recipe: 2 tablespoons*	1.2	7.6	1.9	0.1	0+	0	140.3
Snappy Cheddar Topping, *ETW Recipe: 2 tablespoons*	0.9	25.5	0.8	3.2	1.0	3.8	127.5
Tangy Horseradish Dressing, *ETS Recipe: 2 tablespoons*	0.9	6.7	1.8	0.2	0.1	0	43.7
Tarragon Dressing, *FF Recipe: 2 tablespoons*	1.3	19.4	1.9	2.5	0.2	0.9	206.0
Thick and Creamy Herb Dressing, *FF Recipe: 2 tablespoons*	1.2	30.3	1.7	2.9	1.3	3.9	186.7
Thousand Island Dressing, *ETW Recipe: 2 tablespoons*	1.3	33.8	5.5	2.6	0.3	0.9	137.6
Thousand Island Dressing, regular, w/salt: 2 tablespoons	1.0	114.0	4.6	0.2	10.8	8.0	210.0
Tomato Dressing, *ETS Recipe: 2 tablespoons*	1.3	17.6	1.5	2.0	0.5	1.3	62.0
V-8 Dressing, *ETS Recipe: 2 tablespoons*	1.1	8.6	2.0	0.2	0+	0	5.7
Yogurt Tomato Dressing, *ETW Recipe: 2 tablespoons*	1.9	15.8	2.5	1.1	0.3	0.8	74.9
Zesty Chili Dressing, *FF Recipe: 2 tablespoons*	0.9	10.4	2.0	0.7	0+	0.3	51.0

VEGETABLES

	Weight (oz)	Calories	Carbo. (g)	Protein (g)	Fat (g)	Choles. (mg)	Sodium (mg)
Alfalfa Sprouts, raw: 3½ ounces	3.5	35.4	3.5	3.5	0	0	1.8
Artichoke Hearts, frozen: 3½ ounces	3.5	25.8	6.4	2.6	0.4	0	46.6
Asparagus, raw spears, boiled w/o salt, drained: 1 serving	2.6	17.3	2.8	2.4	0.1	0	0.8
Bamboo Shoots, raw: 1 serving	2.3	18.0	3.5	1.7	0.2	0	3.3
Beans, Heinz Vegetarian: 1 serving	5.3	50.0	9.7	2.6	0.6	0	141.7
Beans, white, raw: 3½ ounces	3.5	337.4	60.8	22.1	1.6	0	18.9
Beet Greens, boiled w/o salt, drained: 1 serving	3.5	18.0	3.3	1.7	0.2	0	76.0
Beets, red, boiled w/o salt, drained: 1 serving	2.9	26.7	6.0	0.9	0.1	0	35.8
Beets, red, canned, drained solids: 1 serving	2.9	30.8	7.3	0.8	0.1	0	196.7
Black Beans, cooked: 3½ ounces	3.5	117.1	21.0	7.7	0.6	0	6.9
Black Beans, dried: 3½ ounces	3.5	339.0	61.2	22.3	1.5	0	25.0
Black-eyed Peas, immature seeds, boiled w/o salt, drained: 1 serving	3.5	130.0	23.5	8.9	0.4	0	39.0
Black-eyed Peas, immature seeds, raw: 3½ ounces	3.5	126.0	21.6	8.9	0.8	0	2.0
Black-eyed Peas, mature seeds, dry, raw: 3½ ounces	3.5	340.3	61.2	22.6	1.5	0	34.7
Broccoli, frozen, chopped, boiled w/o salt, drained: 1 serving	3.5	26.0	4.6	2.9	0.3	0	15.0
Broccoli, raw: 1 serving	3.5	32.0	5.9	3.6	0.3	0	15.0
Broccoli, spears, steamed w/o salt, drained: 1 large	3.5	26.0	4.5	3.1	0.3	0	10.0
Brussels Sprouts, boiled w/o salt, drained: 1 serving	2.9	30.0	5.3	3.5	0.3	0	8.3

Vegetables (*continued*)	Weight (oz)	Calories	Carbo. (g)	Protein (g)	Fat (g)	Choles. (mg)	Sodium (mg)
Butternut Squash, baked w/o salt: 1 serving	3.5	68.0	17.5	1.8	0.1	0	1.0
Butternut Squash, boiled, mashed w/o salt: 1 serving	4.4	51.2	13.0	1.4	0.1	0	1.3
Cabbage, Chinese, raw: 1 serving	0.8	3.1	0.7	0.3	0+	0	5.1
Cabbage, common, boiled w/o salt, large amount of water: 1 serving	2.9	15.0	3.3	0.8	0.2	0	10.8
Cabbage, common varieties, raw: 1 serving	1.8	12.0	2.7	0.6	0.1	0	10.0
Cannellini, canned, rinsed: 3½ ounces	3.5	124.3	22.7	7.9	0.6	0	4.1
Carrots, boiled w/o salt, drained: 1 serving	2.6	23.3	5.3	0.7	0.1	0	24.8
Carrots, canned, drained solids: 1 serving	2.6	22.5	5.0	0.6	0.2	0	177.0
Carrots, raw: 1 serving	3.5	42.0	9.7	1.1	0.2	0	47.0
Cauliflower Curry, ETW Recipe: 1 serving	4.7	91.9	17.7	6.6	0.4	0	36.5
Cauliflower, raw: 1 serving	2.9	22.5	4.3	2.2	0.2	0	10.8
Cauliflower, steamed w/o salt, drained: 1 serving	2.0	12.6	2.3	1.3	0.1	0	5.1
Celery, boiled w/o salt, drained: 1 serving	2.2	8.8	1.9	0.5	0.1	0	55.0
Celery, stalks, raw: 3 small	1.8	10.5	2.4	0.6	0.1	0	78.7
Chard, Swiss, boiled w/o salt, drained: 1 serving	2.9	15.0	2.7	1.5	0.2	0	71.7
"Cheddar" Stuffed Potato, ETW Recipe: ½ average	5.2	145.9	26.7	6.3	1.8	6.2	128.9
Chickpeas, mature seeds, dry, raw: 3½ ounces	3.5	357.2	60.5	20.3	4.8	0	25.8
Chicory, head, raw: 1 serving	2.7	11.5	2.5	0.8	0.1	0	5.4
Chives, chopped, raw: 3½ ounces	3.5	29.8	6.0	2.0	0	0	0

	Weight (oz)	Calories	Carbo. (g)	Protein (g)	Fat (g)	Choles. (mg)	Sodium (mg)
Collards, leaves, boiled w/o salt, large amount water: *1 serving*	3.5	31.0	4.8	3.4	0.7	0	25.0
Corn, canned, cream-style, solids and liquid: *1 serving*	4.4	102.5	25.0	2.6	0.7	0	295.0
Corn, cream-style, low-sodium, canned, solids and liquid: *1 serving*	4.4	102.5	23.1	3.2	1.4	0	2.5
Corn on the Cob, steamed: *1 average*	3.5	100.0	21.0	3.3	1.0	0	1.0
Corn, whole-kernel, canned, solids and liquid: *1 serving*	4.4	82.5	19.6	2.4	0.7	0	295.0
Corn, whole-kernel, low-sodium, canned, drained solids: *1 serving*	4.4	95.0	22.5	3.1	0.9	0	2.5
Corn, yellow, frozen: *1 serving*	3.5	88.0	21.1	3.1	0.7	0	4.0
Cottage Fries, *ETW Recipe: 1 serving*	9.5	231.6	48.9	7.1	1.5	2.0	56.2
Cowpeas, immature seeds, boiled w/o salt, drained: *1 serving*	2.8	86.4	14.5	6.5	0.6	0	0.8
Creamed Corn, *ETS Recipe: 1 serving*	5.8	133.1	30.5	5.1	1.2	0.6	19.5
Cucumber, raw: *½ average*	2.0	7.8	1.8	0.3	0.1	0	3.3
Dandelion Greens, boiled w/o salt, drained: *1 serving*	3.5	33.0	6.4	2.0	0.6	0	44.0
Dilled Corn and Snow Peas, *FF Recipe: 1 serving*	6.6	129.7	28.0	5.6	1.0	0.5	224.8
Dock, boiled, drained: *1 serving*	3.5	19.0	3.9	1.6	0.2	0	3.0
Eggplant, boiled w/o salt, drained: *1 serving*	3.5	19.0	4.1	1.0	0.2	0	1.0
Eggplant, raw: *2 slices*	3.5	25.0	5.8	1.2	0.2	0	2.0
Endive, leaves: *10 small*	0.4	2.5	0.5	0.2	0+	0	1.8
Escarole, leaves: *8 small*	0.9	4.5	0.9	0.3	0+	0	2.5
Garbanzo Beans, canned, *3½ ounces*	3.5	179.0	30.3	10.2	2.4	0	260.0

Vegetables (*continued*)	Weight (oz)	Calories	Carbo. (g)	Protein (g)	Fat (g)	Choles. (mg)	Sodium (mg)
Garbanzos, mature seeds, dry, raw: 3½ ounces	3.5	357.2	60.5	20.3	4.8	0	25.8
Green Beans, boiled w/o salt, drained: 1 serving	3.5	25.0	5.4	1.6	0.2	0	4.0
Green Beans, canned, drained solids: 1 serving	2.2	15.0	3.2	0.9	0.1	0	147.5
Green Beans, raw: 1 serving	2.2	21.9	4.9	1.3	0.1	0	5.0
Green Pepper, raw: 1 large	1.4	9.0	1.9	0.5	0.1	0	5.0
Hash Brown Potatoes, *ETS Recipe:* 1 serving	6.5	121.4	26.4	3.6	0.6	0	150.3
Hot German Potato Salad, *ETW Recipe:* 1 serving	10.1	168.2	35.4	5.8	1.0	0	351.2
Hubbard Squash, baked w/o salt: 1 serving	3.5	50.0	11.7	1.8	0.4	0	1.0
Jerusalem Artichoke, raw: 1 serving	3.5	41.0	16.7	2.3	0.1	0	0
Kale, leaves, boiled w/o salt, drained: 1 serving	3.5	39.0	6.1	4.5	0.7	0	43.0
Kelp, raw: 3½ ounces	3.5	0	0	0	1.1	0	2983.6
Kidney Beans, canned, rinsed: 1 serving	3.2	112.5	20.5	7.1	0.5	0	3.8
Kohlrabi, thickened bulblike stems, boiled w/o salt: 1 serving	2.6	18.0	4.0	1.3	0.1	0	4.5
Leeks, bulb and lower leaf portion, raw: 1 serving	1.8	26.0	5.6	1.1	0.1	0	2.5
Lentils, split, raw: 3½ ounces	3.5	342.3	61.3	24.5	0.9	0	29.8
Lentils, whole, mature seeds, cooked: 1 serving	2.6	79.5	14.5	5.8	0	0	9.8
Lettuce, butterhead varieties, raw: 1 serving	2.0	7.8	1.4	0.7	0.1	0	5.0
Lettuce, Cos or Romaine, raw: 1 serving	2.4	12.0	2.3	0.9	0.2	0	6.0
Lettuce, looseleaf or bunching varieties: 1 serving	2.0	10.0	1.9	0.7	0.2	0	5.0

	Weight (oz)	Calories	Carbo. (g)	Protein (g)	Fat (g)	Choles. (mg)	Sodium (mg)
Lima Beans, boiled w/o salt, drained: *1 serving*	2.8	88.8	15.8	6.1	0.4	0	0.8
Lima Beans, green, frozen: *1 serving*	3.4	128.0	24.5	7.0	0.5	0	125.0
Marinated Potato Salad, *ETW Recipe: 1 serving*	9.9	178.3	39.4	6.1	0.3	0	369.2
Marinated Vegetables, *ETW Recipe: 1 serving*	5.2	22.7	5.2	1.5	0.2	0	6.6
Mashed Potatoes, *ETS Recipe: 1 serving*	11.3	187.8	38.4	7.5	0.9	2.5	138.8
Mixed Vegetables, frozen, boiled w/o salt: *1 serving*	2.9	52.3	10.9	2.6	0.2	0	43.3
Mung Bean Sprouts, raw: *1 serving*	1.8	17.5	3.3	1.9	0.1	0	2.5
Mushrooms, *agaricus campestris,* canned, solids and liquid: *1 serving*	3.5	17.0	2.4	1.9	0.1	0	400.0
Mushrooms, *agaricus campestris,* raw: *5 small*	1.8	14.0	2.2	1.3	0.1	0	7.5
Mustard Greens, boiled w/o salt, drained: *1 serving*	3.5	23.0	4.0	2.2	0.4	0	18.0
Mustard Spinach, boiled w/o salt, drained: *1 serving*	3.5	16.0	2.8	1.7	0.2	0	18.0
Neptune's Potato, *ETS Recipe: 1 average*	10.5	276.6	52.3	13.7	1.8	36.4	117.0
New Zealand Spinach, boiled w/o salt, drained: *1 serving*	3.5	13.0	2.1	1.7	0.2	0	92.0
Okra, boiled w/o salt, drained: *1 serving*	3.5	29.0	6.0	2.0	0.3	0	2.0
Onion, dehydrated, flaked: *3½ ounces*	3.5	347.3	81.5	8.6	1.3	0	87.3
Onions, boiled w/o salt, drained: *1 serving*	3.5	29.0	6.5	1.2	0.1	0	7.0
Onions, raw: *1 average*	3.0	33.0	7.5	1.3	0.1	0	8.6
Parsley, chopped, raw: *1 serving*	0.1	1.8	0.4	0.1	0+	0	1.9
Parsnips, cooked w/o salt: *1 serving*	2.8	51.6	11.6	1.2	0.4	0	6.2

Vegetables (continued)	Weight (oz)	Calories	Carbo. (g)	Protein (g)	Fat (g)	Choles. (mg)	Sodium (mg)
Peas and Carrots, frozen, boiled w/o salt, drained: 1 serving	2.9	44.2	8.4	2.7	0.2	0	70.0
Peas, frozen: 1 serving	2.9	67.5	11.9	4.5	0.4	0	81.7
Peas, green, frozen, boiled w/o salt, drained: 1 serving	3.5	63.0	11.8	5.1	0.3	0	351.0
Pepper, Jalapeño: 1 serving	0.5	13.2	2.6	0.5	0.3	0	1.3
Peppers, hot chili, green, raw pods, w/o seeds: 1 serving	0.5	5.5	1.4	0.2	0+	0	3.7
Pimentoes, canned, solids and liquid: ½ average	0.6	4.2	0.9	0.1	0.1	0	3.9
Pinto Beans, dry: 3½ ounces	3.5	346.2	63.2	22.7	1.2	0	9.9
Potato, baked, w/o skin: 1 average	7.5	203.6	45.2	5.6	0.2	0	8.6
Potato, baked, w/skin: 1 average	9.0	217.1	48.9	6.0	0.3	0	8.6
Potato, boiled, w/o skin: 1 average	9.0	157.9	35.2	4.6	0.2	0	4.9
Potato, boiled, w/skin: 1 average	10.2	217.1	48.9	6.0	0.3	0	8.6
Potato, raw, w/o skin: 1 average	8.5	157.9	35.2	4.6	0.2	0	4.9
Potato, raw, w/skin: 1 average	10.0	215.5	48.6	6.0	0.4	0	9.4
Potatoes, French-fried, w/o salt: 1 serving	3.5	274.0	36.0	4.3	13.2	0	6.0
Potatoes, hash brown: 1 serving	3.5	224.0	29.0	2.0	11.5	0	299.0
Potatoes, mashed, w/milk: 1 serving	3.5	65.0	13.0	2.1	0.7	2.0	301.0
Potatoes Parmesan, ETS Recipe: 1 average	11.5	282.4	54.2	11.9	2.6	6.8	172.5
Potatoes, raw: 1 average	3.5	76.0	17.1	2.1	0.1	0	3.3
Potatoes, scalloped, w/cheese, butter: 1 serving	3.3	135.9	12.8	5.0	7.4	24.0	419.0

	Weight (oz)	Calories	Carbo. (g)	Protein (g)	Fat (g)	Choles. (mg)	Sodium (mg)
Pumpkin, raw: *1 serving*	3.5	26.0	6.5	1.0	0.1	0	1.0
Radish, common, raw: *10 small*	3.5	17.0	3.6	1.0	0.1	0	18.0
Red Beans, cooked: *1 serving*	3.5	118.0	21.4	7.8	0.5	0	3.0
Red Kidney Beans, canned: *1 serving*	4.5	115.0	20.9	7.3	0.5	0	4.0
Red Pepper, raw: *1 large*	1.6	10.2	2.1	0.5	0.1	0	5.7
Rutabaga, boiled w/o salt, drained: *1 serving*	3.5	35.0	8.2	0.9	0.1	0	4.0
Scallions, bulb and tops, raw: *3 average*	1.8	22.5	5.2	0.5	0.1	0	2.5
Shallot, bulbs, raw: *1 serving*	3.5	72.0	16.8	2.5	0.1	0	12.0
Snow Peas, frozen: *3½ ounces*	3.5	89.3	20.2	5.8	0.3	0	119.1
Soybean Curd: *1 serving*	2.9	59.6	2.0	6.5	3.5	0	5.8
Soybeans, mature seeds, cooked: *1 serving*	3.5	130.0	10.8	11.0	5.7	0	2.0
Spinach, boiled w/o salt, drained: *1 serving*	3.5	23.0	3.6	3.0	0.3	0	50.0
Spinach, frozen, chopped, boiled w/o salt, drained: *1 serving*	3.5	23.0	3.7	3.0	0.3	0	52.0
Spinach, raw: *1 serving*	2.0	14.4	2.4	1.8	0.2	0	39.4
Squash Amandine, *ETS Recipe: 1 serving*	8.0	221.4	16.9	11.7	13.1	9.1	293.7
Squash, summer, raw: *1 serving*	3.1	16.7	3.7	0.9	0.1	0	0.7
Squash, summer, steamed w/o salt, drained: *1 serving*	3.5	14.0	3.1	0.9	0.1	0	1.0
Squash, winter, baked w/o salt: *1/4 average*	3.5	126.0	30.8	3.6	0.8	0	2.0
Squash, winter, steamed w/o salt, drained: *1 serving*	3.5	38.0	9.2	1.1	0.3	0	1.0

Vegetables (continued)	Weight (oz)	Calories	Carbo. (g)	Protein (g)	Fat (g)	Choles. (mg)	Sodium (mg)
Steamed Vegetable Platter, ETW Recipe: 1 serving	8.2	98.8	20.4	5.2	0.9	0	35.4
Sweet Potato, baked, w/skin: 1 average	10.5	254.0	58.5	3.8	0.9	0	22.0
Sweet Potato, raw, w/skin: 1 average	11.7	382.7	88.3	5.7	1.3	0	33.6
Sweet Potatoes Discipio, ETS Recipe: 1 serving	10.5	296.6	67.6	4.7	1.2	1.1	30.7
Tofu: 1 serving	2.9	59.6	2.0	6.5	3.5	0	5.8
Tomato Paste, canned, w/salt: 3½ ounces	3.5	81.4	18.5	3.4	0.4	0	783.9
Tomato Puree, canned, regular pack: 3½ ounces	3.5	38.7	8.8	1.7	0.2	0	395.9
Tomato, raw: 1 average	4.7	29.3	6.3	1.5	0.3	0	4.0
Tomato Sauce, canned: 3½ ounces	3.5	36.0	7.2	1.4	0.2	0	523.3
Tomato Sauce, canned, low-sodium: 3½ ounces	3.5	30.8	7.2	1.3	0.3	0	26.8
Tomatoes, canned, solids and liquid: 1 serving	4.4	26.2	5.4	1.2	0.2	0	162.1
Tomatoes, canned, solids only: 3½ ounces	3.5	20.8	4.3	1.0	0.2	0	129.0
Turnip Greens, boiled w/o salt, drained: 1 serving	3.5	20.0	3.6	2.2	0.2	0	50.0
Turnips, boiled w/o salt, drained: 1 serving	3.5	23.0	4.9	0.8	0.2	0	34.0
Two-Bean Bake, FF Recipe: 1 serving	7.4	146.6	29.6	7.8	1.0	0	109.5
Water Chestnuts, Chinese, raw: 16 average	3.5	79.0	19.0	1.4	0.2	0	20.0
Watercress, raw: 1 serving	1.8	9.5	1.5	1.1	0.1	0	26.0
Wax Beans, boiled w/o salt, drained: 1 serving	3.5	22.0	4.6	1.4	0.2	0	3.0
White Beans, cooked: 1 serving	3.5	120.0	23.0	6.3	0.5	0	338.0

	Weight (oz)	Calories	Carbo. (g)	Protein (g)	Fat (g)	Choles. (mg)	Sodium (mg)
Zucchini and Cauliflower Italian, *ETS Recipe: 1 serving*	6.0	47.8	8.0	3.4	0.9	1.3	175.9
Zucchini, raw: *1 average*	3.1	16.7	3.7	0.9	0.1	0	0.7
Zucchini, steamed w/o salt, drained: *1 serving*	3.5	12.0	2.5	1.0	0.1	0	1.0

APPENDIX IV
BIBLIOGRAPHY

Abraham, S., et al. 1980. "Prevalence of severe obesity in adults in the United States." *Am. J. Cl. Nutr.* 33:364–369.

Acheson, K. J., Flatt, J. P., and Jequier, E. 1982. "Glycogen synthesis versus lipogenesis after a 500 gram carbohydrate meal in man." *Metabolism* 31:1234–1240.

Acheson, K. J., et al. 1984. "Nutritional influences on lipogenesis and thermogenesis after a carbohydrate meal." *Am. J. Phys.* 246:62–70.

Acheson, K. J., et al. 1988. "Glycogen storage capacity and *de novo* lipogenesis during massive carbohydrate overfeeding in man." *Am. J. Clin. Nutr.* 48:240–247.

Allen, L. 1979. "Protein-induced hypercalcuria: a long-term study." *Am. J. Clin. Nutr.* 32:741.

Aloia, J. 1978. "Prevention of involutional bone loss by exercise." *Ann. Intern. Med.* 89:356.

Anand, C. 1974. "Effect of protein intake on calcium balance of young men given 500 mg calcium daily." *J. Nutr.* 104:695.

Anderson, J. W., et al. 1980. "Mineral and vitamin status on high-fiber diets: long-term status of diabetic patients." *Diabetes Care* 3:38–40.

Apfelbaum, M. 1976. "The effects of very restrictive high protein diets." *Clin. Endocrinol. Metab.* 5:417–430.

Asp, E. H., et al. 1987. "Reducing total fat intake: Effect on body weights." *Intern. J. Obesity.* 4:397a–397b.

Barnard, R. J., et al. 1981. "Effects of an intensive, short-term exercise and nutrition program on patients with coronary heart disease." *J. Cardiac Rehab.* 1:99–105.

Barrows, C. H., and Kokkonen, G. 1975. "Protein synthesis, development, growth and life span." *Growth* 39:525–533.

Bausman, P. 1981. "Jack Sprat's Legacy: The Science and Politics of Fat & Cholesterol." New York: Richard Marek, p. 29.

Benotti, P. N., et al. 1976. "Role of branched-chain amino acids (BCAA) intake in preventing muscle proteolysis." *Surg. Forum* 27:7–10.

Bingham, S., and Cummings, J. H. 1980. "Sources and intakes of dietary fiber in man." In *Medical Aspects of Dietary Fiber*, Spiller and Kay, eds. New York: Plenum, pp. 261–284.

Bistrian, B. R. 1978. "Clinical use of a protein-sparing modified fast." *JAMA* 240:2299–2302.

Blackburn, G. L., et al. 1979. "Branched-chain amino acid administration and metabolism during starvation, injury and infection." *Surgery* 86(2):307–315.

Bray, G. A. 1976. "The Obese Patient." *Major Problems in Internal Medicine*, vol. IX. Philadelphia: W. B. Saunders.

Bray, G. A., ed. 1979. "Obesity in America." *Bethesda: National Institutes of Health*. Available from Publications Unit, Fogarty International Center, Bldg. 16A, Rm. 205, National Institutes of Health, Bethesda, MD 20205 (NIH Publication No. 79–359).

Brenner, B. M., et al. 1982. "Dietary protein intake and the progressive nature of kidney disease: The role of hemodynamically mediated glomerular injury in the pathogenesis of progressive glomerular sclerosis in aging, renal ablation, and intrinsic renal disease." *N. Eng. J. Med.* 307:652–669.

Bricker, M. 1947. "The protein requirements of the adult rat in terms of the protein contained in egg, milk, and soy flour." *J. Nutr.* 34:491.

Bricker, M., et al. 1945. "The protein requirements of adult human subjects in terms of the protein contained in individual foods and food combinations." *J. Nutr.* 30:269–284.

Brown, G. D., Whyte, L., et al. 1984. "Effects of two lipid lowering diets on plasma lipid levels of patients with peripheral vascular disease." *J. Am. Dietetic Assoc.* 84:546–550.

Brown, J. M., et al. 1978. "Cardiac complications of protein-sparing modified fasting." *JAMA* 240:120–122.

Burkitt, D. P., ed. 1975. "Refined Carbohydrate Foods and Disease: Some Implications of Dietary Fibre." New York: Academic Press.

Burkitt, D. P., et al. 1972. "Effect of dietary fibre on stools and transit-times, and its role in the causation of disease." *Lancet* 2:1408–1412.

Buxe, M. G., et al. 1972. "Oxidation of branched-chain amino acids by isolated hearts and diaphragms of the rat. The effect of fatty acids, glucose, and pyruvate respiration." *J. Biol. Chem.* 24(24):8085–8096.

Carroll, K. K. 1978. "The role of dietary protein in hypercholesterolemia and atherosclerosis." *Lipids* 13:360–365.

Cerqueira, M. T., et al. 1979. "The food and nutrient intakes of the Tarahumara Indians of Mexico." *Am. J. Clin. Nutr.* 32:905–915.

Cerra, F., et al. 1982. "Branched-chains support post-operative protein synthesis." *Surgery* 92(2):192–199.

Charney, E., et al. 1976. "Childhood antecedents of adult obesity: do chubby infants become obese adults?" *N. Eng. J. Med.* 295:6–9.

Clark, H. 1973. "Nitrogen balances of adult human subjects fed combinations of wheat, beans, corn, milk, and rice." *Am. J. Clin. Nutr.* 26:702.

Clin. Nutr. 1980. "Diet and urinary calculi." 38:75–76.

Community Nutrition Institute. 1980. "Diet aids boom." *CNI Weekly Report* 10(14):4.

Connor, W. 1964. "The interrelated effects of dietary cholesterol and fat upon human serum lipid levels." *J. Clin. Invest.* 43:1691.

Connor, W. E., et al. 1978. "The plasma lipids, lipoproteins, and the diet of the Tarahumara Indians of Mexico." *Am. J. Clin. Nutr.* 31:1131.

Consumer Reports. 1978. "Too much sugar?" March.

Council on Foods and Nutrition, American Medical Association. 1974. "A critique of low-carbohydrate ketogenic weight reduction regimens: a review of Dr. Atkins' Diet Revolution." *JAMA* 224:15–22.

Cummings, J., 1979. "The effect of meat protein and dietary fiber on colonic function and metabolism, changes in bowel habit, bile acid excretion, and calcium absorption." *Am. J. Clin. Nutr.* 32:2086.

Currens, J. H., et al. 1951. "Metabolic effects of rice diet in treatment of hypertension." *N. Eng. J. Med.* 245:354–359.

Danforth, E. 1985. "Diet and obesity." *Am. J. Clin. Nutr.* 84:546–550.

Dayton, S., et al. 1962. "A controlled clinical trial of a diet high in unsaturated fat." *N. Eng. J. Med.* 266:1017–1023.

Dayton, S., et al. 1969. "A controlled clinical trial of a diet high in unsaturated fat in preventing complications of atherosclerosis." *Circ.* 40, Suppl. II:1–63.

DeHaven, J., et al. 1980. "Nitrogen and sodium balance and sympathetic-nervous-system activity in obese subjects treated with a low calorie protein or mixed diet." *N. Eng. J. Med.* 302:477–482.

"Diet and Urinary Calculi." 1980. *Nutr. Rev.* 38:74.

Dwyer, J. 1982. "Nutritional status of vegetarian children." *Am. J. Clin. Nutr.* 35:204.

Edwards, C. 1971. "Utilization of wheat by adult man: nitrogen metabolism, plasma amino acids and lipids." *Am. J. Clin. Nutr.* 24:181.

Ellis, F. 1970. "Veganism, clinical findings, and investigations." *Am. J. Clin. Nutr.* 23:249.

Ellis, F. 1971. "The health of vegans." *Pl. Fds. Hum. Nutr.* 2:93.

FDA Drug Bulletin. 1978. "Liquid protein and sudden cardiac deaths—an update." May–July.

Felig, P. 1971. "Amino acid metabolism in exercising man." *J. Clin. Invest.* 50:2703.

Felig, P. 1978. "Four questions about protein diets." *N. Eng. J. Med.* 298:1025–1026.

Fisher, H., et al. 1969. "Reassessment of amino acid requirements of young women on low nitrogen diets. I. 'Lysine and tryptophan'." *Am. J. Clin. Nutr.* 22:1190–1196.

Fisher, H., et al. 1971. "Reassessment of amino acid requirement of young women on low nitrogen diets. II. 'Leucine, methionine, and valine'." *Am. J. Clin. Nutr.* 24:1216–1223.

Flatt, J. P. 1985. "Effects of dietary fat on postprandial substrate oxidation and on carbohydrate and fat balances." *J. Clin. Invest.* 76:1019–1024.

Flatt, J. P., et al. 1987. "Dietary fat, carbohydrate balance, and weight maintenance: Effects of exercise." *Am. J. Clin. Nutr.* 45:296–306.

Franklin, B. A., et al. 1980. "Losing weight through exercise." *JAMA* 244:377.

Frattali, V. P. 1979. "Deaths associated with the liquid protein diet." *FDA,* by-lines No. 4.

Freund, H., et al. 1978. "The role of the branched-chain amino acids in decreasing muscle catabolism in vivo." *Surgery* 83(6):611–618.

Freund, H., et al. 1979. "Infusion at the branched-chain amino acids in postoperative patients." Anticatabolic properties, *Ann. Surg.* 190(1):18–23.

Furese, K. 1987. "Vitamin E: Biological and clinical aspects of topical treatment." *Cosmetics & Toiletries* 102:99–115.

Garn, S., et al. 1975. "Does obesity have a genetic basis in man?" *Ecol. Food Nutr.* 4:57.

Genuth, S. M. 1976. "Effect of high fat versus high carbohydrate feeding on the development of obesity in weanling ob/ob mice." *Diabetologia* 12:155–159.

Golden, M. H. N. 1982. "Protein deficiency, energy deficiency and the oedema of malnutrition." *Lancet* 1:1261–1265.

Goldrick, R. B., et al. 1970. "An assessment of coronary heart disease and coronary risk factors in a New Guinea highland population." In *Atherosclerosis:*

Proceedings of the Second International Symposium, Jones, R. J., ed. Berlin: Springer-Verlag, pp. 366–368.

Greenberg, I., et al. 1979. "Obesity: facts, fads, and fantasies." *Compr. Ther.* 5:68–76.

Greenberg, J. 1978. "The fat American." *Science News* 113(12):188–189.

Griggs, R. C., et al. 1981. "Treatment of myopathic carnitine deficiency: quantitation of response to prednisone and carnitine." *Trans. Am. Neurol. Assoc.* 106:199–202.

Grinker, J. 1978. "Obesity and sweet taste." *Am. J. Clin. Nutr.* 31:1078–1087.

Haber, G. B., et al. 1977. "Depletion and disruption of dietary fiber: effects on satiety, plasma, glucose and serum insulin." *Lancet* 2:679–682.

Hall, J. A., et al. 1982. "Effects of diet and exercise on peripheral vascular disease (case report)." *Phys. and Sportsmed.* 10:90.

Harper, A. 1972. "Adaptive changes to low nutrient intake, metabolic adaption to adequate and inadequate amino acid supply." *Proc. 9th Int. Congr. Nutr.* Mexico 1:1.

Hartroft, W. S. 1960. "The pathology of obesity." In *The Prevention of Obesity,* ed. R. L. Craid, pp. 32–41. Dallas: American Heart Association.

Hartz, A., et al. 1977. "Relative importance of the effect of family environment and heredity on obesity." *Ann. Human Genet.* 41:185–193.

Hegsted, C. 1946. "Protein requirements of adults." *J. Lab. Clin. Med.* 31:261.

Hegsted, D. 1955. "Lysine and methionine supplementation of all-vegetable diets for human adults." *J. Nutr.* 56:555.

Hegsted, D. M. 1968. "Minimum protein requirements of adults." *Am. J. Clin. Nutr.* 21:352–357.

Hegsted, D. M., et al. 1946. "Protein requirements of adults." *J. Lab. Clin. Med.* 31:261–284.

Hornstra, G., et al. 1979. "Fish oils, prostaglandins, and arterial thrombosis." *Lancet* 2:1080.

Huenemann, R. L., et al. 1980. "Cultural factors in the development, maintenance, and control of obesity." *Cardiovascular Reviews & Reports* 1:21–26.

Hultman, E. 1976. "Adverse effects of high fat, low CHO diet on performance." *American Heart Association Monograph* 15:106.

"Humans as walking legumes." 1971. *Nutr. Rev.* 29:223–226.

Insull, W., et al. 1969. "Studies of arteriosclerosis in Japanese and American men. I. 'Comparison of fatty acid composition of adipose tissue'." *J. Clin. Invest.* 48:1313–1327.

Irwin, M. 1971. "A conspectus of research on protein requirements of man." *J. Nutr.* 10:385.

Irwin, M. I., and Hegsted, D. M. 1971. "A conspectus of research on protein requirements of man." *J. Nutr.* 101:385–430.

Jakubczak, L. F. 1976. "Behavioral aspects of nutrition and longevity in animals." In *Nutrition, Longevity, and Aging*, Rockstein, M., and Sussman, M. L., eds. New York: Academic Press, pp. 103–122.

JAMA. 1977. "Obesity in children: environment or genes?" 238:2009.

Jayarajan, P., et al. 1980. "Effect of dietary fat on absorption of B-carotene from green leafy vegetables in children." *Indian J. Med. Res.* 71:53–56.

Johnson, D., et al. 1977. "Therapeutic fasting in morbid obesity: long-term follow-up." *Arch. Intern. Med.* 137:1381–1382.

Jowsey, J. 1976. "Osteoporosis: its nature and the role of diet." *Postgrad. Med.* 60:75–79.

Jowsey, J. 1976. "Prevention and treatment of osteoporosis." In *Nutrition and Aging*, ed. M. Winick, New York: John Wiley, pp. 131–144.

Jurgensen, K. A., and Dyerberg, J. 1983. "Platelets and atherosclerosis." *Adv. Nutr. Res.* 5:57–75.

Kannel, W., et al. 1967. "Relation of adiposity to blood pressure and development of hypertension. Framingham study." *Ann. Intern. Med.* 67:48–59.

Karam, J. H. 1979. "Obesity: fat cells—not fat people." *West. J. Med.* 130(2):128–132.

Keller, W., and Kraut, H. 1959. "Work and Nutrition." *World Rev. Nutr. Diet.* 3:65–81.

Kempner, W. 1949. "Treatment of heart and kidney disease and of hypertensive and arteriosclerotic vascular disease with the rice diet." *Ann. Int. Med.* 31:821–856.

Kempner, W., et al. 1975. "Treatment of massive obesity with rice/reduction diet program." *Arch. Intern. Med.* 135:1575–1584.

Kennedy, D., et al. 1978. "Protein diets." *FDA Drug Bulletin.* January–February.

Kofranyi, E. 1970. "The minimum protein requirements of humans, tested with mixtures of whole egg plus potatoes and maize plus beans." *Z. Physiol. Chem.* 351:1485.

Kolata, G. B. 1977. "Obesity: a growing problem." *Research News* (December), pp. 905–906.

Kon, S. 1928. "The value of whole potatoes in human nutrition." *Biochem. J.* 22:258.

Korycka, M., et al. 1970. "Influence of fat level in the diet on carotene and Vitamin A utilization." *Acta Physiol. Pol.* 20:662–667.

Kudo, Y., et al. 1983. "Study on the risk factors of ischemic heart disease in patients with chronic hemodialysis, with special reference to the role of plasma L-carnitine." *Nippon Jinzo Gakkai Shi* 25:429–438.

Kummerow, F. 1977. "The influence of egg consumption on the serum cholesterol level in human subjects." *Am. J. Clin. Nutr.* 30:664.

Kuthra, A. 1970. "The nutritional, clinical, and economic aspects of vegan diets." *Pl. Fds. Hum. Nutr.* 2:13.

Lala, V. R., and Reddy, V. 1970. "Absorption of B-carotene from green leafy vegetables in undernourished children." *Am. J. Clin. Nutr.* 23:110–113.

Lampman, R. M., et al. 1980. "Type IV hyperlipoproteinemia: Effects of a caloric restricted type IV diet versus physical training plus isocaloric type IV diet." *Am. J. Clin. Nutr.* 33:1233–1243.

Lantigua, R. A., et al. 1980. "Cardiac arrhythmias associated with a liquid protein diet for the treatment of obesity." *N. Eng. J. Med.* 303:735–738.

Lawlor, T., et al. 1969. "Metabolic hazards of fasting." *Am. J. Clin. Nutr.* 22:1142–1149.

Lee, C. J., et al. 1971. "Nitrogen retention of young men fed rice with or without supplementary chicken." *Am. J. Clin. Nutr.* 24:318–323.

Lemon, P. 1981. "Effects of exercise on protein and amino acid metabolism." *Med. Sci. Sports Exerec.* 13:141.

Lennon, D. L., et al. 1983. "Effects of acute moderate-intensity exercise on carnitine metabolism in men and women." *J. Appl. Physiol.* 55:489–495.

Leto, S., et al. 1976. "Dietary protein, life-span, and physiological variables in female mice." *J. Geront.* 31:149–154.

Levine, L., et al. 1983. "Fructose and glucose ingestion and muscle glycogen use during submaximal exercise." *J. Appl. Physiol.* 55(6):1767–1771.

Lewis, M. F., and Ferraro, D. P. 1973. "Flying high: The aeromedical aspects of marihuana." *FAA* No. AD775889.

Linkswiler, H. M., et al. 1974. "Calcium retention of young adult males as affected by level of protein and of calcium intake." *Trans. N.Y. Acad. Sci.*, Ser. II 30:333–340.

Lissner, L., et al. 1987. "Dietary fat intake and the regulation of energy intake in human subjects." *Am. J. Clin. Nutr.* 46:886–892.

Lopez de Romana, G. 1980. "Utilization of the protein and energy of the white potato by human infants." *J. Nutr.* 110:1849.

Lopez de Romana, G. 1981. "Fasting and postprandial plasma free amino acids of infants and children consuming exclusive potato protein." *J. Nutr.* 111:1766.

Lowry, O. H., et al. 1951. "Protein measurement with the folin phenol reagent." *J. Biol. Chem.* 193:265–275.

Luyken, R., et al. 1964. "Nutrition studies in New Guinea." *Am. J. Clin. Nutr.* 14:13–27.

Mahalko, J. R., et al. 1983. "Effect of a moderate increase in dietary protein on the retention and excretion of Ca, Cu Fe, Mg, P, and Zn by adult males." *Am. J. Clin. Nutr.* 37:8–14.

Makinodan, T., et al. 1974. "Aging and the Immune Function." MSS Information Corp., New York, N.Y.

Margen, S. 1974. "Studies in calcium metabolism, the calciuretic effect of dietary protein." *Am. J. Clin. Nutr.* 27:584.

Marquis, N. R., and Fritz, I. B. 1964. "Enzymological determination of free carnitine concentrations in rat tissues." *J. Lipid Res.* 5:184–187.

Mattson, F. 1972. "Effects of dietary cholesterol on serum cholesterol in man." *Am. J. Clin. Nutr.* 25:589.

Mayhowk, J. C. 1981. "Prediction of body density, fat, weight, and lean body mass." *J. Sports Med.* 21(4):385.

Mazess, R. 1974. "Bone mineral content of North Alaskan Eskimos." *Am. J. Clin. Nutr.* 27:916.

McCarty, M. F. 1986. "The unique merits of a low-fat diet for weight control." *Med. Hypoth.* 20:183–197.

Mclaren, D. 1966. "A fresh look at protein-calorie malnutrition." *Lancet* 2:485.

Metzner, H. L., et al. 1977. "The relationship between frequency of eating and adiposity in adult men and women in the Tecumseh Community Health Study." *Am. J. Clin. Nutr.* 30:712–715.

Michiel, R. R., et al. 1978. "Sudden death in a patient on a liquid protein diet." *N. Eng. J. Med.* 298:1005–1007.

Nash, D. T., et al. 1979. "Progression of coronary atherosclerosis and dietary hyperlipidemia." *Circulation* 56:363–365.

Neely, J. R., and Morgan, H. E. 1974. "Relationship between carbohydrate and lipid metabolism and the energy balance of heart muscle." *Annu. Rev. Physiol.* 36:413–459.

Nelson, R. A. 1974. Quoted in "Are we eating too much protein?" *Med. World News,* November 8, p. 106.

Nutr. Rev. 1978. "The nature of weight loss during short-term dieting." 36(3):72–74.

Nutr. Rev. 1980. "Urinary calculi and dietary protein." 38:9–10.

O'Brien, B. 1980. "Human plasma lipid response to red meat, poultry, fish and eggs." *Am. J. Clin. Nutr.* 33:2573.

Pellett, P. 1980. "Nutritional evaluation of protein foods." *Food and Nutrition Bulletin*, supplement 4, United Nations University Press, pp. 1–6.

Rabinowitz, D. 1970. "Some endocrine and metabolic aspects of obesity." *Ann. Rev. Med.* 21:241–258.

Richardson, D. P., et al. 1979. "Quantitative effect of an isoenergetic exchange of fat for carbohydrate in dietary protein utilization in healthy young men." *Am. J. Clin. Nutr.* 32:2217–2226.

Rickman, F., et al. 1974. "Changes in serum cholesterol during the Stillman diet." *JAMA* 228:54–58.

Riopelle, A. M., and Shell, W. F. 1978. "Protein deprivation in primates. XI. 'Determinants of weight change during and after pregnancy'." *Am. J. Clin. Nutr.* 31:394–400.

Rizek, R. L., and Jackson, E. M. 1980. "Current Food Consumption Practices and Nutrient Sources in the American Diet." Hyattsville, MD: *USDA*.

Roberts, S. 1981. "Does egg feeding (i.e., dietary cholesterol) affect plasma cholesterol levels in humans? 'The results of a double-blind study'." *Am. J. Clin. Nutr.* 34:2092.

Robertson, W. 1979. "Should recurrent calcium oxalate stone formers become vegetarians?" *Br. J. Urol.* 51:427.

Rodin, J. 1978. "The puzzle of obesity." *Human Nature* (February), pp. 38–47.

Rodin, J. 1984. "Taming the Hunger Hormone." *American Health*. January–February.

Ross, M. H. 1959. "Protein, calories and life expectancy." *Fed. Proc.* 18:1190–1207.

Sanders, T. 1978. "Studies of vegans: the fatty acid composition of plasma choline phosphoglycerides, erythrocytes, adipose tissue and breast milk, and some indicators of susceptibility to ischemic heart disease in vegans and omnivore controls." *Am. J. Clin. Nutr.* 31:805.

Schuette, S. A., et al. 1980. "Studies on the mechanism of protein-induced hypercalciuria in older men and women." *J. Nutr.* 110:305–315.

Schwartz, R. S., et al. 1978. "Increased adipose-tissue lipoprotein lipase activity in moderately obese men after weight reduction." *Lancet* 1:1230–1231.

Sedar, A. W., et al. 1978. "Fatty acids and the initial events of endothelial damage seen by scanning and transmission electron microscopy." *Atherosclerosis* 30:273–284.

Sinclair, H. M. 1980. "Prevention of coronary heart disease: The role of essential fatty acids." *Postgrad. Med. J.* 56:579–584.

Sinnett, P. R., and Whyte, H. M. "Epidemiological studies in a highland population of New Guinea: Environment, culture, and health status." *Human Ecol.* 1:245–277.

Slater, J. 1976. "Plasma cholesterol and triglycerides in men with added eggs in the diet." *Nutr. Rep. Int.* 14:249.

Smith, R., 1966. "Epidemiologic studies of osteoporosis in women of Puerto Rico and southeastern Michigan with special reference to age, race, national origin, and to other related and associated findings." *Clin. Orthop.* 45:31.

Srivastava, K. C. 1980. "Effects of dietary fatty acids, prostaglandins and related compounds on the role of platelets in thrombosis." *Biochem. Exp. Biol.* 16:317–338.

Storey, R., et al. 1982. "Popular Diets: How They Rate." Los Angeles District, California Dietetic Assoc.

Stunkard, A. J. 1977. "Obesity and the social environment: current status, future prospects." New York Academy of Science, *Food and Nutrition in Health and Disease* 300:298–320.

Sumner, E. 1938. "The biological value of milk and egg protein in human subjects." *J. Nutr.* 16:141.

Truswell, A. 1962. "The nutritive value of maize protein for man." *Am. J. Clin. Nutr.* 10:142.

"Urinary Calcium and Dietary Protein." 1980. *Nutr. Rev.* 38:9.

Van Itallie, T. B. 1980. "'Morbid' obesity; a hazardous disorder that resists conservative treatment." *Am. J. Clin. Nutr.* 33:358–363.

Van Itallie, T. B., et al. 1979. "Appraisal of excess calories as a factor in the causation of disease." *Am. J. Clin. Nutr.* 32:2648–2653.

Walker, A. 1965. "Osteoporosis and calcium deficiency." *Am. J. Clin. Nutr.* 16:327.

Walker, A. R. P., et al. 1948. "Studies in human mineral metabolism. I. 'The effect of bread rich in phytate phosphorus on the metabolism of certain mineral salts with special reference to calcium'." *Biochem. J.* 42:452–462.

Walker, R. 1972. "Calcium retention in the adult human male as affected by protein intake." *J. Nutr.* 102:12–97.

Watkins, D. M. 1977. "Aging, nutrition and the continuum of health care." New York Academy of Science. *Food and Nutrition in Health and Disease* 300:290–297.

Watt, B. K., et al. 1963. "Composition of foods: Raw, Processed, Prepared." Rev. ed. *USDA Agri. Handbk.* No. 8.

Weisinger, J. R., et al. 1974. "The nephrotic syndrome: a complication of massive obesity." 81:440–447.

Weltman, A., et al. 1980. "Caloric restriction and/or mild exercise effects on serum lipids and body composition." *Am. J. Clin. Nutr.* 33:1002–1009.

Wentz, A. E. 1964. "Studies on aging in aviation personnel." *FAA* No. AD456652.

West, K. M., et al. 1966. "Glucose tolerance, nutrition, and diabetes in Uruguay, Venezuela, Malaya, and East Pakistan." *Diabetes* 15:9–18.

Whitescarver, S. A., et al. 1984. "Salt-sensitive hypertension: contribution of chloride." *Science*, pp. 223–1430.

Winitz, M., et al. 1970. "Studies in metabolic nutrition employing chemically defined diets. I. 'Extended feeding of normal human adult males'." *Am. J. Clin. Nutr.* 23:525–545.

Wotecki, C. E. 1982. "Uses and limits to the use of RDA for diet planning and food selection." Speech delivered to the Food and Nutrition Board, National Research Council, Washington, D.C., December 13.

Wretlind, A. 1982. "Standards for nutritional adequacy of the diet: European and WHO/FAO viewpoints." *Am. J. Clin. Nutr.* 36:366–375.

Wynder, E. L. 1977. "Nutritional Carcinogenesis." New York Academy of Science. *Food and Nutrition in Health and Disease* 300:360–378.

Yamamura, Y., and Folkers, K. 1980. I to Y. "Biomedical and Clinical Aspects of Co-enzyme Q, Volume 2." Elsevier Publishing.

Young, J. B., et al. 1977. "Suppression of sympathetic nervous system during fasting." *Science* 196:1473–1475.

INDEX

Page numbers of photos appear in *italics*.

INDEX OF RECIPES